The Essence of COM and ActiveX

A Programmer's Workbook

David S. Platt, M.E.

President, Rolling Thunder Computing, Inc.

**Instructor in Computer Science,
Harvard University Extension School**

http://www.rollthunder.com

To join a Prentice Hall PTR Internet mailing list, point to
http://www.prenhall.com/mail_lists/

ISBN 0-13-079989-0

90000

**Prentice Hall PTR
Upper Saddle River, NJ   07458**

9 780130 799890

Library of Congress Cataloging-in-Publication Data
Platt, David S.
     The essence of COM and ActiveX : a programmer's workbook / by
  David S. Platt. -- [2nd ed.]
        p.   cm.
     Previously published under title: The essence of OLE with ActiveX.
     Includes index.
     ISBN 0-13-079989-0
     1.   Object-oriented programming (Computer science) 2. OLE.
  Computer file) I. Platt, David S. Essence of OLE with ActiveX.
  II. Title
  QA76.64.P62 1997
  005.7--dc21   97-35515
                                             CIP

Editorial/Production Supervision: *Eileen Clark*
Acquisitions Editor: *Mike Meehan*
Marketing Manager: *Stephen Solomon*
Buyer: *Alexis R. Heydt*
Cover Design: *Kiwi Design*
Cover Design Direction: *Jayne Conte*
Editorial Assistant: *Barbara Alfieri*

 © 1998 Prentice Hall PTR
Prentice-Hall, Inc.
A Simon & Schuster Company
Upper Saddle River, NJ 07458

Prentice Hall books are widely used by corporations and government agencies for training, marketing, and resale. The publisher offers discounts on this book when ordered in bulk quantities.

For more information, contact
            Corporate Sales Department,
            Phone: 800-382-3419; FAX: 201-236-7141
            E-mail (Internet): corpsales@prenhall.com
Or write: Prentice Hall PTR
            Corp. Sales Department
            One Lake Street
            Upper Saddle River, NJ 07458

Chapter 13 is based on "Give ActiveX-based Web Pages a Boost with the Apartment Threading Model,"
Microsoft System Journal, February 1997, and "Fashionable App Designers Agree: The Free Threading Model
Is What's Hot This Fall," Microsoft Systems Journal, August 1997. © Miller Freeman, Inc. To learn more about MSJ, visit
the web site www.microsoft.com/msj.

Printed in the United States of America

10 9 8 7 6 5 4 3 2 1

ISBN 0-13-079989-0

Prentice-Hall International (UK) Limited, *London*
Prentice-Hall of Australia Pty. Limited, *Sydney*
Prentice-Hall Canada Inc., *Toronto*
Prentice-Hall Hispanoamericana, S.A., *Mexico*
Prentice-Hall of India Private Limited, *New Delhi*
Prentice-Hall of Japan, Inc., *Tokyo*
Simon & Schuster Asia Pte. Ltd., *Singapore*
Editora Prentice-Hall do Brasil, Ltda., *Rio de Janeiro*

To my parents, Ellen and Ben Platt

Table of Contents

This page intentionally contains no text other than this sentence.

Preface

On the Teaching and Learning of OLE

WHY I WROTE THIS BOOK

OLE has a reputation for being hard to learn. A client once told me that he knew of only two programmers in the entire world who understood it, both of whom worked for Microsoft and spent their days writing puzzles for each other. But really, nothing could be further from the truth. OLE has an elegant simplicity to its architecture and an internal self-consistency that the Windows API lacks. It's just a different way of looking at the world. This book is an attempt to clear things up, to present in a simple and easily digested fashion the stuff I had to learn the hard way.

As I hope to demonstrate in this book, learning OLE isn't that hard. It may take you a little while to get the basic concepts, though I've done my best to build easily accessible ramps into it. But once the light bulb goes off, probably after about two weeks, you have the keys to all of OLE. Learning the Windows API was largely a matter of memorizing arbitrary function calls without any central organizing principle, sort of like memorizing all those boring equations in college organic chemistry. Learning OLE as presented in this book is more like learning the basic principles that cause the entire universe to operate. Remember college physics? The simplest equations, such as $F = MA$, describe all macroscopic motion, from the falling of a feather to the collision of galaxies.

HOW TO TEACH OLE AND HOW NOT TO

Part of OLE's nasty rap results from its debut at a Microsoft professional developers' conference in Seattle in May 1993. It was a disaster. Never in my life had I seen so many people scratching their heads in the same place at the same time, myself included. Microsoft technical evangelists wear red shirts at these affairs so attendees can identify them and ask questions. At this conference the students were so annoyed that the evangelists changed into camouflage. The organizers made every mistake it was possible to make in the transfer of technical information. None of the attendees thought they had learned anything, except maybe to examine their options for career changes.

At the time I was hopping mad, as I had paid my own money to attend. But my teaching practice was starting to take off and I soon realized that I had really learned much more about instruction from the conference's abject failure to communicate anything useful than I would have had it actually taught me something about OLE. Thinking about how OLE should have been explained led me to the classes that I teach at Harvard, and to writing this book.

The first big mistake that the conference made was trying to explain OLE from the top down, a good approach for application development but not for instruction. OLE is so big that the first problem is figuring out where to grab it. This book starts with the simplest example I could think of, pasting text from the Clipboard into your app by means of OLE. It takes exactly 12 lines of code from start to finish. When you understand that, the chapter moves on to explain transferring text via drag and drop, which uses exactly the same mechanism for transferring the data but adds some support for the user interface. In the next chapter, you write your own object for placing data onto the Clipboard, and so on until you've digested all of OLE.

The second big mistake the conference organizers made was that they didn't even attempt to distill the important points from the sea of documentation. For example, when discussing an interface (a set of related functions, see Chapter 1), the presenter would simply list the functions in arbitrary order and discuss each one. The signal-to-noise ratio approached zero. In real life, an interface's functionality usually depends on and is best illustrated by one or two key functions. For example, in Chapter 2, when you write an object interface to put text into the Clipboard, you only have to write code for three of the interface's nine functions, and only one of these takes much work. The other six don't do anything useful in this instance and can be stubbed out to empty shells. If you ever need them, you can easily pick them up using the principles you learned while implementing the three important functions. I've done my best to concentrate my explanations on the important pieces and distill this sour mash into high-test moonshine.

The conference made many other small mistakes as well, which I have done my best to fix. They showed not a single code example, just neat little slides with bullet charts – a complete waste of time, the bandwidth of the medium is far too narrow to communicate anything useful. Programmers think in code, not bullets. Almost every page in this book has a code example on it. The conference presenters never told us where objects came from. "Assume you have an object," they would say, "and you want to do this or that with it. Never mind where it came from, just assume you have one." It made me very disoriented. Every chapter of this book starts by explaining where the objects that it deals with came from. The conference didn't have Kraig Brockschmidt's book to refer to. Whenever there is a topic that I thought some readers might want explained in more detail, I placed a reference to the exact page numbers in the second edition of *Inside OLE* by Kraig Brockschmidt (Microsoft Press, ISBN 1-55615-843-2) on which that topic is discussed.

THE MFC OR NOT THE MFC

This book covers both the API and the MFC implementation of OLE. The MFC prefabricates a lot of the plumbing between apps, allowing you to concentrate on the faucets on either end. The more complex the objects you are writing, the more useful this becomes. For simple text data transfer, it doesn't buy you much. For ActiveX controls, it's indispensable.

The problem with the MFC is that it's frequently marketed by people who ought to know better as a replacement for knowledge of the underlying API. It isn't; instead, it's a tool that amplifies your API knowledge or the lack thereof. If you simply use the MFC without any knowledge of what it's really doing, it's like not knowing how to swim, but using an inner tube to paddle into the middle of Boston Harbor. It's great until you spring a leak, then you are, as we say in Boston, "scrod." The MFC frequently doesn't work as advertised, or you need to do something different than what the MFC designers thought you would. Then you need to take it apart and see what it's really doing in its heart of hearts, possibly changing it, and you can only do that if you know the foundation on which it's built. In the Clipboard example in Chapter 1, the MFC expects the Clipboard to behave in a certain way. Unfortunately, the Clipboard doesn't work the way the MFC thinks it ought to. The workaround is fairly simple but it isn't documented anywhere. Unless you knew enough about the API to step into the MFC and decipher the source code, see what it was saying to the Clipboard and see what the Clipboard was saying back to it, you'd be scrod. So use the MFC, but learn what it's doing.

HOW TO USE THIS BOOK

If you are new to OLE, **READ CHAPTERS 1 AND 2 FIRST!!** Do not attempt to jump to other chapters until you feel comfortable with these. In these chapters I introduce the new programming model and vocabulary of OLE without which subsequent chapters will make no sense. I hate the term "paradigm shift;" it's been so badly overused as to have lost all meaning, but OLE does turn your head around.

You don't really own your knowledge of software until you've written some yourself. The end of each chapter contains self-study programming exercises with detailed instructions. The prepackaged labs pretty much follow the text, so they aren't hard. The extra credit sections at the end of each lab are designed to stretch your mind a bit more.

When you are actually writing your programs, keep this book handy on your desk. My students tell me that it is the first source they refer to, because it's easy to find what they want and easy to absorb it when they do find it. They only go off to a thicker book when they can't find what they want in this book. One student even has two copies, one at home and one at work.

WHY ALL THE EMPTY PAGES?

The reason I have them is to align the two-page sound bites over a spread of two facing pages. When a topic doesn't fit on a single page, such as the explanation of IDataObject::GetData( ) on pages 34 and 35, my experience has shown that students find the material much easier to absorb if it is spread across two facing pages. But the explanation of IDataObject::QueryGetData( ) on page 33 occupies only a single page. So page 32 has no point on it, so QueryGetData( ) goes on an odd-numbered page, so the following section properly spreads across two facing pages.

By the way, I can't stand pages that say "This page intentionally left blank." Does it never occur to anybody that this statement is self-negating? THE %$#^$@ PAGE ISN'T BLANK, IT CONTAINS THAT ONE LYING SENTENCE!! If the author can't even get that dinky little piece right, how can I believe anything else he says? Instead, my empty pages truthfully say, "This page intentionally contains no text other than this sentence." Call me a curmudgeon.

SEND ME FEEDBACK

I'd love to hear from readers, to find out which parts of the book were most useful. Also, I guarantee that, despite my best efforts and those of my reviewers, that some errors remain in this book, and I'd sure appreciate it if you'd tell me about them so they can be fixed in the next edition. My e-mail address is dplatt@rollthunder.com. My web page, http://www.rollthunder.com, will contain updates and corrections to the book.

PROGRAMMING CLASSES AVAILABLE

A self-study guide like this one is great (I hope), but the fastest way to get going in programming is to have an in-house hands-on class. I'll come to your company and teach the subjects that you care about. In addition to OLE, I also teach the MFC and the Win32 API. Look for my other book, *The Win32 API from Scratch* (Prentice-Hall, ISBN 0-13-121484-5). Contact me by e-mail at the addresses in the preceding paragraph.

ACKNOWLEDGMENTS

I need to thank the following people, without whom this book would never have been completed. Mehrdad Givehchi, who did a great job reading the book and finding errors. If he ever gets sick of programming, he's got a great future as a technical editor. Pat Duggan, who found so many typos in my previous book that he earned a free copy of this one. Kraig Brockschmidt, for discussions on the philosophy of OLE and of life in general. My wife Linda, for being there. And Mike Meehan, my editor at Prentice Hall, whom I have now forgiven for talking me into writing it.

— David S. Platt

This page intentionally contains no text other than this sentence.

Preface to the Second Edition

WHAT A DIFFERENCE A YEAR MAKES

I sent the first edition of this book to press at the end of August 1996, just about a year ago. That's an awfully long time in the software business. I occasionally envy my Harvard colleagues in the Department of Classics, whose material hasn't changed in 2000 years. This area of software is really snowballing. COM is everywhere, at the foundation of everything. This book is my attempt to keep up with it, and keep you up with it as well.

CHANGES IN THIS EDITION

Obviously, the title has changed. Microsoft is trying to repair their mistake and let the term "OLE" return to its original meaning as an acronym for "object linking and embedding". COM is now the generic term for binary interaction of one component with another. The root directory for the sample code on the CD-ROM is still "EssenceOfOle", however. The term was hard wired into too many registry files to go back and fix each one.

The first twelve chapters of this book are the original ones, updated to take the latest changes into account. I completely rewrote Chapter 10 on DCOM. I had written the first edition using the Beta 2 release, which changed unrecognizably by the final release, unfortunately after press time. I've added four new chapters, on threads, the ATL, Java, and the user interface shell. I've also added two appendices, covering containment and aggregation, and also smart pointers. Overall, the size of the second edition increased by about 50% over the first edition.

MORE ACKNOWLEDGMENTS

I need to thank all those people that helped me figure out things about COM in the last year. The staff at Microsoft Systems Journal and Microsoft's Developer Relations Group were especially helpful when I was researching COM threading for a couple of MSJ articles on the topic (February and August 1997). Thanks to Dave Edson, Sara Williams, Charlie Kindel, Nat Brown, Dave D'Sousa, and Eric Maffei. When I teach at Boston University's WinDev conferences, I learned much from attending talks presented by the other presenters. Thanks go to Don Box, Jeffery Richter, Jeff Prosise, Ken Ramirez, Joe Najjar, and Richard Hale Shaw. Thanks also to Charles Parker, who did technical editing for this edition, Mike Meehan at Prentice-Hall, and my wife, Linda. Last but not least (to coin a phrase), thanks to everyone who bought or recommended the first edition, on behalf of my creditors. I hope you like this one as much.

— David S. Platt

This page intentionally contains no text other than this sentence.

Chapter 1

Introduction
Using Data Objects

A. CONCEPTS AND DEFINITIONS

1. COM, the *Component Object Model*, is Microsoft's top-level, all-encompassing binary and wire specification for the interoperation of one software component with another, across multiple processes, machines, and (one day, Microsoft hopes) hardware and operating systems. OLE is a collection of higher-level functionality, primarily related to the user interface, that uses COM for communicating between components. It is not always clear exactly where COM stops and OLE begins. Philosophical debate on the topic is about as productive as debating how many pinheads can dance on an angel. This book uses the terms more or less interchangeably, leaning towards "OLE" where there is human user interaction involved and towards "COM" where there isn't.

2. The nomenclature of the OLE/COM/ActiveX world is confusing to say the least. If you search through the Microsoft Developer Network CD-ROM, you will see an incredible array of different meanings attached to the various terms, changing drastically over time and occasionally returning to their starting points. There is no single set of meanings for them and there never really was. Here are the derivations of the terms as you will see them used in the literature today:

OLE first shipped in 1991 with Windows 3.1 and used Dynamic Data Exchange (remember good ol' DDE?) as its underlying communication protocol. OLE originally stood for "Object Linking and Embedding", because that's what it did and that's all it did. Then OLE 2.0 came out in 1993, significantly enhancing the original object linking and embedding functionality, containing such cool enhancements as in-place activation and linking that actually worked. OLE 2.0 replaced DDE with COM as its underlying communication protocol, and as such was the first major use of COM. It also added the programmability of OLE Automation, described in Chapter 3, which nobody was quite sure how to use yet. At this point, Microsoft declared that OLE was no longer an acronym for object linking and embedding. Instead, it was just a combination of random syllables that Microsoft liked enough to trademark, that referred to the entire set of technologies built on top of COM. Here matters stood for a couple of years. Kraig Brockschmidt's book *Inside OLE*, published in 1995, dealt with the entire set of COM-based technologies and refers to them all as OLE. The first edition of the book you are now holding, written beginning in 1995, was entitled *The Essence of OLE with ActiveX*.

Around 1996, when most developers started writing 32-bit apps for Windows 95, they noticed that the way OLE used COM was a cool way of architecting software. Developers started writing their own objects and their own interfaces in a similar manner. Also, the operating system started requiring the use of COM technology, for example, for programming the Windows 95 user interface (see chapter 16). It wasn't object linking and embedding and it wasn't automation, what the heck was it? The term COM started to be used more and more frequently on its own, which is probably what should have happened in the first place. The term OLE is no longer used as the catch-all it once was. Some writers are trying to make it revert to its original meaning, object linking and embedding, but that would leave COM-related user interface technologies, such as drag and drop and Clipboard handling, without a term.

The term ActiveX is another winner. In Chapter 5, I expound at length on the origin and subsequent diluting into oblivion of this term. To quickly summarize here, the term "ActiveX" has no technical meaning whatsoever, although it did have several different meanings at various times. It is today a branding prefix, the same as the letters "Mc" in front of all the food at the restaurant with the golden arches. It means "Microsoft-warm-fuzzy-good", no more and no less.

3. When you start an app that uses OLE or COM, you must first initialize it in your app by calling the API function **OleInitialize( )** or **CoInitialize( )**. The former calls the latter internally, as well as setting up support for the user interface portions of OLE. If you don't need this user interface support, then the latter function is all you need. The include files for all OLE and COM functions are supplied via the header file "windows.h", and the import library is "ole32.lib".

If and only if this call succeeds, as shown below, should your app uninitialize the OLE libraries via the function **OleUninitialize( )** or **CoUninitialize( )**. when it shuts down. The return type of OleInitialize( ), and of almost every other OLE-related function, is of type HRESULT, which is typedefed as a LONG. The high bit of the long is cleared if the call succeeded, set if the call failed. The macro SUCCEEDED( ) tests this bit and returns TRUE if the call was successful. Thus:

```
#include <windows.h>          // includes all OLE and COM files

int WINAPI WinMain(HINSTANCE hInstance, HINSTANCE hPrevInstance,
    LPSTR lpCmdLine, int nCmdShow)
{
    MSG msg;

/*
Initialize OLE Libraries.
*/

    HRESULT hr = OleInitialize (NULL) ;

/*
Run the app.
*/

    <all the other WinMain stuff>


/*
If they were initialized successfully, shut down the OLE Libraries.
S_OK is a constant defined in the sytem header files.
*/
    if (SUCCEEDED(S_OK))
    {
      OleUninitialize ( ) ;
    }

    return (msg.wParam);

}
```

3

B. COMPONENT-OBJECT MODEL

1. OLE uses the *Component-Object Model*, switching from a function-oriented view of the world to an object-oriented view. In this model, an app does not manipulate the world via API functions, such as ShowWindow( ). Rather, the universe consists of *objects*, which expose one or more *interfaces* to the world. An interface is a group of related functions which operate on the object that exposes them. Some interfaces are standard, others are defined by the programmer. You cannot access an object's data directly, but only through the functions of the object's interface(s). This model is conceptually somewhat similar to C++ classes with all member variables private.

2. You will frequently hear the term "pointer to an object." Although the term gets used a lot as a convenient shorthand, it is really a misnomer. In COM, there ain't no such thing as a pointer to an object. What you have is *a pointer to an interface on the object*. In physical binary terms, you have a pointer to another pointer. This second pointer points to a table of pointers to the interface's member functions. This table of functions is known as a VTBL ("Vee-table"). One of the main advantages to implementing your objects in the C++ language is that the compiler will automatically set up the VTBL for you. However, when you have a pointer to an interface on someone else's object, you cannot assume anything at all about the internal organization of the object. It may well have been written in COBOL. In the following diagram, the location of the VTBL pointer and the object's private data are both shown amorphously, to re-emphasize the fact **that you cannot assume anything at all about the internal organization of an object. When you have a pointer to an interface on an object, you can call that interface's methods. That's all.** You cannot manipulate the internal reference count m_RefCount directly, but only by calling the IUnknown interface methods AddRef( ) and Release( ).

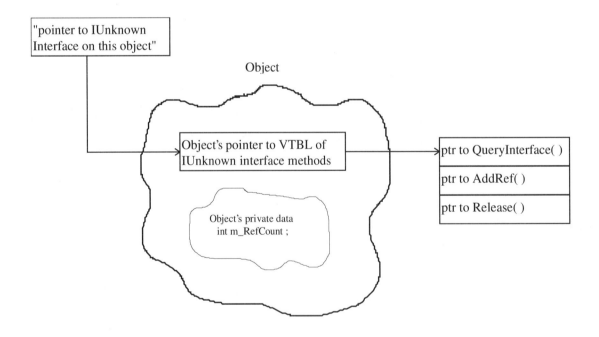

4

3. Once you have a pointer to an object (remember, this is shorthand for having a pointer to some interface on the object), you communicate with the object directly by calling the interface's member functions. But how do you get the first pointer to an object? There are several different ways. You might call an COM/OLE API function that returns a pointer to an object, such as the following:

```
CoCreateInstance( )      // look in registry, launch COM server and get object from it
OleLoad( )               // read embedded or linked object from a document file
OleGetClipboard( )       // return an IDataObject interface pointer to the clipboard's contents
```

Some interfaces have methods that create new objects and return pointers to them. If you have an object of one of these types, you can call the object's method, for example:

```
IDataObject::EnumFormatEtc( )    // return an object that enumerates formats the data object has
IClassFactory::CreateInstance( )  // create a new object of the class manufactured by the factory
```

You might register a callback object whose methods OLE will call and pass you a pointer to an object that OLE has created, for example:

```
RegisterDragDrop( )      // register callback functions for drag-and-drop operations
```

Or you might instantiate a C++ object whose VTBL conforms to the requirements of an OLE interface, for example:

```
new CSomeClass( )        // instantiate an object that implements a COM interface
```

C. IUNKNOWN INTERFACE

1. Every OLE and COM object, without exception, exposes an interface called *IUnknown* which contains the methods **AddRef( )**, **Release( )**, and **QueryInterface( )**. Each and every interface, without exception, is derived from IUnknown and has pointers to these functions as the first three entries in its VTBL. No matter which interface pointer you have, no matter how you got it, you can always call these three methods, and you frequently will.

The first two methods manipulate an internal reference count that controls an object's lifetime. When an object is first created, its creator must call the object's AddRef( ) method to increment the count. Whenever another user is given a pointer to the object, the object's AddRef( ) method must be called again. When the user is finished with the object, he calls that object's Release( ) method, thereby decrementing the reference count. When the last user calls the object's Release( ) method, the count will reach 0, causing the object to destroy itself.   A simple implementation of the methods IUnknown::AddRef( ) and IUnknown::Release( ) might look like this:

```
/*
Increment member variable containing reference count.
*/

ULONG CUnknown::AddRef (void)
{
    return ++m_RefCount ;
}


/*
Decrement member variable containing reference count.  If 0, destroy
object.
*/

ULONG CUnknown::Release (void)
{
    --m_RefCount ;
    if (m_RefCount == 0)
    {
      delete this ;
      return 0 ;
    }
    return m_RefCount ;
}
```

2. Who is responsible for calling AddRef( ) and Release( )? There are two simple rules:

A.   Whenever YOU CALL any function or method that returns a pointer to an object, such as OleGetClipboard( ) or any object's QueryInterface( ) method, the object's AddRef( ) method has already been called for you by the code that supplies the pointer. You must call that object's Release( ) method when you are finished with the object even if you don't do anything with it. It is the object's responsibility to make sure that it continues to exist until you do so.

B. When SOMEONE CALLS YOU and passes an object pointer as a parameter to one of your own callback functions, for example, in drag-and-drop operations, the object's AddRef( ) method has not been called for you. You must call the object's AddRef( ) if you want to use the object, and Release( ) it only if you have done so.

3. When you get a pointer to an object, what you really have is a pointer to one of its interfaces. Which interface you have depends on how you got the pointer. The object might or might not support other interfaces that interest you; there's no way of telling *a priori*. But since every object is guaranteed to support the IUnknown interface, you can ask the object if it supports some other interface that you care about via the method **IUnknown::QueryInterface( )**.

Interfaces are identified by means of *Interface ID's* 16-byte constants. Standard interfaces have their own IID's defined in the system header files, such as IID_IUnknown for the IUnknown interface. When you call QueryInterface( ), you pass it the IID of the interface that you want, and a pointer to an output parameter. If the object supports the requested interface, it will return the success code S_OK (defined as 0) and fill the supplied output parameter with a pointer to the requested interface. If the object does not support the requested interface, it will return a nonzero error code and set the output parameter to NULL. A simple implementation of IUnknown::QueryInterface( ) might look like this:

```
HRESULT CUnknown::QueryInterface(REFIID riid, LPVOID *ppv)
{

/*
Check the IID to see if we support the requested interface.  If we do,
increment the reference count, fill the supplied output variable with a
pointer to the interface, and return the success code.
*/

    if (riid == IID_IUnknown)
    {
        *ppv = (LPVOID)this;
        AddRef();
        return S_OK ;          // success code is 0, repeat zero
    }

/*
We don't support the interface.  Set the supplied output variable to
NULL and return an informative error code.
*/

    else
    {
      *ppv = NULL;
      return  E_NOINTERFACE ; // failure codes are nonzero
    }
}
```

D. DATA TRANSFER

1. Data transfer in OLE is handled by means of *data objects*, which are objects that support the *IDataObject* interface. A data source application creates a data object and makes it available to the consumer via drag-and-drop, the Clipboard, or other channels. In addition to the IUnknown methods supported by every object, the IDataObject interface contains the following methods:

IDataObject::GetData	*// Get object's data in callee-supplied medium*
IDataObject::GetDataHere	*// Get object's data in caller-supplied medium*
IDataObject::QueryGetData	*// Can data be rendered in specified format?*
IDataObject::GetCanonicalFormatEtc	*// Get formats that produce identical data*
IDataObject::SetData	*// Set object's data*
IDataObject::EnumFormatEtc	*// Get enumerator of object's supported data formats*
IDataObject::DAdvise	*// Establish advise loop on this data object*
IDataObject::DUnadvise	*// Unestablish advise loop on this data object*
IDataObject::EnumDAdvise	*// Get enumerator of advise loops on this data objects*

2. Data objects are conceptually similar to individual moveable Clipboards that use delayed rendering and have taken steroids. The single integer that identified a data format in the Clipboard API has been expanded into a FORMATETC structure, allowing the requester of data to be much more specific in indicating its desires. In addition to the original Clipboard format, the caller may specify the type of medium through which the data is to be transferred (global memory, file, metafile, structured storage, etc.), the aspect (level of detail) of the data representation transferred (iconic, thumbnail sketch, or full content), and the output device for which the transferred data is to be formatted.

For the purposes of this book, we will always be using the aspect level DVASPECT_CONTENT, which means "all the data." We will also set the target device to be NULL, which specifies the object's default rendition. For more detailed discussion of the options available in a FORMATETC structure, see Brockschmidt, pp. 497-501. The example on the facing page uses a FORMATETC structure to transfer simple text through an HGLOBAL.

```
typedef struct FARSTRUCT tagFORMATETC
{
    CLIPFORMAT          cfFormat;   // Clipboard format, same as CB API
    DVTARGETDEVICE FAR* ptd;        // target device to format data for
    DWORD               dwAspect;   // level of detail for data
    LONG                lindex;     // reserved, must be -1
    DWORD               tymed;      // type of medium for transfer
} FORMATETC ;
```

3. One potential source of a data object is the existing Windows Clipboard. If your app already handles data objects, it is probably easiest to use the same code for handling data from the Clipboard, rather than write a separate handler using the Clipboard API. The OLE API function **OleGetClipboard( )** synthesizes a data object containing the current contents of the Clipboard, whether or not they were put there by an OLE-aware app. The method **IDataObject::QueryGetData( )** interrogates the data object to see if it can supply data in a specified format and medium, conceptually similar to the API function IsClipboardFormatAvailable( ). Finally we release the object by calling its **Release( )** method.

In the following example, we use OLE to check the Clipboard's contents before displaying the app's menu. If the Clipboard contains text, we enable the "Paste Text" menu item; otherwise we gray it out. The working app may be found in the sample app \CHAPTER1\DONE\DATA1.EXE. Thus:

```
case WM_INITMENU:
{

/*
Get a data object pointer to the current Clipboard contents.
*/
    LPDATAOBJECT lpd ;
    HRESULT hr ;

    hr = OleGetClipboard (&lpd) ;

/*
Fill out a FORMATETC structure, see if the Clipboard data object
contains text.  Gray out EDIT-PASTE menu item if it doesn't, or if
Clipboard is empty (returned data object pointer is NULL).  Otherwise
enable menu item.
*/
    FORMATETC fe ;

    fe.cfFormat = CF_TEXT ;
    fe.ptd = NULL ;
    fe.tymed = TYMED_HGLOBAL ;
    fe.dwAspect = DVASPECT_CONTENT ;
    fe.lindex = -1 ;

    if (!lpd || lpd->QueryGetData (&fe) != S_OK)
    {
      EnableMenuItem ((HMENU)wParam, ID_DEMO_PASTETEXT, MF_GRAYED) ;
    }
    else
    {
      EnableMenuItem ((HMENU)wParam, ID_DEMO_PASTETEXT, MF_ENABLED) ;
    }

/*
Release Clipboard data object.
*/
    if (lpd) lpd->Release( ) ;

    return 0 ;
}
```

4. Actually fetching the object's data is done via the methods **IDataObject::GetData( )** and **IDataObject::GetDataHere( )**. They are conceptually identical, except that in the former, the callee both provides and fills the transfer medium, whereas in the latter, the caller provides the transfer medium and the callee fills it. The former is more common; the latter is used primarily in embedding and linking situations. The example on the facing page shows the use of the former in the DATA1.EXE example when the user picks "Paste Text" from the menu.

Transferred data is held in a structure of type STGMEDIUM. This contains space for the supplier of data to specify and supply the storage medium through which the data is being transferred. Since there are several types of storage media with different rules for their release, the function **ReleaseStgMedium( )** is provided, which is guaranteed to properly dispose of a used STGMEDIUM, no matter what its contents. Thus:

```
typedef struct tagSTGMEDIUM {
    DWORD           tymed;             // flags for self-description

// actual data storage

    union {
    HBITMAP         hBitmap;           // Bitmap
    HMETAFILEPICT   hMetaFilePict;     // METAFILEPICT structure
    HENHMETAFILE    hEnhMetaFile;      // 32-bit enhanced Metafile
    HGLOBAL         hGlobal;           // Global memory
    LPOLESTR        lpszFileName;      // File name
    ISTREAM         *pstm;             // OLE stream  (see chapter 3)
    ISTORAGE        *pstg;             // OLE storage (see chapter 3)
    };

    IUNKNOWN        *pUnkForRelease;   // IUnknown for release of data
} STGMEDIUM;
```

NOTE: In the example on the facing page, it is still necessary to call GlobalLock( ) and GlobalUnlock( ) as shown on the HGLOBAL returned by the method IDataObject::GetData( ). This is because the Clipboard data object's implementation of this method returns a handle to moveable memory rather than fixed memory. This means that the returned handle is actual an index in a table rather than a pointer, and the function GlobalLock( ) is necessary to fetch the actual memory pointer to which the handle refers. I think this is a hangover from Win16, but it exists and must be dealt with nonetheless.

```c
/*
User has picked the EDIT-PASTE command off the menu.  Get data object
from Clipboard and paste its text into our app.
*/

char DisplayText [128] ;

case ID_EDIT_PASTE:
{

/*
Get Clipboard's current contents wrapped in an OLE data object.
*/
    LPDATAOBJECT lpd ;

    OleGetClipboard (&lpd) ;

/*
Get data in text format, transferred in an HGLOBAL.
*/

    STGMEDIUM stg ; FORMATETC fe ;

    fe.cfFormat = CF_TEXT ;
    fe.ptd = NULL ;
    fe.tymed = TYMED_HGLOBAL ;
    fe.dwAspect = DVASPECT_CONTENT ;
    fe.lindex = -1 ;

    lpd->GetData (&fe, &stg) ;

/*
Paste data into our app.  GlobalLock( ) and GlobalUnlock( ) are
required because the handle supplied by the data object is to moveable
memory.
*/

    LPSTR cp = (LPSTR) GlobalLock (stg.hGlobal) ;
    lstrcpyn (DisplayText, cp, sizeof(DisplayText)) ;
    GlobalUnlock (stg.hGlobal) ;
    InvalidateRect (hWnd, NULL, TRUE) ;

/*
Release storage medium and data object.
*/

    ReleaseStgMedium (&stg) ;
    lpd->Release( ) ;

    return 0 ;
}
```

11

E. DRAG AND DROP

1. To accept data via OLE's drag-and-drop mechanism, an app must provide the operating system with a *Drop Target Object*. This is a C++ object that supports OLE's *IDropTarget* interface, providing methods that OLE will call for different situations during a drag-and-drop operation. You must write the code for this object's methods yourself. The object must be created, AddRef( )'d, locked in memory via the function **CoLockObjectExternal**( ), and registered with OLE via the function **RegisterDragDrop**( ). Thus:

```
#include "cdroptgt.h"

CDropTarget *lpDropTarget ;

case WM_CREATE:
{

/*
Set up a drop target.  Instantiate a CDropTarget object and CoLock it
to keep it in memory.  Register it with OLE.
*/

    lpDropTarget = new CDropTarget ( ) ;

    CoLockObjectExternal (lpDropTarget, TRUE, FALSE) ;
    RegisterDragDrop (hWnd, lpDropTarget) ;

    return 0 ;

}
```

When the app no longer wishes to be a drop target, it revokes its drop registration via the function **RevokeDragDrop**( ), unlocks it from memory via the function **CoLockObjectExternal**( ), and releases it with its own Release( ) method, thus:

```
case WM_CLOSE:
{
    RevokeDragDrop (hWnd) ;
    CoLockObjectExternal (lpDropTarget, FALSE, TRUE) ;
    lpDropTarget->Release( ) ;

    DestroyWindow (hWnd) ;
    return 0 ;
}
```

Note: The function CoLockObjectExternal is nonintuitive but necessary. If you leave it out, your drop target will work correctly the first time, but not on subsequent drag operations. You can just put it in as shown and stop worrying about it. Or, for a detailed discussion of the reasons it is needed, see Brockschmidt, pp. 298-300.

2. The drop target object belongs to a class that you have to write yourself. If you write in C++, inheriting from the public Microsoft-supplied class IDropTarget defined in the system header files, the compiler will properly set up all your VTBLs and your life will be relatively simple. All of IDropTarget's methods (and those of all the other standard interfaces) are defined as pure virtual, which means that you have to implement all of them yourself and you can't change any parameters or leave anything out. Your header file CDROPTGT.H will look something like this:

```
class CDropTarget : public IDropTarget
{

    protected:
        ULONG           m_RefCount ;
        LPDATAOBJECT    m_pIDataSource ;

    public:

        CDropTarget(void);
        ~CDropTarget(void);

//IUnknown interface members

        STDMETHODIMP    QueryInterface(REFIID, LPVOID FAR *);
        STDMETHODIMP_(ULONG)  AddRef(void);
        STDMETHODIMP_(ULONG)  Release(void);

//IDropTarget interface members

        STDMETHODIMP DragEnter(LPDATAOBJECT, DWORD, POINTL, LPDWORD);
        STDMETHODIMP DragOver(DWORD, POINTL, LPDWORD);
        STDMETHODIMP DragLeave(void);
        STDMETHODIMP Drop(LPDATAOBJECT, DWORD, POINTL, LPDWORD);

};
```

The class constructor and destructor will look like this:

```
CDropTarget::CDropTarget(void)
{
    m_RefCount = 1 ;              // calling constructor implies AddRef( )
    return;
}

CDropTarget::~CDropTarget(void)
{
    return;
}
```

Note: I like to set my objects' reference counts to 1 in my class constructors. My reasoning is that the constructor is a function that returns a pointer to an object, and any time you call a function that returns a pointer to an object, the pointer has already been AddRef( )'d for your convenience. This is an implementation detail that you can choose to follow or not. If I didn't do it this way, I would have to AddRef( ) my object on the preceding page immediately after constructing it.

3. The IDropTarget interface contains four methods in addition to the standard IUnknown. The first is **IDropTarget::DragEnter( )**, which is called only once when the mouse first enters the target window with a drag operation in progress. You can use this to examine the offered data object and decide if it contains a data format that your app knows how to handle. Note the similarity of this code to that used in the Clipboard data object example on page 9. The main difference is that in the DragEnter( ) method, since OLE called us, we have to AddRef( ) the data object pointer if we want to keep it. This drop target accepts only plain text and doesn't do anything clever with it.

Your drop target signals the result that would happen if the object was dropped by setting the value pointed to by the last parameter, *pdwEffect*. Since this operation is performed in the DragOver( ) method on the facing page, the DragEnter( ) method simply calls DragOver( ) instead of duplicating its code. Thus:

```
STDMETHODIMP CDropTarget::DragEnter(LPDATAOBJECT pIDataSource,
    DWORD grfKeyState, POINTL pt, LPDWORD pdwEffect)
{

/*
Check to see if the data is in a format we can handle (in this case,
only text).  If so, keep a copy of the data object pointer, which means
that we must AddRef( ) it. Note similarity to Clipboard example.
*/

    FORMATETC fe ;

    fe.cfFormat = CF_TEXT ;
    fe.ptd = NULL ;
    fe.tymed = TYMED_HGLOBAL ;
    fe.dwAspect = DVASPECT_CONTENT ;
    fe.lindex = -1 ;

    if (pIDataSource->QueryGetData (&fe) == S_OK)
    {
      m_pIDataSource = pIDataSource ;
      m_pIDataSource->AddRef( ) ;
    }
    else
    {
      m_pIDataSource = NULL ;
    }

/*
Call our own DragOver( ) method to set the effect code.
*/

    DragOver(grfKeyState, pt, pdwEffect) ;

    return S_OK ;
}
```

4. The method **IDropTarget::DragOver( )** is called every time the mouse is moved in the target window during a drag operation, similar to a WM_MOUSEMOVE message. The target's job is to signal back to the source the operation (move, copy, link, nothing, etc.) that would take place if the user dropped the data object at the current mouse location. The target does this by setting the output variable pointed to by the parameter pdwEffect to a specified flag as shown below. On input, this parameter contains flags describing the actions that the source will allow. For example, Winhlp32.exe, being a read-only app, allows a copy operation but not a move. Winword.exe allows copy and move operations, but not link. The state of the mouse, CTRL, and SHIFT keys are provided to the drop target in the parameter grfKeyState.

This method is called frequently, so you want to make it as fast and efficient as possible. You don't have to check if the data is acceptable; you did that when it first entered. DragOver( ) is always called, regardless of the effect code returned from your DragEnter( ) method. Thus:

```
STDMETHODIMP CDropTarget::DragOver(DWORD grfKeyState, POINTL pt,
    LPDWORD pdwEffect)
{

/*
If data is in a format we couldn't handle, then set effect code to
indicate nothing would happen if data was dropped here.
*/
    if (m_pIDataSource == NULL)
    {
      *pdwEffect = DROPEFFECT_NONE ;
    }
/*
Otherwise, if CTRL key is up and permitted effects (supplied by drop
source) allow a move, set the effect code to indicate a move.
*/
    else if (!(grfKeyState&MK_CONTROL) && (*pdwEffect&DROPEFFECT_MOVE))
    {
      *pdwEffect = DROPEFFECT_MOVE ;
    }


/*
Otherwise, if effect permits a copy, set effect code to indicate that.
*/
    else if (*pdwEffect & DROPEFFECT_COPY)
    {
      *pdwEffect = DROPEFFECT_COPY ;
    }
/*
Otherwise, even though the data is in a format that we could accept,
the effect code isn't. Set the effect code to indicate that nothing
would happen if data was dropped here.  Unlikely to actually get here
in real life.
*/
    else
    {
      *pdwEffect = DROPEFFECT_NONE ;
    }
    return S_OK;
}
```

5.   The user may drop the data object on the target, which will cause the method **IDropTarget::Drop( )** to be called. Your app takes the data object and does whatever it wants with its data. This signals the end of a drag operation, so you also have to undo any initialization here. Note the similarity of the pasting code to that used in the Clipboard data object operation on page 11. Thus:

```
extern int xText, yText ;
extern char DisplayText[ ] ;
extern HWND hMainWnd ;

STDMETHODIMP CDropTarget::Drop(LPDATAOBJECT pIDataSource,
    DWORD grfKeyState,  POINTL pt, LPDWORD pdwEffect)
{
    if (m_pIDataSource)
    {

/*
Get point on screen where data was dropped.  Convert to client
coordinates, store in global variables xText and yText, which will
cause main window to display the text where it was dropped.
*/

        ScreenToClient (hMainWnd, (POINT *)(&pt)) ;
        xText = pt.x ;
        yText = pt.y ;

/*
Fetch text from data object.
*/

        STGMEDIUM stg ; FORMATETC fe ;


        fe.cfFormat = CF_TEXT ;
        fe.ptd = NULL ;
        fe.tymed = TYMED_HGLOBAL ;
        fe.dwAspect = DVASPECT_CONTENT ;
        fe.lindex = -1 ;

        m_pIDataSource->GetData (&fe, &stg) ;


/*
Copy data into string for display in main window and Invalidate to
cause a repaint.
*/
        LPSTR cp = (LPSTR) GlobalLock (stg.hGlobal) ;
        lstrcpyn (DisplayText, cp, 127) ;
        GlobalUnlock (stg.hGlobal) ;
        InvalidateRect (hMainWnd, NULL,  FALSE) ;
```

```
/*
Release data object and storage medium.
*/

        ReleaseStgMedium (&stg) ;
        m_pIDataSource->Release( );

    }

/*
Call our own DragOver( ) method to set the effect code.
*/

    DragOver(grfKeyState, pt, pdwEffect) ;
    return NOERROR;
}
```

6. When the mouse leaves the target window without dropping, your app's **IDropTarget::DragLeave( )** method is called. You use this to undo any initialization that you had done during the DragEnter( ) method. Thus:

```
STDMETHODIMP CDropTarget::DragLeave(void)
{
    if (m_pIDataSource)
    {
      m_pIDataSource->Release();
    }

    return NOERROR;
}
```

F. Using Data Objects in the MFC

1. The Microsoft Foundation Classes provide an implementation of the IDataObject and IDropTarget interfaces that we need to make an MFC version of our simple text client app. To use data objects alone in an MFC app, do not select any of the OLE options in App Wizard; they will pull in many large pieces of the MFC that you don't care about, making your app bigger and slower. Instead, simply add the header file "**afxole.h**" to your "stdafx.h" file. You must also call the function **AfxOleInit( )**, which calls OleInitialize( ) and sets up the MFC's own internal OLE bookkeeping, in your app's CWinApp::InitInstance( ) method. Thus:

```
<file stdafx.h>

// stdafx.h : include file for standard system include files,
//  or project-specific include files that are used frequently, but
//      are changed infrequently
//

#define VC_EXTRALEAN

#include <afxwin.h>          // MFC core and standard components
#include <afxext.h>          // MFC extensions
#include <afxole.h>          // MFC OLE stuff

#ifndef _AFX_NO_AFXCMN_SUPPORT
#include <afxcmn.h>
#endif // _AFX_NO_AFXCMN_SUPPORT


<file mfcdata1.cpp>

BOOL CMfcdata1App::InitInstance()
{

/*
Add this function to initialize OLE in the MFC.
*/

    AfxOleInit ( ) ;

    <rest of InitInstance( ) method>
}
```

WARNING: If you have not already read the cautionary note in the preface about dependency on the MFC, go back and do it now.

2. The client side of a data object in the MFC is represented by the class *COleDataObject*, an MFC wrapper that encapsulates an IDataObject pointer. To obtain a COleDataObject that represents the current contents of the Clipboard, you instantiate an object of this class and call its **AttachClipboard( )** method. The method **COleDataObject::IsDataAvailable( )** is the wrapper for the IDataObject::QueryGetData( ) method, asking the object whether or not it could render the data in a specified format. We turn the sample app's "Paste Text" menu item on or off based on the object's reply.

```
/*
Called when the app's menu is about to be shown.
*/


void CMfcdata1View::OnUpdateDataobjectPastetext(CCmdUI* pCmdUI)
{

/*
Instantiate   a   COleDataObject.    Tell   it   to   attach   itself   to   the
Clipboard.
*/
    COleDataObject dataobj ;

    dataobj.AttachClipboard ( ) ;

/*
Ask the COleDataObject attached to the Clipboard if it could supply us
with text.  Turn the "Paste Text" menu item on or off accordingly.
*/

    pCmdUI->Enable (dataobj.IsDataAvailable (CF_TEXT)) ;

/*
The COleDataObject is automatically detached from the Clipboard by its
destructor as it goes out of scope.
*/

}
```

3. We obtain data from a COleDataObject via its **GetData( )** method. When the user selects "Paste Text" from the sample app's menu, the command handler shown below is executed. We instantiate a COleDataObject, attach it to the Clipboard, and paste the text from it into our document. Because the drag-and-drop operation supplies us with the same object, I have placed the pasting code in a separate method of my CView class to be called from both Clipboard and drag-and-drop operations.

```
void CMfcdata1View::OnDataobjectPastetext()
{
    COleDataObject dataobj ;

    dataobj.AttachClipboard ( ) ;

    PasteTextIntoMyDocument (&dataobj) ;
}
```

The code for the pasting operation is shown on the facing page. It illustrates the fact that data transfer using OLE is identical no matter where the data object comes from. It also illustrates the fact that the MFC sometimes gets too clever for its own good, and that you will not, repeat NOT, be able to ship a working app without understanding what OLE is doing in its heart of hearts. (You may be able to make plenty of money from half-working apps, but that's another issue.)

Why do I need to fill out a FORMATETC structure when I call COleDataObject::GetData( )? Why can't I just say :

```
pData->GetData (CF_TEXT, &stg) ;
```

and use the default FORMATETC supplied by the MFC ? If you do this in Windows NT version 3.51, your sample app will not paste text from the Clipboard. It will accept text via drag-and-drop from WinWord, but not from WinHelp. (Try this on the sample app.) Why is this, and what do I do to fix it?

If you use the debugger to step down into the COleDataObject::GetData( ) source code, you will find that when it fills out its default FORMATETC, it sets the `tymed` element to 0xFFFFFFFF. If you look in the documentation for IDataObject::GetData( ), you will find that this is allowed, in fact, encouraged; the caller is saying that it will accept any tymed that the object is able to render and that the object should choose the most appropriate tymed for the requested format and aspect. OK, sounds fine, but the data objects provided by the Clipboard and WinHelp do not support this feature even though the docs say they are supposed to and the data objects supplied by WinWord do. When presented with a choice of tymed, they will choke and supply nothing. As a guess, I'd say they are using the == operator to check the requested tymed rather than the & operator (see page 33). This is the kind of bug that you see in OLE all the time. No matter what the docs say an object ought to do, objects do whatever their programmers wrote code to make them do.

But we checked the object first! Why did the default work in the IsDataAvailable( ) method but not in the GetData( ) method? It's because the MFC got a little too clever. If you use the debugger to step down into the IsDataAvailable( ) method, you will see that if the COleDataObject is connected to the Clipboard, the MFC uses the Clipboard API to check for format availability instead of going through OLE, presumably for speed. That's fine, but the GetData( ) method does not use the Clipboard API, it always uses OLE even to access the Clipboard. The channel the MFC checked for availability is not the channel used for transfer, and the results are different.

How do we fix it? Once we figure out what's happening, it's quite simple; just explicitly provide a FORMATETC requiring the data to be transferred through an HGLOBAL, which is all our sample app knows how to use anyway. But it shows that the MFC is not a magic bullet, there ain't no such thing as a magic bullet in software. It is a very powerful tool, but like all powerful tools, it is double-edged and you need to understand fully what it's really doing before you can make a profit wielding it.

20

```
/*
Pasting function.  Default values are provided for last two parameters;
see header file on next page.
*/

BOOL CMfcdata1View::PasteTextIntoMyDocument(COleDataObject *pData,
    DROPEFFECT de, CPoint point)
{
    STGMEDIUM stg ;

/*
Fill  out  a  FORMATETC  structure  describing  how  we  want  the  data
transferred.
*/
    FORMATETC fe ;
    fe.cfFormat  = CF_TEXT ;
    fe.tymed = TYMED_HGLOBAL ;
    fe.lindex = -1 ;
    fe.dwAspect = DVASPECT_CONTENT ;
    fe.ptd = NULL ;

/*
Attempt to get the data from the COleDataObject.
*/
    if (pData->GetData (CF_TEXT, &stg, &fe))
    {
/*
Copy data from STGMEDIUM into document's CString.
*/
      CMfcdata1Doc* pDoc = GetDocument();
      pDoc->m_String = (char *) GlobalLock (stg.hGlobal) ;
      GlobalUnlock (stg.hGlobal) ;
/*
Copy supplied point into member variable used by OnDraw( ).  Invalidate
to force a repaint.
*/
      m_DropPoint = point ;
      Invalidate ( ) ;

/*
Return success or failure code as appropriate.
*/
      return TRUE ;
    }
    else
    {
      return FALSE ;
    }
}
```

4. Now we want to make our app accept text by means of drag-and-drop as well as the Clipboard. From reading the first part of this chapter, you know that we need a drop target. The MFC has provided a default implementation of the IDropTarget interface in the class *COleDropTarget*. We add a member variable of this class to our view. Then in the view's OnCreate( ) handler, call the method **COleDropTarget::Register( )**, passing it a pointer to the view, which causes the drop target to register and lock itself. Thus:

```
class CMfcdata1View : public CView
{
    COleDropTarget m_DropTarget ;
    BOOL m_bCanDrop ;
    CPoint m_DropPoint ;

    BOOL PasteTextIntoMyDocument (COleDataObject *,
      DROPEFFECT de = DROPEFFECT_COPY, CPoint point = CPoint(0,0));

    < rest of view header file >
} ;



/*
When the view is created, register the drop target.
*/

int CMfcdata1View::OnCreate(LPCREATESTRUCT lpCreateStruct)
{
    if (CView::OnCreate(lpCreateStruct) == -1)
      return -1;

    m_DropTarget.Register (this) ;

    return 0;
}
```

5. The base class CView contains the methods **OnDragEnter( )**, **OnDragOver( )**, and **OnDrop( )** that are called from the registered COleDropTarget when these events happen. The default implementations don't do anything. We use Class Wizard to override them in our view, supplying our own version of what ought to happen when these take place. Thus:

6. Our view's **OnDragEnter( )** method is called once, when the drag operation first enters our view. The COleDataObject that represents the data being dragged is supplied to us as the first parameter. As in the API, we check the data object to see if it contains a format that our view knows how to use, in this case, only text. We signal the effect that would take place if the drop occurred here by returning a DROPEFFECT, the code for determining which lives in our OnDragOver( ) method. Thus:

```
DROPEFFECT CMfcdata1View::OnDragEnter(COleDataObject* pDataObject,
    DWORD dwKeyState, CPoint point)
{

/*
Check to see if the offered data object is capable of supplying text.
Remember its capability in a BOOL member variable.
*/
    if (pDataObject->IsDataAvailable(CF_TEXT))
    {
      m_bCanDrop = TRUE ;
    }
    else
    {
      m_bCanDrop = FALSE ;
    }

/*
Rather than duplicate code for determining drop effects, call our own
OnDragOver( ) method and return its result.
*/

    return OnDragOver (pDataObject, dwKeyState, point) ;

}
```

7. Our view's **OnDragOver( )** method gets called every time the mouse moves in our view while a drag operation is in progress. We determine what operation would take place if the drop took place at the specified point with the specified state of the keys and return a DROPEFFECT code to signal this back to the drop source app.

```
DROPEFFECT CMfcdata1View::OnDragOver(COleDataObject* pDataObject,
    DWORD dwKeyState, CPoint point)
{
/*
If data object contains a format we can use, as determined previously
in OnDragEnter( ), check to see if the control key is down.  If so,
return effect code to signal copy operation, otherwise return effect
code to signal move operation. We don't bother looking at the drop
location; our view does the same thing at every point.
*/
    if (m_bCanDrop)
    {
      if (!(dwKeyState & MK_CONTROL))
      {
            return DROPEFFECT_MOVE ;
      }
      else
      {
            return DROPEFFECT_COPY ;
      }
    }
/*
Data object does not contain a format we can use; return the DROPEFFECT
code that signals this.
*/
    return DROPEFFECT_NONE ;
}
```

8. In our view's **OnDrop( )** method, we copy the data out of the supplied object and make use of it. We already have a helper function in our view class that does this. Thus:

```
BOOL CMfcdata1View::OnDrop(COleDataObject* pDataObject,
    DROPEFFECT dropEffect, CPoint point)
{
    return PasteTextIntoMyDocument (pDataObject, dropEffect, point) ;
}
```

Lab Exercises
Chapter 1
Data Transfer Object Consumer

Directory: \EssenceofOLE\chap01\data1\templ

This lab creates an app that accepts simple text data from the Clipboard by means of a data object. It also implements a drop target object that accepts simple text via drag and drop. A skeleton app is supplied for you in the directory listed above; you may want to build it and run it first (it won't do much) to make sure that your development environment is properly configured.

1. Your app must first initialize the OLE libraries. In the file WINMAIN.CPP, add a call to OleInitialize( ) at the start of the function WinMain( ). Add a call to OleUninitialize( ) at the end of WinMain( ).

2. The Demo-Paste Text menu item starts out grayed. We would like to make it respond to the contents of the Clipboard, enabling the menu item if the Clipboard contains text and disabling it otherwise. In the file MAINWIND.CPP, in the WM_INITMENU message handler, add the following code: Call the function OleGetClipboard( ) to get a data object that encapsulates the current contents of the Clipboard. Allocate a FORMATETC structure and fill its fields with the correct parameters for requesting data in the CF_TEXT format via an HGLOBAL transfer medium. Use the data object's QueryGetData( ) method to ask the object if it can supply data in this manner. If it can, enable the menu item, otherwise gray it out. The menu modification code has been supplied for you. Release the Clipboard data object when you are finished.

3. When the user chooses the Demo-Paste Text menu item, we need to get the text from the Clipboard and paste it into the app. In the file MAINWIND.CPP, in the ID_DEMO_PASTETEXT case of the WM_COMMAND message handler, use the function OleGetClipboard( ) to get the Clipboard's contents wrapped in a data object. Allocate a FORMATETC structure and also an STGMEDIUM structure; fill out the fields of the former. This time, use the object's GetData( ) method to actually retrieve the data in text format. Copy the new data from the STGMEDIUM structure into the global string array named DisplayText[ ], which is provided for you. Finally, release the storage medium via the function ReleaseStgMedium( ) and release the Clipboard data object via its own Release( ) method. Your app should now properly paste text from the Clipboard into the upper left corner of its window.

4. Our app now supports the Clipboard, we would like to make it do the same thing via drag-and-drop. A skeleton of a drop target class, called CDropTarget, has been provided for you in the file CDROPTGT.CPP. Examine this file and its header file CDROPTGT.H. You will find the IUnknown methods have been written for you, but the other four methods are empty shells. In the file MAINWIND.CPP, in the WM_CREATE message handler, instantiate a CDropTarget object and use the function CoLockObjectExternal( ) to lock it into memory. Use the function RegisterDragDrop( ) to notify OLE that your app will accept drop operations. In the WM_CLOSE message handler, use the function RevokeDragDrop( ) to notify OLE that your window will no longer accept drop operations, unlock it from memory via the function CoLockObjectExternal( ), then free it with its own Release( ) method.

5. Our drop target is connected. Its methods will be called when a drag operation takes place over our window, but so far they don't do anything. Now we have to start implementing the code to make it do what we want. The first method, CDropTarget::DragEnter( ), is called when the mouse first enters the target window. What we need to do here is check if the data object that the operation contains (passed as the first parameter) can supply the data in the format that we need. Use the object's QueryGetData( ) method to ask the object if it can render its data in CF_TEXT via an HGLOBAL medium. This code will bear an uncanny resemblance to what you did in step 2 above. If the data can be so rendered, save the data pointer in the member variable m_pIDataSource and AddRef( ) it to make sure it will stay valid until we

26

need it. Otherwise, set the member variable to NULL. You can set the effect code yourself, or, to save duplication, call your own DragOver( ) method described in the next paragraph.

6. The next method is CDropTarget::DragOver( ), which is conceptually similar to the WM_MOUSEMOVE message. In this case, simply check the value of the data pointer m_pIDataSource. If it is NULL, then our DragEnter( ) method initially decided that the object couldn't supply the data in a format that we wanted, so set the effect to DROPEFFECT_NONE. If it is non-NULL, then we can accept the data. Check the state of the control key, passed in the first parameter. If it's up, and the source permits a move (check the last parameter), then set the effect code to DROPEFFECT_MOVE. Otherwise, if the source permits a copy, then set it to DROPEFFECT_COPY.

7. The DragLeave( ) method is trivial. If the m_pIDataSource pointer is valid, release the object via its Release( ) method. That's all.

8. Now we are left with the Drop( ) method. First, convert the point from the screen coordinates it comes in to the client coordinates that your window wants via the API function ScreenToClient( ). The main window's handle is supplied for you in the global variable hMainWnd. Set the drop point's X value into the global variable xText and its Y value into the global yText. This will cause the WM_PAINT message handler to draw it at the place on the screen where it was dropped. Next, use the data object pointer to get the data from the object in the CF_TEXT format. This will be very similar to step 3 above, including the release of both data object and storage medium. Finally, call your own DragOver( ) method to set the effect code.

EXTRA CREDIT: When dragging text inside your window, use a focus rectangle to show the size of the string being dragged. In your DragEnter( ) method, get the data from the dragged object via its GetData( ) method, then use the function DrawText( ) with the flag DT_CALCRECT to calculate the rectangle that the text would occupy if drawn. Store the rectangle in a member variable. Then in your DragOver( ) method, use the function DrawFocusRect( ) to put a focus rectangle on the screen at the point where the mouse is, showing the rectangle that the text would occupy. You will also have to add another member variable to your drop target for storing the point at which you drew the last focus rectangle, so you can remove it before you draw the new one.

Lab Exercises
Chapter 1
MFC Data Transfer Object Consumer

Directory: \EssenceofOLE\chap01\mfcdata1\templ

This lab uses the MFC to do the same thing as the data1 lab did in the API. It creates an app that accepts simple text data from the Clipboard by means of a data object. It also implements a drop target object that accepts simple text via drag and drop. A skeleton app is supplied for you in the directory listed above; you may want to build it and run it first (it won't do much) to make sure that your development environment is properly configured.

1. First, we need to include the necessary header files and initialize OLE. Add the header file "afxole.h" to the other #include files in your "stdafx.h" master header file. In the function CMfcdata1App::InitInstance( ), add a call to AfxOleInit( ).

2. We want to turn the "Paste Text" menu item on and off to indicate whether the Clipboard contains text, and we want to implement this feature using OLE. In the UpdateCommandUI handler CMfcdata1View::OnUpdateDataobjectPastetext( ) supplied for you, instantiate a COleDataObject and attach it to the Clipboard via its AttachClipboard( ) method. Use the data object's IsDataAvailable( ) method to find out if it can supply us with text or not. Use the pCmdUI->Enable( ) method to turn the menu item on or off based on this result.

3. Now we want to paste data into our app from the Clipboard using the COleDataObject. In the command handler CMfcdata1View::OnDataobjectPastetext( ), instantiate a COleDataObject and attach it to the Clipboard. A function CMfcdata1View::PasteTextIntoMyDocument( ) is supplied for you; pass it a pointer to the Clipboard data object. Only the skeleton of this function is supplied for you, you have to provide the guts of the function yourself. Instantiating and setting the necessary structures, call the data object's GetData( ) method to retrieve the text. Your document contains a CString member variable called "m_String", the contents of which are drawn by the supplied CMfcdata1View::OnDraw( ) method. Copy the data from the STGMEDIUM in which the data object supplies it into this variable and invalidate( ) to force a repaint.

4. Now we want to make our app accept text via drag and drop. In the header file "mfcdata1view.h", add a member variable of class COleDropTarget to your view class. In the handler function CMfcdata1View::OnCreate( ), call the drop target's Register( ) method to register it with OLE.

5. We now need to override the OnDragEnter( ), OnDragOver( ), and OnDrop( ) methods of our view class in order to add our own handling for these events. Use Class Wizard to override these member functions.

6. In your view's OnDragEnter( ) member function, use the method COleDataObject::IsDataAvailable( ) to see if the object is capable (or thinks it is capable) of rendering its data in text format. Remember its response in a BOOLean member variable. Call your own OnDragOver( ) member function to get the DROPEFFECT code to return.

7. In your view's OnDragOver( ) member function, check to see what the effect would be if the user dropped the data object in your view. If the object contains a format you can use, then return DROPEFFECT_COPY if the control key is down and DROPEFFECT_MOVE if it is up. Otherwise, return DROPEFFECT_NONE.

8. In your view's OnDrop( ) member function, use the helper function that you added in step 3 to paste the dropped text into your app's window.

28

Chapter 2

Sourcing Data Objects

A. Data Objects, Part 2: Sourcing Data

1. To make your app a source of data objects, you must derive a class from the public class *IDataObject*, the definition of which is found in the system header files. The methods of a data object are conceptually similar to the code that you would have to write for an app that used delayed rendering on the Clipboard. You header file might look like this:

```
class CTextData : public IDataObject
{

    private:
      ULONG        m_RefCount ;
      UINT         m_length ;
      LPSTR        m_cp ;

    public:

      CTextData(LPSTR);        // constructor needs text pointer
      ~CTextData(void);

// IUnknown methods

      STDMETHODIMP        QueryInterface(REFIID, LPVOID *);
      STDMETHODIMP_(ULONG)    AddRef(void);
      STDMETHODIMP_(ULONG)    Release(void);

// IDataObject methods

      STDMETHODIMP GetData (LPFORMATETC, LPSTGMEDIUM) ;
      STDMETHODIMP GetDataHere (LPFORMATETC, LPSTGMEDIUM) ;
      STDMETHODIMP QueryGetData (LPFORMATETC) ;
      STDMETHODIMP GetCanonicalFormatEtc (LPFORMATETC, LPFORMATETC) ;
      STDMETHODIMP SetData (LPFORMATETC, STGMEDIUM *, BOOL) ;
      STDMETHODIMP EnumFormatEtc (DWORD, LPENUMFORMATETC *) ;

      STDMETHODIMP DAdvise (FORMATETC *, DWORD, LPADVISESINK, DWORD*) ;
      STDMETHODIMP DUnadvise  (DWORD) ;
      STDMETHODIMP EnumDAdvise  (LPENUMSTATDATA *);

};
```

Of the nine methods required by the IDataObject interface, only the three shown in bold above are required for a simple one-way data transfer object of the type used for drag-and-drop or the Clipboard. The remainder can be stubbed out, as described on page 37.

2. Consider the case of a data object that encapsulates text data, but offers it to the consumer in either text or metafile format. This is the object provided by the sample app in the directory \chap02\data2. You instantiate such an object by passing the desired text string to the class constructor, thus:

```
#include "ctxtdata.h"
extern char DisplayText[ ] ;

case ID_DEMO_COPYTEXT:
{
    LPCTEXTDATA lpd = new CTextData (DisplayText) ;
    etc...
```

The class constructor allocates a piece of global memory in which to store the text data. This is the object's own internal storage, represented by the inner amorphous figure on page 4. It has nothing to do with how the object does or doesn't render the data to a consumer. The class destructor frees the memory. Thus:

```
/*
Constructor -- allocate global memory to hold text string.  Initialize
other member variables.
*/


CTextData::CTextData(LPSTR lpString)
{
    m_RefCount = 1 ;
    m_length = lstrlen (lpString) + 1;
    m_cp = (LPSTR) GlobalAlloc (GMEM_FIXED, m_length) ;
    lstrcpy (m_cp, lpString) ;
}

/*
Class destructor -- free internal storage to avoid a memory leak.
*/

CTextData::~CTextData(void)
{
    GlobalFree (m_cp) ;
}
```

31

This page intentionally contains no text other than this sentence.

3. The simplest method of a data object is **IDataObject::QueryGetData( )**, which specifies whether the object can or cannot be rendered in the format specified by FORMATETC structure supplied by the caller. It is conceptually similar to the API function IsClipboardFormatAvailable( ). You look at the contents of the FORMATETC, and if your object is smart enough to supply its data in the requested format, you return the success code S_OK. If not, you return the error code DATA_E_FORMATETC.

Note that the TYMED enumeration may contain more than one flag ORed together. In this case, the client is saying that it can accept any of the specified TYMED choices, and the object should pick whichever it thinks is most appropriate. Because of this, we need to use the **&** operator as shown below. Our class which can render both CF_TEXT and CF_METAFILEPICT implements this method thus:

```
STDMETHODIMP CTextData::QueryGetData (LPFORMATETC lpfe)
{

/*
We'll give you text, transferred through a global, with aspect
content.  If the user is asking for this, return success code.
*/
    if (lpfe->cfFormat == CF_TEXT
      && (lpfe->tymed & TYMED_HGLOBAL)
      && lpfe->dwAspect == DVASPECT_CONTENT)
    {
      return S_OK ;
    }


/*
Or we'll give the same text drawn in a metafile, also with aspect
content.  Return success code.
*/

    else if (lpfe->cfFormat == CF_METAFILEPICT
      && (lpfe->tymed & TYMED_MFPICT)
      && lpfe->dwAspect == DVASPECT_CONTENT)
    {
      return S_OK ;
    }

/*
But we won't give you anything else
*/

    return DATA_E_FORMATETC ;

}
```

4. The primary method used for actually transferring data is **IDataObject::GetData( )**. In this method, the object itself allocates the medium through which the data is transferred. The recipient is responsible for freeing the transfer medium by calling the function ReleaseStgMedium( ).   Our text/metafile object implements it thus:

```
/*
GetData Method.  Caller demanding that we supply data in a given
format and medium.
*/

STDMETHODIMP CTextData::GetData (LPFORMATETC lpfe, LPSTGMEDIUM lpstg)
{

/*
We support text format, transferred through a global, with aspect
content. Allocate a new global, copy our text into it.
*/
    if (lpfe->cfFormat == CF_TEXT
      && (lpfe->tymed & TYMED_HGLOBAL)
      && lpfe->dwAspect == DVASPECT_CONTENT)
    {
      LPSTR cpout ;

      cpout = (LPSTR) GlobalAlloc(GMEM_FIXED, m_length);
      if (!cpout)
      {
            return E_OUTOFMEMORY ;
      }

      lstrcpy (cpout, m_cp) ;

/*
Fill in the elements of the STGMEDIUM structure that we were passed.
*/
      lpstg->tymed = TYMED_HGLOBAL ;          // flag specifying data type
      lpstg->hGlobal = (HGLOBAL) cpout ;      // HGLOBAL containing data
      lpstg->pUnkForRelease = NULL ;          // caller must free memory

      return S_OK ;

    }
```

```
/*
We also support the metafile format (in tasteful colors of yellow on
green).
*/

    else if (lpfe->cfFormat == CF_METAFILEPICT
      && (lpfe->tymed & TYMED_MFPICT)
      && lpfe->dwAspect == DVASPECT_CONTENT)
    {
      HMETAFILE hMF ; HDC hDC ;

/*
Create a DC mapped to a metafile, draw our text on the DC, then close
the DC to convert it into a memory metafile.
*/
      hDC = CreateMetaFile (NULL) ;

      SetBkColor (hDC, RGB (0, 255, 0)) ;
      SetTextColor (hDC, RGB (255, 255, 0)) ;
      TextOut (hDC, 0, 0, m_cp, m_length) ;

      hMF = CloseMetaFile (hDC) ;

/*
Allocate a METAFILEPICT structure to describe the picture. Fill in its
elements.
*/
      METAFILEPICT *pMF = (METAFILEPICT *) GlobalAlloc (GPTR,
            sizeof (METAFILEPICT));

      pMF->hMF = hMF ;
      pMF->mm = MM_TEXT ;
      pMF->xExt = 100 ;
      pMF->yExt = 100 ;

/*
Fill in the elements of STGMEDIUM structure to return data to caller.
*/
      lpstg->tymed = TYMED_MFPICT ;          // flag specifying data type
      lpstg->hMetaFilePict = (HMETAFILEPICT) pMF ;    // data itself
      lpstg->pUnkForRelease = NULL ;         // caller must free memory

      return S_OK ;

    }

/*
User asked for a format that we couldn't supply.  Return error code.
*/

    return DATA_E_FORMATETC ;
}
```

5. Your data object must also support the method **IDataObject::EnumFormatEtc( )**, which is conceptually similar to the API function EnumClipboardFormats( ). Your data object must create and return an *Enumerator Object*, which is an object that supports the following methods for iterating along a list of FORMATETC structures:

IEnumFORMATETC::Next
IEnumFORMATETC::Skip
IEnumFORMATETC::Reset
IEnumFORMATETC::Clone

The easiest thing to do is to swipe an already written format enumerator from the sample code supplied with this book. I have written a generic enumerator object which works with any structure. You will find it in the files cenum.cpp and cenum.h in the data2 sample. You simply instantiate an object of the supplied class CEnumerator, passing the constructor an array of the FORMATETC structures that your object supports along with other necessary administrative information. You may use this code freely in your products provided you tell everyone who asks about the cool book from which you shamelessly pirated it. Anyone interested in more information about format enumerators may find it in Brockschmidt, pp. 508-511. The caller is responsible for releasing the enumerator object when finished with it. Thus:

```
#include "cenum.h"

FORMATETC feArray []= {
    { CF_TEXT, NULL, DVASPECT_CONTENT,  -1, TYMED_HGLOBAL },
    { CF_METAFILEPICT, NULL, DVASPECT_CONTENT,  -1, TYMED_MFPICT }
    };


STDMETHODIMP CTextData::EnumFormatEtc (DWORD dwDir,
    LPENUMFORMATETC * lpEnum)
{

/*
Create format enumerator object from providentially supplied sample
code, and store a pointer to it in the supplied output variable. We
must make sure that the enumerator's AddRef( ) method is called before
we give the pointer back to the caller.  This is done for us
automatically in the CEnumerator's constructor.
*/

    *lpEnum = (LPENUMFORMATETC) new CEnumerator (
      this,              // object whose formats enumerator describes
      feArray,           // array of FORMATETC structures
      2,                 // number of structures in array
      sizeof (FORMATETC),    // size of each structure
      IID_IEnumFORMATETC) ;   //interface supported by enumerator obj

    if (*lpEnum == NULL)
    {
    return E_FAIL ;
    }

    return S_OK ;
}
```

6. The IDataObject interface contains six other methods that this particular object chooses not to support. It is entirely up to the provider of the object to decide which methods it will or won't support.

Not implementing a method means that the object will be somewhat less useful. For example, an object that doesn't implement the IDataObject::SetData( ) method will be able to transfer data in only one direction. This is frequently all the functionality you need.

We have to provide entries in the VTBL for all methods in the interface specification, whether or not our object does anything useful with them, as the user of this object has no idea which methods the object does and doesn't support. The unimplemented methods can be empty shells that return only an error code, but the user has to be able to call all the methods without crashing. As my old rabbi used to say, "God answers all prayers, but sometimes the answer is 'No'." Thus:

```
STDMETHODIMP CTextData::GetDataHere (LPFORMATETC lpfe,
    LPSTGMEDIUM lpst)
{
    return E_NOTIMPL ;
}


STDMETHODIMP CTextData::SetData (LPFORMATETC lpfe, STGMEDIUM * lpst,
    BOOL fRelease)
{
    return E_NOTIMPL ;
}


STDMETHODIMP CTextData::GetCanonicalFormatEtc (LPFORMATETC lpout,
    LPFORMATETC lpin)
{
    return E_NOTIMPL ;
}


STDMETHODIMP CTextData::DAdvise (FORMATETC *lpfe, DWORD dw,
    LPADVISESINK lpas, DWORD * lpdw)
{
    return E_NOTIMPL ;
}


STDMETHODIMP CTextData::DUnadvise   (DWORD dw)
{
    return E_NOTIMPL ;
}


STDMETHODIMP CTextData::EnumDAdvise   (LPENUMSTATDATA * lpen)
{
    *lpen = NULL ;
    return E_NOTIMPL ;
}
```

NOTE: Methods whose parameter lists contain output parameters for returning pointers to objects must set the pointer value to NULL in addition to returning the error code, as shown in the method IDataObject::EnumDAdvise( ) above. The specifications call for this, and a number of consumer apps depend on it and will croak if you fail to do it. Consult the documentation for the stubbed method to be sure.

B. SETTING THE CLIPBOARD WITH DATA OBJECTS

1. Once you have a data object, you can make it available to other apps by placing it on the Clipboard via the function **OleSetClipboard( )**. The Clipboard will enumerate the formats from your object and make an entry for each of them, thereby making your data available to other apps that do not necessarily support OLE. Thus:

```
#include "ctxtdata.h"

extern char DisplayText [ ] ;

/*
User picked EDIT--COPY from the menu.  The Clipboard itself will be
responsible for releasing it.  Thus:
*/

case ID_DEMO_COPYTEXT:
{

/*
Create a new data object encapsulating the current display text and
place it on the Clipboard. The Clipboard is responsible for calling the
object's AddRef( ) method if it wants to retain the object's pointer
longer than the duration of this call.
*/

    LPCTEXTDATA lpd = new CTextData (DisplayText) ;
    OleSetClipboard (lpd) ;

/*
We have no further use for this object, so we release our pointer on
it. When the Clipboard is also finished and releases all of its
pointers, the reference count will drop to zero and the object will
destroy itself. We can't delete the object ourselves because we don't
know how long the Clipboard needs to keep it.
*/

    lpd->Release( ) ;
    return 0 ;
}
```

C. DROP SOURCING

1. Sourcing a drag-and-drop operation is controlled by the *IDropSource* interface. When an app wants to begin a drag operation, it calls the API function **DoDragDrop( )**, passing a pointer to an IDropSource object to control the operation, and also a data object which contains the data being offered. This function causes OLE to capture the mouse and begin the drag operation. It does not return until the drag operation completes. Its return code indicates whether the user has dropped the data on a willing target, and the output parameter indicates the effect code set by the target. Thus:

```
#include "ctxtdata.h"
#include "cdropsrc.h"

case WM_LBUTTONDOWN:
{
    DWORD dwEffect ;

/*
Create a data object encapsulating the currently displayed text, and
also a drop source object.
*/

    LPCTEXTDATA lpd = new CTextData (DisplayText) ;
    LPDROPSOURCE lps = new CDropSource ( ) ;

/*
Perform the drag operation.  If the return code indicates a successful
drop and the output effect code indicates that the user said to move
the text (DROPEFFECT_MOVE) as opposed to copying it, then remove the
text from our window.
*/
    if (DoDragDrop (lpd,        //data object containing offered data
      lps,                      // drop source controlling operation
      DROPEFFECT_COPY | DROPEFFECT_MOVE,  // permitted effect codes
      &dwEffect)                // effect code output parameter
      == DRAGDROP_S_DROP)
    {
      if (dwEffect & DROPEFFECT_MOVE)
      {
          DisplayText [0] = 0x00 ;
          InvalidateRect (hWnd, NULL, TRUE) ;
      }
    }

/*
Release data object and drop source object.
*/

    lpd->Release ( ) ;
    lps->Release ( ) ;
    return 0 ;
}
```

2. The IDropSource interface has only two methods, and they're both pretty simple. Since DoDragDrop( ) doesn't return until the drag operation is finished, your app will not be processing messages during this time. The method **IDropSource::QueryContinueDrag( )** is your app's chance to control the drag operation while it is in progress. OLE will call this method in response to each WM_MOUSEMOVE message that it receives while dragging.

If the user presses the escape key, or your app detects other cancellation criteria (not shown), returning the value DRAGDROP_S_CANCEL causes the operation to be canceled. If the left mouse button has been released, then returning DRAGDROP_S_DROP causes the drop operation to take place. Otherwise, returning S_OK allows the operation to continue unchanged. Thus:

```
STDMETHODIMP CDropSource::QueryContinueDrag(BOOL fEsc,
    DWORD grfKeyState)
{

/*
Escape key pressed, cancel drag operation.
*/
    if (fEsc)
    {
        return DRAGDROP_S_CANCEL ;
    }

/*
Left mouse button released, perform drop operation.
*/

    if (!(grfKeyState & MK_LBUTTON))
    {
        return DRAGDROP_S_DROP ;
    }

    return NOERROR;
}
```

3. The method **IDropSource::GiveFeedback( )** allows you to examine the effect code returned by the drop target's methods. If you want to show your own cursors you can do so here, otherwise returning the value DRAGDROP_S_USEDEFAULTCURSORS causes OLE to use the standard ones. In a real-life app, this method frequently contains only the last line. Thus:

```
extern HWND hMainWnd ;

STDMETHODIMP CDropSource::GiveFeedback(DWORD dwEffect)
{
    POINT p ;

/*
If the cursor is over our own window, show a different cursor.
*/

    GetCursorPos (&p) ;
    if (WindowFromPoint (p) == hMainWnd)
    {
      SetCursor (LoadCursor (NULL, IDC_SIZE)) ;
      return S_OK ;
    }

/*
Cursor is not over our own window, so show default cursor.
*/

    return  DRAGDROP_S_USEDEFAULTCURSORS ;
}
```

D. DATA OBJECT SERVERS

    1. A data object server does not have to be running for you to obtain its object. Via the API function **CoCreateInstance( )**, you can ask COM to wake up a registered server app or DLL and create an object for you. You identify the object you want by means of its *globally unique ID* (GUID), also known as a *class ID* (CLSID). This is a 16-byte constant provided by the supplier of the server, who in turn created it with the utility app GUIDGEN.EXE that comes with your development environment.

    When you call CoCreateInstance( ), you can specify whether you want to load the object from a *local server* (.EXE) or an *in-proc server* (.DLL). Most servers come in only one or the other flavors; it is rare to find both together. Combining the context flags as shown below causes COM to look for an in-proc server first, and use a local server only if unable to find an in-proc server.

    COM looks in the system registry to find the server that has registered to supply this class of object. COM then loads the server, has the server create an object of the requested class, and give you back a pointer to the requested interface on the newly created object. You will find the sample code for this app in the directory \chap02\data3. Thus:

```
/*
Globally unique ID of the object we want to create.  Supplied by the
vendor who made the server.
*/

static const GUID GUID_TimeData = { 0xe7767a70, 0xa409, 0x11ce,
    { 0xad, 0xf, 0x0, 0x60, 0x8c, 0x86, 0xb8, 0x9c } };


/*
User made menu selection telling us to create an object of the
specified type, using either an in-proc or a local server.  Tell COM to
find the server, wake it up, make it create an object, and give us back
a pointer to its IDataObject interface.
*/

LPDATAOBJECT lpd = NULL ;

case ID_DATAOBJECT_CREATE:
{
    HRESULT hr ;

    hr = CoCreateInstance (
        GUID_TimeData,              // GUID of desired object
        NULL,                       // outer wrapper, here none
        CLSCTX_LOCAL_SERVER |       // try in-proc server first, use
          CLSCTX_INPROC_SERVER,     // local server if unavailable
        IID_IDataObject,            // interface pointer desired
        (void **) &lpd) ;           // output variable

    return 0 ;
}
```

2. Servers must make entries in the system registry so that COM knows where to find them. This is most commonly done with a .REG file, of the type supplied with this book's sample code. You run the registry editor REGEDIT.EXE, and choose "File -- Merge Registration File..." from the main menu. When the dialog box pops up, simply type in the name of the .REG file containing the registration entries. The keys that you must set are:

```
HKEY_CLASSES_ROOT
    CLSID
            <your object's class ID>
                    LocalServer32 = <full path to server .EXE>
                    InProcServer32 = <full path to server .DLL>
```

In the Data3 example, the entries are:

```
HKEY_CLASSES_ROOT
    CLSID
            {E7767A70-A409-11ce-AD0F-00608C86B89C}
                    LocalServer32 = c:\EssenceofOLE\chap02\data3\server\data3sv.exe
                    InProcServer32 = c:\EssenceofOLE\chap02\data3\inprocsv\data3ips.dll
```

After all of your registration entries are made, you can view or edit them with the more sophisticated registry editor/viewer REGEDIT.EXE. Thus:

Note: Production apps these days are tending to perform self-registration. This is also done by server apps created with the MFC and ATL, and is required for COM controls. Rather than having a separate .REG file as shown here, the app will make registry API calls to register itself every time it runs. This technique is discussed in Appendix A, and in Brockschmidt, pp. 228-229 and 268-269.

3. In addition to the required settings under the CLSID key, most servers choose to provide a human-readable name to identify the class ID. This has the form

```
HKEY_CLASSES_ROOT
    <your app's human-readable name>
            CLSID = <your app's class ID>
```

In the Data3 example, these entries are:

```
HKEY_CLASSES_ROOT
    EssenceofOLE.Data3
            CLSID = {E7767A70-A409-11ce-AD0F-00608C86B89C}
```

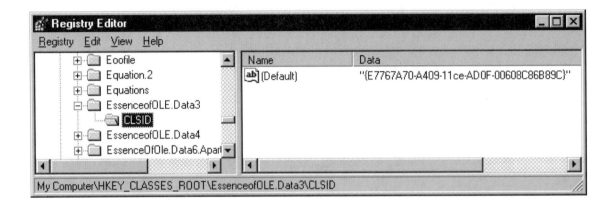

4. If you don't know the object's class ID but do know its registered name, or perhaps have the user pick it from a list, you can fetch the class ID via the function **CLSIDFromProgID( )**. This function finds the specified key under HKEY_CLASSES_ROOT, looks for the CLSID subkey, reads the string value of the subkey and converts it into a CLSID. It requires a wide character string, as do all COM functions and interface methods that take strings as their parameters. A wide character string is a string of 16-bit characters which uses the Unicode character set. A full explanation of the Unicode/ANSI dilemma appears in Appendix A. For now, prepending the character 'L' to the string in quotes causes the compiler to treat the string as wide characters, whether the rest of your app uses wide characters or not. Thus:

```
case ID_DATAOBJECT_CREATEDLL:
{
    HRESULT hr ;

/*
Read class ID from registry key.
*/

    CLSID clsid ;
    hr = CLSIDFromProgID (L"EssenceofOLE.Data3", &clsid) ;

/*
Create object based on class ID read from registry.
*/

    hr = CoCreateInstance (clsid, ...) ;

    <rest of creation case>
}
```

5. When the client calls CoCreateInstance( ), COM goes to the registry, finds the server for the object's class, and loads the server. COM then gets from the server a *class factory*, an object that supports the *IClassFactory* interface. This interface is somewhat misnamed, as it manufactures objects rather than classes. Each class of object requires its own class factory object.

In addition to IUnknown, the IClassFactory interface has only two methods. The method **IClassFactory::CreateInstance( )** is called by COM to create a new object and get a pointer to an interface on it, thus:

```
extern int LockCount, ObjectCount ;

STDMETHODIMP CClassFactory::CreateInstance(LPUNKNOWN pUnkOuter,
    REFIID riid, LPVOID* ppvObj)
{

/*
Check for aggregation request. COM is asking us to create a new object
inside another object provided by COM.  This simple example doesn't
support this feature, and neither do most real-world apps.
*/
    if (pUnkOuter != NULL)
    {
      *ppvObj = NULL ;
      return CLASS_E_NOAGGREGATION ;
    }

/*
Create a new data object.  Query the new object for the interface
requested by the caller.  If found, release our reference on the object
and return success code.
*/

    CTimeData * pTD = new CTimeData ( ) ;

    if (pTD->QueryInterface (riid, ppvObj) == S_OK)
    {
      pTD->Release ( ) ;
      ObjectCount ++ ;
      return NOERROR ;
    }

/*
The new object could not support the requested interface.  Delete the
newly created object and return an error code.
*/
    else
    {
      delete pTD ;
      return E_NOINTERFACE ;
    }
}
```

6. A client that creates and destroys many objects might want to keep the server running, ready for fast action, instead of frequently loading and unloading it. The client can get a pointer to the class factory itself via the API function **CoGetClassObject( )** (not shown), and call its **IClassFactory::LockServer( )** method. If your class factory implements the method, as does this one, you simply increment or decrement a lock count and refuse to shut down the server until all objects created by the server have been destroyed AND the lock count is zero. Many apps simply stub this one out. Thus:

```
extern HWND hMainWnd ;

STDMETHODIMP CClassFactory::LockServer(BOOL bLock)
{

/*
Increment or decrement the lock count, based on the parameter passed to
this method.
*/

    if (bLock == TRUE)
    {
      LockCount ++ ;
    }
    else
    {
      LockCount -- ;

/*
If lock count is decremented to 0 and there are no outstanding objects,
shut down the server app.
*/
      if (LockCount == 0 && ObjectCount == 0)
      {
            PostMessage (hMainWnd, WM_CLOSE, 0, 0) ;
      }
      else
      {
            InvalidateRect (hMainWnd, NULL, TRUE) ;
      }
    }
    return NOERROR ;
}
```

7.   When COM launches a local server app, it passes the string "-Embedding" on the server's command line. When a server finds this on its command line, it must register its class factory interface with COM via the function **CoRegisterClassObject( )**. This interface provides COM with the methods it needs to create new objects of the specified class. When the server app shuts down, it must unregister its class factory via the function **CoRevokeClassObject( )**.   The sequence of events is shown in the block diagram below. The code executed by the local server is shown on the facing page.

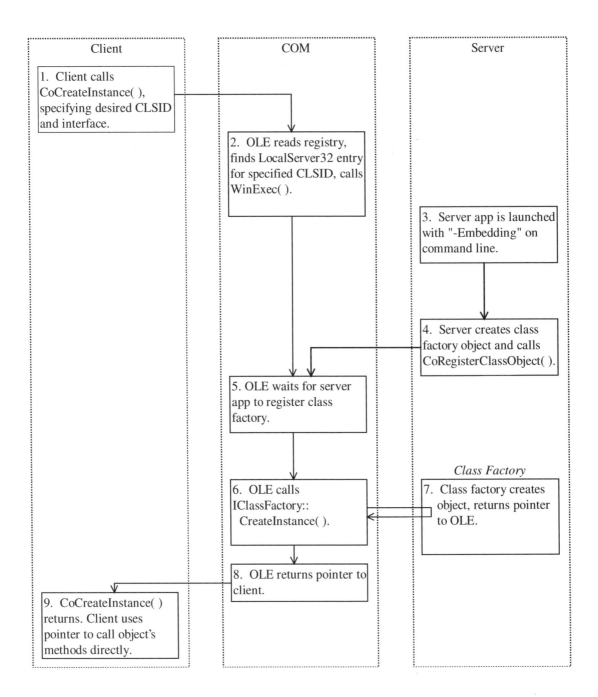

```c
int WINAPI WinMain(HINSTANCE hInstance, HINSTANCE hPrevInstance,
    LPSTR lpCmdLine, int nCmdShow)
{

    <initialize, register classes, create main window>

/*
Check command line to see if launched as an COM server.   If so,
register
the class factory for this app.
*/

    DWORD dwRegister ;

    if (strstr (lpCmdLine, "-Embedding"))
    {
      LPCLASSFACTORY pCF = new CClassFactory ( ) ;

      CoRegisterClassObject(
            GUID_TimeData,          // GUID of object mfd by this fy
            pCF,                    // ptr to IClassFactory object
            CLSCTX_LOCAL_SERVER,    // context, here a local server
            REGCLS_MULTIPLEUSE,     // more flags
            &dwRegister) ;          // output variable

    }

    <standard message loop >

/*
App going down, revoke down class factory
*/

    CoRevokeClassObject (dwRegister) ;


    <standard app shutdown>
}
```

8. You may provide your server in an in-proc (.DLL) server instead of a separate .EXE program. The primary advantage of this is greater speed. Since a DLL is mapped into the address space of the process that loads it, COM does not need to copy (marshal) the method calls and their data from the client's address space into the server's and back again. The "Data Object -- GetData Time Test" menu item on the data3cl.exe sample app's menu provides an easy way of measuring this performance advantage on your system. It's usually in the ballpark of 100 times faster in an in-proc object.

An in-proc server has two disadvantages. First, if you are adding COM support to an existing app, it may be hard to extract server functionality from your existing .EXE into a DLL. Second, since it is mapped into the client's address space, a badly behaved in-proc server can kill a client app in a way that a local server cannot. Most vendors choose the speed. The sequence of events when an object is created from an in-proc server is shown in the following block diagram. The server's code is on the facing page.

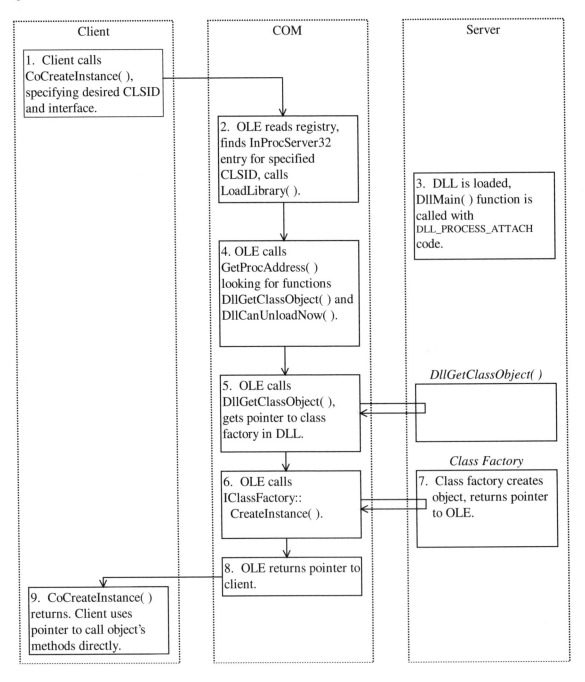

9. The connection between COM and your in-proc server is made differently than for a local server. The server DLL must provide two exported functions for COM to call. The first, **DllGetClassObject( )**, provides COM with a pointer to the class factory object that creates objects of the server's class. This is the same class factory as we passed to CoRegisterClassObject( ) in the local server example previously shown. Thus:

```
CClassFactory cf ;        // IClassFactory interface for this server

STDAPI DllGetClassObject(REFCLSID rclsid, REFIID riid, LPVOID *ppv)
{

/*
Check to make sure that COM is asking for the CLSID that we support.
Maybe someone got the registry entry wrong.
*/

    if (rclsid !=  GUID_TimeData)
    {
      *ppv = NULL ;
      return E_FAIL ;
    }

/*
Take our hard-wired class factory and call QueryInterface( ) on it, on
behalf of the COM that called this function.
*/

    return cf.QueryInterface (riid, ppv) ;

}
```

A local server is responsible for shutting itself down, but an in-proc server will be unloaded by COM. It must provide a function called **DllCanUnloadNow( )**, which tells COM whether or not there are any outstanding references on this server's objects. Thus:

```
STDAPI DllCanUnloadNow(void)
{
/*
If no outstanding objects or lock counts, tell COM that it is now safe
to unload this DLL.  Otherwise, say it isn't.
*/
    if (ObjectCount == 0 && LockCount == 0)
    {
      return S_OK ;
    }
    else
    {
      return S_FALSE ;
    }
}
```

WARNING: The examples shown here have to be exported from the DLL via a .DEF file. The combination of STDAPI and __declspec(dllexport) in the function declaration does not work. The DLL will compile and link, but the function names will not be listed in the DLL's name table. COM's call to GetProcAddress( ) will therefore fail, and so will CoCreateInstance( ).

E. ADVISE LOOPS

1. Once you have a pointer to a data object, you can subscribe to be notified when the object's data changes, conceptually similar to a hot link in DDE. You accomplish this by calling the data object's method **IDataObject::DAdvise( )**. In this method, you specify the FORMATETC in which you want data updates rendered, and provide the data object's server an *advise sink* object. The latter is a generic callback notification object that supports the *IAdviseSink* interface discussed on the facing page. The server will call your advise sink's methods to notify you of changes to the data object. When you are finished with the advise loop, you terminate it via the method **IDataObject::DUnadvise( )**. Thus:

```
extern DWORD dwAdviseConnection ;
LPADVISESINK pAdvSink ;

/*
User has told us to start an advise loop.  Create an advise sink, and
call the method IDataObject::DAdvise( ).
*/

case ID_DATAOBJECT_DADVISE:
{
    FORMATETC fe ;
    HRESULT hr ;

    fe.cfFormat = cfTimeData ;
    fe.ptd = NULL ;
    fe.dwAspect = DVASPECT_CONTENT ;
    fe.lindex = -1 ;
    fe.tymed = TYMED_HGLOBAL ;

    pAdvSink = new CAdviseSink ( ) ;
    hr = lpd->DAdvise (&fe, 0, pAdvSink, &dwAdviseConnection) ;
    return 0 ;
}

/*
User told us to stop the advise loop.  Call the method
IDataObject::DUnadvise( ) and destroy the advise sink object.
*/

case ID_DATAOBJECT_DUNADVISE:
{
    lpd->DUnadvise (dwAdviseConnection) ;
    pAdvSink->Release ( ) ;
    return 0 ;
}
```

52

2. The advise sink contains methods which the server will call to tell the client that the data has changed. It is a generic object used in many different situations callback throughout COM. In this simple data object case, you only need to implement one method, **IAdviseSink::OnDataChange( )**. The server will call this method when the data changes, passing you the FORMATETC structure describing the data's format and the STGMEDIUM structure containing the data itself. You process this in a manner similar to what you did when you got the data from calling IDataObject::GetData( ). The server won't call the other methods, and you wouldn't care if it did, so they are stubbed out. Thus:

```
/*
This method is called when the data object's data changes, with the new
data passed in its parameters.  We take the data, copy it into global
storage, and invalidate the window to force a repaint.
*/

STDMETHODIMP_(void) CAdviseSink::OnDataChange(LPFORMATETC pFEIn,
    LPSTGMEDIUM pSTM)
{

    char *cp ;
    cp = (char *)GlobalLock (pSTM->hGlobal) ;
    memmove (&st, cp, sizeof (st)) ;
    GlobalUnlock (pSTM->hGlobal) ;
    ReleaseStgMedium (pSTM) ;
    InvalidateRect (hMainWnd, NULL, TRUE) ;
    return;
}


/*
The other change methods are of no interest to us in this application.
*/

STDMETHODIMP_(void) CAdviseSink::OnViewChange(DWORD dwAspect,
    LONG lindex)
{
    return;
}


STDMETHODIMP_(void) CAdviseSink::OnRename(LPMONIKER pmk)
{
    return;
}


STDMETHODIMP_(void) CAdviseSink::OnSave(void)
{
    return;
}


STDMETHODIMP_(void) CAdviseSink::OnClose(void)
{
    return;
}
```

3. On the server side, a data object that supports advise loop connections must keep track of all the connections that it currently has open, along with their desired FORMATETC structures and advise sinks. It must add a connection to the list in response to the IDataObject::DAdvise( ) method, remove a connection from the list in response to the IDataObject::DUnadvise( ) method, and provide an enumerator object listing all current connections in response to the method IDataObject::EnumDAdvise( ).

This sounds like a pain in the ass, and it would be if we had to write all this ourselves. Fortunately, COM provides a standard class called a *data advise holder* (an object that implements the *IDataAdviseHolder* interface) that does all of this bookkeeping for us. All we have to do is create one via the API function **CreateDataAdviseHolder( )**, and delegate calls to the data object's three advise loop methods to it. The advise holder knows how to add and remove connections and provide an enumerator. Thus:

```
/*
Create advise holder for this data object.
*/

CTimeData::CTimeData()
{
    m_RefCount = 1 ;
    CreateDataAdviseHolder (&m_pDataAdviseHolder) ;
    return;
}


/*
Delegate all advise method calls to the advise holder.   "Hey, I don't
deal with this stuff. Here, talk to my agent."
*/

STDMETHODIMP CTimeData::DAdvise (FORMATETC * lpfe, DWORD dw,
    LPADVISESINK lpas, DWORD * lpdw)
{
    return  m_pDataAdviseHolder->Advise (this, lpfe, dw, lpas, lpdw) ;
}


STDMETHODIMP CTimeData::DUnadvise   (DWORD dw)
{
    return  m_pDataAdviseHolder->Unadvise (dw) ;
}


STDMETHODIMP CTimeData::EnumDAdvise   (LPENUMSTATDATA * lpen)
{
    return  m_pDataAdviseHolder->EnumAdvise (lpen) ;
}
```

4. When the server's data changes, it needs to signal the change to any clients that have a current advise loop connection. The data advise holder contains the list of connections. Simply calling the method **IDataAdviseHolder::SendOnDataChange( )** will cause the advise holder to run through its list of current connections. For each connection, the advise holder will call the IDataObject::GetData( ) method to get the object's newly changed data in the FORMATETC specified when the connection was established. The advise holder will then call the connection's IAdviseSink::OnDataChange( ) method, passing the data to the waiting client, simply and elegantly. Thus:

```
LPDATAOBJECT lpFirstObj ;

/*
Server's data has changed. Use the object's internal method to tell it
to send the data change to any watching client.
*/

case WM_TIMER:
{
    GetLocalTime (&lt) ;
    InvalidateRect (hWnd, NULL, FALSE) ;

    if (lpFirstObj)
    {
      lpFirstObj->SendDataChangeToClient( )   ;
    }
    return 0 ;
}


/*
Call the data advise holder's SendOnDataChange( ) method. This handles
all the heavy lifting of sending the newly changed data to all waiting
clients.
*/

void CTimeData::SendDataChangeToClient ( )
{
    m_pDataAdviseHolder->SendOnDataChange (this, 0, 0) ;
}
```

F. SOURCING DATA OBJECTS IN THE MFC

1. The MFC provides a prefabricated generic implementation of the IDataObject interface in its **COleDataSource** class. This class supports all of the IDataObject functionality (such as the format enumerator) except for advise loops. An example of using the MFC for data object operations is found in the directory \chap02\mfcdata2.

To use this class to place data on the Clipboard, we use the `new` operator to create a COleDataSource object and place our text data inside it via its **CacheGlobalData( )** method. The method **COleDataSource::SetClipboard( )** places the object on the Clipboard. The object will be destroyed when the Clipboard finally releases it. Thus:

```
void CMfcdata2View::OnDataobjectCopytoclipboard()
{
    CMfcdata2Doc* pDoc = GetDocument();

/*
Create a new COleDataSource object.
*/

    COleDataSource *pds = new COleDataSource ( ) ;

/*
Cache our text string inside the data object.
*/
    char *cp = (char *) GlobalAlloc (GMEM_FIXED,
      pDoc->m_String.GetLength( )+1) ;
    lstrcpy (cp, (LPCTSTR)pDoc->m_String) ;

    pds->CacheGlobalData (CF_TEXT, cp) ;

/*
Place our data object on the Clipboard.  It will be destroyed when the
Clipboard finally releases it.
*/

    pds->SetClipboard ( ) ;
}
```

2. The COleDataSource class is also the basis for a drag operation. We construct and fill a COleDataSource as before, then call its **DoDragDrop( )** method. Internally, this causes the MFC to create a default drop source object and call the API function DoDragDrop( ) as shown previously in this chapter. The return value tells us the operation (move, copy, etc.) that the drop target wants us to perform. Since the drag operation will take place solely within the boundaries of this function, we do not allocate the COleDataSource object with new, but simply instantiate it on the stack. Thus:

```
void CMfcdata2View::OnLButtonDown(UINT nFlags, CPoint point)
{
    CMfcdata2Doc* pDoc = GetDocument();

/*
Create COleDataSource object and fill with data formats.
*/
    COleDataSource ds ;

    char *cp = (char *) GlobalAlloc (GMEM_FIXED,
      pDoc->m_String.GetLength( )+1) ;
    lstrcpy (cp, (LPCTSTR)pDoc->m_String) ;
    ds.CacheGlobalData (CF_TEXT, cp) ;

/*
Perform drag operation.  If effect code is MOVE, then erase string from
our own app.
*/
    if (ds.DoDragDrop () == DROPEFFECT_MOVE)
    {
      pDoc->m_String = "" ;
      Invalidate ( ) ;
    }
}
```

Note: The examples on these two pages do not use the IClassFactory interface. Any reader wanting to see how the MFC implements a class factory will find it in Chapter 9, "Custom Interfaces."

Lab Exercises
Chapter 2
Data Transfer Object Server

Directory: \EssenceofOLE\chap02\data2\templ

This lab is a continuation of the app you worked on in lesson 1. We continue working on the same app, adding code to make it be a source of data objects as well as a consumer of them. As always, a skeleton app is supplied in the above directory. The skeleton app contains a menu item called "Edit Text...", which allows you to change the app's text string from within.

1. Your app must be able to create its own data objects encapsulating its DisplayText[ ]. Your object must implement an IDataObject class that accepts text and renders it either in CF_TEXT or CF_METAFILEPICT. The files CTXTDATA.H and CTXTDATA.CPP contain a skeleton of this class. The IUnknown methods have been written for you, the rest are present but stubbed out. When your object is created, you must create a snapshot of the data which will live inside the object. The class constructor accepts a string pointer as its single parameter. In the constructor, allocate a global memory handle and store the string in it, adding member variables as necessary. Free the global memory handle in the class destructor.

2. Next, implement the QueryGetData( ) method. This takes a single parameter which is a pointer to a FORMATETC structure. Examine the structure to see if the caller is asking for renderings that we support — either CF_TEXT in a TYMED_HGLOBAL, or CF_METAFILEPICT in a TYMED_MFPICT. Return the success code if your object can support the requested rendering, otherwise return an error code.

3. The most important method of this object is GetData( ), which is the method that actually supplies the data when the caller asks for it. Check the supplied FORMATETC structure as you did in step 2. If the user is asking for data in CF_TEXT, allocate a global memory block and copy the member string contents into it. Then store the memory handle in the STGMEDIUM structure, set its other elements, and return success. If the user is asking for data in metafile format, create a metafile DC via the function CreateMetaFile( ), maybe set its colors with SetBkColor( ) and SetTextColor( ), draw the text on the DC with TextOut( ), then convert the DC into a metafile via the function CloseMetaFile( ). Allocate a structure of type METAFILEPICT and fill in its elements. Then store the METAFILEPICT structure's memory handle (not the metafile handle itself) in the STGMEDIUM structure, set its elements, and return success.

4. You must now implement the EnumFormatEtc( ) method. The file CENUM.CPP and .H have been already included in your project. Examine these files so that you understand them, then write your method to instantiate an object of this type using an array of FORMATETC structures that contain the format that your data object supports. Give the user a pointer to it, and return success.

5. You now have a data object but no real way of looking at it or using it. Implement the "Demo -- Copy Text" menu item in the WM_COMMAND case of file MAINWIND.CPP. Instantiate an object of your new data class, using as its starting parameter the global array DisplayText[ ] which contains the text string shown in your app. When you have the object created, put it onto the Clipboard via the function OleSetClipboard( ). You should now be able to use the Clipbook Viewer in your Main application folder to see the data that your app has put onto the Clipboard. You should be able to paste it into WinWord in either text or metafile format.

6. Now that we have our data object, we want to make it do drag and drop. A skeleton IDropSource object has been supplied for you in the file CDROPSRC.CPP and .H. Examine these files until you feel comfortable with them. In file MAINWIND.C, in response to the WM_LBUTTONDOWN message, create an IDropSource object and a CTextData object. Then use the function DoDragDrop( ) to perform

58

the drag-and-drop operation. Check the return code, and if it is DROPEFFECT_DROP, signaling a successful drop operation, check the effect code. If this is DROPEFFECT_MOVE, then rub out the data in your window by setting DisplayText[0] to 0x00 and invalidating.

7. Drag operations in your own window are often special-cased. Modify your IDropSource::GiveFeedback( ) method to check if the drag operation is over your own window (use the functions GetCursorPos( ) and WindowFromPoint( )). If it is, use the function SetCursor( ) to show a special cursor, perhaps the window moving/sizing 4-way arrow (IDC_SIZE).

EXTRA CREDIT: Add more data formats to your object.

EXTRA EXTRA CREDIT: Check whether your data transfer object will work with an Enhanced Metafile, a new type of metafile added to Win32. This behavior would seem reasonable; the Clipboard automatically synthesizes either type of metafile when the other type is placed inside it, but the behavior is not documented and might not exist. I suspect that it will work in the Clipboard but not in drag-and-drop.

EXTRA EXTRA EXTRA CREDIT: The drop source object is in charge of showing the cursor, but sometimes the drop target might want to do it instead. For example, a wastebasket program might want to show a cursor that looks like a shredder. You can't require the drop source to have specific knowledge of every other app it might want to drop on. Try to think of a way either for the drop target to signal the drop source that the former wants to show the cursor so the latter shouldn't, or for the drop target to wrest control of the cursor from the drop source so that the former can display whatever cursor it wants. Any way that works well will be featured in the next edition of this book; I'm not sure that there is one. The target app could, however, draw its own picture around the cursor location; for example a slavering, shark's mouth or a chain saw.

EXTRA EXTRA EXTRA EXTRA CREDIT: It is probably more convenient for the user if a drag operation doesn't begin exactly at the left button mouse click, but rather when the mouse has moved a small number of pixels, thereby clearly differentiating the selection operation from the start-drag operation. Save the last click position in the WM_LBUTTONDOWN message case. Then move the drag operation to the WM_MOUSEMOVE message, happening only if the left button is down and the position has moved from the location of the original click. Experiment with different numbers of pixels and see what feels good.

EXTRA EXTRA EXTRA EXTRA EXTRA CREDIT: You probably noticed that if you click the left mouse button in your app, the text string in it disappears. Why is that, and how would you fix it ? Hint: In what order are the drop source and drop target operations performed?

Lab Exercise
Lesson 2
MFC Data Transfer Object Server

Directory: \EssenceofOLE\chap02\mfcdata2\templ

This lab uses the MFC to do the same thing as the data2 lab did in the API. A skeleton app is supplied for you in the directory listed above.

1. Our app's document class contains a string member variable named CMfcdata2Doc::m_String that is initialized to a default value. When the user selects "Data Object -- Copy to Clipboard" from the main menu, we want to use OLE to place this string onto the Windows Clipboard. In the command handler method CMfcdata2View::OnDataobjectCopytoclipboard( ), which you will find near the bottom of the file mfcdata2view.cpp, use the new operator to allocate an object of class COleDataSource. Use the API function GlobalAlloc( ) to allocate a block of global memory and copy the contents of the document's m_String variable into it. Use the method COleDataSource::CacheGlobalData( ) to place the global into the data object. Then use the method COleDataSource::SetClipboard( ) to place it on the Clipboard.

2. Next, we want to offer our text string to other apps by means of drag and drop as well as the Clipboard. Create and fill a COleDataSource as described above, except this time, instantiate it on the stack instead of using new. Use the method COleDataSource::DoDragDrop( ) to perform the drag operation. If the drop target signals a drop effect code of DROPEFFECT_MOVE, then empty the document's m_String variable and invalidate your view to force a repaint that will display its new empty contents.

EXTRA CREDIT: Examine the extra credit suggestions in the API lab example and implement them in the MFC.

Chapter 3

OLE Automation

A. CONCEPTS AND DEFINITIONS

1. *OLE automation* is the process whereby one application or DLL (the *automation server*) creates and exposes *automation objects* for use by another app (the *automation controller*). It was originally conceived as a way for app writers to expose their internal macro programming languages to external programming tools. App vendors could thus have all the advantages of macro programming without having to develop and maintain the tools to do it, and customers could use whatever tools they liked and were familiar with for programming all of their applications. The architecture of OLE automation was dictated by the need to accommodate Microsoft Visual Basic (VB), the first programming environment at which it was targeted. OLE automation has since expanded into a generalized mechanism for one app to control another.

2. An automation object may expose *methods*, which are functions that optionally accept arguments and return values. An automation object may also expose *properties*, which are data values within the object that the controller may set and get. The set of methods and properties is exposed to the world as a custom interface, conceptually similar to those used in other parts of OLE. Unlike the VTBL interfaces that we have been using so far, to facilitate the runtime binding required for interpreted languages such as VB, all methods and properties of an automation object are accessed through the single, deceptively simple-looking *IDispatch* interface. Its methods are:

```
IDispatch::GetIDsOfNames   // Maps a single member name and an optional set of argument names
                           // to a set of integer DISPIDs for use by IDispatch::Invoke().
IDispatch::GetTypeInfo     // Get ITypeInfo interface describing an object.
IDispatch::GetTypeInfoCount   //Get  number of ITypeInfo interfaces in an object.
IDispatch::Invoke          // Access property or method exposed by the object.
```

WARNING: If you have picked up this book for the first time and jumped straight to this chapter because OLE automation is the only piece of OLE you care about, **STOP!** Unless you are already familiar with the component-object model, including interface VTBLs and class factories, go back and read at least the first half of Chapter 1 and the second half of Chapter 2. Otherwise this chapter will make no sense, and you will only get frustrated and send me nasty e-mail, to which I will reply "RTFC1AC2."

NOTE: At the time of this writing, one part of Microsoft is trying to replace the term "OLE Automation" with simply "automation", and another part wants the term "automation" to go away entirely, although they don't have a replacement. Until they A) find a term that is more descriptive rather than less, and B) use it consistently throughout the company for more than 15 minutes, I will stick to the term that readers will recognize.

3. Hey, wait a minute, where are the custom methods and properties in the IDispatch interface? They are all accessed through the single method IDispatch::Invoke( ). Each method or property is identified by a *dispatch ID*, an integer constant. This ID is passed to the Invoke( ) method, along with any required parameters. The server's implementation of the Invoke( ) method looks at the dispatch ID and executes the code specified by that ID. Parameters and return values are passed in VARIANT structures, self-describing structures used extensively in Visual Basic, which OLE knows how to marshal across process boundaries. When you call the method IDispatch::Invoke( ), you are in essence saying, "Hey, Mr. Object, do thing number 1 (or 2, or 3, etc.) and here's the data for it." Thus:

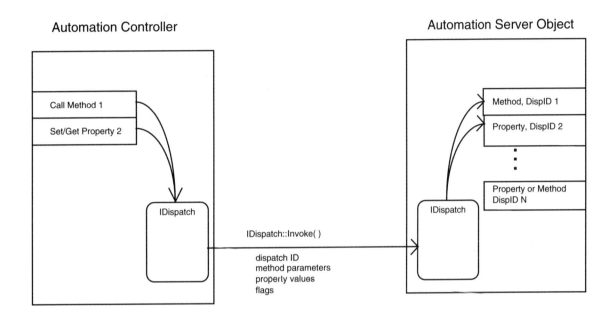

4. Although all automation objects are accessed through the same IDispatch interface, it is clear that the same dispatch ID may mean different things to different objects. A dispatch ID of 1 may instruct one object to save all of its data carefully to disk, whereas to another object, the same dispatch ID may mean to format its hard drive and everyone else's on the network without asking for confirmation. The meaning of the set of IDs accessed through an IDispatch interface to which an object responds is called a *dispinterface*. It is conceptually similar to a custom interface, except the dispinterface's VTBL does not vary from one object to another. It is the interpretation of the data supplied to the IDispatch::Invoke( ) method that makes it custom. Making sure you have the right methods and parameters for the dispinterface you are using is the primary challenge of OLE automation programming.

B. BASIC CONTROLLER FUNCTIONALITY

1.   Building an automation controller is conceptually simple, although the exact syntax of the methods can be tricky. To ease the task of the application programmer, you probably want to encapsulate the controller's interface to the automation object in a C++ wrapper, in this example called CHelloDriver. This also makes it much easier to supply dummy or test data while the server is still under development. A smart component vendor would provide this class along with its server. In the following chapter, we will see how automated tools can generate this wrapper class for us.

In the following examples, we want to create a dedicated controller app that manipulates a very simple automation server. The server object displays a text string in a window on the screen. The object exposes a single method called "SayHello( )", which draws the object's current string in an edit control. It also exposes that current string as a property named "HelloMessage", whose value controllers may set and get. In this example, we pretend we knew all this from reading the documentation provided by the vendor that sold us the server. The source code for this example is in the directory \chap03\helloau\hlodrv32. The controller app's WinMain( ) looks like this:

```
extern BOOL WINAPI HelloDlgProc (HWND, UINT, WPARAM, LPARAM) ;

/*
Controller object that encapsulates the interface to the server's
automation object.
*/

CHelloDriver chd ;

int WINAPI WinMain(HINSTANCE hInst, HINSTANCE hPrevInstance,
    LPSTR lpCmdLine, int nCmdShow)
{
    MSG msg ;
    OleInitialize (NULL) ;

/*
Try to connect to the automation object.  If unsuccessful, terminate
app.
*/
    if (chd.Create( ) == FALSE)
    {
      MessageBox (NULL, "Can't hook up hellodrv", "Error", 0) ;
      return -1 ;
    }

/*
Connection made to automation object.  Pop up dialog box that will call
object's methods in response to dialog box's controls.
*/

    DialogBox (hInst, MAKEINTRESOURCE(IDD_DIALOG1), NULL,
      HelloDlgProc);

    OleUninitialize ( ) ;
    return msg.wParam;
}
```

64

2. The class *CHelloDriver* is the controller's wrapper for the exposed automation object. Its header files, constructor, and destructor will look like this:

```
/*
Wrapper class for the controller side of the Hello automation object.
*/

class CHelloDriver
{
    private:
      LPDISPATCH m_pDisp ;            // IDispatch interface from server
      DISPID m_dSayHelloId ;          // Say hello method ID
      DISPID m_dHelloPropID ;         // string set/get ID

    public:
      CHelloDriver( ) ;
      ~CHelloDriver( ) ;

      BOOL Create(LPSTR) ;            // set up dispatch with server
      HRESULT SetString (LPOLESTR) ;// tell server what string to use
      HRESULT GetString (LPOLESTR) ;// ask what string server is using
      HRESULT SayHowdy(void) ;        // tell server to output its string
      HRESULT BadSetString (void) ; // intentional error for demo
} ;

CHelloDriver::CHelloDriver( )
{
    return ;
}

/*
Class destructor.  If we have a pointer to an IDispatch interface,
release it.
*/

CHelloDriver::~CHelloDriver( )
{
    if (m_pDisp)
    {
      m_pDisp->Release( );
    }
    return ;
}
```

3. To start the automation process, the controller must first cause an automation object of the appropriate class to be created and get a pointer to the object's IDispatch interface. We do exactly the same thing as we did to get a data object in Chapter 2, call the API function **CoCreateInstance( )**. The only difference is that this time we ask for the IDispatch interface pointer. Thus:

```
BOOL CHelloDriver::Create( )
{
    HRESULT hr ;

    CLSID clsid ;

    < read class ID from the registry >


/*
Try to create an instance of the Hello object and get a pointer to its
IDispatch interface.
*/

    hr = CoCreateInstance (
      clsid,                      // class ID of object
      NULL,                       //
      CLSCTX_LOCAL_SERVER,        // context
      IID_IDispatch,              // type of interface ptr wanted
      (LPVOID *) &m_pDisp) ;      // output variable

    if (!SUCCEEDED(hr))
    {
      return FALSE ;
    }
```

4. The IDispatch interface provides access to all the methods and properties exposed by the automation object. Each method or property is identified by a DWORD *dispatch ID*, which we will need to access via the method IDispatch::Invoke( ). The vendor might have given us a header file with those IDs predefined, but maybe was too lazy or wanted to reserve the right to change them later. Since we don't have them at compile time, we must query the object for them at run time via the method **IDispatch::GetIDsOfNames( )**. This is a somewhat misnamed method, as it provides the ID of only a single method or property at a time. The designers gave it a plural name because it can also get the IDs of any named parameters (dealt with later) that a single method might support. Note that as for all strings in OLE, the names provided to this method must always use wide (Unicode) characters, even if neither controller nor server are wide character apps. Thus:

```
/*
Get the ID numbers associated with the names in the IDispatch
interface.
SayHello( ) is a method.
*/

    WCHAR *Name = L"SayHello" ;

    hr = m_pDisp->GetIDsOfNames (
      IID_NULL,                       // reserved
      &Name,                          // Array of names to get IDs for
      1,                              // # of names in the array
      LOCALE_SYSTEM_DEFAULT,          // System locale
      &m_dSayHelloId) ;               // Array of IDs to fill on output

    if (hr)
    {
      return FALSE ;
    }


/*
HelloMessage is a property.
*/
    Name = L"HelloMessage" ;

    hr = m_pDisp->GetIDsOfNames (
      IID_NULL,                       // reserved
      &Name,                          // Array of names to get IDs for
      1,                              // # of names in the array
      LOCALE_SYSTEM_DEFAULT,          // System locale
      &m_dHelloPropID) ;              // Array of IDs to fill on output

    if (hr)
    {
      return FALSE ;
    }

    return TRUE ;
}
```

This page intentionally contains no text other than this sentence.

5. A method is called in an automation object via the method **IDispatch::Invoke( )**, specifying the dispatch ID of the object's method that you want to call. We also specify a flag that tells the server that what we are doing is calling a method on the object, as opposed to getting or setting a property. The arguments required by the object's method are passed in a structure of type **DISPPARAMS**, which is defined thus:

```
typedef struct  tagDISPPARAMS
{
    VARIANTARG *rgvarg;         // array of VARIANT structs holding args
    DISPID  __*rgdispidNamedArgs;   // array of DISPIDs naming args
    UINT cArgs;                 // number of VARIANTS in array
    UINT cNamedArgs;            // number of names in array
} DISPPARAMS;
```

All parameters in OLE automation are passed by means of VARIANT structures, which are described in more detail on the next page. The DISPPARAMS structure is a holder for VARIANTs and the items that describe their use, containing pointers to two arrays and the counts of the items in each array. In this example, the object's method does not require any arguments, so we set both pointers in the DISPPARAMS to NULL and both counts to zero. Thus:

```
/*
Invoke the server's SayHello( ) method.
*/

HRESULT CHelloDriver::SayHowdy(void)
{
    HRESULT hr ;
    EXCEPINFO ei ;
    UINT uiErr ;
    DISPPARAMS dispparamsNoArgs = {NULL, NULL, 0, 0};

    hr = m_pDisp->Invoke (
        m_dSayHelloId,               // ID of function to call
        IID_NULL,                    // reserved
        LOCALE_SYSTEM_DEFAULT,       // system locale
        DISPATCH_METHOD,             // we are calling a method
        &dispparamsNoArgs,           // no parameters are being passed
        NULL,                        // no return value expected
        &ei,                         // exception information
        &uiErr ) ;                   // error information

    return hr ;
}
```

6. The value of a property is fetched via the same IDispatch::Invoke( ) method with slightly different parameters. We pass the dispatch ID of the property that we want to fetch and the flag that says that what we are doing is getting the value of a property. We declare a structure of type **VARIANT** and pass it as the sixth parameter; the server will place the property's value into it.

All parameters and return values in OLE automation are passed by means of VARIANT structures, the definition of which is shown on the facing page. Used extensively throughout VB, a VARIANT is a structure containing a self-describing union supporting 13 different data types which OLE knows how to marshal both by value and by reference. You can pass essentially any type of single-variable value, including arrays (via the SAFEARRAY type). You can pass pointers to IDispatch interfaces directly, and pointers to any other interface by passing the object's root IUnknown interface and then querying it at the destination for the desired interface. A VARIANT does not support structures, so if you need to pass structures to automation objects, you will have to either write a custom interface (see Chapter 7), pack it up as a SAFEARRAY, or think of something else. See Brockschmidt, pp. 647-653 for a fuller discussion of VARIANT data types.

Strings in OLE automation are always passed in the form of a BSTR, again a structure used in VB. You can use it in C++ as if it were a regular null-terminated string, however, you must allocate it via the function SysAllocString( ) and free it via the function **SysFreeString( )**. Thus:

```
HRESULT CHelloDriver::GetString (LPOLESTR pOut)
{
    HRESULT hr ;
    VARIANT var ;          // holder for return value
    EXCEPINFO ei ;
    UINT uiErr ;
    DISPPARAMS dispparamsNoArgs = {NULL, NULL, 0, 0};

    var.vt = VT_EMPTY ;

/*
Try to get the string from the object.
*/

    hr = m_pDisp->Invoke (
      m_dHelloPropID,               // ID of property
      IID_NULL,                     // reserved
      LOCALE_SYSTEM_DEFAULT,        // system locale
      DISPATCH_PROPERTYGET,         // flag
      &dispparamsNoArgs,            // no parameters passed
      &var,                         // holder for returned value
      &ei,                          // exception info
      &uiErr ) ;                    // error info

/*
If string was successfully retrieved, it is in the buffer pointed to by
the variant's bstrVal element.  Copy it into our local buffer and free
the string.
*/
    if (SUCCEEDED(hr))
    {
      wcscpy (pOut, var.bstrVal) ;
      SysFreeString (var.bstrVal) ;
    }
    return hr ;
}
```

```
typedef struct tagVARIANT VARIANTARG;
typedef struct tagVARIANT VARIANT;

typedef struct tagVARIANT
{
    VARTYPE vt;
    unsigned short wReserved1;
    unsigned short wReserved2;
    unsigned short wReserved3;

    union
    {
      short         iVal;               /* VT_I2                    */
      long          lVal;               /* VT_I4                    */
      float         fltVal;             /* VT_R4                    */
      double        dblVal;             /* VT_R8                    */
      VARIANT_BOOL  bool;               /* VT_BOOL                  */
      SCODE         scode;              /* VT_ERROR                 */
      CY            cyVal;              /* VT_CY                    */

      DATE          date;              /* VT_DATE                   */
      BSTR          bstrVal;           /* VT_BSTR                   */
      IUnknown      FAR* punkVal;      /* VT_UNKNOWN                */
      IDispatch     FAR* pdispVal;     /* VT_DISPATCH               */


      short         FAR* piVal;         /* VT_BYREF|VT_I2           */
      long          FAR* plVal;         /* VT_BYREF|VT_I4           */
      float         FAR* pfltVal;       /* VT_BYREF|VT_R4           */
      double        FAR* pdblVal;       /* VT_BYREF|VT_R8           */
      VARIANT_BOOL  FAR* pbool;         /* VT_BYREF|VT_BOOL         */
      SCODE         FAR* pscode;        /* VT_BYREF|VT_ERROR        */
      CY            FAR* pcyVal;        /* VT_BYREF|VT_CY           */
      DATE          FAR* pdate;         /* VT_BYREF|VT_DATE         */
      BSTR          FAR* pbstrVal;      /* VT_BYREF|VT_BSTR         */
      IUnknown FAR* FAR* ppunkVal;      /* VT_BYREF|VT_UNKNOWN      */
      IDispatch FAR* FAR* ppdispVal;    /* VT_BYREF|VT_DISPATCH     */


      SAFEARRAY     FAR* parray;        /* VT_ARRAY|*               */
      VARIANT       FAR* pvarVal;       /* VT_BYREF|VT_VARIANT      */

      void          FAR* byref;         /* Generic ByRef            */
    };
} ;
```

7. Setting a property is slightly more complicated. We use the same IDispatch::Invoke( ) method, passing the dispatch ID of the property that we want to set. We also pass a flag saying that what we are doing is setting a property.

The trick in setting a property is packaging up the parameters in the DISPPARAMS structure. The DISPPARAMS structure, as previously shown, has an element called `rgvarg` which points to an array of VARIANTS containing the parameters that are passed to the method. It also has an element called `cArgs`, which contains the number of VARIANTS in the array, in this case one. We allocate a VARIANT and initialize it to default values via the function **VariantInit( )**. We use the function **SysAllocString( )** to allocate a BSTR containing the string we want to pass, place it in the VARIANT, and set the VARIANT's `vt` element to the flag **VT_BSTR**, indicating that this VARIANT contains a BSTR so that OLE will know how to marshal it. Finally, we set `rgvargs` to point to the VARIANT. Similar footwork is required when calling a method that requires parameters.

You would think this would be all we have to do, but it isn't. Parameters in OLE automation can be passed either by position, as in a compiled language, or by name. See Brockschmidt, pp. 752-753 for a discussion of named arguments. In a DISPPARAMS structure, the element `rgdispidNamedArgs` is a pointer to an array of dispatch IDs specifying the name of each argument in the `rgvargs` array, and the element `cNamedArgs` is the number of elements in the array. For historical reasons, when setting a property, it is necessary to provide an ID for the VARIANT containing the property's value, and the ID must have the reserved value **DISPID_PROPERTYPUT** (-3). The element `rgdispidNamedArgs` must point at an integer whose value is this, and the count of named arguments must be set to 1. Hey, I didn't design it. A working code example is shown on the facing page.

```
HRESULT CHelloDriver::SetString(LPOLESTR cp)
{
    HRESULT hr ;                DISPPARAMS dp ;
    VARIANTARG vString ;        EXCEPINFO ei ;
    UINT uiErr ;                DISPID dPutID ;
/*
Allocate a string from the system memory allocator.  Place it into the
element of a VARIANT structure, and set the flags.
*/

    BSTR bstr = SysAllocString (cp) ;
    VariantInit (&vString) ;
    vString.vt = VT_BSTR ;
    vString.bstrVal = bstr ;


/*
Set up the DISPPARAMS structure.  Point to the array of VARIANTs that
contains the parameters, and set the count in the array (here only 1).
*/

    dp.rgvarg = &vString ;            // variant array containing params
    dp.cArgs = 1 ;                    // # of elements in the array

/*
Now set the elements that identify the parameter passed to the method.
*/

    dPutID = DISPID_PROPERTYPUT ;    // use SET property function
    dp.rgdispidNamedArgs = &dPutID ; // needs it by reference
    dp.cNamedArgs = 1 ;              // number of elements

/*
Invoke the function.
*/
    hr = m_pDisp->Invoke (
      m_dHelloPropID,               // ID of property
      IID_NULL,                     // reserved
      LOCALE_SYSTEM_DEFAULT,        // system locale
      DISPATCH_PROPERTYPUT,         // set value of property
      &dp,                          // array of parameters to pass
      NULL,                         // no return value expected
      &ei,                          // exception info
      &uiErr ) ;                    // error info
/*
If function was successful, recipient should free string; otherwise we
have to.
*/
    if (!SUCCEEDED(hr))
    {
      SysFreeString (bstr) ;
    }
    return hr ;
}
```

C. BASIC SERVER FUNCTIONALITY

1. An automation object must provide the *IDispatch* interface, which is the means whereby the controller invokes the methods and accesses the properties of the object. To create and provide the server's objects to the world, the server must implement the *IClassFactory* factory interface, as was done in the previous chapter. The server may be either an in-proc (DLL) or local (.EXE) server. Thus:

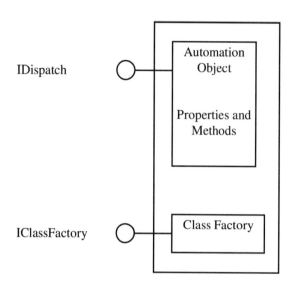

OLE Automation Interfaces

74

2. Exposing an automation object means writing your own dispinterface. Consider a very simple automation object used in the controller example. It exposes a single method called "SayHello( )", which draws a text string in a window on the screen. It also exposes a single property called "HelloMessage", which is the string drawn on the screen when the SayHello( ) method is invoked. We want to expose these features to other apps, which means wrapping them in an IDispatch interface. As we did when providing our own implementation of the IDataObject interface in Chapter 2, we would define our own C++ class derived from the predefined interface. The source code for this example is in the directory \chap03\helloau\hello32. We would call it CHelloDispatch, and its header file would look like this:

```cpp
#include <windows.h>

class CHelloDispatch : public IDispatch
{
 public:

/*
Data members
*/

    BSTR m_bstrHelloMsg;                // HelloMessage property
    ULONG m_RefCount;                   // Reference count

 /*
 Class constructor and destructor
 */

    CHelloDispatch();
    ~CHelloDispatch();

 /*
 IUnknown methods
 */

    STDMETHODIMP QueryInterface (REFIID riid, void FAR* FAR* ppv);
    STDMETHODIMP_(ULONG) AddRef (void);
    STDMETHODIMP_(ULONG) Release (void);

/*
IDispatch methods
*/

    STDMETHODIMP GetTypeInfoCount(UINT *pctinfo) ;
    STDMETHODIMP GetTypeInfo(UINT, LCID, ITypeInfo **pptinfo) ;
    STDMETHODIMP GetIDsOfNames(REFIID, LPOLESTR *, UINT, LCID,DISPID*);
    STDMETHODIMP Invoke(DISPID, REFIID, LCID lcid, WORD, DISPPARAMS *,
      VARIANT *, EXCEPINFO *, UINT *) ;

};
```

3. The class constructor, destructor, and QueryInterface( ) methods look like this:

```
#include "resource.h"
#include "hello.h"

extern HWND hMainWnd ;

/*
Class Constructor
*/

CHelloDispatch::CHelloDispatch()
{
    m_RefCount = 1;
    m_bstrHelloMsg = SysAllocString(TEXT("Hello, world"));
}

/*
Class Destructor
*/

CHelloDispatch::~CHelloDispatch()
{
    SysFreeString(m_bstrHelloMsg);
}


STDMETHODIMP CHelloDispatch::QueryInterface(REFIID riid, void ** ppv)
{

/*
Someone is asking us for our IDispatch or IUnknown.   Return a pointer
to our VTBL.
*/

    if (riid == IID_IUnknown  || riid == IID_IDispatch)
    {
      *ppv = this ;
      AddRef();
      return NOERROR;
    }

/*
Caller asked for an interface that we don't support.
*/
    else
    {
      *ppv = NULL;
      return E_NOINTERFACE;
    }
}
```

4. Now we have to implement the methods of the IDispatch interface. As before, some can be stubbed out completely, and some others are trivial. The methods **GetTypeInfoCount( )** and **GetTypeInfo( )** are optional, and can be stubbed out, thus:

```
STDMETHODIMP CHelloDispatch::GetTypeInfoCount(UINT *pNtypeInfo)
{
    *pNtypeInfo = 0;
    return E_NOTIMPL ;
}


STDMETHODIMP CHelloDispatch::GetTypeInfo(UINT itinfo, LCID lcid,
    ITypeInfo **pptinfo)
{
    *pptinfo = NULL ;
    return E_NOTIMPL ;
}
```

The method **GetIDsOfNames( )** is fairly simple. We are passed the name of a property or method, and simply return the dispatch ID to which it refers. If we do not support a member with that name, we return an error code. Note that the names are always passed in wide character strings. Thus:

```
STDMETHODIMP CHelloDispatch::GetIDsOfNames(REFIID riid,
    LPOLESTR *pNames, UINT cNames, LCID lcid, DISPID *pDispID)
{
    if (_wcsicmp (*pNames, L"SayHello") == 0)
    {
      *pDispID = 2 ;
      return NOERROR ;
    }
    else if (_wcsicmp (*pNames, L"HelloMessage") == 0)
    {
      *pDispID = 1 ;
      return NOERROR ;
    }

    return DISP_E_UNKNOWNNAME ;
}
```

5. As usual, there is one interface method that requires a significant amount of programming, and in this case it's the **Invoke( )** method. This method is passed the ID of the property or method being accessed, and the data that has been marshaled from the caller in an array of self-describing VARIANT structures. The method figures out what to do, and does it.

Unlike the normal implementation of a VTBL-based interface, you cannot assume that the compiler has checked for the correct number and type of parameters. The main drawback of OLE automation's late-bound architecture is that such checking must be done at run time. If an error is found, we return the appropriate error code and hope the controller has some mechanism to present the error to the user/programmer so it can be corrected. Thus:

```
STDMETHODIMP CHelloDispatch::Invoke(DISPID dispidMember, REFIID riid,
    LCID lcid, WORD wFlags, DISPPARAMS *pDispParams,
    VARIANT *pVarResult, EXCEPINFO *pexcepinfo, UINT *puArgErr)
{
/*
Caller wants to get or set the HelloMessage property.
*/
    if (dispidMember == 1)
    {
/*
Caller wants to get the HelloMessage property.
*/
      if (wFlags & DISPATCH_PROPERTYGET)
      {
/*
Check that the caller hasn't passed us any parameters.  That would be
an error.
*/
            if (pDispParams->cArgs != 0)
            {
                  return DISP_E_BADPARAMCOUNT ;
            }
/*
Allocate a string containing it, and place it in the VARIANT used for
the return value.
*/
            pVarResult->vt = VT_BSTR ;
            pVarResult->bstrVal = SysAllocString(m_bstrHelloMsg);
      }

      <continued on facing page>
```

78

```c
/*
Caller wants to set the HelloMessage property.
*/
      else if (wFlags & DISPATCH_PROPERTYPUT)
      {
/*
Check parameter count and type.  If either is incorrect, return
appropriate error code.
*/
            if (pDispParams->cArgs != 1)
            {
                  return DISP_E_BADPARAMCOUNT ;
            }
            if (pDispParams->rgvarg[0].vt != VT_BSTR)
            {
                  return DISP_E_BADVARTYPE ;
            }
/*
Copy the new value from the array of VARIANTS holding the calling
parameters.
*/
            SysReAllocString(&m_bstrHelloMsg,
                  pDispParams-> rgvarg->bstrVal);
      }
      return NOERROR ;
    }
/*
Caller wants to call the SayHello( ) method.
*/

    else if (dispidMember == 2)
    {
/*
Check that there are no parameters.  If not, return an error code.
*/
      if (pDispParams->cArgs != 0)
      {
            return DISP_E_BADPARAMCOUNT ;
      }

/*
Put the current HelloMessage property into the edit control and beep to
signal the user.
*/
      MessageBeep (0) ;
      SetDlgItemText(hMainWnd, IDC_HELLOAREA, m_bstrHelloMsg);
      return NOERROR ;
    }

    return DISP_E_MEMBERNOTFOUND ;
}
```

D. OLE AUTOMATION IN THE MFC

1. The preceding implementation in the API may seem exceedingly bloody, and you may be wondering, "Isn't this stuff very similar from one app to another? Couldn't the plumbing somehow be pre-fabricated, requiring me to implement only the faucets on either end? Specifically, instead of hardwiring data such as member names and IDs directly into the code, couldn't data be abstracted into an array of self-contained structures and removed from the code? The code could then be written once and for all, and the differences from one app to another specified only in simple localized changes to data structures ? And wouldn't it be cool if there were some intelligent tools to manage these data structures? And wouldn't it be extra cool if it took care of all the nonsense about wide versus ANSI strings?" Yes it would be, and it has mostly been done for you in the MFC.

Suppose we want to make an MFC version of the simple automation server used in the preceding pages, exposing a string called "HelloMessage" and a method called "SayHello". The source code for this example is in the directory \chap03\helloau\mfchelloausv. To provide MFC support for OLE automation, choose the "Ole automation" check box while generating the project in App Wizard. The "OLE compound document support" on the tab refers to embedding and linking and has no bearing on automation; you can leave it unchecked. Thus:

2. You may also provide an automation server in a DLL by checking the appropriate box when building an App Wizard DLL. Thus:

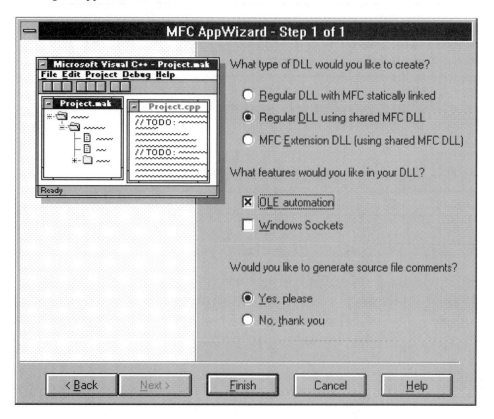

3. When you do this, the following changes are added to your app. The file **<afxdisp.h>** is added to your standard includes in the file stdafx.h, thus:

```
// stdafx.h : include file for standard system include files,
//  or project specific include files that are used frequently, but
//      are changed infrequently
//

#define VC_EXTRALEAN          // Exclude rarely used stuff from headers

#include <afxwin.h>           // MFC core and standard components
#include <afxext.h>           // MFC extensions
#include <afxdisp.h>          // MFC OLE automation classes
#ifndef _AFX_NO_AFXCMN_SUPPORT
#include <afxcmn.h>           // MFC support for Win 95 Common Ctrls
#endif // _AFX_NO_AFXCMN_SUPPORT
```

4. Your CWinApp::InitInstance( ) method initializes the OLE libraries via the function **AfxOleInit( )**. App Wizard generates a CLSID for your automation object, which also appears in your CWinApp file. Thus:

```
<file mfchelloausv.cpp>

CMfchelloausvApp theApp;

// This identifier was generated to be statistically unique for yr app.
// You may change it if you prefer to choose a specific identifier.

// {79B3AC80-92C6-11CF-8A22-00AA00A58097}
static const CLSID clsid =
{ 0x79b3ac80, 0x92c6, 0x11cf, { 0x8a, 0x22, 0x0, 0xaa, 0x0, 0xa5, 0x80,
0x97 } };

//////
// CMfchelloausvApp initialization

BOOL CMfchelloausvApp::InitInstance()
{
    // Initialize OLE libraries
    if (!AfxOleInit())
    {
      AfxMessageBox(IDP_OLE_INIT_FAILED);
      return FALSE;
    }
    <rest of InitInstance( )>
}
```

NOTE: App Wizard also generates the code that your automation server needs to provide a class factory. Since this is a general-purpose feature used for any MFC server, it is dealt with in Chapter 9, "Custom Interfaces."

5. The MFC support for OLE servers is implemented in the class CCmdTarget, from which your CDocument class is derived. App Wizard makes modifications to your CDocument class for supporting automation. The function **CCmdTarget::EnableAutomation**( ), called from the document's constructor, constructs internally an object of class *COleDispatchImpl*, which contains the actual code of MFC's IDispatch implementation. The functions **AfxOleLockApp**( ) and **AfxOleUnlockApp**( ) respectively increment and decrement an app's reference count, thereby keeping the app running as long as a document exists that is being used by OLE. Thus:

```
/*
Document constructor.
*/


CMfchelloausvDoc::CMfchelloausvDoc()
{

/*
My document's own initialization.
*/

     m_helloMessage = "Hello, World" ;

/*
OLE initialization added by App Wizard.
*/

    EnableAutomation();

    AfxOleLockApp();
}

/*
Document destructor.
*/


CMfchelloausvDoc::~CMfchelloausvDoc()
{
    AfxOleUnlockApp();
}
```

6. The MFC supports OLE automation by means of a *dispatch map*, an array of structures conceptually and operationally similar to the message map used for routing messages. The dispatch map contains an array of data structures, each of which contains all the elements needed to describe a single method or property. The dispatch ID for an entry is implied from the entry's position in the array. The entries between the //{AFX_DISPATCH_MAP comment blocks are maintained by Class Wizard. You may manually add entries outside this block if you wish. The following example is shown indented and commented for clarity; Class Wizard will place each entry on a single line. Thus:

```
BEGIN_MESSAGE_MAP(CMfchelloausvDoc, CDocument)
    //{{AFX_MSG_MAP(CMfchelloausvDoc)
        // NOTE - ClassWizard will add and remove mapping macros here.
        //    DO NOT EDIT what you see in these blocks of generated code!
    //}}AFX_MSG_MAP
END_MESSAGE_MAP()


BEGIN_DISPATCH_MAP(CMfchelloausvDoc, CDocument)
    //{{AFX_DISPATCH_MAP(CMfchelloausvDoc)
    DISP_PROPERTY_NOTIFY(          // macro specifying automation property
        CMfchelloausvDoc,          // class containing property
        "HelloMessage",            // name of property
        m_helloMessage,            // member variable
        OnHelloMessageChanged,     // notification function called on change
        VT_BSTR)                   // type of property

    DISP_FUNCTION(                 // macro specifying automation method
        CMfchelloausvDoc,          // class containing method
        "SayHello",                // name of method
        SayHello,                  // function to be called
        VT_EMPTY,                  // return type of function
        VTS_NONE)                  // parameter list of fn, here empty
    //}}AFX_DISPATCH_MAP
END_DISPATCH_MAP()
```

7. When the controller calls IDispatch::Invoke( ), the server code lives in the Invoke( ) method of the COleDispatchImpl object that the CDocument inherited from CCmdTarget. This code first checks for generic errors (1), such as the controller requesting a dispatch ID that doesn't exist or failing to set reserved fields to their required values. Next, it fetches the dispatch map entry describing the requested method or property (2). The code then checks for errors relating to the specific method or property being invoked, such as the wrong number or type of parameters. It will attempt to perform type conversion if necessary. Some conversions will succeed, such as ints to floats; some will fail, such as strings to IDispatch pointers (3). The code then sets or gets the specified property or calls the specified method (4). Finally, the results are reported to the controller. Thus:

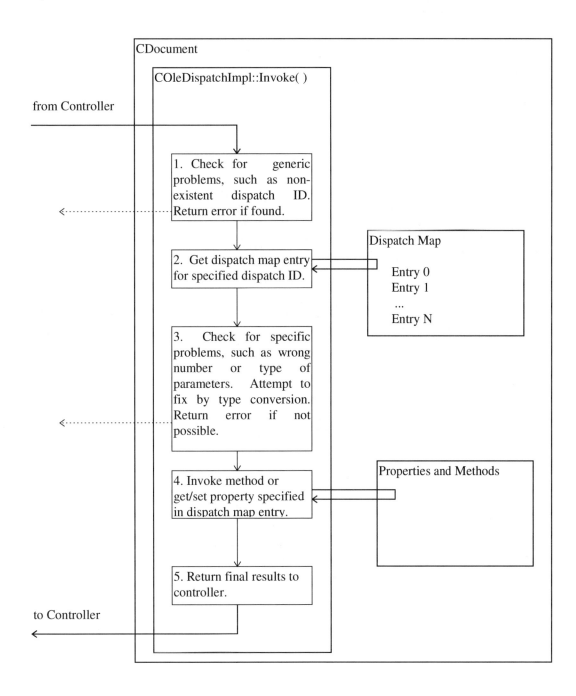

8. You add entries to your document's dispatch map with Class Wizard. The "Ole Automation" tab contains the necessary buttons. The process and its results are very similar to adding a message handler. Class Wizard makes entries in the dispatch map as shown on the preceding pages. It also makes entries in the document's header file. Thus:

< header file showing entries made by Class Wizard >

```
class CMfchelloausvDoc : public CDocument
{
    < rest of header file omitted>

public:
    CString m_HelloMessage ;

protected:
    // Generated OLE dispatch map functions
    //{{AFX_DISPATCH(CMfchelloausvDoc)
    afx_msg BSTR GetHelloMessage();
    afx_msg void SetHelloMessage(LPCTSTR lpszNewValue);
    afx_msg void SayHello();
    //}}AFX_DISPATCH

    DECLARE_DISPATCH_MAP()
    DECLARE_INTERFACE_MAP()
};
```

9. When you add a method, you must specify its name, return type, and parameters if any. Class Wizard adds the method's declaration to your document's header file as shown on the previous page and generates a function skeleton for you as shown below, exactly as was done for a message handler. Thus:

```
/*
Function shell added by Class Wizard.
*/


void CMfchelloausvDoc::SayHello()
{

/*
My own code added.
*/

    UpdateAllViews (NULL) ;
}
```

10. When you add a property, you specify its name and type. You have the choice of two ways to handle the controller's access to the property. You can use the traditional Get and Set( ) method pair as shown below, which is useful if you want to validate the new property value before allowing it to be used. Or you can have Class Wizard add a member variable and automatically handle requests to set and get its value. Class Wizard will generate a notification function which will be called when a controller changes the property's value. In either case, Class Wizard makes the necessary additions to the dispatch map and the header files, and generates skeletons of the required functions. Note in the sample code how the MFC handles all of the conversion between wide and narrow character strings. Thus:

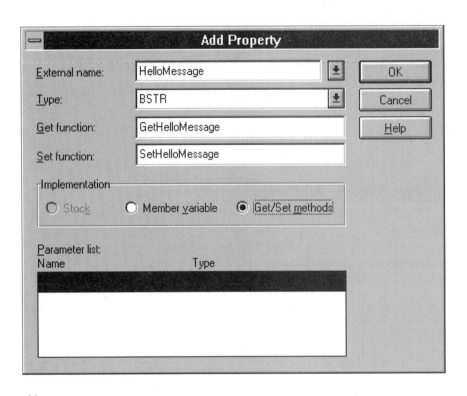

```
/*
Function skeletons generated by Class Wizard.
*/

BSTR CMfchelloausvDoc::GetHelloMessage()
{
    CString strResult;
/*
Next line only added by me:
*/
    strResult = m_HelloMessage ;
    return strResult.AllocSysString();
}

void CMfchelloausvDoc::SetHelloMessage(LPCTSTR lpszNewValue)
{
/*
Next line only added by me.
*/
    m_HelloMessage = lpszNewValue ;
}
```

11. You may generate as many automation-supporting classes as you wish by using Class Wizard to derive a class from CCmdTarget. Since an MFC DLL does not provide a document class, this is the only way to specify the automation object in an in-proc server.

When you generate your new class, you must choose one of the radio buttons to specify how the class is to be exposed to the world. If you pick "Createable by type ID" as shown below, Class Wizard will generate the code to add a class factory for your new class, thereby making it accessible to controllers via CoCreateInstance( ). However, if you simply pick "Automation," Class Wizard will not generate the class factory code and your new class will not be accessible via CoCreateInstance( ). This is customarily done to implement an object hierarchy. Only the top-level object, such as the application, is createable. Objects lower in the hierarchy are provided by calling the methods of higher objects, such as providing a file object by calling a method on the application object. Thus:

89

12. Our SDK server apps to this point have required separate .REG files to make the entries in the system registry that clients need to locate them. An MFC server contains code to make it register itself via the method **COleObjectFactory::UpdateRegistryAll( )**. In an app, this is provided in the CWinApp::InitInstance( ) method. The function is called every time the app is run as a standalone program, but not when it is run as an automation server. Thus:

```
BOOL CMfchelloausvApp::InitInstance()
{
    // Initialize OLE libraries
    if (!AfxOleInit())
    {
      AfxMessageBox(IDP_OLE_INIT_FAILED);
      return FALSE;
    }

    COleObjectFactory::UpdateRegistryAll();

    // Dispatch commands specified on the command line
    if (!ProcessShellCommand(cmdInfo))
      return FALSE;

    return TRUE;
}
```

In an in-proc server, the call to COleObjectFactory::UpdateRegistryAll() is placed in the function DllRegisterServer( ), which the server DLL exports by name. A development tool or setup program will load the library, call GetProcAddress( ) to obtain a pointer to DllRegisterServer( ), and call it. Thus:

```
STDAPI DllRegisterServer(void)
{
    AFX_MANAGE_STATE(AfxGetStaticModuleState());
    COleObjectFactory::UpdateRegistryAll();
    return S_OK;
}
```

E. EXCEPTION INFO

1. The **EXCEPINFO** structure passed as part of the method IDispatch::Invoke( ) is a holder for extensive error information that a friendly OLE automation server can return to a controller for the purpose of informing the user exactly what is wrong with a failed Invoke( ) call. The server can specify an error code and a human-readable string. Most powerfully, the server can specify the help file in which further information can be found and even the context ID of the specific topic within the help file. It's like saying to the caller, "RTFM, and here's the page, you #$%@ idiot !" The structure looks like this:

```
typedef struct FARSTRUCT tagEXCEPINFO
{
    unsigned short wCode;        // app-specific error code
    unsigned short wReserved;    // reserved, must be 0
    BSTR bstrSource;             // server app in which error occurred
    BSTR bstrDescription;        // text description of error
    BSTR bstrHelpFile;           // server's help file path
    unsigned long dwHelpContext;  // server's help context ID for error
    void FAR* pvReserved;        // reserved, must be NULL
    HRESULT (STDAPICALLTYPE FAR* pfnDeferredFillIn)(EXCEPINFO *);
                                 // ptr to function for delayed fill-in
    SCODE scode;                 // SCODE describing error
} EXCEPINFO
```

2. An EXCEPINFO structure is passed to the server by the controller as one of the parameters in the IDispatch::Invoke( ) method. If the server at any time finds an error in the invocation of the desired action, it fills in the fields of the EXCEPINFO structures and returns the code DISP_E_EXCEPTION. In the example on the next page, when the controller tries to set the HelloMessage property, the server uses the API function **VariantChangeType( )** to attempt to convert whatever data the caller actually passed us into a BSTR. If an error is found, the method fills in the EXCEPINFO structure with data describing the error. It is up to the controller to present that data to the user in a meaningful manner. Thus:

```
STDMETHODIMP CHelloDispatch::Invoke(DISPID dispidMember, REFIID riid,
    LCID lcid, WORD wFlags, DISPPARAMS *pDispParams,
    VARIANT *pVarResult, EXCEPINFO *pExcepInfo, UINT *puArgErr)
{

/*
Caller wants to set the HelloMessage property.
*/
    if (dispidMember == 1)
    {
      else if (wFlags & DISPATCH_PROPERTYPUT)
        {

/*
Perform type checking on the passed VARIANT.  If it can't be converted
into  a BSTR, then fill out the EXCEPINFO structure and return the
failure code that says the EXCEPINFO contains valid information.
*/

            VARIANT vResult ; HRESULT hr ;

            hr = VariantChangeType (&vResult,    // output variant
                pDispParams->rgvarg,             // input variant
                0,                               // flags
                VT_BSTR) ;                       // desired output type

            if (hr != S_OK)
            {
                pExcepInfo->wCode = 0 ;
                pExcepInfo->wReserved = 0 ;
                pExcepInfo->pvReserved = NULL ;
                pExcepInfo->pfnDeferredFillIn = NULL ;

                pExcepInfo->bstrSource = SysAllocString(
                    L"Hello32.exe");
                pExcepInfo->bstrDescription = SysAllocString(
                    L"Expecting string parameter") ;
                pExcepInfo->scode = DISP_E_TYPEMISMATCH ;
                pExcepInfo->bstrHelpFile = SysAllocString (
                    L"c:\\hello32.hlp") ;
                pExcepInfo->dwHelpContext = 1 ;

                return DISP_E_EXCEPTION ;
            }

/*
Successful set of the property.
*/
            SysReAllocString(&m_bstrHelloMsg, vResult.bstrVal);
        }
      return NOERROR ;
    }
```

3. The controller needs to check the return value for the Invoke( ) method. If it returns the code that says there is information in the EXCEPINFO, it is up to the controller to package the information and present it to the user. One such way is in a dialog box. Thus:

```
if (!SUCCEEDED(hr))
{

/*
No EXCEPINFO provided by server.
*/
    if (hr != DISP_E_EXCEPTION)
    {
      MessageBox (hMainDlg, TEXT("Unsuccessful, and no EXCEPINFO."),
            TEXT("Error"), MB_ICONSTOP) ;
    }
/*
Server provided EXCEPINFO extended error information. Assemble       the
app's name and error into a string, and pop it up in a dialog box.
*/

    else
    {
      TCHAR out [256] ;
      wsprintf (out,
            TEXT("The app %s reported the following error:%c%c%s"),
            ei.bstrSource, 0x0d, 0x0a, ei.bstrDescription) ;
      int ret = DialogBoxParam (hInstance,
            MAKEINTRESOURCE(IDD_DIALOG2),
            hMainDlg, (DLGPROC) ErrorDlgProc, (long) out) ;

/*
If user clicked the HELP button, invoke WinHelp on the help file and
help context supplied in the EXCEPINFO.
*/
      if (ret == IDC_HELP)
      {
            WinHelp (hMainDlg, ei.bstrHelpFile, HELP_CONTEXT,
                  ei.dwHelpContext) ;
      }

/*
Controller is responsible for freeing the BSTR elements.
*/
      if (ei.bstrHelpFile) SysFreeString(ei.bstrHelpFile) ;
      if (ei.bstrSource) SysFreeString(ei.bstrSource) ;
      if (ei.bstrDescription) SysFreeString (ei.bstrDescription) ;
    }

}
```

4. In the MFC, you can throw an EXCEPINFO in any function called from an automation handler via the function **AfxThrowOleDispatchException( )**. This fills out an EXCEPINFO structure with the app-specific error code, a human-readable string, and the help context ID. The name of the help file is retrieved from the CWinApp base class. Thus:

```
void CMfchelloausvDoc::SetHelloMessage(LPCTSTR lpszNewValue)
{

/*
Check the new value of the property passed by the controller before
allowing it to be used. This controller will not accept any string that
contains the word "bad".  If it does, fire back an EXCEPINFO and don't
set the value.
*/
    if (strstr (lpszNewValue, "bad"))
    {
      AfxThrowOleDispatchException (
            1,                       // app error code
            "I can't take bad news",// human-readable string
            99) ;                    // help context

      return ;
    }

/*
String was acceptable.  Set the value of our property.
*/
    m_HelloMessage = lpszNewValue ;
}
```

When called from a Visual Basic controller, the EXCEPINFO is presented to the user as shown below. The MFC sample app does not contain a help file; this is left as an exercise for the student. Thus:

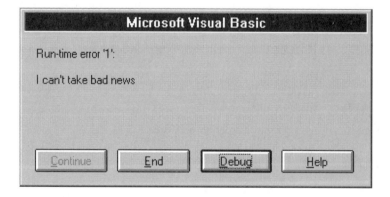

F. ACCESSING AUTOMATION OBJECTS FROM VISUAL BASIC

1. The reason OLE automation got started, and one of the main reasons it caught on, is that it allows programmers to write relatively simple programs in Visual Basic which connect together sophisticated components purchased from other vendors. Real programmers of the type who purchase this book tend to look down their noses at anything having the word "basic" in it, but let's face it:

A) There's lots of money to be made in quickly gluing together components purchased from other vendors, and

B) We like making lots of money.

2. Consider the following very simple VB project. It contains a single form with two edit controls ("text boxes" in VB parlance) and three pushbuttons. It took all of 30 seconds to put together from the VB control palette. You can find the VB source code in the directory \chap03\helloau\vbhelloclient.

3. To create an object, you must first use the `Dim` keyword in the form's general declarations section to declare a variable as an object. Thus:

4. Once you have declared the object, you create it via the VB function **CreateObject( )**. This takes the human-readable name of the object and hey, presto, wakes up the server and creates the object. Since you have studied the guts of OLE to this point, you know that internally, this function is reading the registry to find the class ID value under the human-readable name, then calling CoCreateInstance( ) to make OLE find the server identified with the class ID, deal with the class factories, and return a pointer to the object's IDispatch interface. Thus:

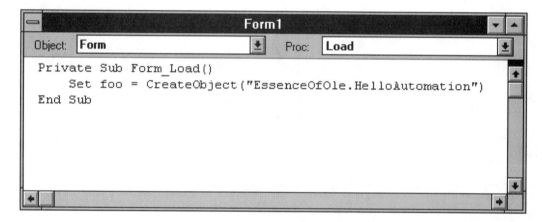

5. To call the object's SayHello( ) method in response to a button click, you simply access the method using the dot notation, as if it were a member of the local object. VB will use the IDispatch interface to query for the dispatch ID, then invoke it. All the heavy lifting is done for you by VB.

```
Private Sub Command1_Click()
    foo.SayHello
End Sub
```

6. To get the object's HelloMessage property, you simply access it using the dot notation as if it was a local property. VB does all of the negotiation with the IDispatch interface. Thus:

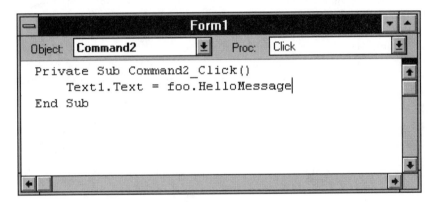

```
Private Sub Command2_Click()
    Text1.Text = foo.HelloMessage
End Sub
```

7. To set the object's HelloMessage property, you simply assign into it on the left-hand side of the equals sign. Again, VB does all the negotiation with the IDispatch interface. Thus:

```
Private Sub Command3_Click()
    foo.HelloMessage = Text2.Text
End Sub
```

97

Directory: \EssenceofOLE\chap03\helloau\hlodrv32\templ

In this lab, we'll create the automation controller discussed in the first part of this chapter. All of the interesting code will take place in the file HELLODRV.CPP.

1. To develop and test the controller, it is necessary to have a server to interact with. Go to the root directory of this example and run the registry file HELLO32.REG. This will make the necessary entries in the system registry to connect the server HELLO32.EXE in the \helloau\hello32\done directory as the automation server for the object whose human-readable name is "EssenceofOLE.HelloAutomation". If the root directory you are using for your samples is anything other than C:\, you will have to edit the .REG file to make the LocalServer32 entry point to the exact path location of the server file.

2. The method CHelloDriver::Create( ) is the place where the connection is first made between the automation controller and the object provided by the server. The first thing the controller needs to do is create the automation object by calling the API function CoCreateInstance( ). The class ID of the object has already been read from the registry for you and may be found in the variable "clsid". The interface that you need returned is IID_IDispatch. Store the returned object pointer in the member variable "m_pDisp". You should build and run your app at this point. The server should appear, but none of the automation methods should work because you have not yet gotten the dispatch IDs needed to identify them. If the server does not come up, you probably have the registry path wrong.

3. Having gotten the IDispatch interface, we need to get the IDs within it that correspond to the named dispatch elements via the method IDispatch::GetIDsOfNames( ). You will have to do this twice, once for the property "HelloMessage" and once for the method "SayHello". Store the IDs in the member variables "m_dHelloPropID" and "m_dSayHelloId" respectively. Remember that the strings you pass to GetIDsOfNames( ) must always be a wide character string, even if your app is not a wide character app.

4. The first actual invocation of the automation object's method takes place in the method CHelloDriver::SayHowdy( ). Use the method IDispatch::Invoke( ) to call the automation object's SayHello( ) method. Pass an empty parameter array to the function and expect no return value.

5. Next implement the CHelloDriver::GetString( ) method. This uses the IDispatch interface to get the value of the automation object's HelloMessage property. You must allocate and initialize a VARIANT structure to receive the return value. The code to put it into the dialog box's edit control has already been written for you.

6. Finally, implement the CHelloDriver::SetString( ) method. You must now allocate a VARIANT to hold the input parameters, and a DISPPARAMS structure to hold the variant and other flags. Initialize them and set their values as shown in the text. Use the IDispatch::Invoke( ) method to set the value of the automation object's HelloMessage property.

EXTRA CREDIT: Examine the CHelloDriver::BadSetString( ) method until you feel comfortable with the processing of the EXCEPINFO structure. The first time you select the "Help" button in the dialog box, WinHelp will probably not be able to find the specified file. You will have to locate it yourself, in the directory \helloau\hello32\help. The operating system will then remember where it lives, so subsequent calls to WinHelp will find it.

Directory: \EssenceofOLE\chap03\helloau\hello32\templ

1. Now that your controller is working, you have something to test the server with. Before starting to work on the server, you must change the entries in the registry so that the controller will use the new server that you are developing rather than the finished one supplied in the \done directory. You can do this either by editing the .REG file to point to the new server's path (in the directory \templ\windebug) and reregistering the whole thing, or by using the registry editor and changing only the path itself.

2. The server app is a small one. All the interesting code takes place in the file HELLO.CPP. As you are already conversant with the concepts, the class factory registration has been done for you, as have the two trivial methods of the IDispatch interface. First, you must implement the method IDispatch::GetIDsOfNames( ). Compare the name supplied by the caller with the names "HelloMessage" and "SayHello". The ID for the former is 1, and that of the latter is 2. Note that the caller always supplies these names in a wide character string, even though it might not be a wide character app and you might not be either.

3. Now you must implement the IDispatch::Invoke( ) method. Since it's complex, we'll do it a piece at a time. First, let's handle the property get case. Check the wFlags element for DISPATCH_PROPERTYGET. If found, the caller is trying to get the HelloMessage property. Set the vt element of the pVarResult parameter to the proper value to indicate a string. Use the function SysAllocString( ) to allocate a new BSTR containing the string in the member variable m_bstrHelloMsg. Place this BSTR in the return variant and return the success code. Test with your controller; you should now be able to get the value of this property.

4. Next, let's implement the set operation. Check the wFlags element for DISPATCH_PROPERTYPUT. If found, the caller is trying to set the HelloMessage property. Check the vt element of the supplied variant to make sure it contains a BSTR. If so, use the function SysReAllocString( ) to reset the value of the member variable m_bstrHelloMsg to the new value supplied in the VARIANT. Return success or failure code. The SayHello( ) method has been implemented for you so you will be able to see the results.

5. Finally, let's implement the EXCEPINFO structure. Use the function VariantChangeType( ) to attempt to coerce the passed parameter into a BSTR. If this function doesn't succeed, then fill out the fields of the EXCEPINFO structure passed in the parameter list. Your app comes with a help file called "hello32.hlp". The context for the topic inside it that explains this error is 1. Return the error code DISP_E_EXCEPTION to indicate to the controller that extended error information can be found in the EXCEPINFO structure.

Directory: \EssenceofOLE\chap03\helloau\mfchelloausv

The MFC is a powerful development environment that lets us construct OLE automation servers in a fraction of the time it would take to hardwire one in the API. No \templ directory is provided for this exercise, as the MFC will generate all the code you need. The \done directory contains a finished example.

1. Start VC++ and generate a new project using App Wizard. On the appropriate App Wizard pane (number 3 at the time of this writing), check the "OLE automation" box. You can choose the "Finish" button after this selection. Build your app and run it; it will register itself.

2. Now we need a controller for the MFC server app. We can use the controller built in the first part of this lab. If you haven't done that part, use the controller from the \done directory. The controller is hardwired to use the server whose class ID is in the registry under the key HKEY_CLASSES_ROOT\ EssenceofOLE.HelloAutomation\CLSID. Open your MFC app's .CPP file that contains the CWinApp-derived class. You will find a variable named "clsid". Just above that variable, in a comment line, you will find the same class ID as a string inside curly braces. Take this string, curlies and all, and place it in the CLSID key listed above, replacing the previous contents. This will cause your controller to launch the MFC server when it starts up. Run your controller and test it. The controller's call to CoCreateInstance( ) will succeed, but its call to GetIDsOfNames( ) will fail because the server currently contains no methods or properties with the names the controller is querying for. The server should not become visible, as this is the user interface convention for servers.

3. In your MFC server's project, go to Class Wizard and select the "Ole Automation" tab. Select your document class in the list box if it isn't already. Use Class Wizard to add a method called "SayHello" and a CString property called "HelloMessage" to your app. Build it and test it with the controller, which should at this point find everything it needs.

4. In the previous step, Class Wizard generated function skeletons for you. Add whatever code you want to implement these features, perhaps by drawing the string on your server's main window. If you want the server window to be visible, go to the CWinApp::InitInstance( ) method and just after the call to COleTemplateServer::RegisterAll( ), comment out the line that says "return TRUE;".

Chapter 4

Type Libraries

A. CONCEPTS AND DEFINITIONS

1. Any type of COM server, especially an OLE automation server can greatly enhance its usability by providing self-description information for the use of intelligent tools that program it, such as VB or VC++. Another way to look at a type library is as a language-independent header file. You will never be able to sell an object server that doesn't provide one. Such a description usually contains:

The types of objects the server supports

Each object's methods with their parameters and types

Each object's properties with their types

References to specific items of on-line documentation

2. An object provides a description of itself by means of a *type library*, a collection of static data structures provided by the object vendor and accessed via the *ITypeLib* interface. A type library is a container for one or more *type infos*. A type info is a static data structure provided by the object vendor that contains information about a single automation object in a binary machine-readable format, accessed via the *ITypeInfo* interface. Thus:

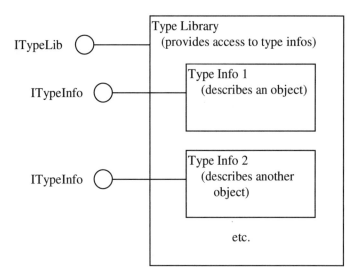

WARNING: A type library and its contents are nothing but a fancy software manual. They are not generated by runtime examination of an object's binary code; they contain whatever descriptive information the author decided to put in them and are only as good as their contents. What's the first law of computer science? Garbage in, garbage out. If the library contains misinformation, you are, as we say here in Boston, "scrod."

3. Type libraries are used for a great many purposes, such as the following. I'm sure you'll think of more.

Instead of having to write the CHelloDriver wrapper class shown in the previous chapter for accessing the methods and properties of a dispatch object, you can have Visual C++ read a type library and automatically generate it for you. It will even regenerate it if the type library changes. This is shown on page 112.

When writing an automation server, you can actually use the type library to implement the IDispatch::GetIDsOfNames( ) and IDispatch::Invoke( ) methods. You don't have to write them manually as shown in the preceding chapter. This is demonstrated in the dual interface section of Chapter 9.

When you use Visual Basic to access an automation object as in the previous chapter, writing simply `Dim foo as Object`, VB uses IDispatch::GetIDsOfNames to find the dispatch IDs of the requested properties and methods. However, if provide VB with a type library, it will use the dispatch IDs from the type library and save the overhead of that call. This is shown on page 120.

Better yet, if you have a VTBL interface defined in a type library, VB can use that VTBL interface directly. It's not restricted to using IDispatch, provided it has a valid type library at compile time. This is demonstrated in the dual interface section of Chapter 9.

When you write your own custom interfaces, you usually have to provide the code that marshals the call from client to server and back again. If you have a type library that describes your custom interface, and if that custom interface uses only parameter types supported by OLE Automation, you can avoid having to write any marshaling code. You can simply make a few registry entries which tell the operating system to perform the marshaling at runtime based on the information in the type library information. This is shown on page 118 and in Chapter 9.

A Java applet that wants to use a COM object must have a special Java class that wraps the COM object. The Java Type Library Wizard generates this wrapper class from a type library that describes the COM object. This is shown in Chapter 15.

When you download a control from the Web, your browser needs to find out the methods and properties that it contains and the events it fires in order to execute scripts. As described on page 110 and in Chapter 5, a control contains its own type library bound inside it as a resource. This allows the browser to discover the control's information at runtime.

Finally, a type library makes it possible for intelligent development environments such as Visual Basic to provide user interface support that makes a developer's life much easier. Some developers look down their noses at this, but time to market is the number one constraint in development today, and anything that saves you time flipping through paper manuals is a great feature. This is shown on page 120.

This page intentionally contains no text other than this sentence.

B. BUILDING TYPE LIBRARIES

1. A type library is created by writing a file in *Object Descriptor Language* or *Interface Descriptor Language* containing statements which describe your objects. ODL is the older way, still used by the MFC. IDL is a superset of ODL, somewhat newer and more versatile, and is used by the ATL. The file will have the extension .ODL or .IDL and is added to the VC++ project. When the project is built, the descriptor file is compiled into a type library file with extension .TLB. Thus:

Note: Type libraries are most conveniently built at compile time as shown above, but if you need to roll one on the fly at runtime, you can do it via the API function **CreateTypeLib( )**.

2. The example shown on the facing page is "hello32.odl", the .ODL file that compiles into the type library describing the simple Hello32 automation server created in the previous chapter. Each of the sections of the .ODL file contains a set of *attributes* enclosed in square brackets, followed by the *definitions* of the objects to which the attributes apply. Attributes used in the sample file include **uuid**, the globally unique ID of the object being defined.

The file starts off with the attributes block of the library itself, which contains the library's uuid and its version number. Next appears the definition of the library, which consists of the keyword **library** followed by the name of this library ("hello32") and a set of curly braces. Everything appearing between the opening and closing curly braces will be compiled into the library.

The first statement inside the library is **importlib**. This is the .ODL equivalent of #include, used to incorporate other type libraries by reference. The file "stdole32.tlb" is the .ODL equivalent of "windows.h".

Next appear a number of .ODL code blocks, each of which describes a type info that we want the library to contain. The first one we encounter is that of the dispinterface IDHello. Remembering from the previous chapter, a dispinterface is the set of properties and methods accessed through a specific IDispatch interface. First we see the attributes of dispinterface, which at present contain only its uuid. Next comes the keyword **dispinterface**, followed by its name and a set of curly braces. Everything appearing within the curly braces will be exposed as an element of the IDHello type info.

A dispinterface contains properties and methods, which are respectively denoted in .ODL via the keywords **properties** and **methods**. Each property and method has its own attributes section, in this case containing only its dispatch ID, denoted via the keyword **id**. Then follows the name of the property or method, its type, and its parameters if any. The dispinterface IDHello contains a single property, of type BSTR, called "HelloMessage", whose dispatch ID is 1. It also exposes a single method called "SayHello( )", whose parameter list and return type are both void and whose dispatch ID is 2.

The final type info that we see in this library is **coclass**, which denotes an object that is creatable via the API function CoCreateInstance( ). Our coclass attributes contain the uuid of the creatable object, which if you check back to the sample code for the previous chapter, you will find matches the class ID passed to CoCreateInstance( ) in the controller program. Inside the coclass is a reference to the dispinterface IDHello, which is telling the programmer that he ought to be able to create an object of the coclass and successfully query it for the dispinterface IDHello. The attribute **default** signifies that IDHello is what the caller will get if he queries for the default IDispatch interface.

A more in-depth description of the .ODL language can be found in Brockschmidt, pp. 150-154 and 160-168. The complete reference for it is in the Win32 SDK documentation.

```
// attributes of the type library itself, here uuid and version.

[uuid(6CED2901-A1DD-11cf-8A33-00AA00A58097), version(1.0)]

// Definition of library.

library hello32
{

// Standard types incorporated by reference.

    importlib("stdole32.tlb");

// A dispinterface is a custom set of methods and properties accessed
// via the IDispatch interface mechanism.

    [ uuid(6CED2902-A1DD-11cf-8A33-00AA00A58097)]
    dispinterface IDHello
    {

// properties and methods contained in the dispinterface with their
// dispatch ids and types.

        properties:
            [id(1)] BSTR HelloMessage;

        methods:
            [id(2)] void SayHello();
    };


// A coclass is an object that can be created by calling
// CoCreateInstance( ).

    [ uuid(6CED2900-A1DD-11cf-8A33-00AA00A58097)]
    coclass HelloApplication
    {

// If you create an object of this coclass, you ought to be able to
// successfully query it for IDHello. And if you query it simply for
// IDispatch, IDHello is what you will get.

        [default] dispinterface IDHello ;

    };
};
```

3. The type libraries we have seen so far have listed only the types and names of an object's properties, methods, and parameters. This isn't anywhere near enough to be able to program it intelligently. A type info may provide a *help string*, a small string provided within the type info itself. In the VB Object Browser example on page 123, the string "Make server output its HelloMessage property" is a help string. To place a help string in a type info, add the ODL attribute **helpstring( )** within the square brackets enclosing a type description as shown below. The string that you want to display is placed inside the parentheses in quotes. A development environment that wants to display the string can retrieve it via the ITypeLib and ITypeInfo interfaces as shown in the latter part of this chapter.

4. A help string is generally displayed in a cramped location inside a development environment, so there is a fairly low limit on the amount of explanation it can usefully provide, perhaps a dozen words or so. To provide more detailed explanation of a property or method, you can place references in the type library to specific topics within your object's on-line help file (which you must provide anyway if you expect anyone to buy it). A smart development environment will provide the programmer with a button that launches WinHelp (via the API function WinHelp( )) and jumps directly to the specified topic. You specify the help file that contains the help topics via the ODL attribute **helpfile( )**, containing the name of the help file in parentheses. This attribute must appear only once in the library's attributes section. Any attributes section within the library may contain the ODL attribute **helpcontext( )**, which specifies the context integer of the topic within the specified help file that (you hope) explains the item. The development environment retrieves these elements via the ITypeLib and ITypeInfo interfaces as shown in the latter part of this chapter. Thus:

```
// Help file for library specified here.

[ uuid(6CED2901-A1DD-11cf-8A33-00AA00A58097), version(1.0),
    helpfile ("Hello32.hlp") ]

library hello32
{
    importlib("stdole32.tlb");

// Help string explaining this type info specified here.

    [ uuid(6CED2902-A1DD-11cf-8A33-00AA00A58097),
      helpstring ("IDispatch for Hello32 Object") ]

    dispinterface IDHello
    {

// Help string explaining this property and help context of further
// explanation specified here.

    properties:
            [id(1), helpstring ("Displayed message"), helpcontext(1)]
                BSTR HelloMessage;

    <rest of .ODL file>
```

108

5. When you add methods or properties to an OLE Automation object in the MFC by using Class Wizard, entries are also made in the .ODL file. The ATL provides similar functionality. Thus:

```
// mfchelloausv.odl : type library source for mfchelloausv.exe
// This file will be processed by the Make Type Library (mktyplib) tool
// to produce the type library (mfchelloausv.tlb).

[ uuid(79B3AC81-92C6-11CF-8A22-00AA00A58097), version(1.0) ]
library Mfchelloausv
{
    importlib("stdole32.tlb");

    // Primary dispatch interface for CMfchelloausvDoc

    [ uuid(79B3AC82-92C6-11CF-8A22-00AA00A58097) ]
    dispinterface IMfchel
    {
      properties:
            // NOTE - ClassWizard will maintain property information
            //     Use extreme caution when editing this section.
            //{{AFX_ODL_PROP(CMfchelloausvDoc)
            [id(1)] BSTR HelloMessage;
            //}}AFX_ODL_PROP

      methods:
            // NOTE - ClassWizard will maintain method info here.
            //     Use extreme caution when editing this section.
            //{{AFX_ODL_METHOD(CMfchelloausvDoc)
            [id(2)] void SayHello();
            //}}AFX_ODL_METHOD

    };

    // Class information for CMfchelloausvDoc
    [ uuid(79B3AC80-92C6-11CF-8A22-00AA00A58097) ]
    coclass Document
    {
      [default] dispinterface IMfchel;
    };
    //{{AFX_APPEND_ODL}}
};
```

NOTE: The .ODL file generated by the MFC does not contain any of the help-related attributes shown on the preceding page, even if you check the "Context-sensitive Help" box in App Wizard while generating the project. You must add them manually.

WARNING: Class Wizard assigns dispatch IDs in alphabetical order, first to properties and then to methods. When you add a new property or method, it will be inserted into the dispatch map at its alphabetical location and the dispatch IDs of all elements which follow it will change. Class Wizard will properly maintain the .ODL file, but any external code that depends on a hardwired class ID will have to be rewritten or regenerated.

C. DEPLOYING AND REGISTERING TYPE LIBRARIES

1. An object may deploy its type libraries in several ways. You can ship a separate .TLB file along with your application. This is especially good if your type library is large. Microsoft Excel, for example, comes with a type library file named "xl5en32.olb", which is 223 Kbytes long.

2. If you do not want to provide the type library in an external file, you can bind it into your .EXE or .DLL as a resource, thereby making your app self-contained. This is the method used by OCX controls. To bind the type library as a resource, add a **TYPELIB** directive to your .RC file, specifying the name of the typelib you want included. **The resource id of the type library within your .EXE or .DLL must be 1, as shown here, or the system's type library access functions will have difficulty finding it.** This probably means that you will have to add it to your .RC file by hand.

```
<.RC file>

//////////////////////////////////////////////////////////////////
//////
//
// TYPELIB
//

1            TYPELIB DISCARDABLE        "hello32.tlb"
```

3. However you decide to distribute your type library files, you must make entries in the system registry so that client applications and development tools can find the correct type library for your object. The registry does not contain the type library itself; rather, it contains references to the file in which the type library can be found. First, under the automation object's CLSID key, you must place the subkey "TYPELIB" with a value of the uuid which identifies the type library in which the type info describing the specific automation object can be found. Thus:

```
HKEY_CLASSES_ROOT
  CLSID
    <your app's clsid>
      TYPELIB=<uuid of your object's type library>
```

In the hello32 example, these entries are:

```
HKEY_CLASSES_ROOT
  CLSID
    {6CED2900-A1DD-11cf-8A33-00AA00A58097}
      TYPELIB={6CED2901-A1DD-11cf-8A33-00AA00A58097}
```

4. The TYPELIB section of the registry contains an entry for every type library registered on the system. The entry structure provides the capability of specifying different type libraries for different version numbers, language IDs, and 16- or 32-bit servers. Since the type library frequently contains references to an object's on-line help files, the registry entry structure also contains an entry specifying the directory in which these may be found. Its keys will look like this:

```
HKEY_CLASSES_ROOT
  TYPELIB
    <type library uuid> >
      <version> = <human-readable name of your type library
        <language id, 0 == any language>
          Win32 = <your type library file name>
          HelpDir = <directory containing help files>
```

In the hello32 example, these entries are:

```
HKEY_CLASSES_ROOT
  TYPELIB
    {6CED2901-A1DD-11cf-8A33-00AA00A58097}
      1.0 = OLE Automation Hello 1.0 Type Library
        0
          Win32 = c:\EssenceofOLE\chap03\helloau\hello32\done\hello32.tlb
          HelpDir = c:\EssenceofOLE\chap03\helloau\hello32\help
```

Note: Brockschmidt, p. 170 gives a slightly different layout for the registry entries; however, the ones shown above are the ones that you will see if you actually go and look at the registry.

D. Using Type Libraries for C++ Automation Clients

1. One of the cooler features added to VC++ in version 5 is its ability to automatically generate C++ wrapper classes for a particular dispinterface based on the dispinterface's description in a type library. The preprocessor now automatically translates the language-independent object and interface definitions in a type library into C++ classes that you can use directly from your source code. As always, you need to have an accurate type library at compile time. The example shown in this section uses this feature to generate a class that replaces the CHelloDriver wrapper class that we wrote manually in the previous chapter. The source code may be found in the directory "\EssenceOfOle\chap04\typelibhellodrv".

To import a type library, you use the new Microsoft-specific **#import** C++ preprocessor directive, specifying the type library file that you want to import. This causes the compiler to read the specified type library, generate C++ language header files based on its contents, and include those header files in the C++ source file. The new header files are stored in the project's output file directory (such as \Debug or \Release), and regenerated whenever the type library changes.

2. The wrapper class generated by this directive is based on the new standard C++ class **_com_ptr_t**, also known as a "smart com pointer," described in Appendix D. This is a template-based class that you will probably not use directly. Instead, you will usually derive your own classes from it, as the automatic import mechanism does in this example.

Looking back at the type library definition on page 107, you will see that it contains a dispinterface named "IDHello". When you import the type library, the preprocessor will use the _com_ptr_t class to create a wrapper class based on this dispinterface. The name of this class is always the name of the dispinterface with the characters "Ptr" appended to it, in this case "**IDHelloPtr**".

The imported class is by default placed into its own C++ namespace, which has the name specified in the "library" attribute of the type library. This was done to avoid possible name conflicts with your existing C++ code, but I find it more confusing than helpful. To turn this feature off, add the keyword **no_namespace** to the #import directive as shown on the facing page. If I had not done this, I would have to refer to my IDHello pointer by its full namespace name, "hello32::IDHelloPtr".

As in the original example, simply instantiating the pointer does not create the server object to which it refers. This requires a separate method, **CreateInstance( )**, which belongs to the class _com_ptr_t. Internally this calls CoCreateInstance( ) and assigns the resulting pointer to the smart pointer. The directive **__uuidof( )** returns the class ID of the HelloApplication object, which you will also see in the generated wrapper class. Thus:

```
/*
Tell the preprocessor to read in this type library and generate a
wrapper class based on it.
*/

#import "hello32.tlb" no_namespace

/*
This is the smart pointer class, based on com_ptr_t that wraps the
IDHello dispinterface specified in the type library.
*/

IDHelloPtr pHello ;

extern BOOL CALLBACK HelloDlgProc (HWND, UINT, WPARAM, LPARAM) ;


int WINAPI WinMain(HINSTANCE hInst, HINSTANCE hPrevInstance,
    LPSTR lpCmdLine, int nCmdShow)
{
    MSG msg ;
    OleInitialize (NULL) ;

/*
Create the driver object based on COM's smart pointer classes generated
by the #import directive.
*/


    HRESULT hr = pHello.CreateInstance (__uuidof(HelloApplication)) ;

    if (hr != S_OK)
    {
      char out [256] ;
      wsprintf (out, "Couldn't create object, hr == 0x%x", hr) ;
      MessageBox (NULL, out, "", 0) ;
    }

/*
Pop up dialog box giving user interface to automation object. This
function returns when the user clicks "Exit".
*/

    DialogBox (hInst, MAKEINTRESOURCE(IDD_DIALOG1), NULL, (FARPROC)
      HelloDlgProc) ;

    OleUninitialize ( ) ;

    return msg.wParam;
}
```

3. The file "hello32.tlh" is the main type library header generated by the preprocessor in response to the #import directive. It contains C++ specific classes based on the language-independent information provided by the type library. Here you will find the C++ declaration of the wrapper class for the dispinterface IDHello. The new C++ keyword __**declspec(uuid)** attaches a uuid to a structure which you can read later with the __uuidof() directive as shown on the previous page. Simplified and commented for clarity, the C++ files look like this:

```cpp
// C++ source equivalent of Win32 type library hello32.tlb
// compiler-generated file created 06/21/97 at 10:06:17 - DO NOT EDIT!

#include <comdef.h>

// Forward references and typedefs

struct            __declspec(uuid("6ced2902-a1dd-11cf-8a33-00aa00a58097"))
IDHello;

// Smart pointer typedef declarations. This line actually generates the
// IDHelloPtr class from com_ptr_t

_COM_SMARTPTR_TYPEDEF(IDHello, __uuidof(IDispatch));

// Type library items

struct __declspec(uuid("6ced2902-a1dd-11cf-8a33-00aa00a58097"))
IDHello : IDispatch
{
    // Properties

    __declspec(property(get=GetHelloMessage,put=PutHelloMessage))
    _bstr_t HelloMessage;

    // Methods:

    HRESULT SayHello ( );

    // Property accessor functions

    _bstr_t GetHelloMessage ( );
    void PutHelloMessage ( _bstr_t _val );
};

struct __declspec(uuid("6ced2900-a1dd-11cf-8a33-00aa00a58097"))
    HelloApplication;

// Wrapper method implementations

#include "Debug/hello32.tli"
```

4. The file "hello32.tli" contains the type library implementations for the wrapper class's methods and properties. It uses the new library functions **_com_dispatch_method( )**, **_com_dispatch_propget( )**, and **_com_dispatch_propput( )** to handle the standard cases of accessing properties and methods through an IDispatch interface. Thus:

```
//
// Wrapper implementations for Win32 type library hello32.tlb
// compiler-generated file created 06/21/97 at 10:06:17 - DO NOT EDIT!

//
// dispinterface IDHello wrapper method implementations
//

inline HRESULT IDHello::SayHello ( )
{
    return _com_dispatch_method(this, 0x2, DISPATCH_METHOD, VT_EMPTY,
        NULL, NULL);
}

inline _bstr_t IDHello::GetHelloMessage ( )
{
    BSTR _result;
    _com_dispatch_propget(this, 0x1, VT_BSTR, (void*)&_result);
    return _bstr_t(_result, false);
}

inline void IDHello::PutHelloMessage ( _bstr_t _val )
{
    _com_dispatch_propput(this, 0x1, VT_BSTR, (BSTR)_val);
}
```

5. The dialog box response function shown below has been modified to use the smart pointer wrapper class. Remember that the _com_ptr_t object is itself a C++ object that contains a pointer to the COM interface as a member variable. To access this COM interface pointer, you must use the overloaded arrow operator as shown; not the dot operator used in the CreateInstance( ) method a few pages ago.   Thus:

```
#import "hello32.tlb" no_namespace
extern IDHelloPtr pHello ;

BOOL WINAPI HelloDlgProc (HWND hDlg, UINT msg, WPARAM wParam,
    LPARAM lParam)
{

    switch (msg)
    {
      case WM_COMMAND:
      {
            switch (LOWORD(wParam))
            {
/*
User clicked "Say Hello" button.  Call driver object's SayHello( )
method, which uses the IDispatch interface to control the server's
automation object and invoke its "SayHello( )" method.
*/
                case ID_SAYHELLO:
                {

                    pHello->SayHello( ) ;
                    return TRUE ;
                }
```

<continued on next page>

6. Automation requires you to pass strings in the form of BSTRs, manipulating which is a complete pain in the ass using the function based API. Microsoft VC++ v5.0 now provides the native class **_bstr_t**, which encapsulates the functionality of a BSTR into an intelligent class. In particular, the = operator and cast operators have been overloaded so as to work smoothly and logically. It also provides automatic conversion between ANSI and Unicode. Thus:

```
<continued from previous page>

/*
User    clicked    "Get    String"    button.    Call    driver    object's
GetHelloMessage() method, which  uses  the  IDispatch interface to read
the value of the server object's "HelloMessage" property.  Convert the
returned string from wide characters to ANSI and place in edit control.
*/
                        case ID_GETSTRING:
                        {
                                _bstr_t bstrHello = pHello->GetHelloMessage ();
/*
The (char *) cast operator of the _bstr_t class automatically performs
conversion from the BSTR's native Unicode to ANSI.
*/
                                SetDlgItemText (hDlg, IDC_EDIT1,
                                        (char *) bstrHello) ;
/*
BSTR's memory freed when it goes out of scope.
*/
                                return TRUE;
                        }
/*
User  clicked  "Set  String"  button.  Fetch  the  desired  string from  the
edit control where the user has typed it. Assigning it to the _bstr_t
object  automatically  converts  it  from  ANSI  into  the  wide  characters
required by OLE. Call driver object's SetHelloMessage( ) method, which
uses  the  IDispatch  interface  to  set  the  value  of  the  server  object's
"HelloMessage" property.
*/
                        case ID_SETSTRING:
                        {
                                char out [128] ;
                                GetDlgItemText (hDlg, IDC_EDIT2, out,
                                        sizeof(out)) ;
/*
Assigning ANSI string to the _bstr_t class invokes  the  overloaded  =
operator that automatically converts it into Unicode.
*/
                                _bstr_t bstrHello  = out ;
                                pHello->PutHelloMessage (bstrHello) ;
                                return TRUE ;
                        }
                }
            return FALSE ;
        }
}
```

E. TYPE LIBRARIES FOR IDENTIFYING DISPATCH INTERFACES

1. It is very important for an automation client to make sure that it connects to the right dispatch interface. If the client just queries for IDispatch, every automation server in the world provides it and they all do different things. Each standard VTBL interface is identified with a unique 16-byte UUID. We would like to extend this safety mechanism to the IDispatch world, so the client doesn't think that a dispatch ID of 1 means to order coffee while the server thinks it means to launch nuclear missiles.

You have probably noticed that each dispinterface in a type library has its own UUID. The way a client ensures that it has connected to this specific IDispatch and no other is to query the server not for the generic IDispatch, but rather for this specific dispinterface. That's what VB does when you dim a variable as a specific type of object such as HelloApplication, instead of the generic "Object".

To make this work, the automation server has to modify its QueryInterface( ) to respond to the specific dispinterface. It is customary to also keep support for the generic IDispatch, in case your client isn't paying that much attention. Thus:

```
STDMETHODIMP CHelloDispatch::QueryInterface(REFIID riid, void **ppv)
{

/*
Someone is asking us for our IDispatch or dispinterface. They get a
pointer to this object.
*/

    if (riid == IID_IUnknown
      || riid == IID_IDispatch
      || riid == IID_IDHello)
    {
      *ppv = this ;
      AddRef();
      return NOERROR;
    }

/*
Caller asked for an interface that we don't support.
*/
    else
    {
      *ppv = NULL;
      return E_NOINTERFACE ;
    }
}
```

118

2. IDispatch is a standard interface so the operating system knew how to set up marshaling for it when connecting to a local or remote server. The dispinterface's UUID is not a standard part of the operating system, so when the client queries for it, the operating system won't know how to marshal it so the call will fail. You can tell the operating system how to marshal the dispinterface by making a few entries in the registry, one of which identifies the type library describing the dispinterface.

In the HKEY_CLASSES_ROOT\Interface section, you make an entry for the dispinterface's UUID. Under this, you add the key "ProxyStubClsid32 = {00020420-0000-0000-C000-000000000046}". This CLSID identifies the generic marshaler for OLE Automation, which is where the actual marshaling code lives. You also add the key "TypeLib = <uuid of your type lib>", which tells the automation marshaler where to look for the description of the dispinterface that it needs to marshal. The specified type library must be registered as shown previously in this chapter. Thus:

```
HKEY_CLASSES_ROOT
    \Interface
      \<uuid of dispinterface>
            \ProxyStubClsid32 = {00020420-0000-0000-C000-000000000046}
            \TypeLib = <uuid of type lib describing the dispinterface>
```

or in this case,

```
HKEY_CLASSES_ROOT
    \Interface
      \{6CED2902-A1DD-11cf-8A33-00AA00A58097}
            \ProxyStubClsid32 = {00020420-0000-0000-C000-000000000046}
            \TypeLib = {6CED2901-A1DD-11cf-8A33-00AA00A58097}
```

119

F. USING TYPE LIBRARIES IN VISUAL BASIC

1. VB version 5 is an excellent example of the user interface support that an intelligent environment can provide to make programming easier. VB reads the type libraries that describe the objects your project is using, and presents their contents at strategic times and places. If you are an object vendor and don't provide a type library, and your competitors do, users will get this support from VB for their products but not for yours. They'll clean your clock.

To make VB use a particular type library, you need to add it to your project configuration by selecting "Project — References" from the main menu. This will pop up a dialog box offering the choice of all the type libraries registered on the system. You select the type library that you want to have added to your project. In this case, I select the type library describing the Hello32 server in Chapter 3. Thus:

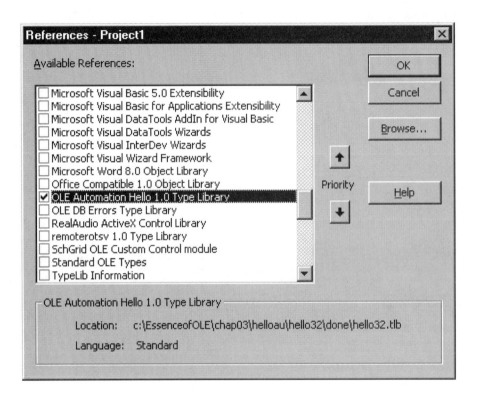

2. When you start typing "Dim <something> as", VB will look in all of its currently loaded type libraries and offer you the choices of all the different objects that it knows about from its collection of type libraries. You select the one you want. Thus:

3. Once you've told it that the objcct foo is a HelloApplication, VB knows which type library to look in for its methods and properties. When you type the name of an object and then type a dot for accessing a property or method, VB will look in the type library and provide you with a list of the properties and methods that this object supports. Thus:

4. In the object browser view, VB shows the objects that it knows about. When you select HelloApplication in the left pane, its methods and properties appear on the right pane. When you select a method or property, VB displays the help string from its type library in the bottom pane. If you press F1, VB will read the help file name and help context from the type library and launch WinHelp, opening it to the specific topic describing the selected property or method. It's like saying, "RTFM, AND HERE'S THE PAGE, YOU $%#%$# IDIOT!"

G. WRITING TYPE LIBRARY BROWSERS

1. Writers of programming tools or other apps that use type libraries need to be able to open the type libraries and read their contents. This section discusses the objects and interfaces provided by the operating system for this purpose. You will find the source code for this sample app in the directory \chap04\typlib32. Because of the frequency of dealing with text strings, this is a Unicode app and will run only under Windows NT.

2. If the user specifies a file name containing the type library, you can load the type library via the function **LoadTypeLib( )**. This returns a pointer to an interface of type *ITypeLib*, which provides access to the newly opened type library. Thus:

```
/*
User clicked "By File Name..." button.
*/

case IDC_BYFILENAME:
{
    OPENFILENAME of ;    TCHAR File [128] ;        HRESULT hr ;
    LPTYPELIB pTypeLib ;
    < fill OPENFILENAME struct with needed values>
/*
Pop up common dialog box, get user's selection of the name.
*/
    if (GetOpenFileName (&of))
    {
/*
Load the type library from the file specified by the user. Get back a
pointer to the ITypeLib interface controlling the new type library.
*/
        hr = LoadTypeLib (File,        // name of file containing type lib
            &pTypeLib) ;               // ptd to output variable
/*
If file name is successfully loaded, create dialog box to display its
contents, passing a pointer to the ITypeLib interface as its lParam.
*/
        if (SUCCEEDED(hr))
        {
            CreateDialogParam (hInst, MAKEINTRESOURCE(IDD_BROWSE),
                NULL, (FARPROC)TypeBrowseProc, (LPARAM)pTypeLib) ;
            pTypeLib->Release( ) ;
        }
/*
Otherwise, display error box.
*/
        else
        {
            MessageBox (hDlg, TEXT("Couldn't open type lib file"),
                TEXT("Error"), MB_ICONSTOP) ;
        }
    }
    return TRUE ;
}
```

3. The user may specify a type library by means of its registered ID, generally acquired by reading the registry. If you have a type library ID, you can load it via the function **LoadRegTypeLib( )**, which returns a pointer to the ITypeLib interface. Thus:

```
/*
User clicked on the "Open Selected" button.
*/


extern TYPEINFOBLOCK tib[ ] ;

case IDC_OPENSELECTED:
{
    LPTYPELIB pTypeLib ;

/*
Get the current selection in the list box.
*/
    LRESULT lr = SendDlgItemMessage (hDlg, IDC_LIST1, LB_GETCURSEL,
            0, 0L) ;

/*
Current selection is an index in an array of TYPEINFOBLOCK structures.
Use the class ID from the current selection to load a type library from
the registry.
*/

        HRESULT hr = LoadRegTypeLib (
                tib[lr].clsid,          // class ID of type library
                tib[lr].wVerMajor,      // version number, major
                tib[lr].wVerMinor,      // version number, minor
                0,                      // locale ID, 0 == any
                &pTypeLib) ;            // output variable
/*
If file name successfully loaded, create dialog box to display its
contents, passing a pointer to the ITypeLib interface.
*/
    if (SUCCEEDED(hr))
    {
      CreateDialogParam (hInst, MAKEINTRESOURCE(IDD_BROWSE), hDlg ,
            (DLGPROC)TypeBrowseProc , (LPARAM)pTypeLib) ;
      pTypeLib->Release( ) ;
    }
/*
Otherwise, display error box.
*/

    else
    {
      MessageBox (NULL,TEXT("Couldn't load type lib"),
            TEXT("Error"), 0);
    }
    return TRUE ;
}
```

4. A type library is manipulated by means of the *ITypeLib* interface. Its methods are:

ITypeLib::FindName	*// Finds name of a type description in a type library.*
ITypeLib::GetDocumentation	*// Get library's documentation strings.*
ITypeLib::GetLibAttr	*// Get attributes of library.*
ITypeLib::GetTypeComp	*// Get pointer to the ITypeComp for a compiling a type library.*
ITypeLib::GetTypeInfo	*// Get a type description from the library.*
ITypeLib::GetTypeInfoCount	*// Get the number of type descriptions in the library.*
ITypeLib::GetTypeInfoType	*// Get the type (function or variable) of a type description in the lib.*
ITypeLib::GetTypeInfoOfGuid	*// Get type description corresponding to the specified GUID.*
ITypeLib::IsName	*// Does lib contain member of this name?*
ITypeLib::ReleaseTLibAttr	*// Release TLIBATTR structure obtained from ITypeLib::GetLibAttr.*

5. Once you have a type library, you can look inside it to see what sorts of type info objects it contains. The method **ITypeLib::GetTypeInfoCount( )** returns the number of type info objects contained within the type library. The method **ITypeLib::GetDocumentation( )** retrieves descriptive information about an item. This function will give you the name of the object, a short descriptive help string, the name of the on-line help file in which more detailed information may be found, and the help context (an index value) within that file. It returns its information in the form of BSTRs, which we must release via the function **SysFreeString( )**. Thus:

```
BOOL InitTypeLib (ITypeLib *pTypeLib, HWND hParent)
{
    unsigned int utypeinfoCount, i;
    BSTR bstrDoc, bstrHelpFile ;     DWORD dwHelpContext ;
    TCHAR out [256], *psz;

/*
Get help string, help file, and help context for type library itself
and place into text controls. The strings come in the form of a BSTRING
which we must free.
*/

    pTypeLib->GetDocumentation(
      (unsigned int)-1,         // index of type in lib
      NULL,                     // output ptr to item name
      &bstrDoc,                 // output ptr to item help string
      &dwHelpContext,           // output ptr to item help context
      &bstrHelpFile);           // output ptr to item help file

    wsprintf(out, TEXT("%ld"), dwHelpContext);
    SetDlgItemText (hParent, IDC_HELPCONTEXT, out);

    psz = (bstrDoc != NULL) ? bstrDoc : TEXT("<none>");
    SetDlgItemText (hParent, IDC_HELPSTRING, psz);
    if (bstrDoc) SysFreeString (bstrDoc) ;

    psz = (bstrHelpFile != NULL) ? bstrHelpFile : TEXT("<none>") ;
    SetDlgItemText (hParent, IDC_HELPFILE, psz) ;
    if (bstrHelpFile) SysFreeString (bstrHelpFile) ;
    <continued on next page>
```

126

```
/*
Get the number of type infos this type lib contains.
*/
    utypeinfoCount = pTypeLib->GetTypeInfoCount();


/*
For each type info in the library, get its name and add it to the type
list control in the dialog box.
*/

    BSTR bstrName;

    for(i = 0; i < utypeinfoCount; i++)
    {
      pTypeLib->GetDocumentation(i, &bstrName, NULL, NULL, NULL);

      SendDlgItemMessage (hParent, IDC_TYPELIST,  LB_ADDSTRING, 0,
        (LPARAM)bstrName);
      SysFreeString(bstrName);
    }

    return TRUE;
}
```

6. When you have selected a type info within the type library, you can find the type of typeinfo it describes via the method **ITypeLib::GetTypeInfoType( )**. The method **ITypeLib::GetDocumentation( )** now gets information describing the selected type, thus:

```c
char * TypeKind[] = {
    "Enum",              /* TKIND_ENUM */
    "Struct",            /* TKIND_RECORD */
    "Module",            /* TKIND_MODULE */
    "Interface",         /* TKIND_INTERFACE */
    "Dispinterface",     /* TKIND_DISPATCH */
    "Coclass",           /* TKIND_COCLASS */
    "Typedef",           /* TKIND_ALIAS */
    "Union",             /* TKIND_UNION */
};

void SetSelectedType(LPTYPELIB pTypeLib, DWORD dwIndex, HWND hParent)
{
    BSTR bstrDoc, bstrHelpFile ;
    TCHAR FAR* psz;
    TCHAR szBuf[40];
    unsigned long dwHelpContext;
    TYPEKIND tkind;

/*
Find the type of typeinfo this one is -- interface, class, etc.  Set
into dialog item text control.
*/

    pTypeLib->GetTypeInfoType(
        (unsigned int)dwIndex,          // index within type lib
        &tkind);                         // output ptr

    SetDlgItemText(hParent, IDC_TYPEKIND, TypeKind[tkind]);

/*
Get the documentation string and help context from the type lib.
Place into their dialog items.
*/

    pTypeLib->GetDocumentation((unsigned int)dwIndex,
        NULL, &bstrDoc, &dwHelpContext, &bstrHelpFile);

    wsprintf(szBuf, TEXT("%ld"), dwHelpContext);
    SetDlgItemText (hParent, IDC_HELPCONTEXT, szBuf);

    psz = (bstrDoc != NULL) ? bstrDoc : TEXT("<none>");
    SetDlgItemText (hParent, IDC_HELPSTRING, psz);
    psz = (bstrHelpFile != NULL) ? bstrHelpFile : TEXT("<none>") ;
    SetDlgItemText (hParent, IDC_HELPFILE, psz) ;
    SysFreeString(bstrDoc);
    SysFreeString(bstrHelpFile) ;
}
```

This page intentionally contains no text other than this sentence.

7. A type library is a container for type info objects. Each type info describes a single type of object. A type info is created via the method **ITypeLib::GetTypeInfo( )**. Thus:

```
/*
User clicked the "Open Type Info" button.
*/

case IDC_OPENTYPEINFO:
{
    LPTYPEINFO pTypeInfo ;

/*
Ask the list box for its current selection.
*/

    LRESULT lr = SendDlgItemMessage (hDlg, IDC_TYPELIST, LB_GETCURSEL,
        0, 0L) ;

/*
Open the selected type info.  They are conveniently arranged so that
the index in the list box is the number of the type info within the
type lib.
*/

    HRESULT hr = pTypeLib->GetTypeInfo(
            lr,                     // index within type lib
            &pTypeInfo)  ;          // output ptr

/*
If we successfully got the type info, then launch a new dialog box to
show its contents, passing a pointer to the new ITypeInfo in its
lParam.
*/
    if (!SUCCEEDED(hr))
    {

      CreateDialogParam (hInst, MAKEINTRESOURCE(IDD_DIALOG2),
            hDlg , (DLGPROC)TypeInfoDlgProc , (LPARAM)pTypeInfo) ;
      pTypeInfo->Release( ) ;
    }
/*
Otherwise, show an error box.
*/
    else
    {
      MessageBox (NULL,TEXT("Couldn't open type info"),
            TEXT("Error"),0);
    }
    break ;
}
```

8. A type info is manipulated by means of the ITypeInfo interface, which has the following methods:

ITypeInfo::AddressOfMember	*// Get address of static functions or variables*
ITypeInfo::CreateInstance	*// Create a new instance of a component object class (coclass)*
ITypeInfo::GetContainingTypeLib	*// Get type library containing the type info*
ITypeInfo::GetDllEntry	*// Get entry point for a function in a DLL*
ITypeInfo::GetDocumentation	*// Get documentation string describing type info*
ITypeInfo::GetFuncDesc	*// Get description of a function, in a FUNCDESC structure*
ITypeInfo::GetIDsOfNames	*// Map between names and IDs*
ITypeInfo::GetMops	*// Get marshaling information*
ITypeInfo::GetNames	*// Map between IDs and names*
ITypeInfo::GetRefTypeInfo	*// Get type descriptions referenced by other type descriptions*
ITypeInfo::GetTypeAttr	*// Get attributes of a type, in a TYPEATTR structure*
ITypeInfo::GetTypeComp	*// Get ITypeComp interface for a type, used for compilers*
ITypeInfo::GetRefTypeOfImplType	*// Get description of the specified interface types*
ITypeInfo::GetVarDesc	*// Get description of a variable, in a VARDESC structure*
ITypeInfo::Invoke	*// Invokes a method or accesses a property of an described object*
ITypeInfo::ReleaseFuncDesc	*// Releases a FUNCDESC previously returned by GetFuncDesc*
ITypeInfo::ReleaseTypeAttr	*// Releases a TYPEATTR previously returned by GetTypeAttr*
ITypeInfo::ReleaseVarDesc	*// Releases a VARDESC previously returned by GetVarDesc*

9. A type info contains global information, such as GUID, locale, and version, in a structure called a **TYPEATTR**, which you get via the method **ITypeInfo::GetTypeAttr( )**. This allocates and returns a structure, which you must later release via the method **ITypeInfo::ReleaseTypeAttr( )**. Thus:

```
void InitTypeInfo (LPTYPEINFO pTypeInfo, HWND hParent)
{
    MEMBERID memid;
    BSTR bstrName;
    unsigned int i;
    FUNCDESC FAR *pfuncdesc;
    VARDESC  FAR *pvardesc;
    TCHAR out [256], *pStr ;
    HRESULT hr ;

/*
Get the TYPEATTR structure from the type info.
*/
    TYPEATTR *pTypeAttr ;

    pTypeInfo->GetTypeAttr(&pTypeAttr);

/*
Get the GUID from the attributes and set it into its edit control.
*/

    hr = StringFromCLSID(pTypeAttr->guid, &pStr);
    SetDlgItemText(hParent, IDC_GUID, pStr) ;
    SysFreeString (pStr);

/*
Same for the locale.
*/

    wsprintf (out, TEXT("0x%x"), pTypeAttr->lcid) ;
    SetDlgItemText (hParent, IDC_LOCALE, out) ;
/*
Do the same for the version.
*/
    wsprintf(out, TEXT("%u.%02u"),pTypeAttr->wMajorVerNum,
      pTypeAttr->wMinorVerNum);
    SetDlgItemText (hParent, IDC_VERSION, out);

/*
Get the function and variable names, shown later.
*/
    < code omitted, shown on page 134>

/*
Release the type attr.
*/

    pTypeInfo->ReleaseTypeAttr (pTypeAttr) ;
}
```

10. A **TYPEATTR** structure looks like this:

```
typedef struct FARSTRUCT tagTYPEATTR
{
    GUID guid;                          // GUID of the TypeInfo
    LCID lcid;                          // locale of names and doc strings
    unsigned long dwReserved;           // reserved
    MEMBERID memidConstructor;          // ID of constructor
    MEMBERID memidDestructor;           // ID of destructor
    char FAR* lpstrSchema;              // reserved
    unsigned long cbSizeInstance;       // size of an instance of this type
    TYPEKIND typekind;                  // kind of this type
    unsigned short cFuncs;              // number of functions
    unsigned short cVars;               // number of variables/data members
    unsigned short cImplTypes;          // number of implemented interfaces
    unsigned short cbSizeVft;           // size of this type's VTBL
    unsigned short cbAlignment;         // byte-alignment for this type
    unsigned short wTypeFlags;          // flags
    unsigned short wMajorVerNum;        // major version number
    unsigned short wMinorVerNum;        // minor version number
    TYPEDESC tdescAlias;                // type this type is an alias for
    IDLDESC idldescType;                // IDL attributes of the type

} TYPEATTR, FAR* LPTYPEATTR;
```

11. The most interesting thing to see in a type is its list of member functions and variables. These are presented by the **FUNCDESC** and **VARDESC** structures, respectively. We fetch them via the methods **ITypeInfo::GetFuncDesc( )** and **ITypeInfo::GetVarDesc( )**. The structures are allocated dynamically and need to be released via the methods **ITypeInfo::ReleaseFuncDesc( )** and **ITypeInfo::ReleaseVarDesc( )**. The member ID item that each contains is necessary for getting the documentation names for the item via the method **ITypeInfo::GetDocumentation( )**. It also represents the item's Dispatch ID for OLE Automation. Thus:

```
< code excerpted from page 132>

/*
For each function in the TYPEATTR, get its description in a FUNCDESC.
Use the member id from the funcdesc to get the function's name from the
TypeInfo. Place the name into the list box, then release the string and
the funcdesc.
*/
    for(i = 0; i < pTypeAttr->cFuncs; i++)
    {
      pTypeInfo->GetFuncDesc(i, &pfuncdesc) ;
      memid = pfuncdesc->memid;
      pTypeInfo->GetDocumentation(memid, &bstrName, NULL, NULL, NULL);

      SendDlgItemMessage (hParent, IDC_LIST1, LB_ADDSTRING,
            0, (LPARAM)bstrName);
      SysFreeString(bstrName);
      pTypeInfo->ReleaseFuncDesc(pfuncdesc);
    }


/*
For each variable in the TYPEATTR, get its description in a VARDESC.
Use the member ID from the vardesc to get the variable's name from the
TypeInfo. Place the name into the list box, then release the string and
the vardesc.
*/

    for(i = 0; i < pTypeAttr->cVars; i++)
    {
      pTypeInfo->GetVarDesc(i, &pvardesc) ;
      memid = pvardesc->memid;
      pTypeInfo->GetDocumentation(memid, &bstrName, NULL, NULL, NULL);

      SendDlgItemMessage (hParent, IDC_LIST1, LB_ADDSTRING,
            0, (LPARAM)bstrName);
      SysFreeString(bstrName);
      pTypeInfo->ReleaseVarDesc(pvardesc);
    }
```

12. The FUNCDESC and VARDESC contain many interesting entries, thus:

```
typedef struct tagFUNCDESC
{
    MEMBERID memid;             // function member ID
    SCODE FAR* lprgscode;       // legal SCODES for the function
    ELEMDESC FAR* lprgelemdescParam;        // array of param types
    FUNCKIND funckind;          // is fn virtual, static,or dispatch-only
    INVOKEKIND invkind;         // is fn method, prop-get or prop-set
    CALLCONV callconv;          // function's calling convention
    short cParams;              // total number of parameters
    short cParamsOpt;           // number of optional parameters
    short oVft;                 // offset in virtual function table
    short cScodes;              // count of permitted Scodes
    ELEMDESC elemdescFunc;      // return type of the function
    unsigned short wFuncFlags;// flags
}
FUNCDESC;

typedef struct FARSTRUCT tagVARDESC
{
    MEMBERID memid;             // member ID
    char FAR* lpstrSchema;      // reserved
    union
    {
      unsigned long oInst;      // offset of variable within the instance
      VARIANT FAR* lpvarValue;  // value of the constant

    }UNION_NAME(u);
    ELEMDESC elemdescVar;       // Variable data, in a VARIANT
    unsigned short wVarFlags;   // Flags
    VARKIND varkind;            // kind of variable
} VARDESC, FAR* LPVARDESC;
```

13. A function isn't a function without its parameters and return type, which you can get by examining the FUNCDESC structure in detail. Thus:

```
extern LPTYPEATTR pTypeAttribs ;

void SetSelectedMember(LPTYPEINFO pTypeInfo, DWORD index, HWND hParent)
{
    MEMBERID memid;
    TCHAR out [256], *psz ;
    BSTR bstrDoc, bstrHelpFile ;
    DWORD dwHelpContext ;

/*
Get the TYPEATTR structure from the type info.
*/
    TYPEATTR *pTypeAttr ;
    pTypeInfo->GetTypeAttr(&pTypeAttr);

/*
If this is a function, fill the param list.
*/

    if(index < pTypeAttr->cFuncs)
    {
      int i;
      unsigned int cNames;
      FUNCDESC *pfuncdesc;
      const unsigned int MAX_NAMES = 40;
      BSTR rgNames[MAX_NAMES];
/*
Get the funcdesc of the function.
*/
      pTypeInfo->GetFuncDesc((unsigned int) index, &pfuncdesc) ;
      memid = pfuncdesc->memid;
/*
Get the type of the function from our own utility function mapping name
strings to invocation types; set name into text control.
*/

      GetFuncTypeName (pfuncdesc->invkind, out, sizeof(out));
      SetDlgItemText (hMainWnd, IDC_FUNCTYPE, out) ;
/*
Do the same for the return type.
*/
      GetVarTypeName (pfuncdesc->elemdescFunc.tdesc, out) ;
      SetDlgItemText (hParent, IDC_RETURNTYPE, out) ;
```

136

```
/*
Check for number of params; if none, put VOID in listbox.
*/    if (pfuncdesc->cParams == 0)
        {
            SendDlgItemMessage(hMainWnd, IDC_PARAMLIST, LB_ADDSTRING,
                0, (LPARAM)(LPSTR)"[void]") ;
        }


/*
Use the memid of the funcdesc to get the list of names from the
TypeInfo. Loop through them all to put them in the list box.  Free each
when done, and release the funcdesc.
*/
    else
    {
        pTypeInfoCur->GetNames(memid, rgNames, MAX_NAMES, &cNames);
/*
First returned name is the func itself.  If there is more than 1, then
functions parameters are named.  Loop through and put each name in
list.
*/
        if (cNames > 1)
        {
            for(i = 1; i < cNames; i++)
            {
                SendDlgItemMessage(hMainWnd, IDC_PARAMLIST,
                    LB_ADDSTRING, 0, (LPARAM)rgNames[i]);
                SysFreeString(rgNames[i]);
            }
        }
/*
Otherwise, parameters aren't named.  Examine each type, get the name of
the type from our own utility function, and put in list.
*/
        else
        {
            char type [128] ;
            for (i = 0 ; i < pfuncdesc->cParams; i++)
            {
                VARTYPE vtype ;
                vtype = ((pfuncdesc->lprgelemdescParam) + i)->
                    tdesc.vt ;
                GetVarTypeName (vtype, out, sizeof(out)) ;
                wsprintf (type, "[%s]", out) ;
                SendDlgItemMessage(hMainWnd, IDC_PARAMLIST,
                    LB_ADDSTRING, 0, (LPARAM)type);
            }
        }
        SysFreeString(rgNames[0]);
    }
    pTypeInfoCur->ReleaseFuncDesc(pfuncdesc);
}
```

<continued on following page>

14. The type of a variable may be found by examining its VARDESC, thus:

```
/*
Otherwise it's a variable.
*/
    else
    {
            VARDESC FAR *pvardesc;
            char type [128] ;

/*
Get variable descriptor and use memid.
*/

            pTypeInfoCur->GetVarDesc(
                    (unsigned int)(dwIndex - pTypeAttribs->cFuncs),
                    &pvardesc);
            memid = pvardesc->memid;
            UpdateMemberInfo(memid);

/*
Get type of variable; get its name from our utility function.  Set
strings into edit controls.
*/

            VARTYPE vtype = (pvardesc->elemdescVar).tdesc.vt ;
            GetVarTypeName (vtype, out, sizeof(out)) ;
            wsprintf (type, "[%s]", out) ;
            SendDlgItemMessage(hMainWnd, IDC_PARAMLIST, LB_ADDSTRING,
                    0, (LPARAM)type);
            SetDlgItemText (hMainWnd, IDC_FUNCTYPE, (LPSTR)"Variable");
            pTypeInfoCur->ReleaseVarDesc(pvardesc);
    }
}
```

15. To jump to a given context number in a help file, use the function **WinHelp( )** , thus:

```
case ID_DOHELP:
{
  OLECHAR HelpFileName [128], HelpContextName [128] ;
  long HelpContext ;

/*
Get help file name and context number from edit controls.  Convert the
latter into a long integer.
*/
    GetDlgItemText (hDlg, IDC_HELPFILE, HelpFileName,
          sizeof(HelpFileName)) ;
    GetDlgItemText (hDlg, IDC_HELPCONTEXT, HelpContextName,
          sizeof(HelpContextName)) ;
    HelpContext = _wtol (HelpContextName) ;

/*
Invoke the help system for the specified file and context number.
*/

    WinHelp (
          hDlg,                 // owner window
          HelpFileName,         // help file name (.HLP)
          HELP_CONTEXT,         // flags
          HelpContext) ;        // context number

    break ;
}
```

Directory: \EssenceofOLE\chap04\typbro32\templ

1. This lab is the type browser shown in the latter section of this chapter. First, the app queries the registry to see all the type libraries installed on the system, in file MAINDLG.CPP, case WM_INITDIALOG. Examine this code until you feel comfortable with it.

2. When the user clicks the "By File Name" button, the file-open dialog box pops up. This code is in the file MAINDLG.CPP, case WM_COMMAND, subcase IDC_BUTTON1. If the user selects a name from it, attempt to get a type library from the specified file via the function LoadTypeLib( ). Place the pointer to the new type lib in the output variable pTypeLib.

3. If the user clicks "Open Selected" or double-clicks the list box, he has selected a type library from the registry. This code is in the file MAINDLG.CPP, case WM_COMMAND, subcase IDC_BUTTON2. Load the type library via the function LoadRegTypeLib( ). The class ID of the selected type lib is in the array tib[lr].clsid. Store the output pointer in the variable pTypeLib.

4. The type library has now been loaded, so the type library dialog box is on the screen. We need to fill its controls with information describing the type library. In the file TYPELIB.CPP, go to the function InitTypeLib( ). You are passed a pointer to the type library that has just been opened. Use the GetDocumentation( ) method to get the type library's (offset == -1) help file, help string, and help context. The placement of these into the dialog box's controls has been done for you.

5. Now we want to know the names of all the type infos that this type library contains. Use the method ITypeLib::GetTypeInfoCount( ) to get the number of type info objects in the type lib. Then for each type info, use the method ITypeLib::GetDocumentation( ) to get its name. The code that puts it in the list box has been done for you.

6. When the user clicks on a type info in the list box, the function SetSelectedType( ) will be called. This means that the dialog box should now show information relating the selected type info. Use the method ITypeLib::GetTypeInfoType( ) to get the type of the type info. The code to find its name and put it into its edit control has already been written for you. Also, use the method ITypeLib:: GetDocumentation( ) to get the type infos document string, its help context, and its help file. Code is supplied for you to place all of these members into their edit controls.

7. When the user clicks the "Open Type Info" button, or double-clicks a type info name in the list box, it means that he wants to examine the selected type info in more detail. To do this, we must open the type info. In the file TYPEDLG.CPP, case WM_COMMAND, subcase IDC_BUTTON2, use the method ITypeLib::GetTypeInfo( ) to do this. The index of the type info is the same as the index of the list box, which you will find the variable "lr". Store the pointer in the variable "pTypeInfo".

8. Now that the type info is open, we want to start examining it. In the file TYPEINFO.CPP, go to the function InitTypeInfo( ). You are passed a pointer to a type info. Get a TYPEATTR structure describing this type via the method ITypeInfo::GetTypeAttr( ). Store a pointer to the TYPEATTR structure in the variable pTypeAttr. Code is supplied for you that takes the TYPEATTR structure and displays its elements in the dialog box. At the end of the function, release the TYPEATTR via the method ITypeInfo::ReleaseTypeAttr( ).

9. Now that we have selected a type info, we need to show the member functions and variables within it. For each function in the TYPEATTR, get its description in a FUNCDESC. Use the member id from the

funcdesc to get the function's name from the TypeInfo via the method GetDocumentation( ). The placement of the name into the text control has been done for you. Finally, release the string and the funcdesc. Do the same for the variables.

10. The filling of the parameter list for a function was deemed too painful to make you do in the time allotted. In the file TYPEINFO.CPP, go to the function SetSelectedMember( ). Examine the completed code until you feel comfortable with it.

11. Finally, we want to hook up the on-line help to connect to the help files provided by the vendors of the type library. In the file TYPEDLG.CPP, case WM_COMMAND, subcase IDC_DOHELP, use the function WinHelp( ) to bring up the on-line help engine, open to the specified help file and context gotten from the type library. The file name and help context have already been fetched for you.

EXTRA CREDIT: Find more useful things in the typelib, the TYPEATTR, the funcdesc or the vardesc. Place them in their own text controls on the box.

EXTRA EXTRA CREDIT: Add a button to the type info dialog box. When the user clicks it, use the method ITypeInfo::CreateInstance( ) to create one of them. Then start writing code to provide access to its member functions and variables. When you finish this one, you will have written VB4.

This page intentionally contains no text other than this sentence.

Chapter 5
ActiveX Controls

A. Control Theory and History: Buy Components, Don't Make Them

When Windows was first designed, the visual user interface demanded some common set of gizmos to allow the user to provide input or commands to the program. For example, every app needed some form of pushbutton. Rather than force every developer of Windows software to write his own pushbutton from scratch, the providers of Windows wrote a pushbutton global window class that all app designers were able to use. The control was a simple child window so communication between the control and its container was handled by Windows messages. The container would send the control a message such as WM_SETTEXT to set the button's text, and the control would send its parent window a WM_COMMAND message to indicate that the user had clicked on it. This was enormous bang for the buck at the time.

The child window control architecture was a fine first cut, but as the concept took hold and controls' intelligence increased, the bandwidth of the message-based communication channel between child and parent became too narrow. The messages from container to control proliferated and were hard to use, having only two parameters. For example, look at the edit control which has no fewer than 78 custom messages as of this writing. The communication channel from control to container was even tighter since it relied on the WM_COMMAND message, which allows only a single 16-bit int for the control's customized status information, not even enough for a pointer to a structure. The child window control architecture had reached its limit.

The VBX control model, released with Visual Basic, solved the bandwidth problem. Controls could export *methods*, functions that a container could call directly and pass an arbitrary number of parameters. The control could also expose *properties*, data values that the container could directly set or get. Better yet, the control could signal the container of asynchronous *events*, again passing any number and type of parameters. A virtuous cycle began as more and better VBX controls attracted more and richer buyers and more buyers stimulated development of more and better controls. You didn't have to write a calendar control to allow the user to input a date; you could buy a VBX control off the shelf. One of my favorites was an electrocardiogram monitor control (although I wouldn't want to be a patient in a coronary care unit run by a 16-bit VB app on Windows 3.1).

Trouble arose with the switch to 32-bit Windows. The techniques used to make VBX controls efficient in 16-bit Windows were heavily tied not only to the Intel chip, with lots of assembler code, but also into the 16-bit segmented architecture, particularly the stack frame. Porting it to 32 bits and processor independence would have required a complete rewrite and led to other troubles. Microsoft decided to take the top-level concepts of the VBX architecture and implement it using the new OLE 2.0 specification, and they dubbed their new control mechanism OCX. In the spring of 1996, the name was changed to ActiveX.

B. WHAT THE HELL IS ACTIVEX ANYWAY ?

The term "ActiveX" has gotten an enormous amount of airplay since its release in the spring of 1996. As usual, once Microsoft finds an adjective they like, they tack it onto everything in sight until it loses all meaning, as they did with the word "Visual", leading to a great deal of confusion. At the time of this writing, the term is defined, or fails to be defined, thus:

The term *ActiveX* originally referred to an extension of existing OLE and COM technologies, code-named "Sweeper", that allowed OLE-aware apps to do useful things with and over the Internet. A little later, Microsoft declared that *ActiveX Controls* was to be the new name for all OLE controls, whether or not they had anything to do with the Internet. Then *ActiveX Components* meant any in-proc COM or OLE server, and then it meant all of COM except for object linking and embedding. Oh yes, and then ActiveX Documents deal with embedding and linking over the Internet. But the term ActiveX isn't a replacement for the term COM.

At the time of this writing, the term "ActiveX" has no specific, universal technical meaning whatsoever. It is today a branding prefix, the same as the letters "Mc" in front of all the food at the restaurant with the golden arches. It means "Microsoft-warm-fuzzy-good", no more and no less. When someone uses the term "ActiveX" in conversation, they mean one of two things: either they have a specific piece of technology in mind, which the term they use unfortunately doesn't specify, or they are using the latest buzzword for the sake of using it and hoping nobody calls them on it. You have to probe carefully to find out which it is.

As used in this book, the term "ActiveX Control" means the in-proc servers with properties and methods, events, user interfaces and programming support, of the type created by the MFC or ATL and most frequently used by Visual Basic. You can think of it as a replacement for the term ".OCX control." These controls are discussed in this chapter, and the basics of their containers in the following chapter. Downloading and installing these controls from the Internet is discussed in Chapter 11. *ActiveX Scripting* is the ability of apps to execute run-time interpreted scripts in languages such as Java or Visual basic, generally involving ActiveX controls. This allows HTML pages to contain active content. ActiveX Scripting is discussed in Chapter 12. *ActiveX Documents* deal with the embedding and linking of objects which reside on the Internet. As this book does not cover embedding and linking, neither does it cover ActiveX Documents.

The Internet portion of ActiveX was originally developed for use in an HTML environment, and the examples in Chapters 11 and 12 concentrate on this use. However, there is no reason to confine their use to this environment. You really can use them anywhere you want, in any app.

C. ACTIVEX CONTROL ARCHITECTURE

1. An ActiveX control must be an in-process COM server whose objects expose at least the IUnknown interface. As a COM server, it must provide a class factory and export the named functions DllGetClassObject( ) and DllCanUnloadNow( ). A control must also provide the capability of self-registering, exposing the named functions DllRegisterServer( ) and DllUnregisterServer( ). This allows any container app that obtains the control's file to register it programmatically and begin using it. See Appendix A for a detailed description of self-registration functionality. The required pieces of a control are shown graphically below:

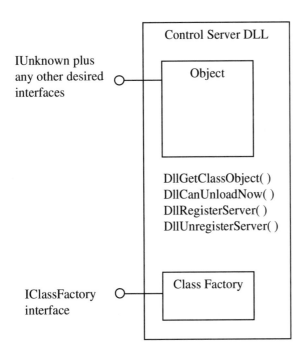

2. If a control wants to have a visible window and receive Windows messages, it must support all the interfaces necessary for being an embedded object server with in-place activation. Fortunately, this support is built into the MFC base class for an ActiveX control, the discussion of which begins on page 149. The container in which the control resides must provide all the functionality of an embedded object container with in-place activation. A discussion of embedding and in-place activation is beyond the scope of this book. See Brockschmidt, Chapters 17, 18, 22, and 23.

Note: Some Microsoft documentation refers to in-place activation as "Visual Editing," no doubt to distinguish it from tactile editing or olfactory editing. This term manages to be ambiguous, misleading, and inaccurate, quite an accomplishment for a two-word phrase. See Brockschmidt, pp. 1011-1012 for a discussion of its origins.

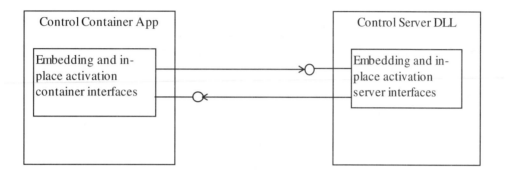

3. A control will generally want to expose methods and properties to its container. It does this by being an automation server supporting the IDispatch interface as discussed in Chapter 3. The container accesses the methods and properties by means of the method IDispatch::Invoke( ). The discussion of control properties and methods begins on page 157.

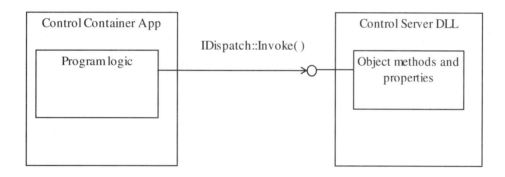

4. A control may also signal events to its container. It does this by being an automation controller and calling the Invoke( ) method of an IDispatch interface provided by its container. The discussion of control events begins on page 168.

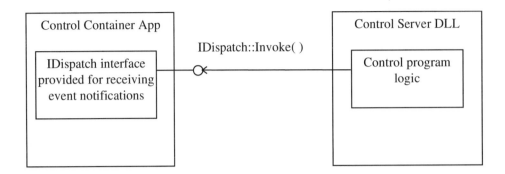

5. A control may also get, but not set, ambient properties provided by its container. An ambient property tells the control about the container environment in which it lives, for example, the color of the form on which it has been placed. A container exposes its ambient properties by providing a second IDispatch interface from which the control reads the desired property. The use of ambient properties by a control is discussed on page 176.

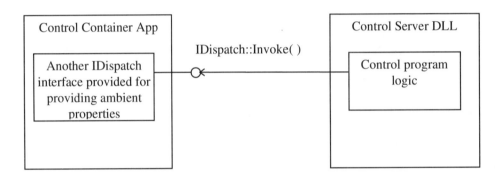

6. A control usually needs to provide a way of remembering its persistent properties from one session to another. This is done by supporting the IPersistStream interface as discussed in Chapter 7. The control's container will query for this interface and use it to store the control's properties in a configuration file or other persistent medium. The use of persistent properties is discussed beginning on page 164.

7. A control may provide programming support, such as type libraries and property pages, for the design time use of its programming environment. The type libraries in an ActiveX control are described on pages 160 and 170; the discussion of property pages begins on page 173. This programming support is the first feature I would expect to see removed when slimming down controls for the Internet. Real-world controls will probably come in two flavors: full-featured design flavor, which will include the programming support, and run-time flavor, which won't.

D. MFC CONTROL BASICS

1. You've probably noticed that many apps including VC++ like to display a clock in the lower right-hand corner of their status bar. In this example, we are going to create an ActiveX control that performs this function for us. Instead of having to write a clock, app designers will be able to buy ours and just drop it in, saving lots of development time. While relatively simple in its own function, this example will demonstrate all of the features of an ActiveX control. You will find the sample code in the directory \chap05\timer.

You create a new control via VC++'s Control Wizard, which you will find on the "New Project Workspace" dialog box as shown below. When you select "Create...", Control Wizard will take you through two wizard sheets allowing you to specify choices for your new control's configuration.   In this sample app, we select only the default options. Thus:

2. When you create a new control project, Control Wizard will derive a new class for you from the base class **COleControl**, which in turn derives from CWnd. An ActiveX control requires a complex support framework. The in-place activation code alone makes strong men weep, but the framework is essentially identical from one control to the next. This lends itself beautifully to the inheritance mechanism of C++ and the MFC. The COleControl class provides most of the nuts-and-bolts functionality common to all ActiveX controls. The derived class declaration looks like this:

```
class CTimerCtrl : public COleControl
{
    DECLARE_DYNCREATE(CTimerCtrl)

// Constructor
public:

// Overrides

    // Drawing function
    virtual void OnDraw(CDC* pdc, const CRect& rcBounds,
      const CRect& rcInvalid);

    // Persistence
    virtual void DoPropExchange(CPropExchange* pPX);

    // Reset control state
    virtual void OnResetState();

// Implementation
protected:
    ~CTimerCtrl();

    DECLARE_OLECREATE_EX(CTimerCtrl)     // Class factory and guid
    DECLARE_OLETYPELIB(CTimerCtrl)       // GetTypeInfo
    DECLARE_PROPPAGEIDS(CTimerCtrl)      // Property page IDs
    DECLARE_OLECTLTYPE(CTimerCtrl)       // Type name and misc status

    <declaration of message, dispatch, and event maps omitted>
};
```

3. Control Wizard will also create two more classes for you. You will find a class derived from **COleControlModule**, which is the control's version of CWinApp. In the timer example, this is called CTimerApp, shown below. App Wizard will override the InitInstance( ) and ExitInstance( ) of this class for you and place their shells in this class's implementation file, here "timer.cpp". You can do app-level initialization and cleanup by placing your own code here, but that is relatively rare and this simple example provides none.

Control Wizard will also create a property page for you, derived from the MFC base class **COlePropertyPage**. This is discussed in more detail on page 173.

```
<file timer.h>

class CTimerApp : public COleControlModule
{
public:
    BOOL InitInstance();
    int ExitInstance();
};

<file timer.cpp>

///////////////////////////////////////////////////////////////////////
////
// CTimerApp::InitInstance - DLL initialization

BOOL CTimerApp::InitInstance()
{
    BOOL bInit = COleControlModule::InitInstance();

    if (bInit)
    {
        // TODO: Add your own module initialization code here.
    }

    return bInit;
}
```

4. All controls must export the named function DllRegisterServer( ), which is the function used by external agencies to order the control to make all the necessary entries in the registry. Control Wizard will generate this function for you; you will find it in your control's App class. If you want to make additional registry entries, you can add the code here to do so. When you build your control, VC++ will automatically find this function and call it, producing registry entries similar to the following:

The key "InProcServer32", with which you are already familiar, identifies the full path to the server which produces objects of the specified class. In this case, you can see that it points to the control DLL "timer.ocx". The presence of the key "Control" identifies this registry entry as belonging to a full-featured ActiveX control. Programming environment apps that want to provide a list of registered ActiveX controls, such as Visual Basic or the test container on page 156, will look for the presence of this key to determine whether or not the registered server is a control.

In the forthcoming ActiveX control architecture, where not every control will support every feature, there will be more registry keys here denoting *component categories*. These entries will specify which interfaces the control supports, so the container will be able to determine the control's capabilities without actually having to create and query the control itself. This can be an expensive operation when the control lives out on the Internet.

152

5. Similar to the CView class, our control contains an **OnDraw( )** method which is called when the control needs to render its appearance. As with the method CView::OnDraw( ), you are provided with a pointer to a CDC object which represents the output device context. When your control is active, this CDC will be mapped to the control's window. When your control is inactive, the CDC will represent a metafile which the container uses to present a picture of your control that looks right even when it isn't active. This is the *presentation format* required in an embedding operation. The beauty of the MFC is that you don't have to do anything different in either case. You simply write code to draw on the CDC to make your control look the way you want it to look, and the MFC magically routes the pixels to the right place.

There are two important differences between drawing in COleControl::OnDraw( ) and drawing in a view. First, in a control you CANNOT assume that the control's drawing area starts at coordinates (0,0) and extends for your window's width and height. If the control is inactive, the provided DC might not be a window, it might actually be a metafile DC with a different bounding rectangle. You must use the bounding rectangle **rcBounds** provided as the second parameter as shown in the source code sample below. The invalid rectangle in the DC is likewise unreliable; if you care about the invalid rectangle, you must use the last parameter, **rcInvalid**. Second, the COleControl base class does not automatically fill the control's background with a default brush as does a view. If you want the background filled with a certain color or pattern, you must do that yourself. This is not shown in the example below, but is demonstrated on page 163 where the background color property is explained.

In the timer example, we get the current time from the operating system, format it into a string, and draw it centered in the control. Thus:

```
void CTimerCtrl::OnDraw(CDC* pdc, const CRect& rcBounds,
    const CRect& rcInvalid)
{

/*
Get current time.
*/
    SYSTEMTIME st ;
    GetLocalTime (&st) ;

/*
Convert time into colon-separated string.
*/
    char out [128] ;
    wsprintf (out, "%2.2d:%2.2d:%2.2d", st.wHour, st.wMinute,
      st.wSecond) ;

/*
Draw within bounding rectangle presented by framework.
*/
    pdc->DrawText (out, -1, (LPRECT)&rcBounds,
      DT_CENTER | DT_VCENTER | DT_SINGLELINE) ;

}
```

153

6. The COleControl class can process messages exactly like any other class derived from CCmdTarget. Simply use Class Wizard to add message handlers to your message map. In this example, we add handlers for the WM_CREATE to start a one-second timer, the WM_DESTROY message to kill the timer, and the WM_TIMER message to repaint our control's window to display the current time. The added code is on the facing page. Thus:

154

```
/*
When window is created, start a one-second timer which will be used to
refresh the display.
*/

int CTimerCtrl::OnCreate(LPCREATESTRUCT lpCreateStruct)
{
    if (COleControl::OnCreate(lpCreateStruct) == -1)
      return -1;

    m_TimerID = SetTimer (0, 1000, NULL) ;

    return 0;
}

/*
When the timer signals, invalidate the window to force a repaint.
*/

void CTimerCtrl::OnTimer(UINT nIDEvent)
{
    Invalidate ( ) ;
}

/*
When the window is destroyed, kill the timer too.
*/

void CTimerCtrl::OnDestroy()
{
    COleControl::OnDestroy();

    KillTimer (m_TimerID) ;
}
```

7. To test your control, you will need to use the test container app TSTCON32.EXE. This will probably appear as "OLE Control Test Container" on the "Tools" menu of VC++. If not, you can add it via the "Tools – Customize" menu item. This app provides easy GUI access to all the standard features of any control. It will allow you to create and destroy controls, activate and deactivate them, set their properties, call their methods, and respond to their events. You place a control into the test container via the "Edit – Insert OLE Control…" menu item, which will bring up a list of all registered controls on your system. Thus:

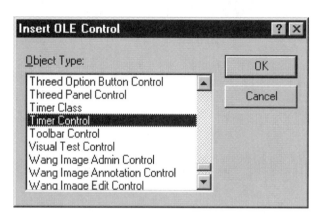

When you choose a control, the test container will create it and activate it. The sizing border and hatching are drawn by the container itself, not by your control. Try inserting several instances of the control and moving them around. You should also experiment with the "Edit – Embedded Object Functions" menu, which provides access to the activation and deactivation of the control. These menu items are actually calling methods on the *IOleObject* interface exposed by the control. You don't have to write code to make it happen, you have inherited all of this functionality from the COleControl base class. Thus:

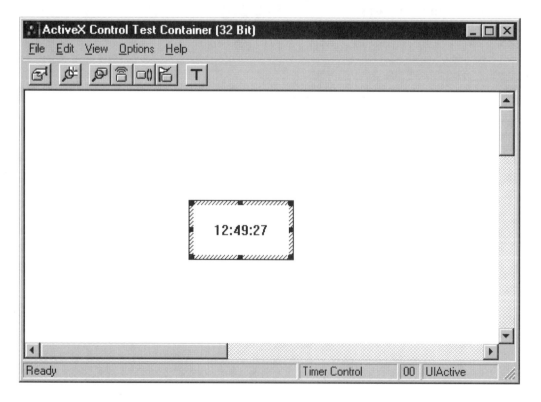

156

E. CONTROL PROPERTIES AND METHODS

1. A control exposes properties and methods to its container by being an OLE automation server, supporting the IDispatch interface as discussed in Chapters 3 and 4. A property in a control is exactly the same as an automation property introduced in Chapter 3, a variable that makes sense to the control and which the control's container may want to set or get.

2. The buyer of any control is a programmer writing an app. We want to make our control as useful as possible so the programmer will buy our control and not someone else's. In order to be versatile, we will give our control the capability of displaying the time either showing the seconds (01:23:45) or not (01:23). We accomplish this by creating a property, called "ShowSeconds", which the programmer will set to TRUE or FALSE. Some programmers will hardwire the property at development time, and some will provide their own UI to allow the user to choose. We expose this property to the world do this exactly as we did in Chapter 3 by using the "OLE Automation" tab of Class Wizard and selecting the "Add Property…" button. The MFC framework adds exactly the same support. Thus:

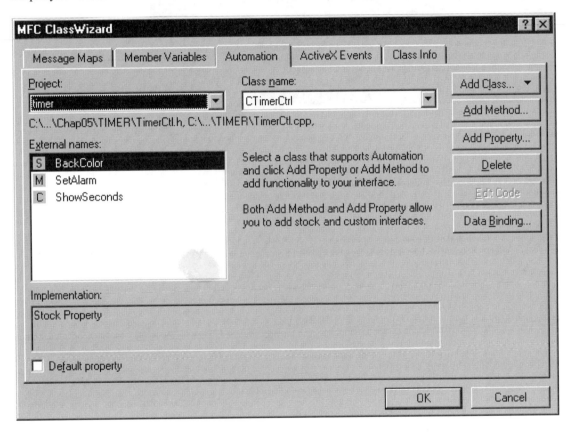

3. When we add a property, we enter its name and type as shown below. Class Wizard will add a member variable added to the control class and automatically connect it to the control's IDispatch::Invoke( ) method. When the property is changed by the container, the specified notification function will be called. Thus:

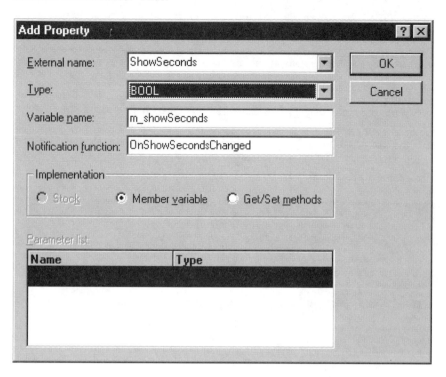

```
/*
This notification function will be called when the ShowSeconds property
is changed by the control's container.  Simply invalidate to force a
repaint.
*/

void CTimerCtrl::OnShowSecondsChanged()
{
    Invalidate( ) ;
    SetModifiedFlag();
}
```

4. Our ShowSeconds property is exposed automatically for us by Class Wizard. It is up to us to write code that uses the property intelligently. In the timer example, we modify the OnDraw( ) method to examine the value of the ShowSeconds property and display the current time with or without the seconds accordingly. Thus:

```
void CTimerCtrl::OnDraw(CDC* pdc, const CRect& rcBounds,
    const CRect& rcInvalid)
{

/*
Get current time.
*/
    SYSTEMTIME st ;
    GetLocalTime (&st) ;

/*
Convert time into colon-separated string. If property is set, then
compose string showing time in seconds.  Otherwise, compose string
showing time to nearest minute.
*/
    char out [128] ;

    if (m_showSeconds)
    {
      wsprintf (out, "%2.2d:%2.2d:%2.2d", st.wHour, st.wMinute,
          st.wSecond) ;
    }
    else
    {
      wsprintf (out, "%2.2d:%2.2d", st.wHour, st.wMinute) ;
    }

    <rest of OnDraw( ) method>
}
```

5. Just as in Chapter 4, our control contains an .ODL file for creating a type library. When we add a property, Class Wizard adds an entry to the .ODL file describing the property. In the case of an ActiveX control, the type library is bound into the control DLL itself as a resource. Thus:

```
#include <olectl.h>

[ uuid(69999370-BD40-11CF-8A6C-00AA00A58097), version(1.0),
  helpstring("timer OLE Control module"), control ]
library TIMERLib
{
    importlib(STDOLE_TLB);
    importlib(STDTYPE_TLB);

    //  Primary dispatch interface for CTimerCtrl

    [ uuid(69999371-BD40-11CF-8A6C-00AA00A58097),
      helpstring("Dispatch interface for Timer Control"), hidden ]
    dispinterface _DTimer
    {
      properties:
            // NOTE - ClassWizard will maintain prop information here.
            //     Use extreme caution when editing this section.
            //{{AFX_ODL_PROP(CTimerCtrl)
            [id(1)] boolean ShowSeconds;
            //}}AFX_ODL_PROP

      methods:
            // NOTE -ClassWizard will maintain method information here.
            //     Use extreme caution when editing this section.
            //{{AFX_ODL_METHOD(CTimerCtrl)
            //}}AFX_ODL_METHOD

            [id(DISPID_ABOUTBOX)] void AboutBox();
    };
```

NOTE: The type library information is useful only at programming time, not at run time. To make controls smaller for better Internet support, I would expect that the type library will be removed from a runtime control in the future.

160

6. To access a property from the test container, create or select a control and select "View – Properties..." from the menu. This will bring up a dialog box that reads the control's type library and lists all of the exposed properties contained therein. When you select a property in the list box, the test container will call IDispatch::Invoke( ) to fetch its value. You can set the property by typing in a value and clicking "Apply", in which case test container will call IDispatch::Invoke( ) to set its value. Thus:

WARNING: The test container and all other programming environments get their information from reading the type library supplied by the control, not by examining the code. If they get out of sync, you're scrod. This would seem unusual because of the automatic .ODL file management provided by the MFC, but you would not believe the amount of money I've made cleaning up after clients who did exactly that. It is especially deadly when you are developing container and control simultaneously.

7. Some properties are so common among controls that they have been designated by Microsoft as *stock properties*. A stock property is a property whose name, type, and dispatch ID are reserved for a specific purpose.

Although the name "stock property" might lead you to think that these were always exposed and functional, this is not the case. A control specifies each stock property that it wants to support via the OLE Automation tab of Class Wizard. When you pick "Add Property", the drop-down combo box contains the names of all the stock properties. When you select one, entries will be made in your control's dispatch map and .ODL file, similar to those used for custom properties. Thus:

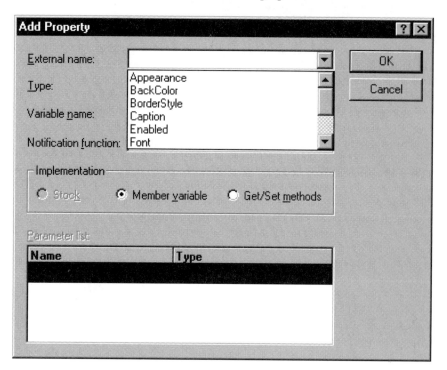

Using a stock property means that when you expose one via Class Wizard, you do not have to add the member variable or notification function; the base class already contains it. The property is available to you via a member function or variable in the COleControl base class. The stock properties and their access mechanisms are:

Property   COleControl member function/variable

Appearancem_sAppearance
BackColor   GetBackColor( )
BorderStyle   m_sBorderStyle.
Caption   InternalGetText( )
Enabled   m_bEnabled
Font   InternalGetFont( )
ForeColor   GetForeColor( )
hWnd   m_hWnd
Text   InternalGetText( ) [same as Caption]

8. Having added a stock property, it is up to the control to use it intelligently. Here we add support for the "BackColor" property to our timer control. Every time we draw our control, we get the current background color via the method **COleControl::GetBackColor( )**, which returns a variable of type **OLE_COLOR**.

The programmer using our control in his container might want to set the background color to a permanently fixed value such as blue. Alternatively, he might want to set it to a system color specified by the user in the Control Panel, such as the button face color, which obviously can vary from one user to another. Look at the color property page shown on page 175 for an example of how a programmer could specify this arrangement. The method **COleControl::TranslateColor( )** looks at the OLE_COLOR and returns the actual COLORREF to use, either the color hardwired by the container programmer or the system color set by the user.

In the example below, we get the background color and translate it. We then create a brush, fill the control's rectangle with it, and set the text background color to use it. Thus:

```
void CTimerCtrl::OnDraw(CDC* pdc, const CRect& rcBounds,
    const CRect& rcInvalid)
{


    <set up string as shown previously>
/*
Having exposed it via Class Wizard, use the stock property
"BackColor" to draw the background of the control.
*/
    OLE_COLOR oc = GetBackColor ( ) ;
    COLORREF cr = TranslateColor (oc) ;

    CBrush BackBrush (cr) ;
    pdc->FillRect(rcBounds, &BackBrush);

    pdc->SetBkColor (cr) ;


/*
Draw within bounding rectangle presented by framework.
*/
    pdc->DrawText (out, -1, (LPRECT)&rcBounds,
      DT_CENTER | DT_VCENTER | DT_SINGLELINE) ;


}
```

163

9. A control must deal with the issue of persistence. The programmer who buys our control sets its properties when he places it into the app he is writing. He then ships to his customer, the end user, an app containing our control. When the end user starts the programmer's app and the control is first created, the control's properties will be those specified in the class constructor that you wrote, not the state to which the programmer set them when he designed the app. The control needs some mechanism to change its properties from these default values to the state specified by the programmer when he used our control to build his app. The control accomplishes this by supporting the IPersistStream interface discussed in Chapter 7.

The control does not know where it will live or what storage resources are available to it. It is up to the container to provide a stream in which the control will store its properties at design time and read them out again at run time. This stream can be in a configuration file, or in the final app's .EXE file. See Chapter 6 for an example of the latter. At design time, the development environment creates the stream, queries the control for IPersistStream, and uses the methods of that interface to make the control write its properties into the stream. At run time, the app will find the stream and use the IPersistStream interface to make the control read its properties from it.

In the COleControl class, the interfaces are written for you and connected to the **COleControl::DoPropExchange(**) method. This method is conceptually similar to the CWnd::DoDataExchange( ) method used for initializing and saving the initial state of a dialog box's member variables. All you have to do is to add code to handle your own properties to the method COleControl::DoPropExchange( ), which does the actual reading or writing when the control is loaded or stored. There are functions beginning with the letters PX_ for storing each type of variable. In this example, the function **PX_Bool(**) is used to fetch or store a BOOL variable to the control's persistent stream. If the stream does not contain the specified element, such as when the control is initially created, then the PX_Bool( ) function will fail and the variable will be unmodified. Thus:

```
void CTimerCtrl::DoPropExchange(CPropExchange* pPX)
{

/*
These two lines were added by Control Wizard.  They store the control's
version number and the stock properties of the base class.
*/
    ExchangeVersion(pPX, MAKELONG(_wVerMinor, _wVerMajor));
    COleControl::DoPropExchange(pPX);

/*
We added this line ourselves to save our custom ShowSeconds property
into the stream provided by the container.
*/

    PX_Bool (pPX, "ShowSeconds", m_showSeconds) ;
}
```

10. To test the persistence of your control, run the test container, insert a control, and change its properties from their default values. Then choose "File – Save to Stream" from the main menu. The container will create a stream internally and serialize your control's properties into it. You can then delete the original control. Selecting the somewhat misnamed "File – Load" item from the menu will cause the test container to create a control of the specified class and call its DoPropExchange( ) method, passing the stream in which the properties were saved. The control that appears in the container should have the previously set property values, not the control's default values. You can examine the contents of the saved stream by selecting the "View – Saved Control Stream" from the test container's menu. Thus:

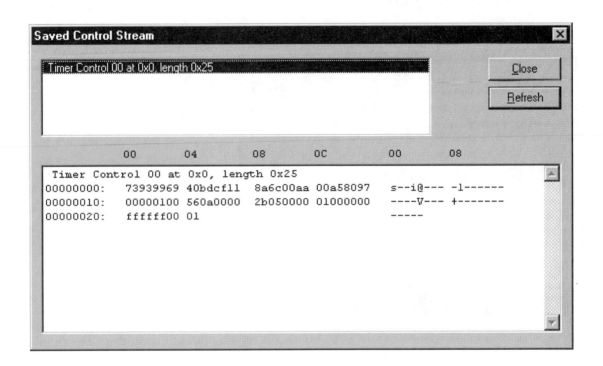

Note: You are not restricted to storing only exported automation properties in your control's stream; you can put anything you want in it. However, there is no guarantee that the container will use this persistence mechanism. It might just save all the property values itself and restore them one by one – kludgey, but legal. Make sure that your control works reasonably if the DoPropExchange( ) method is not used, or is used and fails.

11. In addition to properties, a control may also expose *methods* to its container. These are functions, exposed via the same IDispatch interface that exposes properties. Methods are added via Class Wizard, exactly as they were in Chapter 3. There are two stock methods, Refresh( ) and DoClick( ). The former forces a repaint of the control, the latter simulates a mouse click. Their implementation is similar to stock properties.

In the following example, we add a method called "SetAlarm" to our timer control. It accepts a single parameter, the delay in seconds until an alarm event is fired. Class Wizard handles the plumbing; all we have to do is add the code that we want executed. In this case, we simply calculate the tick count at which the specified delay will have expired and store it in a member variable. Thus:

```
/*
This method is exposed to OLE Automation. Calculate and save expiration
time.
*/

void CTimerCtrl::SetAlarm(long Delay)
{
    m_Expiration = GetTickCount( ) + Delay * 1000 ;
}
```

12. To call a method from the test container, use the "Edit – Invoke Methods…" menu item. This will pop up a dialog box that reads the control's type library. It will show you all the methods the control contains along with their parameters. To invoke the method, enter values for the parameters and click the "Invoke" button. Thus:

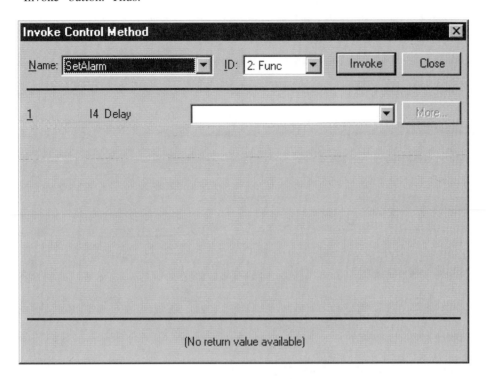

F. EVENTS

1. A control may use *events* to notify its container asynchronously of anything that takes place in the control that it thinks the container might care about. To receive notification of events, a container must create and expose an IDispatch interface. The control will obtain a pointer to this interface from the container and call its Invoke( ) method to signal the event, passing it the ID of the event and whatever parameters the event requires to describe it. You can think of an event as an OLE automation method call in the opposite direction. A container is free to process or ignore events it receives from its controls. A control adds events by using the "OLE Events" tab of Class Wizard. Thus:

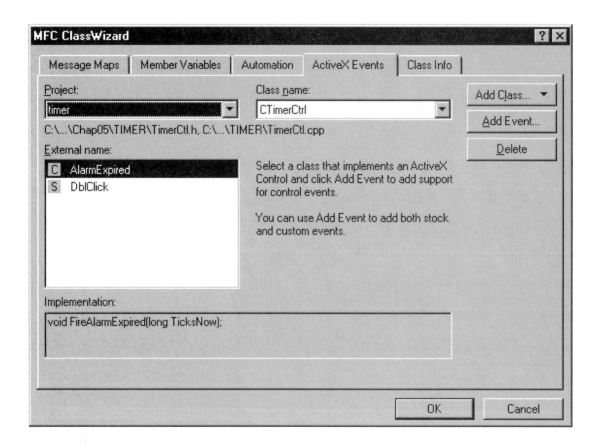

2. When you click "Add Event", Class Wizard will pop up a dialog box for you to enter the name of the event and its parameters. In this example, we define an event named "AlarmExpired", which passes a single LONG parameter named "TicksNow". Class Wizard will add a member function to our control class with the word "Fire" prepended to the name of the event, "FireAlarmExpired( )" in the example below. This code is added inline in the header file. When our control determines that the criteria for the event have been met, we call the appropriate Fire function. Thus:

```
<file TimerCtrl.h>

/*
This function added inline to class definition header file.
*/
void FireAlarmExpired(long TicksNow)
{
    FireEvent(eventidAlarmExpired, EVENT_PARAM(VTS_I4), TicksNow);
}


<file TimerCtrl.cpp>

void CTimerCtrl::OnTimer(UINT nIDEvent)
{
    Invalidate ( ) ;
/*
If system time has passed alarm time, fire the event signaling the
container that the alarm has expired.
*/
    if (m_Expiration != 0 && m_Expiration <= GetTickCount( ))
    {
      FireAlarmExpired (m_Expiration) ;
      m_Expiration = 0 ;
    }
}
```

169

3. The control's .ODL file contains a second typeinfo to describe the events to be fired by the control. In the incoming dispinterface descriptions that we have seen so far in this book, the control has been saying, "When you invoke ID #1 to me, here's what I take it to mean." In the outgoing events dispinterface shown on this page, the control is saying, "When I invoke ID #1 to you, here's what I mean has happened." Class Wizard makes entries in this file to describe the events that you place in the control. Thus:

```
#include <olectl.h>

[ uuid(69999370-BD40-11CF-8A6C-00AA00A58097), version(1.0),
  helpstring("timer OLE Control module"), control ]
library TIMERLib
{
    importlib(STDOLE_TLB);
    importlib(STDTYPE_TLB);

    <primary timer IDispatch definition omitted>

    // Event dispatch interface for CTimerCtrl

    [ uuid(69999372-BD40-11CF-8A6C-00AA00A58097),
      helpstring("Event interface for Timer Control") ]
    dispinterface _DTimerEvents
    {
      properties:
            // Event interface has no properties

      methods:
            // NOTE - ClassWizard will maintain event information here.
            //      Use extreme caution when editing this section.
            //{{AFX_ODL_EVENT(CTimerCtrl)
            [id(DISPID_DBLCLICK)] void DblClick();
            [id(1)] void AlarmExpired(long TicksNow);
            //}}AFX_ODL_EVENT
    };

    // Class information for CTimerCtrl

    [ uuid(69999373-BD40-11CF-8A6C-00AA00A58097),
      helpstring("Timer Control"), control ]
    coclass Timer
    {
      [default] dispinterface _DTimer;
      [default, source] dispinterface _DTimerEvents;
    };


    //{{AFX_APPEND_ODL}}
};
```

170

4. The base class COleControl contains a number of stock events. These are events which are so commonly used that Microsoft has reserved their names, dispatch IDs, and parameters, similar to stock methods and stock properties. The stock events are:

Click	*// Button-up received with capture on and mouse over control.*
DblClick	*// Double-click received with capture on and mouse over control.*
Error	*// Error occurred OLE control.*
KeyDown	*// WM_SYSKEYDOWN or WM_KEYDOWN message received.*
KeyPress	*// WM_CHAR message received.*
KeyUp	*// WM_SYSKEYUP or WM_KEYUP message received.*
MouseDown	*// Any BUTTONDOWN received. Mouse captured just before event fired.*
MouseMove	*// WM_MOUSEMOVE message is received.*
MouseUp	*// Any BUTTONUP is received. Mouse capture is released before event is fired.*

To make your control signal a stock event, simply select the event in Class Wizard's "OLE Events" dialog box tab. Firing the event is handled by the base class in response to the Windows messages that it receives. For example, if you add a handler for the stock event "DblClick" as shown below, the base class will automatically fire it when it receives the WM_LBUTTONDBLCLK message. Thus:

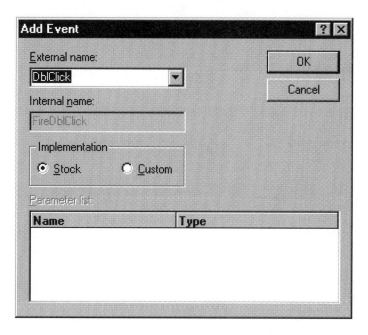

5. To view events from the test container, choose "Options – Event Log" from the main menu. This will show you a modeless dialog box in which events are reported as they occur. The event's parameters, if any, appear in the box as well. Thus:

G. PROPERTY PAGES

1. The programmer who buys a control usually sets the control's properties in some kind of programming environment such as the dialog box editor or Visual Basic. While the programming environment can read the names and types of the control's properties and present them to the user in a contiguous list, a more friendly mechanism for presenting and receiving choices would be a big selling point. Imagine programming the edit control if you had to look up all the style flags and type in a single hex value combining them, instead of having a tabbed dialog box containing nice check boxes for each style flag.

A control can provide its own user interface for accessing its properties by supporting one or more *property pages*, which are the individual panes used in property sheets (tabbed dialog boxes). OLE provides a mechanism for a server such as our control to specify the property pages it supports, and for a client app such as a development environment to create a property sheet containing those property pages. The underlying mechanism is quite involved, see Brockschmidt, pp. 761-774.

By providing property pages, you can make your control much easier to program and therefore much more attractive to buyers. Even in this very simple example, providing a check box for the ShowSeconds property graphically illustrates its boolean nature. Controls with many different properties could group them logically.

The MFC provides support for OLE's property page mechanism via the class *COlePropertyPage*. If you look in the file "TimerPpg.h", you will find the ID of a dialog resource. This is the dialog template that is used for the specified property page. You may add controls to it in the dialog editor for the purpose of manipulating your control's properties. To pop up the property page in the test container, choose "Edit – Properties" from the main menu. After you add a single check box to the supplied dialog template, the test container will show you a property page that looks like this:

NOTE: By convention, property pages are only supposed to have one of two standard sizes, either 250 x 62 dialog box units or 250 x 100 dialog box units. If you make yours any other size, you run the risk that not all of your controls will be visible.

NOTE: Like the type library, the property page mechanism is useful only at programming time, not at runtime. To make controls smaller for better Internet support, I would expect that it will be removed from a runtime control in the future.

173

2. The property page is created by an external app via the IOleObject::DoVerb( ) method, which is automatically handled for you by the COleControl base class. As with a dialog box, the only thing you really care about on a property page is setting the initial state of its controls when it first comes up, and reading the final state of its controls if the user clicks OK. And as with a dialog box, this operation is so highly standardized that it has been automated with MFC support.

To connect an ActiveX property to a dialog control on a property page, use Class Wizard to add a member variable to the property page class in the same manner as you would for a dialog box. Enter the name of the OLE property in the "Optional OLE property name" control at the bottom of the box. When you do this, Class Wizard will add code to the property page's DoDataExchange( ) method that accesses the value of the specified property through the ActiveX control's OLE automation mechanism and either sets the dialog control to the property's value or vice versa. The data movement is accomplished with a function in the DDP_ family, as in the **DDP_Check( )** function in the example below. Thus:

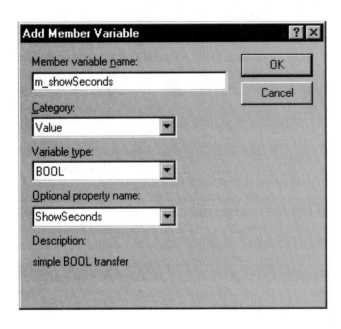

```
/*
Code added by Class Wizard.   Function DDP_Check( ) maps the value of
the property "ShowSeconds" to the member variable m_showSeconds and the
checkbox IDC_CHECK1.
*/

void CTimerPropPage::DoDataExchange(CDataExchange* pDX)
{
    //{{AFX_DATA_MAP(CTimerPropPage)
    DDP_Check(pDX, IDC_CHECK1, m_showSeconds, _T("ShowSeconds") );
    DDX_Check(pDX, IDC_CHECK1, m_showSeconds);
    //}}AFX_DATA_MAP
    DDP_PostProcessing(pDX);
}
```

3. Control Wizard generated a single property page for your control. If you want more, you may create them by using Class Wizard to derive a new class from the base class COlePropertyPage (not CPropertyPage, that is a bare dialog box class that has no connection to OLE). The MFC supplies stock property pages for specifying colors, fonts, and pictures, which you may also use.

Each property page is a separate OLE object with its own class ID, class factory, and registry entries. Your COleControl file will contain a section of property page IDs beginning with the macro **BEGIN_PROPPAGEIDS( )**. This macro specifies the control class and the number of property pages it contains. After this macro, you place one **PROPPAGEID( )** macro for each property page you want your control to support. Inside this macro, you place the class ID of the property page. In the example below, we add the MFC stock property page for colors, whose class ID is the constant **CLSID_CColorPropPage**. This causes the property sheet displayed by the test container to have two pages in it, as shown at the bottom of this page. Thus:

```
<file timerctl.cpp>


/////////////////////////////////////////////////////////////////////
//////
// Property pages

// TODO: Add property pages as needed.  Remember to increase the count!

BEGIN_PROPPAGEIDS(CTimerCtrl, 2)
    PROPPAGEID(CTimerPropPage::guid)
    PROPPAGEID(CLSID_CColorPropPage)
END_PROPPAGEIDS(CTimerCtrl)
```

They work thus:

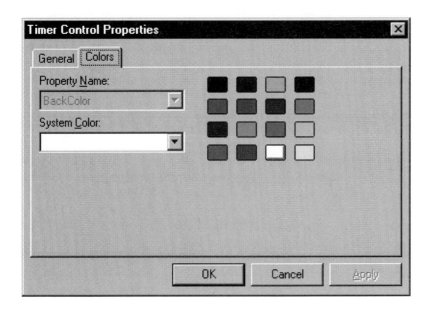

175

H. AMBIENT PROPERTIES

1. A container may choose to expose *ambient properties* to the control. These are standard properties that describe the environment in which a control resides. For example, the ambient background color is the background color of the form containing the control. The container exposes ambient properties via a second IDispatch interface. Connecting to and accessing the ambient IDispatch fortunately is handled by the COleControl base class. A control may get an ambient property's value but may not set it.

An ambient property is sort of like the button face color specified in the control panel – most apps use it for their buttons, but they don't have to if they don't want to, and there's no way to make them use it or even find out if they do or not. The supported ambient properties are:

BackColor
DisplayName
Font
ForeColor
LocaleID
ScaleUnits
TextAlign
UserMode
UIDead
DisplayHatching
DisplayGrabHandles

All ambient properties have helper functions to make them available to the programmer, such as **COleControl::AmbientForeColor( )**, which gets the ambient foreground color. There is no conflict between ambient properties and stock or custom properties with the same name. They represent different properties of different objects and are accessed via different mechanisms.

Exactly what a control is supposed to do with an ambient property is still somewhat murky. For example, should a control set its background color to the container's ambient, or should it choose a contrasting color ? It depends on what the control is for. A text control probably wants to use this information to help it blend in. An alarm control probably wants to use this information to help it stand out. The one important rule is that if the programmer explicitly sets a control property that conflicts with the ambient, then the explicitly set property should govern.

The base class is notified of changes to ambient properties (which ought to be rare) via the method COleControl::OnAmbientChanged( ). The default implementation simply invalidates the control, which is fine for most purposes.

In the following example on the facing page, we use the ambient foreground color to draw the text of our control.

```
void CTimerCtrl::OnDraw(CDC* pdc, const CRect& rcBounds,
    const CRect& rcInvalid)
{

    <set up string as shown previously>
/*
Having subscribed to be notified of it, use the stock property
"BackColor" to draw the background of the control.
*/
    OLE_COLOR oc = GetBackColor ( ) ;
    COLORREF cr = TranslateColor (oc) ;

    CBrush BackBrush (cr) ;
    pdc->FillRect(rcBounds, &BackBrush);

    pdc->SetBkColor (cr) ;

/*
Use ambient foreground color for text.
*/

    oc = AmbientForeColor ( ) ;
    cr = TranslateColor (oc) ;

    pdc->SetTextColor (cr) ;

/*
Draw within bounding rectangle presented by framework.
*/
    pdc->DrawText (out, -1, (LPRECT)&rcBounds,
      DT_CENTER | DT_VCENTER | DT_SINGLELINE) ;
}
```

2. To set ambient properties in the test container, choose "Edit – Set Ambient Properties …" from the menu. The container will pop up the following dialog box, which provides access to all ambient properties.

Lab Exercises
Chapter 5
ActiveX Controls

Directory: \chap05\timer

1. This lab starts from an empty directory. Pick "File — New" from the main menu, then pick "Project Workspace" from the dialog box. In the next dialog box, select "OLE Control Wizard". Pick all the default options from the resulting Control Wizard dialog boxes. Build the resulting control. Run the test container by picking "Tools — OLE Control Test Container" from the main menu. In the test container, pick "Edit — Insert OLE Control" from the main menu. Pick your newly built control from the resulting dialog box. You should see a fairly boring ellipse that doesn't do much. You now know that all of your control development tools are installed and working properly.

2. Next, we want to process timer messages. Bring up Class Wizard. In your COleControl-derived base class, add methods to handle the WM_CREATE, WM_DESTROY, and WM_TIMER methods. In the OnCreate( ) handler, start a timer with an interval of 1 second. In the OnDestroy( ) handler, destroy the timer. In the OnTimer( ) handler, simply invalidate your control's window to force a repaint. Modify your OnDraw( ) method to get the current time via the API function GetLocalTime( ) and draw it centered in your controls window via the method CDC::DrawText( ). Build your control and run it in the test container. You should see it ticking, but the background is transparent, which looks crummy.

3. Now add a stock property to your control. In Class Wizard, pick the "OLE Automation" tab, then click the "Add Property" button. If you click the drop-down list box in the "External Name" field, you will see the property "BackColor". Select it, note the values filled in for the other fields, and click OK. Click OK again to close Class Wizard. Examine your control's header file and .ODL to see the new entries made by Class Wizard. Modify your OnDraw( ) handler to call the function GetBackColor( ), the base class's access function for the stock property. Call TranslateColor( ) to translate it into an RGB value. Instantiate a CBrush of the same color and use it to fill paint the control's background area. Use the method CDC::SetBkColor( ) to set the background color of your timer's text to the specified value before drawing it. Build your control and run it in the test container. Pick "View — Properties" from the test container's main menu. Pick BackColor from the resulting dialog box and choose a value. Your timer's text background should change to the selected color. How did the test container know the property was there and what type it should be ?

4. Now add a custom property to your control. In Class Wizard, pick "Add Property" again. This time, type in your own name "ShowSeconds" for the name of the property. Set its type to BOOL. Modify your OnDraw( ) handler to use the value of this property to show or not show the seconds in the ticking timer. Set this property from the test container and watch your timer show and remove its seconds display.

5. Now we want to show a property page to allow access to our custom property. In your control's .RC file, you will find a dialog box entry whose ID contains the word "PROPPAGE". Open this and add a checkbox to it. Label the check box "Show Seconds". Then bring up Class Wizard and go to the "Member Variables" tab. Add a BOOL variable that binds to the checkbox. Place the "ShowSeconds" property name in the "Optional OLE property name" field. Build your control and run it in the test container. Pick "Edit — Embedded Object Functions — Properties" from the test container's main menu to show the property page.

6. Your control now has most of its features. What it does not have is a way to remember its properties from one session to another. In the method DoPropExchange( ), use the function PX_Bool to save and restore the ShowSeconds property. Build your control and place it in the container. Save its properties into a stream, delete the control, then create another control using the stored set of properties, as explained on page 165.

179

7. Now add a custom method to your control for setting an alarm. In Class Wizard, pick "Add Method". Fill in the fields to add a method named "Set Alarm", which takes a single argument of the number of seconds to wait. Note how this method is added to the dispatch map, header file, source file, and .ODL file. Add code to your method handler to remember the delay variable. Add code to your WM_TIMER message handler to check the delay and determine if it has expired. You can signal the expiration with a beep for now. Pick "Edit — Invoke Methods" from the test container to test your method.

8. Now add an event that your control will fire when the alarm set in the previous section expires. In Class Wizard, pick the "ActiveX Events" tab. Click the "Add Event" button and fill in the fields to add an event named "AlarmExpired". You may add any parameters to it that you think it ought to have. Note the addition to your control's header file of the inline method "FireEventExpired", and the addition to your .ODL file of statements describing the event. In your WM_TIMER message handler, add code to call this function when you determine that the timer has expired. In the test container, choose "View — Event Log" to bring up a window that will display events as they occur. Invoke the "SetAlarm" method as in the previous step, and watch your event appear.

9. Your control contains a bitmap which is used for display in the tool palettes of development environments such as VB. You will find that bitmap in your control's .RC file; it will be the only one. Edit the bitmap to something at least halfway recognizable. Build your control and run it in the test container. When you insert the control, you will see its bitmap appear on the test container's toolbar.

EXTRA CREDIT: Add a second property page to your control. Use the standard property page CLSID_CColorPropPage to manipulate the background color property of your control.

Chapter 6
ActiveX Control Containers

A. SUPPORTING CONTROLS IN YOUR CONTAINER

1. The MFC provided support in version 4.0 for containers of ActiveX controls. To add ActiveX control container support to your app, you must choose the "ActiveX Controls" box in step 3 of App Wizard. Thus:

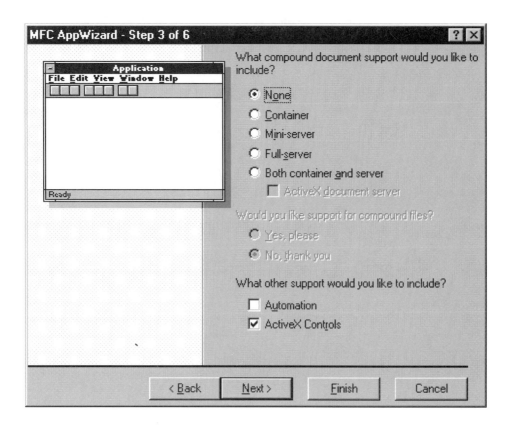

The sample code for this chapter can be found in the directory \chap06\timeruser. It is a container app that uses the timer control we created in Chapter 5. It is meant as a demonstration of what you can do to use controls that you know about at design time. It does not attempt to demonstrate what you have to do to access any arbitrary control, reading the type library and generating support on the fly, which is a problem at least an order of magnitude greater.

2. If you do not check the box when you are generating the project and want to add ActiveX control support after the fact, you must add the include file "**afxdisp.h**" to your stdafx.h file, and call the function **AfxEnableControlContainer( )** from your app's CWinApp::InitInstance( ). Thus:

```
< stdafx.h file>

// stdafx.h : include file for standard system include files,
//  or project specific include files that are used frequently, but
//      are changed infrequently
//

#define VC_EXTRALEAN          // Exclude rarely used stuff

#include <afxwin.h>          // MFC core and standard components
#include <afxext.h>          // MFC extensions
#include <afxdisp.h>          // MFC OLE automation classes
#ifndef _AFX_NO_AFXCMN_SUPPORT
#include <afxcmn.h>              // MFC  support  for  Windows  95  Common
Controls
#endif // _AFX_NO_AFXCMN_SUPPORT


< file containing CWinApp-derived class>

BOOL CTimerUserApp::InitInstance()
{
    AfxEnableControlContainer();

    <rest of InitInstance>

    return TRUE ;
}
```

B. CONTROL CONTAINER ARCHITECTURE

1. ActiveX control containment is built into the CWnd class in a rather cool transparent way. Each control that your container app uses is wrapped by a proxy class derived from CWnd. The creation of this class can be done in several different ways, as discussed on pages 192 and 198. You manipulate the window aspects of the control by calling the CWnd base class methods as for any other CWnd. For example, to move the control, you would call the proxy class's CWnd::MoveWindow( ).

The actual connection of the CWnd methods to the control is provided by the barely documented class *COleControlSite*. Each control proxy CWnd contains a member variable called **m_pCtrlSite**, which is a pointer to an object of this class. For a standard CWnd which is not a control proxy, this value will be NULL. Thus:

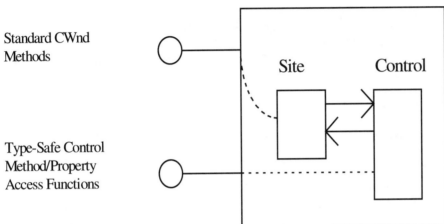

CWnd-based Control Proxy

Standard CWnd Methods

Site   Control

Type-Safe Control Method/Property Access Functions

2. When you call a method such as CWnd::MoveWindow( ), the framework checks this member variable. If it is NULL, then the CWnd is a standard non-ActiveX CWnd, in which case the framework simply calls the API function MoveWindow( ) as before. If this member is not NULL, then the CWnd is a wrapper for an ActiveX control. In this case, the framework calls the COleControlSite::MoveWindow( ), which negotiates with the ActiveX control to move and resize its window. A pseudo-code listing would look somewhat like this:

```
void CWnd::MoveWindow(int x, int y, int nWidth, int nHeight,
    BOOL bRepaint)
{

/*
If this member variable is NULL, then this CWnd is a regular old
common-garden-variety CWnd, not a proxy wrapper for a control.  Execute
the standard call to MoveWindow( ).
*/

    if (m_pCtrlSite == NULL)
    {
        ::MoveWindow(m_hWnd, x, y, nWidth, nHeight, bRepaint);
    }

/*
Otherwise, this CWnd is a wrapper for a control.  Delegate the call to
the COleControlSite's MoveWindow( ) method.
*/

    else
    {
        m_pCtrlSite->MoveWindow(x, y, nWidth, nHeight, bRepaint);
    }
}
```

3. The COleControlSite class is not well documented. Perhaps the developers of VC++ thought that you should never have to touch it directly, as all negotiation with it should have been handled at the CWnd level. Its code is found in the file "OCCSITE.CPP". The method COleControlSite::MoveWindow( ) uses the IOleObject and IOleInPlaceObject interfaces to negotiate the placement of the control's window on the container's window. A pseudo-code listing would look somewhat like this:

```
void COleControlSite::MoveWindow(int x, int y, int nWidth, int nHeight,
    BOOL)
{

/*
Set the proxy's location and size to that specified by the caller.
*/

    CRect rectOld(m_rect);
    m_rect.SetRect(x, y, x + nWidth, y + nHeight);

/*
Call the control's IOleObject::SetExtent( ) method, telling the
embedded control object how big its container wants it to be.
*/

    if (SetExtent())
    {

/*
If that was successful, call the control's
IOleInPlaceObject::SetObjectRects( ) method, telling the control object
how much space it is allowed to have in the in-place container's
window.
*/

        m_rect.SetRect(x, y, x + m_rect.Width(), y + m_rect.Height());
        m_pInPlaceObject->SetObjectRects(m_rect, NULL);
    }
    else
    {
        m_rect = rectOld;
    }
}
```

186

This page intentionally contains no text other than this sentence.

C. ACTIVEX CONTROLS IN DIALOG BOXES

1. One of the primary uses of any type of control is to communicate with the user in a dialog box. The VC++ dialog editor contains extensive support for ActiveX controls, making it quite easy for you to employ them in this manner.

To add an ActiveX control to a dialog box, open the desired dialog box template in the dialog editor. Then click the right mouse button on the dialog box and select "Insert ActiveX Control ..." from the context menu. You will see a dialog box containing all the ActiveX controls currently registered on your system. Select the one that you want, in this case the timer control that we built in the previous chapter. Thus:

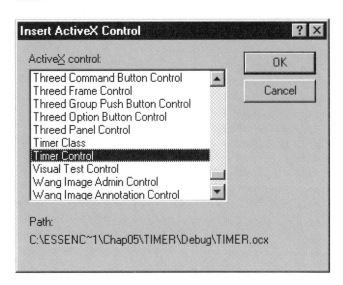

2. When you select a control, the dialog editor will create an instance of it and place it on your template. The control will not be active at this point, so you will not see the timer ticking. The appearance of the control that you see on the screen is the presentation format discussed in the previous chapter, a metafile supplied by your control. Thus:

NOTE: If you want to see your control activated, select "Layout — Test" from the main menu. A test dialog box will appear containing another instance of your control which will be ticking.

189

3. You will probably want to set most, if not all, of the control's properties in the dialog editor. The editor is smart enough to access the control's property pages that we built in the previous chapter. You bring up the "Properties" dialog box in the same manner as for any other control — either double click on the timer control, or right click on the timer control and select "Properties" from the context menu.

The dialog editor creates the "General" and "All" property pages on its own. It then gets all the property pages from the control and places them in the middle. In this example, the "Control" and "Colors" tabs were supplied by the control itself as shown in the previous chapter. Thus:

4. The template of a dialog box containing ActiveX controls is similar to any other dialog template. If you examine your app's .RC file, you will see that the template uses the **CONTROL** statement to generate an ActiveX control, with the control's class ID in place of the registered window class. Thus:

```
IDD_DIALOG1 DIALOG DISCARDABLE  0, 0, 186, 95
STYLE DS_MODALFRAME | WS_POPUP | WS_CAPTION | WS_SYSMENU
CAPTION "Dialog"
FONT 8, "MS Sans Serif"
BEGIN
    DEFPUSHBUTTON    "Close",IDOK,129,7,50,14
    EDITTEXT         IDC_EDIT1,33,52,33,16,ES_AUTOHSCROLL
    PUSHBUTTON       "Set Alarm",IDC_SETALARM,7,74,50,14
    LTEXT            "Delay:",IDC_STATIC,7,56,21,8
    CONTROL          "",IDC_TIMERCTRL1,
                     "{69999373-BD40-11CF-8A6C-00AA00A58097}",
                     WS_TABSTOP,13,12,40,18
END
```

5. The dialog editor also stores the control's properties in the .RC file in a resource type called **DLGINIT**. When the editor saves the template, it creates a stream and goes through the OLE functions that eventually connect to your control's DoPropExchange( ) method, causing your control to write its properties into the stream. The dialog editor then takes the contents of the stream and writes them into the .RC file as shown below. At runtime, when the dialog pops up and the control is created, the dialog box generator will read the DLGINIT resource into a stream and present it to the control in the DoPropExchange( ) method, thereby causing your control to read the property values set by the programmer. Thus:

```
IDD_DIALOG1 DLGINIT
BEGIN
    IDC_TIMERCTRL1, 0x376, 25, 0
0x0000, 0x0000, 0x0000, 0x0001, 0x0634, 0x0000, 0x02ff, 0x0000, 0x0001,
0x0000, 0xc0c0, 0x00c0, "\315"
    0
END
```

6. If all the dialog box ever needs to do with the control is to show it to the user with the properties set at design time, you don't have to do anything else. However, for most controls, you will probably want to access their properties and methods at runtime or respond to their events. To make this happen, you have to generate the proxy wrapper class for that control referred to on page 184. Bring up Class Wizard and select the "Member Variables" tab. In the "Control IDs" list, select your ActiveX control, then click "Add Variable…". Thus:

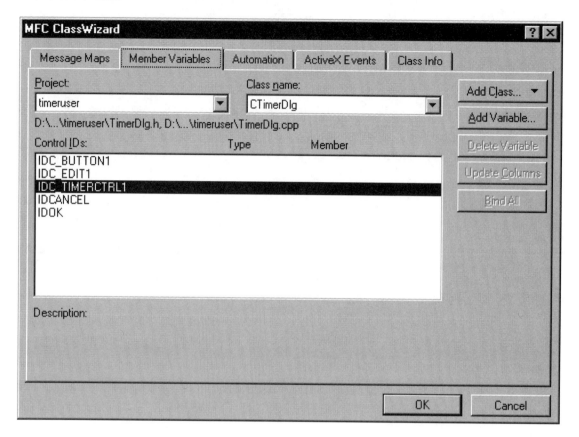

7. When you attempt to add the member variable for the ActiveX control, Class Wizard will automatically detect that this control does not have a wrapper class available, and so will generate one for you. You will see the following dialog box. Select OK and Class Wizard will read your app's type library and generate the proxy class shown on the next page. Thus:

8. When you generate the proxy wrapper class, Class Wizard reads the control's type library and generates type-safe access functions for the properties and methods in the control, in a manner similar to generating an OLE automation controller class as shown in Chapter 4. The wrapper class's header file looks like this:

```
class CTimer : public CWnd
{
protected:
    DECLARE_DYNCREATE(CTimer)
/*
Type-safe access functions for control's properties.
*/

public:
    BOOL GetShowSeconds();
    void SetShowSeconds(BOOL);
    OLE_COLOR GetBackColor();
    void SetBackColor(OLE_COLOR);

/*
Type-safe access functions for control's methods.
*/

public:
    void SetAlarm(long Delay);
    void AboutBox();

/*
Creation methods for this control. Not used in a dialog box, but used
in the nondialog case dealt with on page 198.
*/

public:
    CLSID const& GetClsid()
    {
      static CLSID const clsid = { 0x69999373, 0xbd40, 0x11cf,
            { 0x8a, 0x6c, 0x0, 0xaa, 0x0, 0xa5, 0x80, 0x97 } };
            return clsid;
    }
    virtual BOOL Create(LPCTSTR lpszClassName,
      LPCTSTR lpszWindowName, DWORD dwStyle, const RECT& rect,
      CWnd* pParentWnd, UINT nID, CCreateContext* pContext = NULL)
    { return CreateControl(GetClsid(), lpszWindowName, dwStyle, rect,
            pParentWnd, nID); }

    BOOL Create(LPCTSTR lpszWindowName, DWORD dwStyle,const RECT &rect,
      CWnd* pParentWnd, UINT nID, CFile* pPersist = NULL,
      BOOL bStorage = FALSE, BSTR bstrLicKey = NULL)
    { return CreateControl(GetClsid(), lpszWindowName, dwStyle, rect,
      pParentWnd, nID, pPersist, bStorage, bstrLicKey); }
};
```

9. The wrapper class's member functions that provide access to the control's methods and properties will look similar to those you saw in Chapter 4. The member function which provides the SetAlarm( ) method looks like this:

```
void CTimer::SetAlarm(long Delay)
{
    static BYTE parms[] =
      VTS_I4;
    InvokeHelper(0x2, DISPATCH_METHOD, VT_EMPTY, NULL, parms,
      Delay);
}
```

You use the wrapper class member variables and functions just like you did in Chapter 4. When the user clicks the "Set Alarm" button, we read the requested delay from the edit control and access the wrapper class's "SetAlarm" method. Thus:

```
/*
User clicked the "Set Alarm" button. Use type-safe member function of
wrapper class to access that method on the control.
*/

void CTimerDlg::OnSetalarm()
{
    UINT DelaySeconds = GetDlgItemInt(IDC_EDIT1) ;
    m_Timer.SetAlarm (DelaySeconds) ;
}
```

10. Responding to events is even easier. Simply select the "Message Map" tab of Class Wizard and select the ID corresponding to the ActiveX control. When you generated the wrapper class and added the member variable, Class Wizard read the control's type library, specifically the event typeinfo discussed in the previous chapter, and found the names and parameters of all the events that it supports. The events' names will appear in the "Messages" list box. Simply select the desired event and add a handler function as for any other message. Thus:

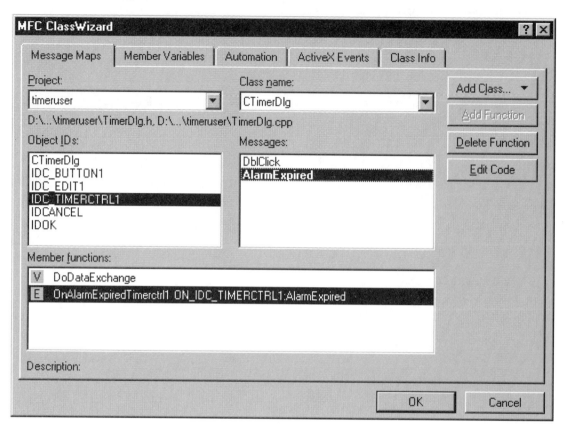

11. As you recall from Chapter 5, the container handles events by exposing an IDispatch interface which the control calls. All the heavy lifting is done for you by the MFC. When you add an event response to your dialog class, Class Wizard will add an event sink map to the dialog class that contains the control. This will look exactly like a dispatch map because it is exactly like a dispatch map. It connects your handler function to the generic IDispatch implementation provided by the container and called by the control. Thus:

```
BEGIN_EVENTSINK_MAP(CTimerDlg, CDialog)
    //{{AFX_EVENTSINK_MAP(CTimerDlg)
    ON_EVENT(CTimerDlg, IDC_TIMERCTRL1, 1, OnAlarmExpiredTimerctrl1,
        VTS_I4)
    //}}AFX_EVENTSINK_MAP
END_EVENTSINK_MAP()

/*
SetAlarm event has been signaled.  Beep to alert user and dismiss the
dialog box.
*/

void CTimerDlg::OnAlarmExpiredTimerctrl1(long TicksNow)
{
    MessageBeep(0) ;
    OnCancel ( ) ;
}
```

D. ACTIVEX CONTROLS ON STANDARD WINDOWS

1. The dialog editor has very nice support for ActiveX controls, but suppose you want to use them outside of a dialog box, for example on a view. The easiest way is to use a CFormView, because then you get the dialog editor back again. But suppose you want to create and destroy the controls dynamically. What do you do?

2. The first thing you need to do is to generate the control's proxy wrapper class if this hasn't been done already. You do this via VC++'s Component Gallery, accessed via the "Project — Add to Project— Components and Controls" menu item. If you select the "Registered ActiveX Controls" tab, you will see a list of all the registered controls on your system along with their toolbar icons, as shown below. Click "Insert" to generate the wrapper class and add it to your project. The wrapper class for the timer control, called CTimer, was generated earlier in this chapter and may be found on page 194.

3. In the TimerUser example program, we add to our view a member variable which points to an object of class CTimer. Thus:

```
class CTimerUserView : public CView
{
protected: // create from serialization only
    CTimerUserView();
    DECLARE_DYNCREATE(CTimerUserView)

    CTimer *m_pTimer ;

    <rest of view class declaration>
} ;
```

4. When the user picks "Control Test — Add to View" from our app's menu, we need to instantiate a CTimer and call its Create( ) method. This is identical to the process used for creating a new child window. Thus:

```
void CTimerUserView::OnControltestAddtoview()
{

/*
Instantiate new CTimer proxy object.
*/
    m_pTimer = new CTimer ( ) ;

/*
Call CTimer::Create( ), which does the actual creation of the proxy
window and its control.
*/
    RECT r = {10, 10, 100, 50} ;

    m_pTimer->Create ("",                    // text
      WS_CHILD | WS_VISIBLE | WS_BORDER,    // style
      r,                                     // window rectangle
      this,                                  // parent CWnd
      1) ;                                   // child window ID
}
```

5. When the user picks "Control Test — Remove from View" from our sample app's menu, we destroy the control by calling its DestroyWindow( ) method. We then destroy the proxy object that wraps it and NULL out the pointer to it. Thus:

```
void CTimerUserView::OnControltestRemovefromview()
{
    m_pTimer->DestroyWindow ( ) ;
    delete m_pTimer ;
    m_pTimer = NULL ;
}
```

6. You access the control's properties and methods simply by calling the type-safe access functions provided in the wrapper class. In the following example, the "Control Test — Show Seconds" menu item is connected to the "ShowSeconds" property. The "Control Test — Wait 5 Seconds" menu item is connected to the SetAlarm( ) method. Thus:

```
/*
User picked "Show Seconds" menu item. Use proxy's access function to
find current setting of this property.  Then if it's on, turn it off
and vice versa.
*/

void CTimerUserView::OnControltestShowsecondsproperty()
{
    if (m_pTimer->GetShowSeconds( ) == TRUE)
    {
      m_pTimer->SetShowSeconds (FALSE) ;
    }
    else
    {
      m_pTimer->SetShowSeconds (TRUE) ;
    }
}


/*
User picked "Wait 5 Seconds" menu item.  Use proxy's access function to
call the SetAlarm( ) method. This function returns immediately.  The
control signals expiration of the alarm by means of an event as shown
on the facing page.
*/

void CTimerUserView::OnControltestWait5seconds()
{
    m_pTimer->SetAlarm (5) ;
}
```

7. Connecting to the events of a control is a little trickier. Remembering back to the dialog box, Class Wizard added an event sink map to the CDialog class when we added a handler function for the first event. You can't make Class Wizard do this for a view, but you can do it in a dummy dialog box and transfer everything by hand. This isn't as hard as it sounds, really about a two-minute job. You add the declaration of your event handler function and the macro **DECLARE_EVENTSINK_MAP( )** to your view's header file. Thus:

```
<file TimerUserView.h>

class CTimerUserView : public CView
{
    < rest of view declaration >

    afx_msg void OnAlarmExpiredTimerctrl1(long TicksNow) ;
    DECLARE_EVENTSINK_MAP()

};
```

You then add the macros **BEGIN_EVENTSINK_MAP( )** and **END_EVENTSINK_MAP( ) to** your view's implementation file. Between them, you place an **ON_EVENT( )** macro for each event that you want to handle. Finally, you add the actual handler function to the header file and implementation as shown here. While this sounds hard, it isn't really. Just create a dummy dialog box, add the control to it and use Class Wizard to add handlers for the events. Then just cut from the dialog box class and paste into the view class. Sounds kludgey and it is, but it's very quick and that makes you money.

```
<file TimerUserView.cpp>

BEGIN_EVENTSINK_MAP(CTimerUserView, CView)
    //{{AFX_EVENTSINK_MAP(CTimerDlg)
    ON_EVENT(CTimerUserView, 1, 1, OnAlarmExpiredTimerctrl1, VTS_I4)
    //}}AFX_EVENTSINK_MAP
END_EVENTSINK_MAP()

void CTimerUserView::OnAlarmExpiredTimerctrl1(long TicksNow)
{
    MessageBeep (0) ;
}
```

201

E. AMBIENT PROPERTIES

1. The container exposes ambient properties by means of an IDispatch interface. The undocumented MFC base class *COleControlContainer*, contained inside CWnd, takes care of creating the IDispatch and connecting a default set of ambient properties to it. The ambient properties exposed by an MFC container are:

Appearance	1 if 3d controls enabled, 0 otherwise
AutoClip	TRUE
BackColor:	background color returned in DC by WM_CTLCOLORSTATIC
DisplayAsDefault	TRUE if button is default, FALSE otherwise
ForeColor	foreground color returned in DC by WM_CTLCOLORSTATIC
Font	result of CWnd::GetFont( )
LocaleID	result of API function GetThreadLocale( )
Message Reflect	TRUE
Scale Units:	pixels
ShowGrabHandle	FALSE
ShowHatching	FALSE
Supports Mnemonics	TRUE
UI Dead	FALSE
User Mode	TRUE

If for some reason you need to change the ambient properties, you can override the method COleControlContainer::GetAmbientProp( ), which you can find in the file OCCCONT.CPP. It's deeply buried and modifications to it are likely to be bloody, but if you can't live without it, that's where to start.

This page intentionally contains no text other than this sentence.

F. Licensing of Controls

1. Controls represent the main product of control developers, who naturally want to be protected against unauthorized use to the extent technically feasible. Remember the three-tier structure in the control business. You build a control and sell it to a programmer. The programmer takes your control, builds it into his apps, and sells them to end users. The programmer has to ship your control DLL with his app in order for the latter to run on the end users' machines. What you don't want is for the end users to take your control and start building it into their own apps without paying for it. You want some way of allowing the control to run in an end user app while blocking it from being used by a development environment.

The ActiveX control spec provides support for a low level of this capability through the *licensing* of controls. In practice, the security provided isn't very tight, and I find the hype over it to be vastly inflated. I discuss it in this book only for the purpose of completeness. It's potentially useful as a reminder for users who download trial versions of your control from the Internet to pay their licensing fees. It isn't protection against a determined assault and can't easily be turned into such. In practice, most controls sell for a few hundred bucks or less. All you need from a licensing scheme is to make it cost more than that for someone to pirate your control. The way licensing works is as follows:

A. You build your ActiveX control with licensing support as shown on the next page. This means that whenever a control of this type is created, the control checks for a *key*, some combination of characters that you specify when you develop the control. If the control does not find the required key, its class factory will refuse to hand over a pointer to it.

B. The key can be supplied to the control in one of two ways. When your customer the programmer buys the control, he gets the control and also a *license file* containing the key. When he inserts the control into the app he is building, the control finds the license file, checks that the key contained therein matches its own internal setting, knows that it is legal to run, and so comes up fully functional.

C. When the programmer compiles his app, his development environment asks the control for the key, which it binds into the app's .EXE file. The programmer ships his app to the end user, including your control DLL but not the license file. When the end user starts the app, the app creates the control using the key that the programmer bound into the app. The control comes up and runs fine. If the end user tries to use your control in VB or VC++, his new app will have neither the key nor the license file, so the control will refuse to allow itself to be created.

2. What protects you against the end user reverse engineering the app and finding the key? Only that the time it takes costs more than buying it legally, and the customer wouldn't get any upgrades (hah!) or support (hah! hah!). What protects you against your customer shipping the license file to the end user or posting it anonymously on the Internet? Nothing at all. I told you this scheme wasn't very secure. It doesn't buy you any more, and possibly less, than creating two versions of the control, one with development support such as property pages and type libraries and one without. The runtime version of the control could be freely distributed. The developer version could contain a serial number so that if one got loose, you'd know who let it go.

3. This section refers to a sample licensed control which you will find in the directory \chap06\lic. It doesn't do anything except draw an ellipse on the screen so you know it's there. If the control finds a satisfactory license on creation, it simply allows itself to be created. If it does not, it allows creation anyway but shows the user a nagging dialog box to encourage him to pay the license fee. This way, if an end user likes your control enough to want to program with it, he can go ahead and try it right away, which might generate more sales. Also, if for some reason a bug appears in the licensing code or the key embedded in the container app gets damaged, the end user isn't completely out of action and you are less likely to be threatened with dismemberment.

4. You create a control with licensing support by clicking the appropriate box in Control Wizard. Thus:

5. At the lowest level, licensing support is provided by the interface *IClassFactory2*, which is similar to IClassFactory except that it adds three additional methods to support licensing. This interface is supplied in the MFC by the class COleObjectFactory. Its additional methods are:

IClassFactory2::RequestLicKey( )   *// get lic key from control to embed in compiled app*
IClassFactory2::GetLicInfo( )   *// get lots of licensing information*
IClassFactory2::CreateInstanceLic( )   *// create object, checking license key*

When you build the control, App Wizard internally generates a *license key*, a combination of characters that the container provides to the control so that the latter can verify that it is being created by an authorized licensee.   At design time, this key is provided in a *license file* supplied by the control vendor. When you are writing a container app and create an instance of a control, your development tool does so by calling the **IClassFactory2::CreateInstanceLic( )** method, passing a license key of NULL. The control will then check for the existence of the licensing file that contains the specified key. If the control fails to find this license file or fails to find the required contents within it, the control will refuse to be created. Thus:

Design Time: Creating Control

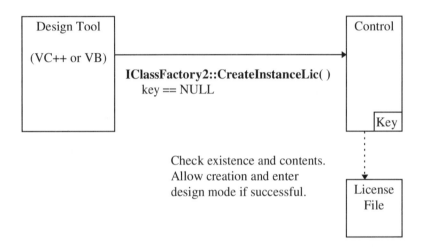

IClassFactory2::CreateInstanceLic( )
key == NULL

Check existence and contents.
Allow creation and enter
design mode if successful.

206

6. The base class COleObjectFactory implements IClassFactory2 in the MFC. The default COleObjectFactory ignores any licensing issues and simply creates the control. When you check the box in App Wizard to request licensing support in your control, this class's methods VerifyUserLicense( ) and GetLicenseKey( ) are overridden and default implementations of them to your control source file. The name of the licensing file and the text of the licensing string are generated and hardwired into your code as shown below.

When a caller attempts to create an instance of your control without passing the proper key, the method **COleObjectFactory::VerifyUserLicense**( ) is called from within the internal IClassFactory2::CreateInstanceLic( ). You place here whatever verification code you want, returning TRUE if your conditions are satisfied, thereby allowing the creation to proceed, or FALSE if they aren't, thereby causing the creation to fail. In the example shown below, creation is always allowed, but unlicensed users are shown a nagging dialog box to encourage them to pay their license fees. The MFC function **AfxVerifyLicFile**( ) checks that the license file with the hardwired name exists and contains the hardwired string. Thus:

```
/*
Name of license file.
*/


static const TCHAR BASED_CODE _szLicFileName[] = _T("lic.lic");

/*
Required license string, either from license file or from container
app.
*/


static const WCHAR BASED_CODE _szLicString[] =
    L"Copyright (c) 1996 Rolling Thunder Computing";

/*
This function is called by the class factory if the container attempts
to create the control without passing the specified license string.
*/


BOOL CLicCtrl::CLicCtrlFactory::VerifyUserLicense()
{
/*
Use MFC function to verify that license file exists and contains the
required string.  If not, then show a nagging dialog box but allow
creation anyway.
*/
    if (!AfxVerifyLicFile(AfxGetInstanceHandle(), _szLicFileName,
      _szLicString))
    {
      CNagDlg dlg ;
      dlg.DoModal ( ) ;
    }
    return TRUE ;
}
```

7. By using the license file, the developer is able to create the control on his machine and embed it in an app that he's building, but we don't want him to ship the license file with the app. That would allow the end users to use our expensive control to develop apps of their own, rather than simply running the control in apps purchased from licensed developers. Somehow the control needs to be able to verify its license from information supplied by the container app, rather than needing the license file. To accomplish this, the design tool has to get the license key from the control at design time and embed it within the container app's own file. It does this by calling the method IClassFactory2::RequestLicKey( ) . Thus:

Design Time: Saving New App

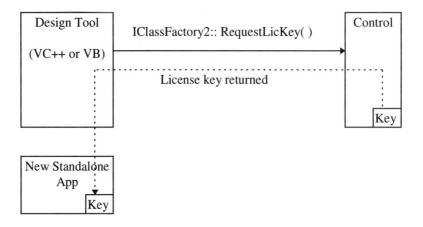

8. In the MFC, this functionality is obtained by calling the method **COleObjectFactory::GetLicenseKey( )**, which returns the license string in the form of a BSTR. The development environment must call this method when we embed a control in a dialog box or a VB form. The default implementation provided by the MFC simply hands over the hardwired license key string. In the case of a dialog box control, this is stored in the container app's .RC file and bound into the compiled app as a resource. Thus:

```
/*
This method is called by the dialog box editor when an ActiveX control
is placed in the dialog box.  Return the hard wired license string in
the form of a BSTR.
*/


BOOL CLicCtrl::CLicCtrlFactory::GetLicenseKey(DWORD dwReserved,
    BSTR FAR* pbstrKey)
{
    if (pbstrKey == NULL)
      return FALSE;

    *pbstrKey = SysAllocString(_szLicString);
    return (*pbstrKey != NULL);
}


<.RC file>

IDD_DIALOG1 DLGINIT
BEGIN
    IDC_LICOCXCTRL1, 0x376, 108, 0
0x002c, 0x0000, 0x0043, 0x006f, 0x0070, 0x0079, 0x0072, 0x0069, 0x0067, // Copyrig
0x0068, 0x0074, 0x0020, 0x0028, 0x0063, 0x0029, 0x0020, 0x0031, 0x0039, //ht (c) 19
0x0039, 0x0035, 0x0020, 0x0052, 0x006f, 0x006c, 0x006c, 0x0069, 0x006e, //95 Rollin
0x0067, 0x0020, 0x0054, 0x0068, 0x0075, 0x006e, 0x0064, 0x0065, 0x0072, //g Thunder
0x0020, 0x0043, 0x006f, 0x006d, 0x0070, 0x0075, 0x0074, 0x0069, 0x006e, //Computin
0x0067, 0x0000, 0x0001, 0x0634, 0x0000, 0x02ff, 0x0000, 0x0000, 0x0000, //g
    0
END
```

9. When the finished container app wants to create a control at run time, it reads the control's license key from wherever it was stored when the app was compiled (the app's internal resources in the preceding example). The container then calls **CWnd::CreateControl( )** specifying the key in the form of a BSTR, which eventually passes the key to method IClassFactory2::CreateInstanceLic( ). Thus:

```
WCHAR key [256] ;
CLSID clsid ;

< read clsid and key from app's file>

BSTR bstrKey = SysAllocString (key) ;

CWnd NewWnd ;        CRect r ;

r.SetRect (100,0,200,50) ;

NewWnd.CreateControl ( clsid,       // class ID of control to create
    "",                             // control's text
    WS_CHILD | WS_VISIBLE,          // window style
     r,                             // window rectangle
     this,                          // parent
     2,                             // child ID
     NULL,                          // persistent state
     FALSE,                         // default
     bstrKey) ;                     // license key

SysFreeString (bstrKey) ;
```

210

Compare key supplied by app with control's embedded key. Allow run-mode creation if successful.

NOTE: There are many wrapper functions in common use that query for the IClassFactory interface which does not support licensing, rather than the IClassFactory2 interface which does. Examples of such functions are CoCreateInstance( ) and OleLoad( ). If you care about backwards compatibility with these widely used functions, you will not be able to use licensing for the components on which you want them to operate.

Lab Exercises
Chapter 6
ActiveX Control Containers

Directory: \chap06\timeruser

1. As with the other MFC labs, this one also starts from an empty root directory. From the main menu of VC++ v4.0, pick "File — New". From the resulting dialog box, pick "Project Workspace", then select "MFC App Wizard .EXE". Continue with your App Wizard selections, picking "Multiple Documents" in step 1. In step 3, check the "OLE Controls" box. Select default options for all other settings. Build and run your app.

2. Start by adding a timer control from the previous lab to your container app's "About" dialog box. Open the dialog box in the resource editor, then click the right mouse button. From the resulting popup menu, pick "Insert OLE Control...". From the resulting dialog box, pick the timer control you created in the previous example, or the completed version of it in the \done directory. Choose "Layout -- Test" from the resource editor's menu. The dialog box will come up with your timer ticking away merrily inside it. Dismiss the test box.

3. In the resource editor, double-click on your timer control. You will see the property page(s) supported by the control, wrapped up between two different tabs supplied by the dialog box editor. Set the properties of the timer control to your satisfaction. Build and run your app, and try the dialog box. Note that the properties of the control are those that you set.

4. Now we want to use an ActiveX control as a regular window. To do this, we need to import it with a wrapper class. Select "Insert — Component" from VC++'s main menu. Pick the "OLE Controls" tab from the Component Gallery dialog box. Find your control and double-click it. Choose OK when the "Confirm Classes" dialog box come up. Note that new header and code files have been added for the generated class.

5. Add a member variable of the new ActiveX wrapper class to your app's CView-derived class. Using Class Wizard, process the WM_CREATE message in the view. In your OnCreate( ) handler, call the control's Create( ) method to create the control as a child of the view.

6. Now we want to use the methods and events of the control. Go to Class Wizard and select the "Member Variables" tab and your CAboutDlg class. Select the control ID for your timer control and pick "Add Variable". The resource editor will automatically add a variable of the wrapper class that has been generated for timer control. Add a button to your dialog box that calls the timer's SetAlarm( ) method with a delay of 5 seconds.

7. Go the "Message Maps" tab of Class Wizard, and in the "Object IDs" field, select the ID of your timer control. In the "Messages:" list, you will find the "AlarmExpired" event for it. Add a handler for this event popping up a simple message box. Build and run your app.

EXTRA CREDIT: Figure out a way to drag an ActiveX control around on a view. It's harder than it looks, because the control gets the mouse clicks rather than the CView that contains it.

Chapter 7

Structured Storage
Persistent Objects

A. CONCEPTS AND DEFINITIONS

1. *Structured storage* is a storage architecture whereby logical divisions <u>within</u> a file can be created and used in a hierarchical manner, similar to the way in which the operating system distributes files among noncontiguous sectors of a disk while presenting a contiguous stream interface to the programmer. Structured storage provides the same tools for organizing the internal contents of your file that the operating system provides for organizing files on your disk, thereby making your life easier.

2. A *storage* is a division within a file analogous to a directory or subdirectory. A storage may contain any number of streams or substorages. A *stream* is a logically sequential block of data within a storage, analogous to a file. Each storage and stream has a name of up to 31 characters.

3. If an app uses structured storage for its files, then any other app has the potential of exploring the internal structure of those files. For example, Microsoft is encouraging apps to place in their data files a stream with the name "\005SummaryInformation", which is to contain a property set providing such information as a document's title, author, and list of keywords. Third-party browsers and the Windows 95 Explorer are able to open the file, read this stream, and present the information to the user without having to launch the app that created the file. You can examine the contents of any structured storage file by using the DocFile Viewer app DFVIEW.EXE that comes with your development environment.

4. Storages and streams may also be used for transferring data from one process to another, as OLE knows how to marshal them across process boundaries. This facility is used extensively in embedding and linking, where each embedded or linked object resides within its own storage in the container's document file. When transferring data via the IDataObject interface, the medium types TYMED_ISTORAGE and TYMED_ISTREAM are used to indicate a storage or a stream medium.

214

5. The code samples in the first half of this chapter refer to the sample app in directory \chap07\strucstr. In the picture below, the viewer is displaying the data file created and used by this app. Each storage is represented by a folder icon, and each stream by a page icon. The root storage has the name of the file itself, in this case "A". The root storage contains a single stream named "DisplayText", and a substorage called "SummaryInfo". The latter storage contains two streams, one named "Author" and one named "Title". In the bottom diagram, the viewer displays the contents of the "Title" stream.

Note: The summary information storage and streams shown in this simple example are not the standard ones used by file viewers in Windows 95. That stream layout is actually quite complicated. You can find the description in Brockschmidt, pp. 789-791.

This page intentionally contains no text other than this sentence.

B. STORAGES

1. A storage is controlled via the *IStorage* interface. You do not have to write this interface or the IStream interface; it is provided by the operating system. All you have to do is obtain a pointer to it via an API function or an interface method and call the methods you want, as you did with the ITypeLib and ITypeInfo interfaces in Chapter 4.

The IStorage and IStream interfaces should seem familiar to you from your work in the API file system. For example, the method IStorage::CreateStream( ) is analogous to the function CreateFile( ), except that the former creates a stream within a structured storage file, while the latter creates a new separate file on the disk. The methods of the IStorage interface are:

IStorage::CreateStream	*// Create a new stream within this storage*
IStorage::OpenStream	*// Open existing stream within this storage*
IStorage::CreateStorage	*// Create new substorage within this storage*
IStorage::OpenStorage	*// Open existing substorage within this storage*
IStorage::CopyTo	*// Copy this storage into another storage*
IStorage::MoveElementTo	*// Move a substorage or stream to another storage*
IStorage::Commit	*// Commit changes made to this storage since last commit*
IStorage::Revert	*// Discard changes made to this storage since last commit*
IStorage::EnumElements	*// Enumerate substorages and streams contained in this storage*
IStorage::DestroyElement	*// Destroy a substorage or stream in this storage*
IStorage::RenameElement	*// Rename a substorage or stream in this storage*
IStorage::SetElementTimes	*// Set last modification time on substorage or stream*
IStorage::SetClass	*// Set Class ID associated with this storage*
IStorage::SetStateBits	*// Set state flags associated with this storage*
IStorage::Stat	*// Get statistics, such as name, for this storage*

2. You may obtain a pointer to a file's root IStorage interface via several API functions or interface methods. The function **StgCreateDocfile( )** creates a new structured storage file and returns a pointer to the IStorage object controlling that file. In the following example, the sample app creates an unnamed working file when it first starts up. Specifying NULL for the file name makes the system pick a unique one, thereby avoiding collisions. Specifying the STGM_DELETEONRELEASE flag means that the file will be automatically deleted when the pointer is released, thereby avoiding cluttering up the disk with a bunch of garbage files. If the user wants to keep the contents, he will do a "Save As" operation, writing the storage's contents into a new named storage. Thus:

```
LPSTORAGE pRootStg ;

case WM_CREATE:
{
    HRESULT hr ;
/*
Create a new structured storage file and get a pointer to the IStorage
interface controlling it.
*/
    hr = StgCreateDocfile (
      NULL,                              // system picks unique name
      STGM_CREATE | STGM_READWRITE |     // flags
      STGM_SHARE_EXCLUSIVE |
      STGM_TRANSACTED |
      STGM_DELETEONRELEASE,
      0,                                 // reserved
      &pRootStg) ;                       // output variable

/*
Create new internal structure in the file (code shown on facing page).
*/
    WriteNewStorageStructure (pRootStg) ;

    return 0 ;
}
```

NOTE: Getting the right combination of flags on calls to structured storage functions or methods can be tricky, and some of them aren't documented very well. If a structured storage function or method isn't working even though you think you have everything right, the odds are that you have the wrong combination of flags.

3. Once you have the initial storage open, you can create your file's internal structure. The method **IStorage::SetClass( )** marks the storage with your app's class ID so that your app can easily identify its own storages. The method **IStorage::CreateStream( )** creates a new stream within a storage, the method **IStorage::CreateStorage( )** creates a new substorage within the original storage. Note that the names of the storage elements, as with all strings passed to OLE, use wide characters. Thus:

```
extern CLSID MyCLSID ;

BOOL WriteNewStorageStructure (LPSTORAGE pNewStg)
{
    DWORD nActual ;      HRESULT hr  ;
/*
Mark the storage with our app's class ID so we can identify it later.
*/

    pNewStg->SetClass (MyCLSID) ;


/*
Create a stream for data in DisplayText[], then release it because we
don't need the pointer until and unless we are ready to save data to
it.
*/

    LPSTREAM pStream ;
    pNewStg->CreateStream (L"DisplayText",// stream name
            STGM_CREATE | STGM_WRITE |    // flags
            STGM_SHARE_EXCLUSIVE,
            0, 0,                         // both reserved
            &pStream) ;                   // output variable

    pStream->Release( ) ;

/*
Create new substorage for summary info.
*/
    LPSTORAGE pSubStg ;

    pNewStg->CreateStorage (L"Summary Info", STGM_CREATE |
      STGM_DIRECT |STGM_READWRITE | STGM_SHARE_EXCLUSIVE,
      0, 0, &pSubStg) ;

/*
Create new stream in substorage. Write default data.
*/
    LPSTREAM pAuthor ;

    pSubStg->CreateStream (L"Author",
      STGM_CREATE | STGM_DIRECT |   STGM_WRITE | STGM_SHARE_EXCLUSIVE,
      0, 0, &pAuthor)    ;
    pAuthor->Write ("Some Bozo", 10, &nActual) ;
    pAuthor->Release ( ) ;
    pSubStg->Release ( ) ;
    return TRUE ;
}
```

4. If we want to open an existing file in response to the "File — Open" menu item, the function **StgOpenStorage( )** opens an existing structured storage file or optionally creates a new one. The function **StgIsStorageFile( )** tells you whether or not a given file is a structured storage file. The method **IStorage::Stat( )** fills in a structure of type **STATSTG** with statistics about a storage, one of which is the storage's class ID, set via the SetClass( ) method in the previous example. Thus:

```
extern CLSID MyCLSID ;

BOOL OpenFileByName (OLECHAR* pName, LPSTORAGE *ppStgOut)
{
    LPSTORAGE pNewStg ;
    LPSTREAM pStream ;

/*
Check to see if this is a structured storage file.  If not, complain
and quit.
*/
    if (StgIsStorageFile (pName) != S_OK)
    {
      MessageBox (NULL, "File is not a structured storage file",
            "Error", MB_OK | MB_ICONSTOP) ;
      return FALSE ;
    }

/*
It is a structured storage file; open it.
*/

    StgOpenStorage (pName, NULL,
      STGM_READWRITE | STGM_SHARE_EXCLUSIVE | STGM_TRANSACTED,
      NULL, 0, &pNewStg) ;

/*
If unable to open file, then complain and quit.  Must convert wide
character name to ANSI before passing it to MessageBox( ).
*/
    if (!pNewStg)
    {
      char AnsiName [256] ;
      WideCharToMultiByte (CP_ACP, 0,
            pName, -1, AnsiName, sizeof (AnsiName), NULL, NULL) ;
      MessageBox (NULL, AnsiName, "Couldn't open file",
            MB_OK | MB_ICONSTOP) ;

      return FALSE ;
    }
```

<continued on next page>

220

```
/*
Check to see if the root storage's class ID is the one we gave it;
i.e., it's one of our app's own files.  If not, complain and quit.
*/

    STATSTG stat ;

    pNewStg->Stat (&stat, STATFLAG_DEFAULT) ;

    if (MyCLSID != stat.clsid)
    {
      MessageBox (NULL, "File's class ID is different from ours",
            "Error", MB_OK | MB_ICONSTOP) ;

      pNewStg->Release ( ) ;
      return FALSE ;
    }


/*
Structured storage file successfully opened; fill output variable with
pointer to IStorage interface that controls the file.
*/
    *ppStgOut = pNewStg ;
    return TRUE ;
}
```

5. The method **IStorage::CopyTo( )** copies the contents of one storage to another storage. It is possible to exclude elements from the copy operation by filling in the first three parameters of this method. In the example shown below, which illustrates the "File -- Save As" operation, specifying NULL for the first three parameters causes all of the streams and substorages contained within the source storage to be copied in their entirety to the destination storage. Thus:

```
LPSTORAGE pRootStg ;
WCHAR WideFileName [256] ;

case ID_FILE_SAVEAS:
{

    <get wide-char file name from user>

/*
Create new storage for saved contents, with name specified by dialog
box.
*/
    LPSTORAGE pNewStg ;

    hr = StgCreateDocfile (WideFileName,
      STGM_READWRITE | STGM_SHARE_EXCLUSIVE |
      STGM_DIRECT | STGM_CREATE,
      0, &pNewStg) ;

/*
Copy the current main storage's contents into the new one.  Then
release the current main storage and make the newly created storage the
main document storage.
*/
    hr = pRootStg->CopyTo (
      NULL,               // number of elements to exclude, here none
      NULL,               // interface ID to exclude, here none
      NULL,               // array of elements to exclude, here none
      pNewStg) ;          // destination storage

    pRootStg->Release ( ) ;
    pRootStg = pNewStg ;

    return 0 ;
}
```

6. A storage may be opened in *transacted* mode by specifying the flag **STGM_TRANSACTED** in the function or method call that creates the storage. In this mode, changes made to any element within the storage are not written directly to the file, but rather are buffered until the storage is committed via the method **IStorage::Commit( )**. At any time you want to discard the changes, you can do so via the method **IStorage::Revert( )**. Streams do not yet support transacted mode, although this is promised for a future version of OLE. Currently, you must commit or revert all the streams within a storage with a single call. Thus:

```c
/*
Save our data to a structured storage file.
*/
extern BOOL bSummaryChanged, bTextChanged ;
extern HWND hEdit ;

case ID_FILE_SAVE:
{

/*
Fetch text from edit control; write into the DisplayText stream.
*/
    LPSTREAM pStream ;
    char buf [4096] ;
    int length ;

    pRootStg->OpenStream (L"DisplayText",  NULL,
      STGM_READWRITE | STGM_SHARE_EXCLUSIVE, NULL,
      &pStream) ;

    length = GetWindowText (hEdit, buf, sizeof(buf)) + 1 ;
    pStream->Write (buf, length, NULL) ;
    pStream->Release ( ) ;

/*
Commit the root storage, thereby saving any changes that have been made
to it, including changes to the Author and Title streams in the Summary
Info substorage.
*/

    pRootStg->Commit (STGC_DEFAULT) ;

    bSummaryChanged = bTextChanged = FALSE ;
    return 0 ;
}
```

7. When you revert a storage, no further operations are possible on that pointer. All methods except Release( ) will fail with an error code. To continue operations on a reverted storage, it is necessary to release and reopen the storage. Thus:

```
extern WCHAR WideFileName [256] ;
extern IStorage *pRootStg ;

case ID_STORAGE_REVERT:
{

/*
Use the IStorage::Revert( ) method to roll back the uncommitted changes
made to any element contained at any level within the main storage.  In
this app, that means the Author and Title streams in the Summary Info
substorage.
*/

    HRESULT hr ;

    pRootStg->Revert( ) ;

/*
Reverted storage can no longer be used.  Release it and reopen storage
file.
*/

    pRootStg->Release ( ) ;

    hr = StgOpenStorage (WideFileName,  NULL,
            STGM_READWRITE | STGM_SHARE_EXCLUSIVE | STGM_TRANSACTED,
            NULL, 0, &pRootStg) ;

    <reload previous file contents>

    return 0 ;
}
```

8. You can enumerate the elements of a storage, conceptually similar to reading a directory, via the method **IStorage::EnumElements( )**. This gives you back an *IEnumSTATSTG* object, which you can step through to receive a STATSTG structure for each element in the storage. Thus:

```
case WM_INITDIALOG:
{
    LPSTORAGE pStg = (LPSTORAGE) lParam ;
    LPENUMSTATSTG pEnum ; STATSTG stat ;
    char out [256] ;

/*
Get a pointer to the IEnumSTATSTG object enumerating the storage that
we were passed in our initial lParam.
*/

    pStg->EnumElements(0, NULL, 0, &pEnum) ;

/*
Step through it until the end, getting a STATSTG structure for each
element contained in that storage.
*/

    while (pEnum->Next(1, &stat, NULL) == S_OK)
    {

/*
Compose a character string containing type, name, and length of the
element and put it in the dialog box's list box.
*/
        if (stat.type == STGTY_STORAGE)
        {
            wsprintf (out, "Strg: ") ;
        }
        else if (stat.type == STGTY_STREAM)
        {
            wsprintf (out, "Strm: ") ;
        }
        wsprintf (out+6, "%ls, %d bytes", stat.pwcsName,
            stat.cbSize.LowPart) ;
        SendDlgItemMessage (hDlg, IDC_LIST1, LB_ADDSTRING,0,(LPARAM)out);
    }

/*
Release the enumerator object.
*/
    pEnum->Release ( ) ;

    return TRUE ;
}
```

9. Streams and storages within a structured storage file may be constantly appearing and disappearing, expanding and contracting. The internal arrangement of the file may get fragmented, reducing efficiency. Standard file defragmenters do not work on the innards of a structured storage file. To defragment a file, use the **IStorage::CopyTo( )** method to copy the fragmented file to a temporary file. This operation will rewrite the internal structures in the most efficient manner possible. Then use the same method to copy it back to the original file, thus:

```
LPSTORAGE pRootStg ;


case ID_STORAGE_DEFRAGMENT:
{
    LPSTORAGE pTempStg ;



/*
Open new temporary storage for defragmenting file.
*/
    StgCreateDocfile (NULL,
      STGM_CREATE | STGM_READWRITE | STGM_SHARE_EXCLUSIVE |
      STGM_DELETEONRELEASE,
      0, &pTempStg) ;


/*
Copy existing storage to new temporary storage, which performs the de-
fragment.  Then copy it right back again and commit the changes.
*/
    pRootStg->CopyTo (NULL, NULL, NULL, pTempStg) ;
    pTempStg->CopyTo (NULL, NULL, NULL, pRootStg) ;
    pRootStg->Commit(STGC_DEFAULT) ;

    pTempStg->Release( ) ;

    return 0 ;
}
```

C. STREAMS

1. A stream is a logically contiguous sequence of bytes within a storage, analogous to a file within a file. The operations that are available for streams should remind you of the functions you are used to using to manipulate the contents of ordinary files. A stream is manipulated via the *IStream* interface, which contains the following methods:

IStream::Read	*// Read bytes from stream to memory*
IStream::Write	*// Write bytes from memory to stream*
IStream::Seek	*// Set position of stream pointer*
IStream::SetSize	*// Preallocate space for stream (streams are expandable anyway)*
IStream::CopyTo	*// Copy bytes from one stream to another*
IStream::Commit	*// Not yet implemented*
IStream::Revert	*// Not yet implemented*
IStream::LockRegion	*// Not yet implemented*
IStream::UnlockRegion	*// Not yet implemented*
IStream::Stat	*// Get statistics about this stream*
IStream::Clone	*// Create new stream pointer accessing same stream*

2. The IStream interface contains the methods Commit( ) and Revert( ), seeming to imply the availability of transacted mode as is supported for storages. It also contains the methods LockRegion( ) and UnlockRegion( ), seeming to imply the availability of this functionality. Both implications are wrong. Neither transacted mode nor region locking is available in the structured storage file implementation supplied with OLE, and these IStream methods don't do anything useful. I keep hearing rumblings about supporting them sometime in the future, but no firm plans have been announced at the time of this writing. Placing them in the interface now, even though they are not supported, means that code depending on this interface will not need to change if and when these methods are ever added.

3. The method **IStream::Read( )** reads in up to a specified number of bytes from a given stream. Here two streams are opened and read, and their contents put into edit controls in a dialog box for the user to examine and modify. Thus:

```
/*
Read them in and set them into the edit controls.  Hang on to objects
until done.
*/

static LPSTORAGE pSubStg ;
static LPSTREAM pTitle, pAuthor ;

case WM_INITDIALOG:
{
    char buf [256] ; DWORD nActual ;

/*
Open substorage and streams where author and title live.
*/
    pMainStg->OpenStorage (L"Summary Info", NULL,
      STGM_DIRECT | STGM_READWRITE | STGM_SHARE_EXCLUSIVE,
      NULL, 0,
      &pSubStg) ;

    pSubStg->OpenStream (L"Author", NULL,
      STGM_READWRITE | STGM_SHARE_EXCLUSIVE,
      0, &pAuthor) ;

    pSubStg->OpenStream (L"Title", NULL,
      STGM_READWRITE | STGM_SHARE_EXCLUSIVE,
      0, &pTitle) ;

/*
Read author and title from streams and set their text into edit
controls.
*/
    pAuthor->Read (buf, sizeof(buf), &nActual) ;
    SetDlgItemText (hDlg, IDC_EDIT1, buf) ;

    pTitle->Read (buf, sizeof(buf), &nActual) ;
    SetDlgItemText (hDlg, IDC_EDIT2, buf) ;

/*
Finish initialization of dialog box.
*/
    SetFocus (GetDlgItem (hDlg, IDC_EDIT1)) ;
    SendDlgItemMessage (hDlg, IDC_EDIT1, EM_SETSEL, 0, -1) ;
    return FALSE ;
}
```

228

4. Using separate streams allows you to save only the changed elements, not the whole thing — rewrite only the author, or only the title, but not both unless they both have changed. The method **IStream::Seek( )** positions the pointer of a stream. The method **IStream::Write( )** writes a specified number of bytes to the current position in the stream, updating the position when finished, extending the stream if necessary. The method **IStream::SetSize( )** sets the length of the stream. Thus:

```
case WM_COMMAND:
{
    if (LOWORD(wParam) == IDOK)        // OK button clicked
    {
      LARGE_INTEGER ZeroL = {0, 0} ;        ULARGE_INTEGER Size ;
/*
If contents of author edit control have changed, write new contents to
stream.
*/
      if (SendDlgItemMessage (hDlg, IDC_EDIT1, EM_GETMODIFY, 0, 0))
      {
          GetDlgItemText (hDlg, IDC_EDIT1, buf, sizeof(buf)) ;
          Size.LowPart = lstrlen (buf) + 1 ;
          Size.HighPart = 0 ;
/*
Find beginning of stream.  Write current contents fetched from edit
control.  Set stream length to size of current data, thereby truncating
stream in case new data is shorter than previous data.
*/
          pAuthor->Seek(ZeroL, STREAM_SEEK_SET, NULL) ;
          pAuthor->Write (buf, Size.LowPart, &nActual) ;
          pAuthor->SetSize (Size) ;
      }
/*
Do the same for the other edit control.
*/
      if (SendDlgItemMessage (hDlg, IDC_EDIT2, EM_GETMODIFY, 0, 0))
      {
          GetDlgItemText (hDlg, IDC_EDIT2, buf, sizeof(buf)) ;
          Size.LowPart = lstrlen (buf) + 1 ;
          Size.HighPart = 0 ;

          pTitle->Seek(ZeroL, STREAM_SEEK_SET, NULL) ;
          pTitle->Write (buf, Size.LowPart, &nActual) ;
          pTitle->SetSize (Size) ;
      }
/*
Release storage and streams.
*/
      pAuthor->Release( ) ;
      pTitle->Release( ) ;
      pSubStg->Release( ) ;

      EndDialog (hDlg, IDOK) ;
      return TRUE ;
    }
    < rest of WM_COMMAND case >
}
```

D. PERSISTENT OBJECTS

1. A *persistent object* is an object which knows how to save itself to a persistent storage device and then restore its exact state from that device during some later instantiation. Since an object's client has no idea how the object is organized internally, it is unable to perform this action without the object's assistance, which the object provides by supporting via QueryInterface( ) one or more of the following interfaces:

IPersistStream	*Save/restore object to/from a stream within a structured storage file*
IPersistStorage	*Save/restore object to/from a storage within a structured storage file*
IPersistFile	*Save/restore object to/from a separate file of any type the object recognizes*

2. The simplest persistent object interface is *IPersistStream*. In addition to IUnknown, the methods of the IPersistStream interface are:

IPersistStream::GetClassID	*// Get CLSID of object to be stored in stream*
IPersistStream::IsDirty	*// Ask object if it thinks it's dirty*
IPersistStream::Load	*// Load object's data from stream*
IPersistStream::Save	*// Store object's data to stream*
IPersistStream::GetSizeMax	*// Ask object how big its data might get*

3. A sample program that uses this interface is supplied for you in the directory \chap07\perstream. It is similar to the data3 sample provided in Chapter 2, except that in this sample, the data object representing the current time has been made persistent by having the data object support the IPersistStream interface. The menu selection "Save to Stream" uses this interface to save the object's state (the current time) into a stream provided by the client. The menu selection "Create from Stream" creates a new object and uses its IPersistStream interface to restore its previous state from the stream.

4. When you have an object which you want to save to a stream, you ask the object if it is capable of doing so by calling its QueryInterface( ) method, asking for the IPersistStream interface. If the object knows how to do this, it will supply a pointer to this interface.

Unless your client app only ever deals with one class of object, you will probably want to record in the stream the class ID of the stored object so you know which class to create when reconstituting the object. You can find the class ID via the method **IPersistStream::GetClassID( )**, and write it to the stream via the API function **WriteClassStm( )**. You then call the **IPersistStream::Save( )** method to tell the object to save its data to the stream. The layout of data in the stream looks like this:

Class ID (written by client)	Object state data written by object's IPersistStream::Save( ) method

0   16 17   ...   N

```
extern IStream *pStream ;        // IStream with stream seek ptr at start

case ID_STREAM_SAVETOSTREAM:
{
    HRESULT hr ;
/*
Query the data object for the IPersistStream interface, to see if the
object is capable of saving itself to a stream.
*/
    IPersistStream *pPerStream ;

    hr = lpd->QueryInterface (IID_IPersistStream,(LPVOID*)&pPerStream);
    if (!SUCCEEDED(hr))
    {
      MessageBox (NULL, "Data object does not support IPersistStream",
            "Error", MB_ICONSTOP) ;
      return 0 ;
    }

/*
Ask the object for its class ID.  Write it into the stream.
*/
    CLSID clsid ;
    pPerStream->GetClassID (&clsid) ;
    WriteClassStm (pStream, clsid) ;

/*
Tell the object to save its data into the stream.
*/

    pPerStream->Save (pStream, TRUE) ;

/*
Release IPersistStream interface pointer when done.
*/
    pPerStream->Release ( ) ;
    return 0 ;
}
```

5. When the client wants to reload the object from its stream, it uses the API function **ReadClassStm( )** to read the class ID that the client wrote to the stream. This retrieves the class ID that the client needs to call CoCreateInstance( ), launching the server and creating a new object with whatever default data the server provides. We then query the newly created object for the IPersistStream interface, and use the **IPersistStream::Load( )** method to make the object read from the stream the state data that it saved in the previous session. Thus:

```
extern IStream *pStream ;        // IStream with stream seek ptr at start

case ID_STREAM_LOADFROMSTREAM:
{

/*
Read the class ID from the stream.  Attempt to create an object based
on it.
*/
    CLSID clsid ;
    ReadClassStm (pStream, &clsid) ;

    hr = CoCreateInstance (clsid, NULL, CLSCTX_LOCAL_SERVER,
            IID_IDataObject, (LPVOID *)&lpd) ;

    if (!SUCCEEDED(hr))
    {
      MessageBox (NULL, "Couldn't create object", "Error",MB_ICONSTOP);
      return 0 ;
    }

/*
Query the object for its IPersistStream interface.  If found, tell
object to load its data from the stream.
*/

    IPersistStream *pPerStream ;

    hr = lpd->QueryInterface (IID_IPersistStream,
      (LPVOID*)&pPerStream);

    if (!SUCCEEDED(hr))
    {
      MessageBox (NULL, "Data object does not support IPersistStream",
            "Error", MB_ICONSTOP) ;
      return 0 ;
    }

    pPerStream->Load (pStream) ;

/*
Release interface pointers when done.
*/
    pPerStream->Release ( ) ;
    return 0 ;
}
```

6. The objects used in this example support both the IDataObject and IPersistStream interfaces. The easiest way of writing an object that supports multiple interfaces is by multiple inheritance. You simply write a class that derives from both the desired interface definitions. Thus:

```cpp
class CPersistTimeData : public IDataObject, public IPersistStream
{

    public:
      ULONG    m_RefCount ;
      BOOL     m_bIsDirty ;

    public:

        CPersistTimeData(void);
        ~CPersistTimeData(void);

    // IUnknown member functions

        STDMETHODIMP     QueryInterface(REFIID, LPVOID *);
        STDMETHODIMP_(ULONG)  AddRef(void);
        STDMETHODIMP_(ULONG)  Release(void);

    // IDataObject member functions

      STDMETHODIMP GetData (LPFORMATETC, LPSTGMEDIUM) ;
      STDMETHODIMP GetDataHere (LPFORMATETC, LPSTGMEDIUM) ;
      STDMETHODIMP QueryGetData (LPFORMATETC) ;
      STDMETHODIMP GetCanonicalFormatEtc (LPFORMATETC, LPFORMATETC) ;
      STDMETHODIMP SetData (LPFORMATETC, STGMEDIUM *, BOOL) ;
      STDMETHODIMP EnumFormatEtc (DWORD, LPENUMFORMATETC *) ;
      STDMETHODIMP DAdvise(FORMATETC *, DWORD, LPADVISESINK, DWORD *) ;
      STDMETHODIMP DUnadvise  (DWORD) ;
      STDMETHODIMP EnumDAdvise  (LPENUMSTATDATA *);

    // IPersistStream member functions

      STDMETHODIMP GetClassID(CLSID *) ;
      STDMETHODIMP IsDirty( void) ;
      STDMETHODIMP Load(IStream *) ;
      STDMETHODIMP Save(IStream *, BOOL) ;
      STDMETHODIMP GetSizeMax(ULARGE_INTEGER *) ;
};
```

7. The only GOTCHA! in this multiple inheritance operation is that every time you use the `this` pointer, you must cast it to specify which of the VTBLs it refers to. Don't worry, the compiler will remind you with an error if you forget. Thus:

```
HRESULT CPersistTimeData::QueryInterface(REFIID riid, LPVOID *ppv)
{

/*
Caller is asking for IUnknown or IDataObject interface.  Respond with a
pointer to our IDataObject VTBL.   IUnknown, as the root class of both
base classes, is available through either VTBL.
*/

    if (riid == IID_IUnknown || riid == IID_IDataObject)
    {
      *ppv = (LPDATAOBJECT) this ;
      AddRef();
      return S_OK ;
    }

/*
Caller is asking for the IPersistStream interface or the IPersist from
which it derives. Respond with a pointer to our IPersistStream VTBL.
*/

    else if (riid == IID_IPersist || riid == IID_IPersistStream)
    {
      *ppv = (LPPERSISTSTREAM) this ;
      AddRef();
      return S_OK ;
    }

/*
Caller is asking for an interface that we don't support.
*/

    else
    {
      *ppv = NULL;
      return  E_NOINTERFACE ;
    }
}
```

8. The methods of the IPersistStream interface are fairly simple. **IPersistStream::GetClassID( )** and **IPersistStream::IsDirty( )** are trivial, thus:

```
/*
Object has been asked for its class ID.   Return in the output variable.
*/


extern GUID GUID_PersistTimeData ;

STDMETHODIMP CPersistTimeData::GetClassID(CLSID * pClsID)
{
    *pClsID = GUID_PersistTimeData ;
    return S_OK ;
}


/*
Object has been asked whether it is dirty or not.  If it is, return
the success code S_OK (which has a numerical value of 0).  Otherwise,
return the error code.
*/


STDMETHODIMP CPersistTimeData::IsDirty( void)
{
    if (m_bIsDirty)
    {
      return S_OK ;
    }
    else
    {
      return S_FALSE ;
    }

}
```

9. **IPersistStream::GetSizeMax( )** is trivial to implement, but takes a little thinking about what you ought to say. The caller is asking how big a buffer is required to save the object in its current state. The estimate that you return should be conservative, because the caller's memory might not be expandable. This example is easy because the object's data is always the same size. Thus:

```
/*
This data object saves its size in a SYSTEMTIME structure.   That's
always exactly how much space we need.
*/


STDMETHODIMP CPersistTimeData::GetSizeMax(ULARGE_INTEGER *pLint)
{
    pLint->LowPart = sizeof (SYSTEMTIME) ;
    pLint->HighPart = 0 ;
    return S_OK ;
}
```

10. The method **IPersistStream::Save( )** instructs the object to save its data in its own native data format into the provided stream. The flag bClearDirty tells the object whether or not to clear its dirty flag. The client might be making a copy of the object, in which case this will be FALSE.

The saving object cannot depend on being the only owner of data in the stream. The client might have class ID or data format information stored in the stream ahead of the object's data, and might have other objects' data stored after it. The client is responsible for having the stream's seek pointer in the proper position, pointing to the beginning of the object's saved data before calling this method. The object is responsible for somehow detecting the end of its own data (in this example, the data is always of a fixed size) and leaving the stream's seek pointer positioned there at the end of this method. An object whose data size varied might write the length of its data as the first DWORD in the stream. Thus:

```
extern SYSTEMTIME LocalTime ;

STDMETHODIMP      CPersistTimeData::Save      (IStream      *pStream,      BOOL
bClearDirty)
{

/*
If the clear flag is set by the caller, clear this object's dirty flag.
*/

    if (bClearDirty)
    {
      m_bIsDirty = FALSE ;
    }

/*
Write our own native data to the provided stream.
*/
    return pStream->Write ((LPVOID) &LocalTime, sizeof (SYSTEMTIME),
    NULL) ;
}
```

236

11. The method **IPersistStream::Load( )** tells the object to read its own native data from the provided stream. The client is responsible for providing a pointer to the stream in which data has been previously saved by the method IPersistStream::Save( ) of this object, with the stream pointer at the beginning of the area in which the object's data resides. Thus:

```
/*
Load our object's data from the provided stream.  Clear the dirty flag,
as the data is now new.
*/

extern SYSTEMTIME LocalTime ;

STDMETHODIMP CPersistTimeData::Load(IStream *pStream)
{
    m_bIsDirty = FALSE ;

    return pStream->Read ((LPVOID) &LocalTime,
      sizeof(SYSTEMTIME), NULL);
}
```

E. STRUCTURED STORAGE IN THE MFC

1. The MFC has its own architecture for persistent objects which was released at least two years before OLE structured storage. It does not use the persistence mechanism described in the latter part of this chapter.

The MFC uses structured storage as part of its prefabricated functionality for embedding and linking, with which this book does not deal. The MFC provides the *COleStreamFile* class which represents the IStream interface in a compound file.

Directory: \EssenceOfOLE\chap07\strucstr\templ

1. Our app begins with a temporary working file. In the file MAINWIND.CPP, case WM_CREATE, use the function StgCreateDocfile( ) to create a new structured storage file with a unique name, using transacted mode. Store the pointer to this file's IStorage interface in the global variable pRootStg.

2. The next thing we need to do with our new file is to create its internal structure. The function WriteNewStorageStructure( ) is provided for you in the file STGUTIL.CPP, but it is an empty shell. First, use the method IStorage::SetClass( ) to write our app's class ID into the main storage so that we can identify our own files. The class ID is provided for you in the external variable MyCLSID. Then create a stream called "DisplayText" and a storage called "Summary Info" in the main storage using the methods IStorage::CreateStream( ) and IStorage::CreateStorage( ), respectively. In the Summary Info storage, create two streams, one named "Author" and another named "Title". Use the method IStream::Write( ) to put some default data into each of the streams. Make sure that you release all your interface pointers at the end of the function, except for the main IStorage pointer that you were passed as the function's parameter. Your new structured storage file now has an internal structure that the rest of the application expects. NOTE: When you write data in text string format, make sure you write the terminating NULL character into the stream. Write lstrlen(pString) + 1 characters, not lstrlen (pString) characters.

3. Now we have a file structure and some default data. We need to be able to save the file to disk. In the file MAINWIND.CPP, WM_COMMAND message, ID_FILE_SAVE case, use the method IStorage::Commit( ) to commit changes made to the file. This is what actually causes any changes that might have been made to the file to be physically written to the file's storage areas on the disk. The write of the DisplayText[ ] to the stream has already been done for you, as has the connection with the Save As... menu command. Use the DocFile Viewer in the OLE SDK to verify proper functionality.

4. We can now create a new file, edit its text, and save it. What we now need to do is to be able to open existing files through the File-Open menu command. The user interface has already been written for you. It calls a helper function called OpenFileByName( ), which lives in STGUTIL.CPP. Naturally, this function is an empty shell left for you to implement. You are passed a pointer to the file name and a pointer to an output variable in which to return the IStorage pointer that controls the file. You must return TRUE if you are able to open the file, FALSE if not. First, use the function StgIsStorageFile( ) to make sure that the requested file is a structured storage file. If it isn't, the skeleton app pops up a message box and returns FALSE. Next, open the file via the function StgOpenStorage( ) using transacted mode, then use the method IStorage::Stat( ) to get the class ID of this storage. If it is not the same as our class ID (MyCLSID, see 2 above), the skeleton pops up a message box and returns FALSE. Once the file is opened, the code to read the data from the stream is provided for you.

5. When the user picks "File - Summary Info..." from the menu, a dialog box appears offering him the chance to edit the author and the title of the document. These items live in separate streams in a substorage, which you created in step 2. The dialog box response function lives in SUMMRDLG.CPP. In response to the WM_INITDIALOG message, open the substorage, open the two streams, read their contents, and set the title into the first edit control (IDC_EDIT1) and the author's name into the second (IDC_EDIT2). In response to the WM_COMMAND message from an OK button, each edit control checks to see if it has been modified. If it has, fetching the data from the edit control has been done for you; you must write it into the appropriate stream. I suggest that you keep open the streams that you opened in the first message, and only release them when you dismiss the dialog box. Position the stream pointer to the beginning via the method IStream::Seek( ), write the data via IStream::Write( ), and truncate the length with IStream::SetSize( ). Make sure that you release all storages and streams before dismissing the dialog box.

6. Users occasionally change their minds and want to discard their changes. Since we are using transacted storage (you did set that flag in steps 1 and 4, didn't you ?), this is easily done via the method IStorage::Revert( ). In MAINWIND.CPP, case WM_COMMAND, subcase ID_STORAGE_REVERT, add a call to this method to discard any changes the user might have made. You must then release the root storage and reopen the file. The reopening has been done for you.

7. The user can pick the "Enumerate..." item from the menu and be shown a dialog box of the elements in the top storage. The dialog box response function lives in ENUMDLG.CPP. In the WM_INITDIALOG message, you are passed a pointer to the main storage in the lParam. Use this to call the method IStorage::EnumElements( ) to get a STATSTG enumerator. Step through this enumerator, calling its Next( ) method until it doesn't return S_OK, at which time you have seen every element in the storage. Each call fills in a STATSTG structure. Code already exists to pick elements of the structure and display them in a list box.

8. I've put a De-fragment option on the menu. By now, you'd probably rather just look at it. Be my guest. It's in MAINWIND.CPP, case WM_COMMAND, subcase ID_STORAGE_DEFRAGMENT. Examine it to make sure you understand what it does.

EXTRA CREDIT: When your app opens a file, it uses the function StgIsStorageFile( ) to check if the file uses structured storage or not. This means that our app can't open a simple text file. Modify your app so that if the user attempts to open a file that doesn't use structured storage, rather than simply rejecting it, you offer the user a choice to convert it. Use the function StgCreateDocfile( ) with the flag STGM_CONVERT to open the file. This will convert the plain vanilla file into a structured storage file, with the previous contents in a single stream called CONTENTS. Write the structure of one of our files into the root storage, then copy the contents into the DisplayText[ ] and then delete the stream.

EXTRA EXTRA CREDIT: Extend the enumeration dialog box. In the file ENUMDLG.CPP, add code to respond to a double-click on a line in the list box. If the user has clicked on a substorage, pop up another instance of the same type of dialog box, showing the elements in the substorage. If the user has double-clicked on a stream, pop up a dialog box showing the stream's contents, perhaps in a multiline edit control.

Chapter 8

Monikers

This page intentionally contains no text other than this sentence.

A. CONCEPTS AND DEFINITIONS

1. It is frequently useful in OLE for a client app to be able to connect to not just an object of a certain class (say, any old Excel spreadsheet), but rather one particular noninterchangeable object that belongs to that class (say, a particular range of cells in a particular sheet in a particular file). To provide this capability, OLE provides a general-purpose facility for the naming of objects. An object that wishes to provide its name to the world, so that a user of the object may at some later time recreate that specific object and no other, identifies itself by supplying a *moniker*, which is an object that supports the *IMoniker* interface.

2. A moniker is an intelligent name. It contains all the code and data necessary to locate the original object's server and instruct the server to recreate the original object. The moniker does not contain the object's data, but rather a reference to it (such as a file name) that is understood by the server. The process by which an object is recreated from its moniker is called *binding*, and is accomplished via the method **IMoniker::BindToObject( )**. Once the client has used the moniker to bind to the object, the client generally has no further use for the moniker and will release it. Thus:

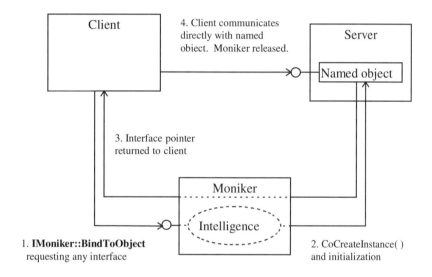

3. Since monikers are used to recreate a specific object at some later time, it is necessary to have some mechanism for storing them from one session to another. OLE accomplishes this by deriving the IMoniker interface from IPersistStream. Therefore, every moniker ever created knows how to save itself into a stream provided by the client app. This will generally live in the client app's data file.

4. Implementing the IMoniker interface can be quite complicated, so we aren't going to do it ourselves. Rather, the portions of this chapter that deal with sourcing monikers will confine themselves to the standard types provided by the operating system and created via simple API functions. We will treat them as atomic, occasionally combining them into molecules. This will suffice for over 95 percent of all applications. See Brockschmidt, pp. 461-470 for notes on implementing your own custom monikers.

B. CLIENT USE OF MONIKERS

1. When a client app opens a file containing a moniker, it first needs to load the moniker from its stream within the file. The stream contains the moniker's class ID followed by the moniker's private data, thus:

Class ID	Moniker's private data ...

The API function **OleLoadFromStream( )** will recreate any class of object that supports the IPersistStream interface and has been saved in the above format. This function reads the class ID from the stream and calls CoCreateInstance( ) to create an object of that class, asking for the IPersistStream interface. It then calls IPersistStream::Load( ) to make the object read its data from the stream. Finally, it calls QueryInterface( ) on the object for the interface ID specified by the caller. Thus:

```
extern IMoniker * pMoniker ;

case ID_MONIKER_OPENMONIKERFILE:
{
    HRESULT hr ;
    IStream *pStream ;

    <get file name from user, open file and stream containing moniker>

/*
Load moniker from the stream in which it was stored.
*/

    hr = OleLoadFromStream (
      pStream,                    // stream containing moniker's data
      IID_IMoniker,               // interface ID wanted on new obj
      (void **) &pMoniker) ;      // output variable

    if (!SUCCEEDED(hr))
    {
      MessageBox (NULL, "Couldn't load moniker from stream",
            "Error", 0) ;
    }
    pStream->Release( ) ;

    <continued on facing page>
```

NOTE: The sample client and server apps referred to in this section can be found in the directory \chap08\monikers. Use of these samples is less obvious than usual, so see the lab exercise instructions at the end of this chapter for directions on how to register and run them.

2. Having reconstituted the moniker, we now want to bind to the object that it names. We do this via the method **IMoniker::BindToObject( )**. This requires us to create a *bind context* object, essentially a memory scratchpad used by the moniker during the binding operation. Direct creation and use of the bind context are shown in the section on the URL moniker on page 261. The API function **BindMoniker( )** combines these operations into a single function call, creating the bind context, calling IMoniker::BindToObject( ), and releasing the bind context. This tells the moniker to do whatever it needs to do to reconstitute the object that it names and return a pointer to the specified interface on the new object. If it succeeds, we can then use the new object to our heart's content. Whether it succeeds or fails, we have no further use for the moniker, so we release it. Thus:

```
<continued from previous page>

/*
Bind to the object named by the moniker. The bind context will be
created and released internally.
*/
    if (pMoniker)
    {
      hr = BindMoniker (
            pMoniker,            // moniker naming desired object
            0,                   // reserved
            IID_IDataObject,     // interface ID wanted on new object
            (void **) &lpd) ;    // output variable

      if (!SUCCEEDED(hr))
      {
            MessageBox (NULL, "Couldn't bind to moniker", "Error", 0) ;
      }
      else
      {
            <use new object>
      }

/*
Release moniker as we no longer need it.
*/
      pMoniker->Release( ) ;
      pMoniker = NULL ;
    }

    return 0 ;
}
```

Note: If the client is able to directly handle the raw data in the file named by the moniker, it can bypass the server and fetch that data directly into a storage or a stream via the method **IMoniker::BindToStorage( )**. This is shown in more detail in the section dealing with the URL moniker on page 261.

3. How does the client app get and save the moniker in the first place? There are a number of ways. If you start with the object whose name you want, you can call its QueryInterface( ) method asking for the IMoniker interface. If the object supports naming, it will return its moniker. Monikers may also be supplied by other mechanisms, such as the method IOleObject::GetMoniker( ) method used in embedding and linking. Monikers may also be transferred via data objects, such as from the Clipboard or drag-and-drop. The data transfer operation for a moniker uses the private Clipboard format "Link Source" and a stream storage medium. The stream will look and behave exactly like the ones on the previous pages; the only difference is that it came out of a data object instead of from a file. The function OleLoadFromStream( ) will recreate the moniker as in the previous example. Thus:

```
UINT cfLinkSource ;
case WM_CREATE:
{
    cfLinkSource = RegisterClipboardFormat ("Link Source") ;
    return 0 ;
}


case ID_MONIKER_PASTEFROMCLIPBOARD:
{
    HRESULT hr ;     LPDATAOBJECT pClip ;
    FORMATETC fe ;   STGMEDIUM stg ;
/*
Get clipboard data object.  Get its data in link source format in
an IStream medium.
*/
    OleGetClipboard (&pClip) ;
    fe.cfFormat = cfLinkSource ;
    fe.tymed = TYMED_ISTREAM ;
    fe.lindex = -1 ;
    fe.dwAspect = DVASPECT_CONTENT ;
    fe.ptd = NULL ;
    hr = pClip->GetData (&fe, &stg) ;

/*
Seek the stream to its beginning. Load the moniker from the stream.
*/

    LARGE_INTEGER li = {0, 0} ;
    stg.pstm->Seek (li, STREAM_SEEK_SET, NULL) ;

    hr = OleLoadFromStream (stg.pstm,        // stream containing object
      IID_IMoniker,                          // interface ID desired
      (void **)&pMoniker);                   // output variable

    if (hr != S_OK)
    {
      MessageBox (NULL, "Couldn't load moniker", "", 0) ;
    }
    ReleaseStgMedium (&stg) ;

    <use moniker to our heart's content>
    pClip->Release ( ) ;
    return 0 ;
}
```

246

4. Once the client app obtains a moniker, it saves the moniker into a stream via the API function **OleSaveToStream( )**, which operates on any object that supports the IPersistStream interface. This function first obtains the object's class ID via the method IPersistStream::GetClassID( ) and writes it to the stream via the function WriteClassStm( ). It then tells the moniker to write its private data into the stream by calling the method IPersistStream::Save( ), thereby producing the stream layout detailed previously. Thus:

```
extern IMoniker *pMoniker ;

case ID_MONIKER_SAVEMONIKERAS:
{
    HRESULT hr ;

    IStream *pStream ;

    <open stream for moniker to live in>
/*
Tell the moniker to save its data into the stream.
*/
    hr = OleSaveToStream (
            pMoniker,                 // IPersistStream-derived object
            pStream) ;                // stream to save object in

    if (!SUCCEEDED(hr))
    {
      MessageBox (NULL, "Couldn't save moniker", "Error", 0) ;
    }

/*
Release interface pointers when done.
*/
    pStream->Release ( ) ;

    return 0 ;
}
```

C. SERVER SUPPORT OF SIMPLE MONIKERS

1. Suppose I have the simplest server app I can think of. The server is so simple that it makes its objects' data available to clients only in text format via the IDataObject interface. Its objects are files containing text that the user enters.

In addition to simply transferring text, the server app also wants to make it possible for a client to preserve not the server object's data itself, but rather a reference the server's object. At some later time, the client wants to be able to reconstitute the object representing that data. In order to accomplish this, the server has to do two things. First, it has to provide to the client a moniker naming its objects. Second, it has to be able to reconstitute the named objects when asked to do so by the monikers. In this manner, if the user runs the server app and makes a change in a file, then the next time a user runs the client app and recreates the object, the object will reflect the changes that have been made by the user of the server.

2. This app has two classes of data objects. The first, CFileTextData, is the data object that contains the actual contents of the file. The second, CMonikerData, is used only for transferring a moniker to a client app via the Clipboard or drag-and-drop. The moniker naming the file object is a *file moniker*, one of OLE's standard types, which you create via the API function **CreateFileMoniker( )**. Thus:

```
#include "cmonikerdata.h"
/*
User picked "Edit -- Copy File Link" from the menu.
*/


WCHAR WideFileName [256] ;

case ID_EDIT_COPYFILELINK:
{
    LPMONIKER pFileMoniker ;    LPDATAOBJECT pData ;

/*
Create moniker naming currently open file.
*/

    CreateFileMoniker (WideFileName, &pFileMoniker) ;

/*
Create a data transfer object that knows how to transfer monikers and
place it on the Clipboard. This object maintains a reference count on
the moniker.
*/
    pData = new CMonikerData (pFileMoniker) ;
    OleSetClipboard (pData) ;

/*
No further business with any of these objects, so release them here.
Final release from Clipboard will destroy them.
*/
    pFileMoniker->Release( ) ;
    pData->Release ( ) ;
    return 0 ;
}
```

3. The method CMonikerData::GetData( ) has to provide the moniker to a client app using "Link Source" Clipboard format in a stream storage medium. We could create a disk file to contain this stream, but that would be slow. It is fastest to create a stream in global memory via the API function **CreateStreamOnHGlobal( )**. The function OleSaveToStream( ) is then used to save the moniker into the global memory stream. Finally, the stream is returned in the STGMEDIUM structure that transfers data in this operation. Thus:

```
extern UINT cfLinkSource ;

STDMETHODIMP   CMonikerData::GetData   (LPFORMATETC   lpfe,   LPSTGMEDIUM
lpstg)
{

/*
We support link source format, transferred through an IStream, with
aspect content.
*/
    if (lpfe->cfFormat == cfLinkSource &&
      lpfe->dwAspect == DVASPECT_CONTENT &&
      lpfe->tymed == TYMED_ISTREAM)
    {
/*
Create a new stream in global memory.
*/
        CreateStreamOnHGlobal (
            NULL,                // allocate new memory block
            TRUE,                //automatically free when stream released
            &lpstg->pstm) ;    // output variable

/*
Save the moniker into the stream.  Moniker provided in class
constructor on previous page, kept in member variable.
*/

        OleSaveToStream (m_pMoniker, lpstg->pstm) ;

/*
Set elements of STGMEDIUM structure for transfer.
*/

        lpstg->tymed = TYMED_ISTREAM ;
        lpstg->pUnkForRelease = NULL ;

        return S_OK ;

    }
/*
User asked for a format that we couldn't supply.  Return error code.
*/
    return DATA_E_FORMATETC ;
}
```

4. When the client binds to the file-based moniker, the OLE-supplied implementation of the file moniker looks for the file whose name is encoded in the moniker and attempts to launch a server based on it. The search for the server of a given file is performed internally via the API function **GetClassFile( )**. The procedure followed by this function is as follows:

A. If the file is a structured storage file, then the moniker will look for the class ID with which the root storage was marked.

B. Failing that, it will look in the registry section HKEY_CLASSES_ROOT\FileType for an entry. The file's contents are checked against each of the class ID subkeys in this section. Each class ID entry has one or more subkeys specifying the byte pattern that a file must contain to be identified as belonging to the server of that class ID. In the example shown below, the file's contents beginning at offset 0, continuing for the next 8 bytes, combined with the mask 0xFF00F9FF0000FFFF using the logical AND operation, must produce the result 0x0900000000002000 to be identified with the server whose class ID is {00020811-0000-0000-C000-000000000046}, which is Microsoft Excel. If the entry contains more than one subkey, a file must match all of them.

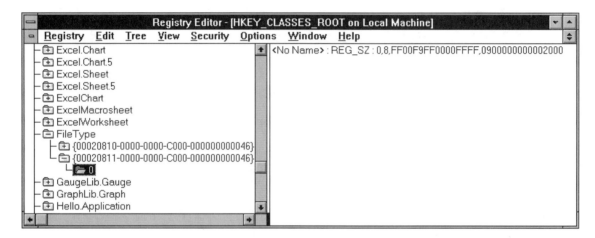

C. Failing that, it will look in the registry for a key that corresponds to the file's extension. If found, this key will contain the name of the object that a file with the specified extension contains. The moniker will then look up the class ID associated with that named object, and launch the server of that class. In the following example, a file with the extension .XLS is thought to contain an Excel.Sheet.5 object.

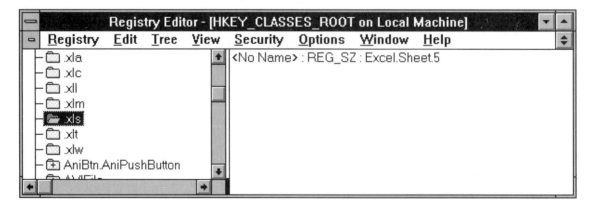

5. When the moniker locates the class ID of the server that handles the file, the moniker will call CoCreateInstance( ) to create an object of this class, asking for the IPersistFile interface, discussed on the following page. Obtaining this, the moniker calls IPersistFile::Load( ) to make the object read its data from the file specified in the moniker. Finally, the moniker calls QueryInterface( ) for the interface specified by the client in the call to BindMoniker( ). A failure at any point terminates the binding operation with an error. The sequence of events is shown graphically below:

6. The *IPersistFile* interface is somewhat similar to the IPersistStream interface seen in the previous chapter. It tells an object to load its data from a standalone file rather than a stream. The methods of this interface are:

GetClassID( )   *// Get class ID of object saved in file.*
IsDirty( )   *// Ask object if it has changed since it was last saved to its current file.*
Load( )   *// Open specified file and initialize object from the file contents.*
Save( )   *// Save object's data to specified file.*
SaveCompleted( ) *// Notify object that it can revert from NoScribble mode to Normal mode.*
GetCurFile( )   *// Get the current name of the file.*

In the sample program, when the moniker calls CoCreateInstance( ), the server's class factory manufactures an object of class CFileTextData, which supports both the IDataObject and IPersistFile interfaces. After creating the object, the moniker will then call the **IPersistFile::Load( )** method, passing it the name of the file contained in the moniker. It is up to the object to open the file and properly reconstitute the object's previous state from the contents of that file. Thus:

```
STDMETHODIMP CFileTextData::Load(LPCOLESTR pFileName, DWORD grfMode)
{

    HRESULT hr ;
/*
Open storage file we are passed. Open stream that contains data within
the storage file.
*/

    IStorage *pStor ;
    IStream *pStream ;

    hr = StgOpenStorage (pFileName, NULL,
      STGM_READWRITE | STGM_SHARE_EXCLUSIVE,
      NULL, 0, &pStor) ;

    if (!SUCCEEDED(hr))
    {
      return E_FAIL ;
    }

    hr = pStor->OpenStream (L"Text", 0,
      STGM_READWRITE | STGM_SHARE_EXCLUSIVE,
      0, &pStream) ;

    if (!SUCCEEDED(hr))
    {
      return E_FAIL ;
    }
```

```
/*
Find length of stream, allocate enough memory to hold its contents.
*/
     ULARGE_INTEGER ul ; LARGE_INTEGER l_zero = {0, 0} ;

     pStream->Seek (l_zero, STREAM_SEEK_END, &ul) ;
     pStream->Seek (l_zero, STREAM_SEEK_SET, NULL) ;

     m_length = ul.LowPart+1    ;
     m_cp = (char *)GlobalAlloc (GMEM_FIXED, m_length) ;
     if (!m_cp)
     {
       return E_OUTOFMEMORY;
     }

/*
Read file text from stream. Make sure it is NULL-terminated.
*/

     pStream->Read (m_cp, m_length-1, NULL) ;
     *(m_cp + ul.LowPart) = 0 ;

/*
Release storage and stream.
*/
     pStor->Release ( ) ;
     pStream->Release ( ) ;

}
```

D. COMPOSITE MONIKERS

1. File monikers are fine, but their granularity is too large for most applications. Suppose the object named by the moniker has a finer granularity, such as a range of cells in a spreadsheet. In our server example, if the user selects a block of text with the mouse, he wants to be able to provide a moniker that refers to only the selected text. The server in this case must supply a *composite moniker*, which is a moniker made up other monikers.

2. A composite moniker is composed from left to right. Each moniker narrows down the field until the desired granularity and determinism are reached. A composite moniker generally begins with a file or URL moniker specifying the root file, then contains one or more *item monikers*. An item moniker is an intelligent persistent name object supporting the IMoniker interface, but whose contents only have meaning to the server application. An item moniker does not know how to stand alone. In the supplied server example, the selected text block is named by an item moniker consisting of the first and last selected characters, separate by a colon. Thus:

3. When the user chooses "Edit -- Copy File!Item" from the main menu, the server constructs a composite moniker based on the current text selection and places it on the Clipboard as before. The API function **CreateItemMoniker( )** makes an item moniker for us. The delimiter character in its first parameter specifies a character that we promise OLE will never appear in this item's name. The item moniker uses it to separate its strings internally. The choice of the bang ('!') character as shown below is customary but not required.

The obtusely named function **CreateGenericComposite( )** takes two monikers and binds them together into a single composite moniker. The left-hand moniker, here the file moniker, is specified first in its parameter list. If you wanted to, you could take the resulting composite moniker, bind another one to its right, and go on to create composite monikers of staggering complexity. Thus:

```
case ID_EDIT_COPYFILEITEMLINK:
{
    LPMONIKER pFileMoniker, pItemMoniker, pCompositeMoniker ;
    LPDATAOBJECT pData ;  char out [256] ; WCHAR wout [256] ;

/*
Create moniker for currently open file.
*/
    CreateFileMoniker (WideFileName, &pFileMoniker) ;

/*
Get selection of text, convert to wide chars, and create item moniker
naming it.
*/
    DWORD dwSel = SendMessage (hEdit, EM_GETSEL, 0, 0) ;
    wsprintf (out, "%d:%d", LOWORD(dwSel), HIWORD(dwSel)) ;
    MultiByteToWideChar (CP_ACP, 0, out, -1, wout, 80) ;

    CreateItemMoniker (L"!",   // delimiter character
      wout,                    // object name
      &pItemMoniker) ;         // output variable

/*
Combine file and item moniker into composite. Place composite moniker
in data transfer object.  Place on Clipboard.
*/
    CreateGenericComposite (
      pFileMoniker,            // leftmost moniker
      pItemMoniker,            // right-hand moniker to add
      &pCompositeMoniker) ;    // output variable

    pData = new CMonikerData (pCompositeMoniker) ;
    OleSetClipboard (pData) ;

/*
Release everything.
*/
    pFileMoniker->Release ( ) ;
    pItemMoniker->Release ( ) ;
    pCompositeMoniker->Release( ) ;
    pData->Release ( ) ;
    return 0 ;
}
```

4. The client that uses the moniker doesn't know or care whether the moniker is simple or composite. All it does is call BindMoniker( ) as shown in the first example. It is up to the server to properly decompose the composite moniker and reconstruct the named object in accordance with the names contained therein.

Composite monikers are decomposed from right to left. When the client calls the composite moniker's BindToObject( ) method, the composite delegates that call to the rightmost moniker in the composite, passing a pointer to the remaining composite to the left of rightmost moniker. The rightmost moniker attempts to recreate the object that it names, but is usually unable to do so without the assistance of the moniker on its left. In the text server example shown previously, the item moniker on the right which indicates the range of selected text is meaningless without the file in which the range resides. The item moniker knows this, so it calls the BindToObject( ) method on the moniker to its left, asking for the IOleContainerItem( ) interface. When this returns, the rightmost moniker calls the method IOleItemContainer::GetObject( ), passing its own item name. This method is where the intelligence resides to create an object based on the file and item names. This process is shown graphically on the facing page:

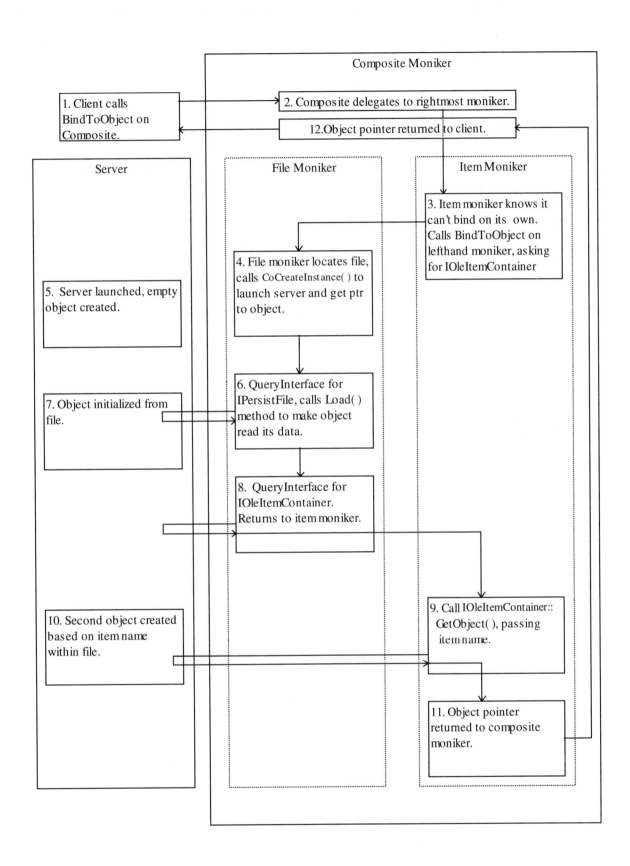

Composite Moniker

1. Client calls BindToObject on Composite.

2. Composite delegates to rightmost moniker.

12. Object pointer returned to client.

Server

File Moniker

Item Moniker

3. Item moniker knows it can't bind on its own. Calls BindToObject on lefthand moniker, asking for IOleItemContainer

4. File moniker locates file, calls CoCreateInstance( ) to launch server and get ptr to object.

5. Server launched, empty object created.

6. QueryInterface for IPersistFile, calls Load( ) method to make object read its data.

7. Object initialized from file.

8. QueryInterface for IOleItemContainer. Returns to item moniker.

9. Call IOleItemContainer:: GetObject( ), passing item name.

10. Second object created based on item name within file.

11. Object pointer returned to composite moniker.

257

5. To properly decompose and bind to composite moniker, the server must support the interface *IOleItemContainer*. The methods of this interface are:

ParseDisplayName( )   *// Parses object's display name to form moniker.*
EnumObjects( )   *// Enumerates objects in a container.*
LockContainer( )   *// Keeps container running until explicitly released.*
GetObject( )   *// Returns a pointer to a specified object.*
GetObjectStorage( )   *// Returns a pointer to an object's storage.*
IsRunning( )   *// Checks whether an object is running.*

The one with which we are most concerned is **IOleItemContainer::GetObject( )**, shown below. In it, we are passed the name of the item from the item moniker. It is up to this code to make sense of the name and create an object based on it. Thus:

```
STDMETHODIMP CFileTextData::GetObject(LPOLESTR pWideItemName,
    DWORD dwSpeed, LPBINDCTX pbc, REFIID riid, VOID **ppv)
{

    HRESULT hr ;
    char ItemName [256] ;

 /*
 Convert item name from wide to the ANSI that we use internally.
 */

    WideCharToMultiByte (CP_ACP, 0, pWideItemName, -1,
      ItemName, sizeof(ItemName), NULL, NULL) ;

 /*
 Parse first and last digit out of item name
 */

    char *pColon  = strchr (ItemName, ':') ;
    *(pColon) = 0x00 ;
    int first = atoi (ItemName) ;
    int last = atoi (pColon+1) ;

 /*
 Instantiate new CFileTextData object, using the overloaded
 constructor that allows us to specify a data pointer and an
 extent.
 */

    CFileTextData *pNewTextData = new CFileTextData (m_cp+first,
      last-first) ;

 /*
 Query new object for requested interface.  Return result code.
 */
    hr = pNewTextData->QueryInterface(riid, ppv);
    pNewTextData->Release();

    return hr ;
}
```

258

This page intentionally contains no text other than this sentence.

E. URL MONIKERS

1. With the advent of Internet support in most apps, the *URL moniker* has been added to the standard types supported by the operating system. This is a standalone moniker that may also be used as the root of composite monikers. It is similar in operation to the file moniker, except a URL moniker binds to an object named by an Internet URL rather than a local file name. You create a URL moniker via the API function **CreateURLMoniker( )**. A sample app that uses the URL moniker to download information from the Internet is provided for you in the directory \chap08\urlmoniker. Thus:

```
void CUrlmonikerDlg::OnBind()
{
    char name [256] ;
    HRESULT hr ;

/*
Get name from combo box control.
*/

    m_URLCombo.GetWindowText (name, sizeof(name)) ;


/*
Use name to create an URL moniker. Store moniker in a member variable.
This function, as do all OLE functions, requires a wide character
string.  The macro A2W( ) is an MFC macro that performs this
conversion.  The macro USES_CONVERSION must be inserted prior to it as
shown.
*/

    USES_CONVERSION ;
    hr = CreateURLMoniker (NULL, A2W(name), &m_pUrlMoniker) ;

    <continued on facing page>
```

260

2. You generally want to bind to a URL moniker asynchronously. Downloading data over the Internet may take a long time or fail completely, and you probably don't want to hang your main app while waiting for it. In the synchronous binding operation shown in the beginning of this chapter, you created a bind context and called IMoniker::BindToObject( ) or IMoniker::BindToStorage( ). When that method returned, the object had been fully reconstituted and you could use it freely.

In asynchronous binding, you create the same bind context and call the same IMoniker method; however, this merely starts the binding process. When the function returns, the object has not been fully reconstituted. The object's data will be retrieved over the Internet and the binding process completed at some later time, possible never.

To bind asynchronously, you must provide the moniker with an *IBindStatusCallback* object, which receives notifications as the binding operation proceeds. This interface is described in more detail on the following pages. You place this object in the bind context via the API function **RegisterBindStatusCallback( )**.

In the first example in this chapter, we used the method IMoniker::BindToObject( ) to launch the server associated with the object named by the moniker and have the server read the object's data and present it to us. In this example, our client knows how to use the raw data of the object named by the moniker without the mediation of a server, so we call **IMoniker::BindToStorage( )** rather than IMoniker::BindToObject( ). This retrieves the data named by the moniker and presents it to us in a stream. Thus:

```
<continued from previous page>

/*
Create a new IBindStatusCallback operation to control the asynchronous
binding operation.
*/

    m_pBindStatusCallback = new CBindStatusCallback (this) ;

/*
Create a bind context.  Register the IBindStatusCallback with it,
*/

    hr = CreateBindCtx (0, &m_pBindCtx) ;

    hr = RegisterBindStatusCallback (
      m_pBindCtx,
      m_pBindStatusCallback,
      BSCO_ALLONIBSC,
      NULL) ;

/*
Tell the moniker to bind to the storage.  This returns the data named
by the moniker.
*/

    hr = m_pUrlMoniker->BindToStorage (
      m_pBindCtx,                // bind context
      0,                         // not used
      IID_IStream,               // interface ID on returned data
      (void **)&m_pStream) ;     // output variable

}
```

261

3. The IBindStatusCallback is used by the moniker to get information from the client about the binding operation and to inform the client about important events in the binding operation as it takes place. Its methods are

GetBindInfo( )	*// provide control information to moniker.*
GetPriority( )	*// provide priority of download operation.*
OnDataAvailable( )	*// provide downloaded data to client.*
OnLowResource( )	*// signals client of low resources.*
OnObjectAvailable( )	*// provide requested interface pointer to client*
OnProgress( )	*// tell client about current progress of this bind operation.*
OnStartBinding( )	*// tells client that bind operation has started.*
OnStopBinding( )	*// tells client that bind operation has completed.*

When binding to the storage, as shown in the supplied example, there are two choices for how the data is downloaded. In the example provided, the moniker downloads data when the client explicitly requests it to do so by reading from a provided data stream. If the client stops reading, the moniker will stop downloading until the client starts reading again. This is called the "data-pull" model and is analogous to the IDataObject::GetData( ) method. Its primary advantage is that the client knows that it will never miss data because of an overrun. The primary disadvantage is that it requires the data to be copied twice, once by the moniker from the net into a buffer, and again by the client from the buffer into the client's own storage.

The other alternative is to use the "data-push" operation, in which the client provides a buffer to the moniker and the moniker downloads data continuously into the stream until the operation completes. This is analogous to the IDataObject::GetDataHere( ) method. It saves the extra copy operation. On the other hand, if the moniker downloads data faster than the client can handle it, you can run into trouble and coding to handle this error may be more trouble than its worth. Implementing this mechanism is left as an extra-credit exercise to the student.

4. Our implementation of the IBindStatusCallback object looks like this. The constructor and destructor don't do anything interesting.

```
class CBindStatusCallback : public IBindStatusCallback
{
  public:

    // Data members

    DWORD               m_RefCount ;
    DWORD               m_LastSize ;
    CUrlmonikerDlg*     m_pDlg ;
    char *              m_pBuf ;
    IBinding *          m_pBinding ;
    BOOL                m_BeganDownload ;

    // constructor/destructor

    CBindStatusCallback(CUrlmonikerDlg *);
    ~CBindStatusCallback();

    // IUnknown methods

    STDMETHODIMP        QueryInterface(REFIID, void **);
    STDMETHODIMP_(ULONG)    AddRef() ;
    STDMETHODIMP_(ULONG)    Release() ;

    // IBindStatusCallback methods

    STDMETHODIMP    OnStartBinding(DWORD, IBinding*);
    STDMETHODIMP    GetPriority(LONG*);
    STDMETHODIMP    OnLowResource(DWORD dwReserved);
    STDMETHODIMP    OnProgress(ULONG, ULONG, ULONG, LPCWSTR);
    STDMETHODIMP    OnStopBinding(HRESULT, LPCWSTR);
    STDMETHODIMP    GetBindInfo(DWORD*, BINDINFO*);
    STDMETHODIMP    OnDataAvailable(DWORD, DWORD, FORMATETC *,
                        STGMEDIUM*);
    STDMETHODIMP    OnObjectAvailable(REFIID riid, IUnknown* punk);
} ;
```

263

5. The first method that the URL moniker will call is **IBindStatusCallback::GetBindInfo( )**. The moniker is asking us for detailed information describing the binding operation that we have just instructed it to perform. We provide this information by filling out the fields of a structure of type **BINDINFO**, which is passed to us in the parameter list. The flag **BINDF_PULLDATA** signifies the use of data-pull mode.

```
/*
Moniker is asking us to fill in a BINDINFO structure describing the
binding operation that is about to occur.
*/


STDMETHODIMP CBindStatusCallback::GetBindInfo (DWORD* pgrfBINDF,
    BINDINFO* pbindInfo)
{

/*
Fill out flags calling for asynchronous binding using the data-pull
mode.
*/

    *pgrfBINDF = BINDF_ASYNCHRONOUS|BINDF_ASYNCSTORAGE|BINDF_PULLDATA ;

/*
Clear out STGMEDIUM structure in BINDINFO, signifying that the moniker
should allocate its own.
*/

    memset(&pbindInfo->stgmedData, 0, sizeof(STGMEDIUM));

/*
Set other elements to their default values.
*/
    pbindInfo->cbSize = sizeof(BINDINFO);
    pbindInfo->szExtraInfo = NULL;
    pbindInfo->grfBindInfoF = 0;
    pbindInfo->dwBindVerb = BINDVERB_GET;
    pbindInfo->szCustomVerb = NULL;

    return S_OK;
}
```

6. Once it has retrieved the BINDINFO structure describing the operation, the moniker will signal the start of the binding operation by calling the method **IBindStatusCallback::OnStartBinding( )**. We put in this method whatever code we want to initialize our downloading operation, in this case allocating a buffer and displaying information to the user. In the parameter list is a pointer to an object of type *IBinding*. This object provides methods giving us control over the download operation, allowing us to suspend or abort it. It is described in more detail on page 269.

The URL moniker does not provide an automatic timeout for the location of the desired resource, and there is no central agency to say that a specified page does not exist. The only way to tell if a resource is unavailable is if the download does not begin within an interval that you feel is reasonable. In this example, we read the interval specified by the user in an edit control on the parent dialog box, and start a timer for that duration. If the download does not begin within that length of time, we will abort the operation as shown on page 269. Thus:

```
STDMETHODIMP CBindStatusCallback::OnStartBinding(DWORD grfBSCOption,
    IBinding* pbinding)
{

/*
Show status to user.
*/

    m_pDlg->SetDlgItemText (IDC_STATUS, "Starting to bind ...") ;

/*
Allocate a large buffer for incoming text.
*/
    m_pBuf = (char *) GlobalAlloc (GMEM_FIXED | GMEM_ZEROINIT,
        BUFSIZE);

/*
AddRef the IBinding and store for later use.
*/
    m_pBinding = pbinding ;
    m_pBinding->AddRef ( )  ;

/*
Start the timeout interval for beginning the download.
*/
    UINT TimeoutSec = m_pDlg->GetDlgItemInt (IDC_TIMEOUTSEC) ;
    SetTimer (m_pDlg->m_hWnd, (UINT)this, TimeoutSec * 1000,
        TimerFunc);

    return S_OK;
}
```

7. During the download operation, the moniker will periodically call the **IBindStatusCallback::OnProgress( )** method to provide us with some idea of the progress of the operation. The first two parameters are unsigned longs, giving us the number of bytes downloaded and total number of bytes expected. In this sample program, we use these to set a progress indicator control on the parent dialog box. The ulStatusCode contains flags telling us the current state of the operation, which we use to choose a status string to show the user. The final parameter is a pointer to a text string containing the name of the data location. Thus:

```
STDMETHODIMP CBindStatusCallback::OnProgress(ULONG ulProgress,
    ULONG ulProgressMax, ULONG ulStatusCode, LPCWSTR szStatusText)
{

/*
Set state of progress indicator bar.  Since its range is only 0-64K,
scale it by factor of 1000.
*/
    m_pDlg->m_Progress.SetRange (0, ulProgressMax/1000) ;
    m_pDlg->m_Progress.SetPos (ulProgress/1000) ;

/*
Find character string that corresponds to status flag.  Place in
edit control for user to look at.
*/
    char *cp ;
    switch (ulStatusCode)
    {
      case BINDSTATUS_FINDINGRESOURCE: cp = "Finding resource"; break;
      case BINDSTATUS_CONNECTING: cp = "Connecting"; break ;
      case BINDSTATUS_REDIRECTING: cp = "Redirecting"; break ;
      case BINDSTATUS_BEGINDOWNLOADDATA: cp="Beginning download";break;
      case BINDSTATUS_DOWNLOADINGDATA: cp = "Downloading"; break ;
      case BINDSTATUS_ENDDOWNLOADDATA: cp = "Download complete"; break;
      default: cp = "Unknown progress flag" ;
    }
    m_pDlg->SetDlgItemText (IDC_STATUS, cp) ;


/*
Put status string with data location into status edit control.
*/
    USES_CONVERSION ;
    m_pDlg->SetDlgItemText (IDC_PROGSTRING, W2A(szStatusText)) ;

    return S_OK ;
}
```

8. As the data is downloaded, the moniker makes it available to us by calling our **IBindStatusCallback::OnDataAvailable( )** method. The data is provided in a storage medium structure using the medium that we requested in the call to IMoniker::BindToStorage( ), in this example a stream. We use the method IStream::Read( ) to read the data from the stream into a buffer. In the data-pull model being used in this example, we must also perform a second IStream::Read( ) operation to signal the moniker to download the next block of data. This will not actually fetch any more data. The return code should be E_PENDING if there is more data to come, or E_FALSE if we have reached the end of the file.

```
STDMETHODIMP CBindStatusCallback::OnDataAvailable(DWORD grfBSCF,
    DWORD dwSize, FORMATETC* pfmtetc, STGMEDIUM* pstgmed)
{

/*
If more data has arrived, read it into our local buffer and place it in
the parent dialog box's edit control for the user to look at.
*/
    DWORD nBytesToRead = dwSize - m_LastSize ;
    DWORD nActual ;

    if (dwSize > m_LastSize)
    {
      pstgmed->pstm->Read (m_pBuf + m_LastSize, nBytesToRead,&nActual);
      m_pDlg->SetDlgItemText (IDC_DATAEDIT, m_pBuf) ;
      m_LastSize = dwSize ;
/*
Set flag saying download has started.
*/
      m_BeganDownload = TRUE ;
    }

/*
Since we are using the data-pull mode, we must do another read to keep
the flow of data coming.
*/
    HRESULT hr = pstgmed->pstm->Read (m_pBuf + m_LastSize, 1, NULL) ;

    return S_OK;
}
```

267

9. The moniker signals the end of the download operation by calling our **IBindStatusCallback::OnStopBinding( )** method. We use this to do any cleanup that might be required, in this case only signaling the parent dialog. All the deallocation of resources is done in our object's destructor, thereby ensuring that it is not done until the final release of our object. Thus:

```
STDMETHODIMP CBindStatusCallback::OnStopBinding (HRESULT hrStatus,
    LPCWSTR pszError)
{
    if (pszError)
    {
      USES_CONVERSION ;
      m_pDlg->SetDlgItemText (IDC_STATUS, W2A(pszError)) ;
    }
    else
    {
      m_pDlg->SetDlgItemText (IDC_STATUS, "Completed") ;
    }

/*
Signal the parent dialog box that the operation has finished. It will
take care of all the UI stuff.
*/
    m_pDlg->BindFinished( ) ;

    return S_OK;
}
```

10. When it called OnStartBinding( ), the moniker provided us with an IBinding object as a means of controlling the download operation while it is in progress. The methods of the IBinding interface are:

Abort( )	// Permanently aborts the bind operation.
Suspend( )	// Suspends the bind operation until further notice.
Resume( )	// Resumes a suspended bind operation.
SetPriority( )	// Establishes the priority for the bind operation.
GetPriority( )	// Retrieves the current priority of this bind operation.

In the example shown below, the timer created in our OnStartBinding( ) method has expired. If the download operation has begun by this time, the flag m_BeganDownload will have been set to TRUE in the OnDataAvailable( ) method. If not, we figure that the requested resource can't be found and abort the operation via the method **IBinding::Abort( )**. This causes the moniker to call our OnStopBinding( ) method, thereby cleaning up nicely. Thus:

```
void CALLBACK TimerFunc(HWND hWnd, UINT msg,  UINT idEvent,
    DWORD dwTime)
{
    CBindStatusCallback *pThis =  (CBindStatusCallback*) idEvent ;

/*
Didn't begin download in time, abort the operation. This should
generate a call to OnStopBinding( ) ;
*/
    if (pThis->m_BeganDownload == FALSE)
    {
      pThis->m_pBinding->Abort( ) ;
    }

    KillTimer (hWnd, idEvent) ;
}
```

269

F. RUNNING OBJECT TABLE

1. If the object that the moniker names is currently active when a binding operation is performed, it would be nice to be able to connect directly to it, without requiring a new server to start up and a new instance of the object to be created. OLE provides the *Running Object Table* to enable exactly this sort of optimization.

2. The ROT is a global table that matches objects with their monikers. You obtain a pointer to the running object table via the function **GetRunningObjectTable( )**. This function returns a pointer the interface *IRunningObjectTable*, by which the ROT is read and manipulated. The member functions of this interface are:

Register( )	*// Place object and associated moniker in ROT.*
Revoke( )	*// Remove object and its moniker from ROT.*
IsRunning( )	*// Check whether an object is in ROT.*
GetObject( )	*// Return a pointer to the object named by specified moniker.*
NoteChangeTime( )	*// Notify the ROT of time at which an object last changed.*
GetTimeOfLastChange( )	*// Return the time at which an object last changed.*
EnumRunning( )	*// Return an enumerator of objects in ROT.*

3.   An object is placed in the ROT via the method **IRunningObjectTable::Register( )**, passing a pointer to the object and to the moniker which names the object. In the following example, the object itself performs the registration in its IPersistFile::Load( ) method, as this is where the object finds out its file name and becomes useful. Thus:

```
STDMETHODIMP CFileTextData::Load(LPCOLESTR pFileName, DWORD grfMode)
{

    <open file and read contents as in previous example>

/*
Create new moniker based on current file name.
*/

    CreateFileMoniker (pFileName, &m_pFileMoniker) ;

/*
Make entry for new file in Running Object Table.
*/
    LPRUNNINGOBJECTTABLE pROT ;

    GetRunningObjectTable (0, &pROT) ;

    pROT->Register (0,              // flags
      (LPDATAOBJECT)this,          // running object
      m_pFileMoniker,              // moniker of running object
      &m_dwRegisterROT) ;          // output variable

    pROT->Release ( ) ;

    return S_OK ;
}
```

4. An object is removed from the ROT via the method **IRunningObjectTable::Revoke( )**. In this example, this is performed in the class destructor.

```
CFileTextData::~CFileTextData(void)
{

/*
Remove ourselves from the running object table.
*/
    if (m_dwRegisterROT != 0)
    {
      LPRUNNINGOBJECTTABLE pROT ;

      GetRunningObjectTable (0, &pROT) ;
      pROT->Revoke (m_dwRegisterROT) ;
      pROT->Release ( ) ;
    }
/*
Release moniker.
*/
    if (m_pFileMoniker)
    {
      m_pFileMoniker->Release ( ) ;
    }

/*
Free data storage.
*/
    GlobalFree (m_cp) ;

    return;
}
```

Directory: \EssenceOfOLE\chap08\monikers\templ\monikercl

In this lab, we'll create the moniker client discussed in the first part of this chapter. It gets a moniker from the Clipboard and uses it to bind to a data object at a later time.

1. To develop and test the client, it is necessary to have a server to interact with. Go to the root directory of this example and run the registry file MONIKERSV.REG. This will make the necessary entries in the system registry to connect the server MONIKERSV.EXE in the directory chap08\monikers\done\monikersv as the automation server for the object whose human-readable name is "EssenceOfOle.Monikersv". If the root directory you are using for your samples is anything other than C:\EssenceOfOLE, you will need to edit the .REG file to make the LocalServer32 entry point to the exact path location of the server file.

2. Run the server app MONIKERSV.EXE mentioned in the previous paragraph. It will come up with an empty edit control in its main window. Type some text of your choosing into the edit control, then use the "File – Save As" menu item to save your text into a named file that the server app knows how to use. The server directory already contains one such with the name 'a'. (That way it appears first on the list). Pick "Edit – Copy File Link" from the server's menu to create a moniker and place it on the Clipboard.

3. In the file MAINWIND.CPP, case WM_COMMAND, subcase ID_MONIKER_PASTEFROMCLIPBOARD, we have to get from the Clipboard the stream containing the moniker that the server has placed there and reconstitute the moniker from the stream. Use the API function OleGetClipboard( ) to get a data object representing the Clipboard contents. Use the method IDataObject::GetData( ) to get the moniker from the Clipboard. Use the Clipboard format cfLinkSource, which has been registered for your in the WM_CREATE case of the client app, and the TYMED_ISTREAM. Once you have gotten the data, use the API function OleLoadFromStream( ) to reconstitute the moniker.

4. Having reconstituted the moniker, use the API function BindMoniker( ) to get the object which the moniker names. Ask for the IDataObject interface, storing it in the global variable lpd. After this call succeeds, the template app contains code that will call IDataObject::GetData( ), thereby transferring the data from the server to the client.

5. Now the client needs to save the moniker into a data file. Onc is constructed for you in the subcase ID_MONIKER_SAVEMONIKERAS which contains a stream named "Moniker". Use the API function OleSaveToStream( ) to save your moniker into this stream. Paste a moniker into the client app from the Clipboard as before, then choose "File – Save As" from the menu and save your file. Then use the DocFile viewer shown in the previous chapter to examine the contents of this file and the "Moniker" stream. You will find that it begins with the class ID of the file moniker, which is 00000303-0000-0000-C000-000000000046, and the contains the name of the server file in wide characters. You don't have to worry about that, it is entirely the moniker's responsibility. Close the client app and the server app.

6. Now the client needs to reconstitute the moniker from its data file. In the subcase ID_MONIKER_OPENMONIKERFILE, the client app opens the file and the "Moniker" stream. Use the API function OleLoadFromStream( ) to load the moniker from this stream, then use the API function BindMoniker( ) to create the object that it names. This should launch the server and make it open the specified file. The template app contains code to transfer the data from the file. Everything is cool. Shut down client and server.

7. Now start the server app again and either open one of its previously saved files or type in new text and save it. Select a range of characters with the mouse, then pick "Edit – Copy File!Item Link" from the menu. Run the client app, paste the link, and save the client file as before. Note that only the selected characters from the server were copied by the paste operation.

8. Save the client file and look at it with the DocFile viewer as before. Note how much larger and more complicated the moniker has become. Note that the client doesn't give a damn, its moniker loading, saving, and binding code works unchanged. The new contents of the moniker are entirely the moniker's problem. That's what we mean when we say that the moniker is an intelligent name.

Lab Exercise
Chapter 8
Moniker Server

Directory: \EssenceOfOLE\chap08\monikers\templ\monikersv

This app is the server side for the moniker client you did in the preceding lab.

1. Now that your controller is working, you have something to test the server with. Before starting to work on the server, you must change the entries in the registry so that the controller will use the new server that you are developing rather than the finished one supplied in the \done directory. You can do this either by editing the .REG file to point to new server's path (in the directory \templ\debug) and reregistering the whole thing, or by using the registry editor and changing only the path itself.

2. The IPersistFile interface has been written for you. You can find it in the file CPERFILE.CPP. Examine it until you feel comfortable with it.

3. When the user picks "Copy File Link" from the menu, we need to create a moniker and place it on the Clipboard for the use of a potential client. In the file MAINWIND.CPP, case WM_COMMAND, subcase ID_EDIT_COPYFILELINK, use the API function CreateFileMoniker( ) to create a file moniker. You will find the name of the currently open file in the variable pFileDataObj->m_wFileName, and you must store the resulting moniker pointer in the local variable pFileMoniker. Note that the moniker is released at the end of the message case.

4. In order to transfer the moniker to the Clipboard, we instantiate an object of class CMonikerData, passing it a pointer to the moniker in its constructor, which calls AddRef( ) on the moniker pointer. In the file CMONIKERDATA.CPP, modify the GetData( ) method. Create a stream on an HGLOBAL via the API function CreateStreamOnHGlobal, place it in the output STGMEDIUM structure. Use the API function OleSaveToStream( ) to instruct the moniker to save itself into the stream. Build and run your server app, paste a link into the client app and save the client's file. Use the DocFile viewer to look at the client's file. You should see a stream named "Moniker" whose contents are similar to those in step 5 of the client example lab.

5. Now we want to do transfer a composite moniker based on a partial selection in the server's edit control. In the subcase ID_EDIT_COPYFILEITEMLINK, create a file moniker as before. Create an item moniker using the string wout, which is a wide character string containing the beginning and ending characters selected by the user. Use the API function CreateGenericComposite( ) to combine the file and item monikers together into a composite moniker. The code to put the composite moniker on the Clipboard has already been written for you.

6. When the client binds to the composite moniker, the IOleItemContainer interface comes into play. It has been written for you in the file ITEMCONT.CPP. Examine it until you feel comfortable.

This page intentionally contains no text other than this sentence.

Chapter 9

Custom Interfaces

A. WHY USE CUSTOM INTERFACES ?

1. Why would you want to expose your app's capabilities to the world by writing your own COM interfaces? What's wrong with just using DLLs, which were touted as the magic bullet of component software for the first seven or eight years of Windows' existence?

When a client app links to a DLL, the DLL's name is hard coded inside the client app. The DLL must be located in the client app's directory or in the system path. With a custom COM interface, the name and location of the server are found in the registry, so servers can be moved or changed without changing the client.

A DLL exposes all of its functions in a flat programming model. There is no notion of hierarchy of functions within a DLL. This makes it hard for a single DLL to provide more than one set of functions to the world. The interface-oriented COM programming model makes it easier to combine several groups of functions within the same DLL without them stepping on each other's toes.

Versioning becomes much, much easier because each new version of an interface has its own ID. A new release of a server can contain within it the code to support any previous versions, thereby eliminating the proliferation of DLLs for each version (VBRUN100.DLL, VBRUN200.DLL, etc.). Because a client app queries at runtime for the interfaces it wants, the server can load code for outdated features only if requested. Conversely, a new client that can use the latest features but finds an old server can gracefully degrade to use only those features supported by the server rather than crashing with an "undefined dynlink" error.

DLL functions by definition had to live in a DLL on the same machine as the client app. A COM object's server can live in an .EXE file as well as a DLL, and even on a different machine somewhere on a network.

Kraig Brockschmidt expounded on these points in much more detail (for example, four full pages on versioning) in two articles entitled "How OLE and COM Solve the Problems of Component Software Design" and "How COM Solves the Problems of Component Software Design, Part II" in the May and June 1996 issues of *Microsoft Systems Journal*.

2. When writing your own interfaces, why would you choose a VTBL-based custom interface over an IDispatch interface as shown in the OLE Automation chapter? The primary drawback of a VTBL-based interface is that it is harder to use from an interpreted language such as a web browser; however, a VTBL interface has three main advantages:

The overhead of a VTBL function call is much lower than that of a dispinterface function call. The client doesn't have to pack up all the parameters into a bunch of VARIANT structures. The server doesn't have to check the number of parameters or their types. All of this gets compiled away instead of being performed at runtime on every function call. The sample app in \chap09\eliza provides an easy way for you to measure this overhead. On a Pentium 120, a call to an in-proc server VTBL interface passing a single string and receiving a single string took 1.8 microseconds, while a call to the same method on an IDispatch interface took 94 microseconds. This doesn't sound like much, but who has microseconds to waste? Also, the IDispatch overhead will get much worse as more and larger parameters are added, whereas the VTBL will not degrade as much, particularly if large parameters are passed by reference.

In a call to a dispinterface function, you can only pass the types of parameters that are contained in a VARIANT structure. The most annoying part of this restriction is that you cannot pass a structure of any type. A VTBL function call does not have this restriction. Think about even a very simple interface such as IDataObject, with its FORMATETC and STGMEDIUM structures. You will have to work hard to implement a workaround for passing these via a dispinterface, costing more performance, and worst of all, delaying ship dates by taking longer to develop.

3. Which do you choose? In practice, an in-proc server with a VTBL interface is easiest for you to write and easiest for your compiled clients to use. If your client apps are going to be compiled, or if you need the last scrap of performance, you probably want a VTBL interface. If your clients are interpreted, marketing considerations will probably require that you provide a dispinterface.

4. If you can't make up your mind, you can supply both a dispinterface and a VTBL interface. You can supply them separately, with different class factories. Or you can use the much-touted dual interface, which is a custom interface derived from IDispatch, allowing interpreted clients to use the dispinterface and compiled clients to use the VTBL interface. Dual interfaces are described beginning on page 294.

I find very few of my customers going this route, however. They find that if they need a dispinterface for marketing reasons, compiled clients can use it fairly easily by generating a wrapper class as shown in Chapter 4, and that providing a VTBL interface in addition is not worth even the small amount of extra development time it takes.

B. ACCESSING AN INTERFACE

1. As shown in the diagram below, when a client process creates or receives an object from an in-proc (DLL) server, the object resides completely within the address space of the client process. Calls made to an object's functions are thus direct VTBL calls with parameters passed on the stack, which makes for very fast, very efficient execution and easy development.

When an object server is a local server (different process, same machine) or remote server (different machine connected via network), the client cannot simply make direct calls to the object's interface methods, as the object's code resides in a different process and possibly a different machine. Rather, when the object is created, COM creates an *object proxy* in the client's address space. The proxy exposes the same functions and accepts the same parameters as the object, but the proxy does not contain the object's actual functionality. Instead, the proxy communicates via remote procedure calls with a *stub* in the server's address space. The stub actually calls the object's methods in the server's address space and passes the results back to the proxy, which in turn passes them back to the client.

When a client calls an object's methods via this proxy/stub mechanism, the transfer of data between client and server is known as *marshaling*. COM provides marshaling support for all of its standard interfaces. If you want to write your own custom interface that can be used from local and remote servers, you must provide marshaling support for this interface. Strangely enough, it isn't that hard.

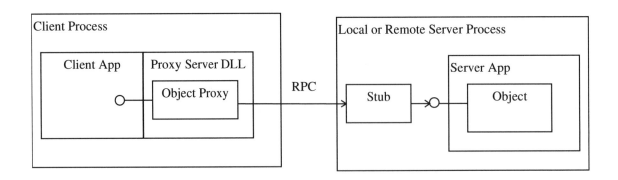

280

C. Simple Custom Interface, In-proc Server

1. Implementing a custom interface in an in-proc server is quite simple. Suppose we have a sample of the old "Eliza" psychotherapy program that we want to provide to the world via COM. Let's create a custom interface called *IEliza*, derived (as all COM interfaces must be) from IUnknown. Our interface will contain a single member function called IEliza::Complain( ), which takes the patient's complaint as an input string, and returns Eliza's response as a string in a caller-supplied buffer.

We use the GUIDGEN.EXE utility program to generate a 16-byte GUID to identify this interface. We then write a C++ class definition file similar to those provided by Microsoft for the standard interfaces. The keyword **interface** is used to denote a COM interface; it is actually #defined as **struct**. Each member function must return an HRESULT, must use the **__stdcall** calling convention, and must be declared as pure virtual. The interface's definition file looks like this:

```
<file IELIZA.H>

#include <windows.h>

/*
Interface ID for the IEliza interface.   Generated via the utility app
GUIDGEN.EXE.
*/

static const GUID IID_IEliza = {0x35fc0c40, 0xc4fa, 0x11ce,
    {0xad, 0x55, 0x0, 0x60, 0x8c, 0x86, 0xb8, 0x9c}} ;


/*
Our custom interface, which only has one method. It is derived, as are
all COM interfaces without exception, from IUnknown.
*/

interface IEliza : public IUnknown
{
    virtual HRESULT __stdcall Complain (LPOLESTR pIn, LPOLESTR pOut) =0;
} ;
```

2. To implement the IEliza interface, we will write our own class called CEliza that provides the member functions required by the definition of IEliza. This is similar to what we did in Chapters 1 and 2, writing our own classes which implemented the IDropTarget and IDataObject interfaces. Our CEliza header file looks like this:

```
<file CELIZA.h>

#include <windows.h>
#include "ieliza.h"

class  CEliza : public IEliza
{
    protected:
        ULONG            m_RefCount;


    public:
        CEliza  (void);
        ~CEliza (void);

        //IUnknown members

        STDMETHODIMP          QueryInterface(REFIID, LPVOID*);
        STDMETHODIMP_(ULONG) AddRef(void);
        STDMETHODIMP_(ULONG) Release(void);

        //IEliza members

        STDMETHODIMP          Complain (LPOLESTR, LPOLESTR);
};
```

3. The implementation of the methods is similar to those we have seen before. In a DLL, it's not that complicated. If you've understood the book to this point, it works like you think it ought to. The QueryInterface( ) and other IUnknown methods look almost identical to those we have seen before, the only difference being the inclusion of our own custom interface ID **IID_IEliza**, in QueryInterface( ). We then implement the methods of our own interface as in the **IEliza::Complain**( ) example shown here. The code for faking the responses of a shrink lives in the sample code file "eliza.c", for anyone interested. Thus:

```
#include <celiza.h>

/*
Standard query interface method, only new thing is our custom interface
GUID IID_IEliza.
*/

STDMETHODIMP CEliza::QueryInterface(REFIID riid, LPVOID *ppv)
{
    if (riid == IID_IUnknown || riid == IID_IEliza)
    {
      *ppv = (LPVOID)this;
      AddRef( ) ;
      return NOERROR;
    }
    else
    {
      *ppv = NULL ;
      return E_NOINTERFACE;
    }

}


/*
This is the only new method in the IEliza custom interface.  The
function Eliza( ), which fakes the role of a psychotherapist, lives in
the file "eliza.c".  The caller's complaint is in the character array
pIn.  Eliza considers it, and places her reply in the buffer pointed to
by pOut.
*/

STDMETHODIMP CEliza::Complain (LPOLESTR pIn, LPOLESTR pOut)
{
    Eliza (pIn, pOut) ;
    return NOERROR ;
}
```

4. That's all we need to do for a single-threaded DLL. WARNING: The seeming simplicity of this case is very attractive, but be WARNED ! It only applies when the server and the client are using the same threading model. See Chapter 13.

D. CUSTOM INTERFACE CLIENT

1. The client who uses the custom interface does not do anything different at all, that's the whole point of COM. The operating system jumps through a few hoops to arrange the connection between the object's client and server, then gets out of the way while they talk to each other. The following code should look almost identical to the IDataObject client code shown in Chapter 2, because it IS almost identical:

```
IEliza *pEliza = NULL ;          // ptr to custom IEliza interface
CLSID CLSID_Eliza ;              // class ID of Eliza object
extern HWND hInWnd, hOutWnd ;

/*
Ask COM to create us an object of the class CLSID_Eliza, and give us
back a pointer to the IEliza interface on the object.
*/

case ID_ELIZA_CREATEINPROC:
{
    HRESULT hr ;

    hr = CoCreateInstance (
      CLSID_Eliza,              // Eliza object ID from registry
      NULL,                     // standalone object, no aggregation
      CLSCTX_INPROC_SERVER,     // in-proc server
      IID_IEliza,               // IEliza custom interface ID
      (LPVOID *) &pEliza) ;     // output variable

    return 0 ;
}


case IDC_SEND:
{
    char WinText [256], in [256]  ;

/*
Get user's complaint from the edit control where he enters it.  Call
the method IEliza::Complain( ) to pass it on to Eliza and get her
response.  Place response in the output window.
*/
    if (pEliza)
    {
        GetWindowText (hOutWnd, WinText, sizeof(WinText)) ;

        pEliza->Complain (WinText, in) ;

        SendMessage (hInWnd, EM_SETSEL, (WPARAM) -1, (LPARAM)-1) ;
        SendMessage (hInWnd, EM_REPLACESEL, 0, (LPARAM) in) ;
    }

    return 0 ;
}
```

E. Local Server, Standard Marshaling

1. Suppose we can't or don't want to place the Eliza server in a DLL. Perhaps we have an existing ELIZA.EXE app that has its own user interface, and we now want to expose its functionality via COM so that other programs can use it. Our 10 year old spaghetti code can't be easily extracted into a DLL, so we have to somehow provide a custom interface directly from our .EXE. Writing the IEliza interface is the same as it was for the DLL in the previous example, but because we now live in an .EXE, we need to provide the proxies and stubs shown on page 280.

2. Proxies and stubs are created by COM when the client calls a function or method that returns an interface pointer, such as CoCreateInstance( ) or IUnknown::QueryInterface( ). After the server returns the interface pointer to COM, but before COM returns the interface pointer to the client, COM creates the proxy and stub for the specified interface and returns to the client a pointer to the proxy. This process is called *marshaling the interface pointer.*

3. COM uses the operating system's RPC mechanism to create proxies and stubs for marshaling its standard interfaces. Suppose a client calls the API function CoGetClassObject( ), which returns a pointer to the class factory object that manufactures a specified class of object. If the class factory is provided by a local or remote server, COM will need to create a proxy and stub and return to the client a pointer to the proxy. In other words, COM needs to marshal the IClassFactory interface pointer into the client's address space. How does COM accomplish this?

After obtaining the pointer to the class factory from the server, but before returning it to the client, COM looks in the HKEY_CLASSES_ROOT\Interface section of the registry for a key containing the interface's IID. Under that key COM will find a subkey "ProxyStubClsid32", containing the class ID of the server that produces the proxies and stubs. In the example below, the IClassFactory interface has the class ID {00000001-0000-0000-C000-000000000046}. Looking in the registry, we see that the proxy and stub for this interface are produced by the server whose class ID is {00000320-0000-0000-C000-000000000046}. Before returning from CoGetClassObject( ), COM will wake up the proxy/stub server registered for the IClassFactory interface, make it create a proxy and stub, and return the proxy pointer to the client.

4. The proxies and stubs are produced at runtime by an object that supports the barely documented interface *IPSFactoryBuffer*. Its member functions are:

CreateProxy( )   *// create client-side proxy for marshaling specified interface*
CreateStub( )   *// create server-side stub for marshaling specified interface.*

As you can see from the registry below, the server that produces the proxies and stubs for the IClassFactory interface is the system DLL OLE32.DLL.

5. To marshal our custom IEliza interface, we need to provide a proxy/stub factory server in a manner similar to that used for the standard interfaces. We could do it the hard way by writing all the code ourselves, but that would be extremely bloody (more than it looks from the simple example shown here, see Brockschmidt, pp. 290-295). Or we could do it the (relatively) easy way by using the programming tools supplied for the operating system's RPC mechanism to generate the server for us.

The tool used in RPC is the MIDL compiler, which comes with the Win32 SDK but not with VC++. We write a source file in Microsoft's *Interface Descriptor Language* (.IDL). We run the MIDL compiler over it, which produces C language source files containing the proxy and stub code. We than add a .DEF file to export the required names and build these into a DLL as shown in the following diagram. We make a few registry entries, and off we go. Sounds simple ? It mostly is.

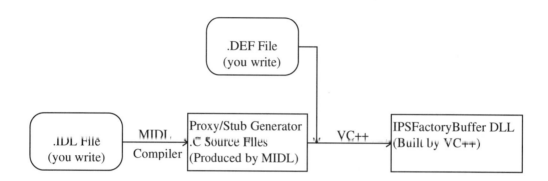

6. IDL language is a strongly typed language used for the description of RPC operations. The ODL language used for type libraries can be considered a subset of it. The .IDL file describing the IEliza interface is shown below. The .IDL for IUnknown is incorporated by reference via the keyword `import`, you will find this file in the directory "mstools\include." The uuid specified is the interface ID for the IEliza interface. The IDL directives for the Complain( ) method describe the type and direction of the data marshaling to be performed. See the .IDL reference manual for further details.

```
<file eliza.idl>

/*
IEliza interface ID
*/

[uuid(35FC0C40-C4FA-11ce-AD55-00608C86B89C), object]

interface IEliza:IUnknown
{

/*
IUnknown methods incorporated by reference.
*/
    import "unknwn.idl" ;

/*
IEliza custom methods.  IDL directives describe the direction of data
marshaling required.
*/

    HRESULT  Complain ([in] LPOLESTR pIn,
      [out, size_is(256)] LPOLESTR pOut) ;
}
```

7. Once you have the .IDL file, you run the MIDL compiler on it. A batch file that does this for the file shown is:

```
<file midlme.bat>

midl /ms_ext /app_config /c_ext eliza.idl
```

8. Running MIDL as shown will produce the .C files "dlldata.c", "eliza_i.c", and "eliza_c.c". The latter is where most of the code resides. You make a new .DLL project in VC++, using these three files. You must also add the import library RPCRT4.LIB, which contains references to the operating system's RPC functions, to the linker input list. Thus:

9. You must also create and include in your project a .DEF file which tells the linker to export by name the functions DllGetClassObject( ), DllCanUnloadNow( ), and GetProxyDllInfo( ), as shown below. You do not have to write any code, all of it is in the proxy/stub code generated for you by MIDL. The first two you have seen before, the last one is new here. It provides the IPSFactoryBuffer interface to COM in the same way that DllGetClassObject( ) provided the IClassFactory interface. The DLL produced by building this project is the proxy/stub generator.

```
LIBRARY     ELIZAPRX
DESCRIPTION IEliza Interface Proxy/Stub DLL

EXPORTS     DllGetClassObject
            DllCanUnloadNow
            GetProxyDllInfo
```

10. Now that we have our custom proxy/stub generator DLL, we need to tell COM where to look for it and how to use it. Once you have done this, COM will support standard marshaling for this interface for the use of any local or remote server. This is exactly the same mechanism as COM uses for its standard interfaces.

As you saw for the standard interfaces, we must make entries in the HKEY_CLASSES_ROOT\Interface section of the registry specifying the server that produces the proxy and stub for marshaling this interface. The requisite keys and values are:

```
HKEY_CLASSES_ROOT
   Interface
     <interface IID>
        BaseInterface = <IID of interface from which this one derives, IUnknown if absent>
        NumMethods = <Total # of methods in your interface, including any base interface(s)>
        ProxyStubClsid32 = <class ID of server providing IPSFactoryBuffer for this interface>
```

In our IEliza example, these entries are:

```
HKEY_CLASSES_ROOT
   Interface
     {35FC0C40-C4FA-11ce-AD55-00608C86B89C} = IEliza Custom Interface
     {35FC0C40-C4FA-11ce-AD55-00608C86B89C}\NumMethods = 4
     {35FC0C40-C4FA-11ce-AD55-00608C86B89C}\ProxyStubClsid32 =
        {35FC0C40-C4FA-11ce-AD55-00608C86B89C}  ;(sic)
```

Note that the interface ID and the proxy/stub server's class ID are identical. This is necessary when using MIDL to generate the proxy/stub code. The last line above is not a typo. They do not conflict because they are used in completely different contexts. See Brockschmidt, pg. 328.

You also need to make the standard InProcServer32 entry in the CLSID section of the registry so that COM can find the IPSFactoryBuffer server. A human-readable app name with a CLSID key is not necessary. Note that the server's CLSID and the interface's IID are the same.

```
HKEY_CLASSES_ROOT
   CLSID
     {35FC0C40-C4FA-11ce-AD55-00608C86B89C} = IEliza Proxy/Stub Factory
     {35FC0C40-C4FA-11ce-AD55-00608C86B89C}\InProcServer32 =
        C:\EssenceOfOle\chap09\eliza\localsv\done\midl\elizaprx.dll
```

F. STANDARD MARSHALING VIA A TYPE LIBRARY

1. The foregoing wasn't too hard to do and it was pretty flexible. The problem with it is that we need to provide a separate proxy/stub DLL to go along with out .EXE server; one more logistical headache. It would be cool if we could somehow describe the interface to COM at run time and have it roll a marshaler on the spot.

It turns out that this isn't very hard to do. COM already has the requisite knowledge for runtime marshaling because it needs to marshal the parameters of OLE Automation calls. We can tap into this same capability for custom interfaces by providing a type library to COM and telling COM to look there for marshaling information. The main drawback of this strategy is that it can only handle parameters of the types that OLE Automation supports; that is, the types that can be held in a VARIANT structure.

2. To take advantage of type library marshaling in our Eliza server, we have to do a couple of things. I first modified the CEliza::Complain( ) method to use BSTRs instead of standard string pointers, because COM's standard marshaler only supports the former. I next added an .ODL file to the project to create a type library for it. This type library contains the description of the custom interface. In this example, I use a new interface called ITypeLibMarshaledEliza to prevent a conflict with the previous IEliza custom interface. The .ODL keyword **oleautomation** signals COM that this interface contains only parameters of the types supported by OLE automation. The sample code is in the directory \chap09\eliza\TypeLibMarshaled. The .ODL file looks like this:

```
[ uuid(088AFA01-DB7C-11d0-9121-00608C86B89C), version(1.0) ]

library TypeLibMarshaledElizaTlb
{
    importlib("stdole32.tlb");

// definition of interface

    [ uuid(088AFA02-DB7C-11d0-9121-00608C86B89C), oleautomation]

    interface ITypeLibMarshaledEliza : IUnknown
    {
      HRESULT Complain (BSTR *pIn, BSTR *pOut) ;
    };

// declaration of coclass

    [ uuid(088AFA00-DB7C-11d0-9121-00608C86B89C) ]

    coclass TypeLibMarshaledEliza
    {
      [default] interface ITypeLibMarshaledEliza ;
    };
};
```

3. To tell COM how to marshal our interface, we need to make registry entries describing it. We place the interface ID of our new custom interface in the \Interface section as before. The ProxyStubClsid32 key will always have the value "{00020424-0000-0000-C000-000000000046}", which is the class ID of COM's standard marshaler.

We now add a new key called "TypeLib", which contains the GUID of the registered type library in which the description of this interface may be found. In this case, the value is "{088AFA01-DB7C-11d0-9121-00608C86B89C}", which as you will see on the preceding page, is the GUID of the type library itself. This type library must also be registered in the standard manner for type libraries, described in Chapter 4. In the supplied example, I bound the type library into my .EXE file as a resource so I wouldn't have the logistical hassle of two different files, so if you look in the .REG file in the sample directory, you will find that the registered type library path points back to the .EXE. Thus:

HKEY_CLASSES_ROOT
   Interface
     <interface IID>
       ProxyStubClsid32 = {00020424-0000-0000-C000-000000000046}
       TypeLib = <GUID of type library describing this interface>

293

G. DUAL INTERFACES

1. What is a dual interface and why do you care ? A dual interface is an interface which supports the same functionality via both an IDispatch and also a VTBL interface. The former allows flexibility from interpreted client; the latter allows speed from a compiled client. The IEliza interface provided via a dual interface would look like this:

```
#include <windows.h>

/*
Interface ID for the IDualEliza interface
*/

static const GUID IID_IDualEliza =
{ 0x98da18b2, 0xdb73, 0x11d0, { 0x91, 0x21, 0x0, 0x60, 0x8c, 0x86,
0xb8, 0x9c } };

interface IDualEliza : public IDispatch
{
    virtual HRESULT __stdcall Complain (BSTR *pIn, BSTR *pOut) = 0;
} ;
```

2. Dual interfaces are pound-for-pound the subject of more hype and more outrageous hype than any other feature of COM. In reality, they just aren't that important, neither in their presence nor in their absence. They don't cost much to put in, but neither do they buy your clients much additional functionality. When some evangelist gets misty-eyed over the glories of supporting both early binding and late binding, ask him, "Oh yeah? How does that make me any money?" The answer will be, "Not all that often, and then not very much." But they should follow up by saying, "But they don't cost much to do, either."

Either your object requires an IDispatch interface for marketing reasons or it doesn't. If it doesn't, then you don't care about dual interfaces at all. The major client app that required an IDispatch used to be Visual Basic, but VB 5 knows how to use a type library to call VTBL interfaces without needing an IDispatch, as demonstrated in the previous section. The major application for run-time connection to interfaces is a Web browser, which doesn't know what objects and what scripts it will be executing until the user surfs to a relevant page.

If you do need an IDispatch interface, then what about compiled clients? They can easily access your IDispatch with a wrapper class, which Class Wizard or other tools will generate in all of ten seconds. As discussed in the beginning of this chapter, this will cost some amount of calling overhead compared to a straight VTBL call. **Eliminating this overhead while retaining compatibility with IDispatch clients is the sole advantage of a dual interface.** How much overhead? Ballpark value, a few hundred microseconds per call. This overhead is small enough that it gets swamped by the larger overhead of marshaling to another process or thread, so **you only collect this advantage in the case where the client has a direct (proxyless) connection to your object**.

3. OK, dual interfaces don't buy me much except the latest buzzword, what do they cost me? Again, the answer is not all that much. There is the relatively small amount of additional work in programming the dual interface. As I will show on the following pages, it is almost free. In the ATL, it actually is free; you would have to work to take it out. The VTBL portion of your interface will only be able to handle automation compatible parameters, which shouldn't be a big problem if you are already supporting an IDispatch. The main drawback is not in development, but in testing and support– since the timing of the two accesses is different, you have to QA them both for each release. When a client reports a bug, you have to find out which entry he's using, which he frequently won't know and which you'll have to train your support staff to ask. It looks cheap, but some of the costs are hidden.

4. Suppose we have decided that we need to support a dual interface for our object. What do we have to do. It's fairly simple. You write a custom interface that is compatible with the automation parameter types as described in the previous section. You derive your custom interface not from IUnknown, but rather from IDispatch, as shown on the previous page. You then use the keyword **dual** in your .ODL file to designate your interface as a dual interface. You also must assign dispatch ID attributes to each of your interface's custom methods. In the example below, we specify that the method IDualEliza::Complain( ) is to be accessed via IDispatch::Invoke( ) with a dispatch ID of 1. Thus:

You write a type library that looks like this:

```
[ uuid(98DA18B1-DB73-11d0-9121-00608C86B89C), version(1.0) ]

library DualElizaTlb
{
    importlib("stdole32.tlb");

// declaration of IDualEliza dual interface

    [ uuid(98DA18B2-DB73-11d0-9121-00608C86B89C), dual, oleautomation ]

    interface IDualEliza : IDispatch
    {
      [id(1)] HRESULT Complain (BSTR *pIn, BSTR *pOut) ;
    };

// declaration of coclass

    [ uuid(98DA18B0-DB73-11d0-9121-00608C86B89C) ]

    coclass DualEliza
    {
      [default] interface IDualEliza ;
    };
};
```

5. Your dual interface server will derive a new class that implements the specified interface. The IDualEliza implementation looks like this:

```
#include <windows.h>
#include "idualeliza.h"

class  CEliza : public IDualEliza
{
    protected:
      ULONG             m_RefCount ;
      ITypeInfo *       m_pTypeInfo ;

    public:
      HWND              m_hWnd ;
      HWND              m_hEdit ;

    CEliza   (void);
    ~CEliza (void);

    //IUnknown members

    STDMETHODIMP        QueryInterface(REFIID, LPVOID*);
    STDMETHODIMP_(ULONG) AddRef(void);
    STDMETHODIMP_(ULONG) Release(void);

    // IDispatch members

    STDMETHODIMP GetTypeInfoCount(UINT *pctinfo) ;
    STDMETHODIMP GetTypeInfo(UINT, LCID, ITypeInfo **pptinfo) ;
    STDMETHODIMP GetIDsOfNames(REFIID, LPOLESTR *, UINT, LCID,DISPID*);
    STDMETHODIMP Invoke(DISPID, REFIID, LCID lcid, WORD, DISPPARAMS *,
      VARIANT *, EXCEPINFO *, UINT *) ;

    //IEliza members

    STDMETHODIMP Complain (BSTR *, BSTR *);

};
```

5. You now have to implement the methods of your interface. It's trivially easy if you delegate to a type info. Thus:

```
extern GUID GUID_DualElizaInterface ;

CEliza::CEliza (void)
{
    m_RefCount = 1 ;
/*
Get the type info of this object.
*/
    ITypeLib* pTypeLib; HRESULT hr ;

/*
Load our type library from the registry.
*/
    hr = LoadRegTypeLib(GUID_DualElizaTypeLib, 1, 0, 0, &pTypeLib);
/*
Get from the library the type info that describes our custom interface.
*/
    hr = pTypeLib->GetTypeInfoOfGuid(GUID_DualElizaInterface,
      &m_pTypeInfo);
    pTypeLib->Release();
}


/*
Method IDispatch::GetIDsOfNames. Delegate it to our object's type info.
*/

STDMETHODIMP CEliza::GetIDsOfNames (REFIID riid, LPOLESTR* rgszNames,
    UINT cNames, LCID lcid, DISPID* rgdispid)
{
    return m_pTypeInfo->GetIDsOfNames(rgszNames, cNames, rgdispid);
}


/*
Method IDispatch::Invoke. Delegate it to our object's type info.
*/

STDMETHODIMP CEliza::Invoke(DISPID dispidMember, REFIID riid,
      LCID lcid, WORD wFlags, DISPPARAMS* pdispparams,
      VARIANT* pvarResult, EXCEPINFO* pexcepinfo, UINT* puArgErr)
{
    return m_pTypeInfo->Invoke(this, dispidMember, wFlags,
      pdispparams, pvarResult, pexcepinfo, puArgErr);
}
```

6. A Visual Basic demonstration program is given in the directory \chap09\eliza\dual\vbdemo.

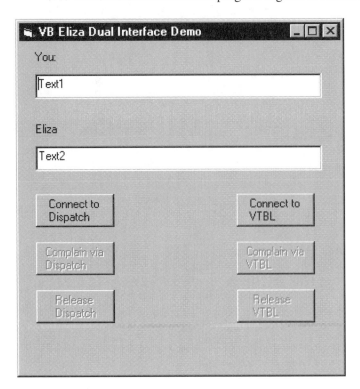

To use a dual interface in VB, you choose "Project — References" from the main menu. It will show you the following dialog box containing all the type libraries currently registered on your system. You check the one that describes your server. Thus:

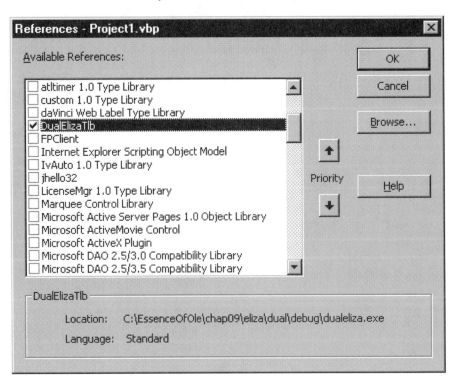

7. To tell VB to use the type library to connect to the object, you DIM the object as the specified type. When you create the object, you don't use the call CreateObject( ), a generic function which would bind to the IDispatch. You use the "new" operator, which examines the type library to figure out how to handle an object of the specified type. In this case, finding that the object is described as having a VTBL, VB is smart enough to use it. The code then looks like this:

```
' Tell VB that the ElizaVTBL object is the type that it finds described
' in the type library.

Dim ElizaVTBL As DualEliza

' User clicked the "Connect VTBL" button. Create the object and connect
' to its VTBL

Private Sub btn_ConnectVTBL_Click()
    If ElizaVTBL Is Nothing Then
        Set ElizaVTBL = New DualEliza

        btn_ComplainVTBL.Enabled = True
        btn_ReleaseVTBL.Enabled = True
        btn_ConnectVTBL.Enabled = False

    End If
End Sub


' User clicked "Complain" button. Call the complain( ) method. Because
' this object is described in a type library, VB will use the VTBL
entry
' and not the dispatch entry. Since the server is in a .EXE in another
' process, it won't be faster enough to notice.

Private Sub btn_ComplainVTBL_Click()
    Dim Complaint As String
    Dim Response As String

    Complaint = Text1.Text
    Call ElizaVTBL.Complain(Complaint, Response)
    Text2.Text = Response

End Sub
```

H. LOCAL SERVER, CUSTOM MARSHALING

1. In the previous section of this chapter, we created standard marshaling support for our IEliza interface in a local server. It works, it's simple, it wasn't that hard to write, but the problem is that it is slow, about a factor of 100 slower than an in-process server which requires no marshaling at all. Suppose we want to try to speed up our local server. Instead of using the standard marshaling that MIDL gives us, we can use our intimate knowledge of the conversation between the client and server to write our own proxies and stubs which will be much faster than the lowest common denominator provided by MIDL. By doing this, we will be able to speed it up by a factor of about 10 compared to standard marshaling, leaving it still about a factor of 10 slower than an in-proc server.

2. Every COM object server has the right to control its own data marshaling if it prefers, rather than accept the standard marshaling that COM provides. You may provide custom marshaling for your own custom interfaces, or even for standard COM interfaces such as IDataObject. You may choose to provide custom marshaling in order to optimize throughput, or to provide features that COM doesn't yet support.

3. The whole point of custom marshaling is that the server vendor provides both proxy and stub. Because these are both written by the same source, they can use their intimate knowledge of their communication mechanism to optimize throughput.

4. Custom marshaling consists of two parts. First, the server app must create and establish communication with the object proxy that resides in the client's address space (marshaling the interface pointer, as explained on page 286). This is done via the *IMarshal* interface, which both server and proxy must support. The use of the IMarshal interface is shown in the diagram on page 302. Whenever a server provides an object pointer to COM, such as in the methods IClassFactory::CreateInstance( ) or IUnknown::QueryInterface( ), before setting up standard marshaling, COM will call that object's QueryInterface( ) method to see if it supports IMarshal. If not, COM will attempt to provide standard interface marshaling as described in the previous section. If the object wants to perform its own marshaling, it does so by returning a pointer to the IMarshal interface, whose methods are:

GetUnmarshalClass ( )	*// get class ID of client-side in-process proxy object*
GetMarshalSizeMax ( )	*// get size of marshaling data packet*
MarshalInterface ( )	*// fill packet with marshaling data and send to proxy*
UnmarshalInterface ( )	*// proxy receives marshaling data from server*
ReleaseMarshalData ( )	*// proxy signals completion of marshaling process*
DisconnectObject ( )	*// inform client that server has disconnected*

5. Once the IMarshal interface establishes communication between the proxy and the object server, it falls out of the picture. The proxy and server communicate via whatever inter-process communication mechanism you decide to write. In the provided example, the IEliza::Complain( ) method is implemented by means of a shared memory-mapped file. The two apps place their data in a shared RAM bank and signal each other by means of events, as shown in the diagram below.

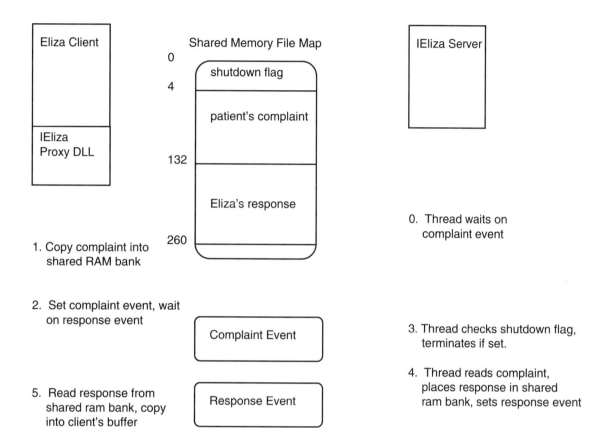

| Eliza Client | | Shared Memory File Map | | IEliza Server |

1. Copy complaint into shared RAM bank

2. Set complaint event, wait on response event

5. Read response from shared ram bank, copy into client's buffer

0. Thread waits on complaint event

3. Thread checks shutdown flag, terminates if set.

4. Thread reads complaint, places response in shared ram bank, sets response event

6. The process of marshaling the interface pointer is controlled by the methods of the IMarshal interface. The sequence of events is shown in the following diagram:

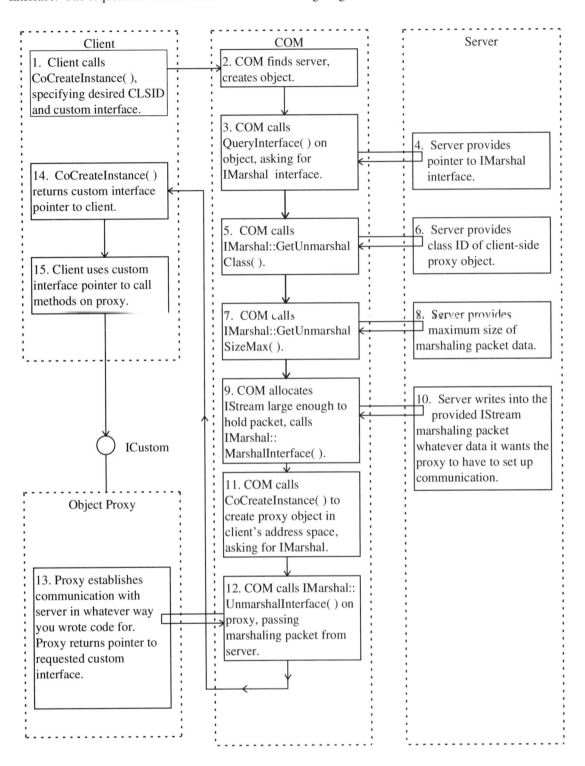

7. To implement our custom marshaling server, we create a class that supports both the IMarshal and IEliza interfaces. It contains member variables for performing the marshaling operation. In this sample app, the stub shown on page 280 is built into the server for simplicity, rather than being a separate entity. Thus:

```
#include <windows.h>
#include "ieliza.h"

/*
Class ID for client-side proxy.
*/

static const GUID CLSID_ElizaProxy =
    { 0x402f6bd0, 0xcb37, 0x11ce, { 0x84, 0x9c, 0xca, 0x8d, 0xf3, 0x9c,
    0x7d, 0x1b } };

class  CElizaServer : public IEliza, public IMarshal
{
    protected:
        ULONG           m_RefCount ;
    public:
      TCHAR       m_ShareName [128] ;
      HANDLE      m_hMap ;
      HANDLE      m_hComplaintEvent ;
      HANDLE      m_hResponseEvent ;
      HANDLE      m_hThread ;
      LPTSTR      m_pSharedMem ;
      DWORD       m_ThreadID ;

      CEliza  (LPOLESTR);
        ~CEliza (void);

    //IUnknown members

    STDMETHODIMP            QueryInterface(REFIID, LPVOID*);
    STDMETHODIMP_(ULONG) AddRef(void);
    STDMETHODIMP_(ULONG) Release(void);

    //IEliza members

    STDMETHODIMP            Complain (LPOLESTR, LPOLESTR);

    // IMarshal members

    STDMETHODIMP GetUnmarshalClass (REFIID, VOID*, DWORD, VOID*, DWORD,
      CLSID *) ;
    STDMETHODIMP GetMarshalSizeMax (REFIID, VOID*, DWORD, VOID*, DWORD,
      DWORD *) ;
    STDMETHODIMP MarshalInterface (IStream *, REFIID , VOID * , DWORD,
      VOID *, DWORD) ;
    STDMETHODIMP UnmarshalInterface (IStream *, REFIID, VOID **) ;
    STDMETHODIMP ReleaseMarshalData (IStream * ) ;
    STDMETHODIMP DisconnectObject ( DWORD ) ;
};
```

8. The first thing that COM will do after getting your object's IMarshal interface pointer is to call the method **IMarshal::GetUnmarshalClass( )**. COM is asking for the class ID of the in-proc server that provides the proxy object. This must be a standard in-proc server DLL with standard registry entries that implements the client side of the custom marshaling interface. Thus:

```
static const GUID CLSID_ElizaProxy =
{ 0x402f6bd0, 0xcb37, 0x11ce, { 0x84, 0x9c, 0xca, 0x8d, 0xf3, 0x9c,
0x7d, 0x1b } };

STDMETHODIMP CElizaServer::GetUnmarshalClass (REFIID riid, VOID* pVoid,
    DWORD dwDestCtx, VOID*, DWORD, CLSID *pClsid )
{

/*
Custom marshaling is provided on a per-interface basis, signaled by the
first parameter.  A different proxy can be used for each interface.
This object only knows how to marshal the IEliza interface.  Anything
else is an error, in which case COM will try to set up standard
marshaling for the requested interface.
*/
    if (riid != IID_IEliza)
    {
      *pClsid = IID_NULL ;
      return E_FAIL ;
    }
/*
The supplied context flags describe the relation between the processes.
The particular scheme we have implemented here depends on the two
objects running on the same machine.  If they aren't, fail with an
error.
*/

    if (dwDestCtx != MSHCTX_LOCAL)
    {
      *pClsid = IID_NULL ;
      return E_FAIL ;
    }

/*
Return the class ID of the server that provides our proxy DLL
*/

    *pClsid = CLSID_ElizaProxy ;
    return S_OK ;

}
```

9. COM will next transmit a block of data from the server to the client proxy. This data block is called the *marshaling packet*, and is transmitted by means of a stream. Its contents can be anything that the server wants the client to know so that they can establish communication. In this example, it is the base name from which the server has generated the names it uses for the shared memory file map and related events.

COM will first call the method **IMarshal::GetMarshalSizeMax( )** to find the maximum amount of memory it needs to allocate for the marshaling packet. Thus:

```
STDMETHODIMP CElizaServer::GetMarshalSizeMax (REFIID riid, VOID* pv,
    DWORD dwDestCtx, VOID* pvReserved, DWORD dwFlags, DWORD *pSize)
{

/*
COM is asking for the maximum size of the marshaling packet.  In this
case, it is the size of the name we are using for the shared file map
and the events.
*/

    *pSize = sizeof(m_ShareName) ;
    return S_OK ;
}
```

10. Next, COM calls the method **IMarshal::MarshalInterface( )**, passing it a pointer to the marshaling packet stream which will be sent to the proxy. The server uses the method IStream::Write( ) to write into the stream whatever data it wants to send to the proxy so that the latter knows how to set up the custom marshaling. In this example, we also use this method to actually create the file mapping, events, and thread that we will use to perform the custom marshaling.

Note that an additional **AddRef( )** is required on the server's object. A standard COM stub keeps a reference count on its object. We need to provide this code in our custom marshaling case.

```
STDMETHODIMP CElizaServer::MarshalInterface (IStream *pStream,
    REFIID riid, void* pv, DWORD dwDestCtx, void *pvReserved,
    DWORD dwFlags)
{

/*
Write the name we will use for the file mapping and event into the
stream provided.  This is the marshaling packet that will be passed
to the client proxy.
*/

    pStream->Write (m_ShareName, sizeof(m_ShareName), NULL) ;

/*
Additional AddRef( ) on this object to make up for the lack of
a system-supplied stub.
*/

    AddRef( ) ;

/*
Create file mapping and map it into our address space
*/

    char out [256] ;
    wsprintf (out, "%sMap", m_ShareName) ;
    m_hMap = CreateFileMapping ((HANDLE)-1, NULL, PAGE_READWRITE,
      0, 1000, out) ;
    m_pSharedMem = (LPTSTR) MapViewOfFile (m_hMap, FILE_MAP_ALL_ACCESS,
      0, 0, 0) ;

/*
Create events that the client proxy will set to signal us that
data has been placed in the shared RAM buffer.  Create a thread to
wait on the event.
*/

    wsprintf (out, "%sComplaintEvent", m_ShareName) ;
    m_hComplaintEvent = CreateEvent (NULL, FALSE, FALSE, out) ;
    wsprintf (out, "%sResponseEvent", m_ShareName) ;
    m_hResponseEvent = CreateEvent (NULL, FALSE, FALSE, out) ;

    m_hThread = CreateThread (NULL, 0, ThreadFunc,
      (LPVOID)this, 0, &m_ThreadID) ;
    return S_OK ;
}
```

11. These three methods are the only ones that COM will call on the server. The others may be stubbed out, thus:

```
STDMETHODIMP CElizaServer::UnmarshalInterface (IStream *pStream,
    REFIID riid, VOID **ppv)
{
    MessageBox (NULL, "Unexpected UnmarshalInterface", "Server", 0) ;
    return S_OK ;
}


STDMETHODIMP CElizaServer::ReleaseMarshalData (IStream *pStream)
{
    MessageBox (NULL, "Unexpected ReleaseMarshalData", "Server", 0) ;
    return S_OK ;
}


STDMETHODIMP CElizaServer::DisconnectObject (DWORD dwReserved)
{
    MessageBox (NULL, "Unexpected DisconnectObject", "Server", 0) ;
    return S_OK ;
}
```

This page intentionally contains no text other than this sentence.

12. Having received all it needs from the server, COM will now call CoCreateInstance( ) and create this proxy in the client's address space, asking for the IMarshal interface. COM knows that the proxy was provided for the purpose of custom marshaling, so if it can't get that interface, the object creation must fail. Once COM has the IMarshal pointer, it will call the method **IMarshal::UnmarshalInterface( )**, passing a pointer to the marshaling packet provided by the server. The proxy reads the data from the marshaling packet's stream and does whatever it needs to do to initialize the custom marshaling. In the provided example, the proxy reads from the marshaling packet the name that the server used to create the shared file mapping and events that are to be used for communication between proxy and server. The proxy provides the target interface pointer (here IEliza) back to COM in the output parameter. Thus:

```
STDMETHODIMP CElizaProxy::UnmarshalInterface (IStream *pStream,
    REFIID riid, VOID **ppv)
{

/*
Read file mapping name from pStream.  Create file mapping and map
memory pointer for that name.  Also open the events that the server
should have already created.
*/

    pStream->Read (m_ShareName, sizeof(m_ShareName), NULL) ;

    char out [256] ;

    wsprintf (out, "%sMap", m_ShareName) ;
    m_hMap = OpenFileMapping (FILE_MAP_ALL_ACCESS, FALSE, out) ;
    m_pSharedMem = (LPTSTR) MapViewOfFile (m_hMap, FILE_MAP_ALL_ACCESS,
      0, 0, 0) ;

    wsprintf (out, "%sComplaintEvent", m_ShareName) ;
    m_hComplaintEvent = OpenEvent (EVENT_MODIFY_STATE, FALSE, out) ;

    wsprintf (out, "%sResponseEvent", m_ShareName) ;
    m_hResponseEvent = OpenEvent (EVENT_ALL_ACCESS, FALSE, out) ;
/*
If we couldn't open the file map or the events, fail construction of
the object.
*/

    if (!m_pSharedMem || !m_hComplaintEvent || !m_hResponseEvent)
    {
      *ppv = NULL ;
      return E_NOINTERFACE ;
    }
/*
Return pointer to IEliza interface.
*/

    return QueryInterface (riid, ppv) ;
}
```

13. The proxy implements its methods that are called directly from the client. Instead of providing the actual object functionality, the proxy communicates with the server in whatever way the writer of both of these has decided to use. In this case, the proxy copies the patient's complaint into a specified area of the shared file memory map and signals the server of a new complaint by setting an event on which the server is waiting. The proxy then waits on a second event with a timeout of 1second. The server will think about the patient's complaint and place its response in another area of the shared memory and signal the proxy by setting this event. The proxy will then copy the response from the shared memory to the buffer provided by the caller. If the server does not respond in time, the proxy's wait will time out, causing the proxy to try to cover up. Thus:

```
STDMETHODIMP CElizaProxy::Complain (LPOLESTR pIn, LPOLESTR pOut)
{

/*
Copy client's complaint into shared ram buffer.  Signal server by
setting an auto-reset event that the server ought to be waiting for.
*/

    lstrcpyn (m_pSharedMem+4, pIn, 128) ;
    SetEvent (m_hComplaintEvent) ;

/*
Wait for server to respond, timeout interval 1 second.  If found, copy
into output buffer.
*/
    if (WaitForSingleObject (m_hResponseEvent, 1000) == WAIT_OBJECT_0)
    {
      lstrcpyn (pOut, m_pSharedMem+132, 128) ;
    }

/*
Otherwise, hem and haw.
*/
    else
    {
      lstrcpy (pOut, "I'm sorry, I spaced out.  What did you say ?") ;
    }

    return NOERROR ;

}
```

14. The proxy knows how to handle internally all the methods of IUnknown, so we don't need to marshal their calls to the server. This is another case of how custom marshaling can save performance, by preventing an unnecessary context switch. The server doesn't care if the proxy's reference count goes from 5 to 6; it only cares when it touches zero, so these calls are handled internally on the proxy. When the proxy object gets its final release, we use its class destructor to signal the server to finally destroy its object. Thus:

```
STDMETHODIMP_(ULONG) CElizaProxy::AddRef(void)
{
    return ++m_RefCount;
}



STDMETHODIMP_(ULONG) CElizaProxy::Release(void)
{
    m_RefCount -- ;

    if (m_RefCount == 0)
    {
        delete this;
      return 0 ;
    }

    return m_RefCount ;
}



CElizaProxy::~CElizaProxy (void)
{

/*
Object being destroyed, signal final release to the server.
*/

    *(DWORD *) m_pSharedMem = 1 ;
    SetEvent (m_hComplaintEvent) ;

/*
Clean up.
*/

    UnmapViewOfFile (m_pSharedMem) ;
    CloseHandle (m_hMap) ;
    CloseHandle (m_hResponseEvent) ;
    CloseHandle (m_hComplaintEvent) ;

    return;
}
```

311

I. CUSTOM INTERFACES IN THE MFC

1. The MFC also supports custom interfaces. Implementing one may feel painful at first compared to the easy point-and-click support that the MFC provides for OLE automation. It took me a few tries to figure it out, but if you read through this section a few times and let it settle, it ought to make sense. In any event, the code is provided here for you to cut and paste. As you remember from Chapter 2, implementing an interface is identical for a local or in-proc server except the mechanism by which the class factory is exposed to the world, and this holds true in the MFC as well. Exposing the class factory is demonstrated on pages 318 and 319. Samples of the IEliza custom interface can be found in the directories \chap09\mfcipsv for an in-proc server and \chap09\mfclosv for a local server.

2. When you use App Wizard to generate your project, select no OLE support. Otherwise you will wind up with a bunch of stuff that doesn't help you and only gets in the way. As shown in previous chapters, include the header file **<afxdisp.h>** in your stdafx.h, and add a call to AfxOleInit( ) in your CWinApp::InitInstance( ) method.

3. All COM interfaces must derive from IUnknown. In the MFC, IUnknown is built into the class CCmdTarget. So, to write a custom interface in the MFC, begin by using Class Wizard to derive a class from CCmdTarget, leaving the "OLE Automation" selection at "None". Thus:

312

4. You must manually add several elements to your new class's header file. First, you must include the header file which defines the custom interface that you are implementing, in this case "**ieliza.h**". You must also include the macros **BEGIN_INTERFACE_PART** and **END_INTERFACE_PART**. Between these, you place the declaration of your custom interface's methods, omitting the IUnknown methods which are automatically declared by the former macro. This macro creates inside your CCmdTarget object a nested class which implements the member functions required by your custom interface. The name of the nested class is the first name specified in the macro with the letter 'X' prepended to it. The expansion of these macros is shown in the comment block of the source code sample below.

You must also include the macro **DECLARE_INTERFACE_MAP**, which declares an array of structures that IUnknown::QueryInterface( ) will use to keep track of the IDs and locations of the interface(s) you support. Finally, you must also declare a static variable of class *COleObjectFactory*, which is the MFC implementation of the class factory for your new COM class. Thus:

```
<file mfceliza.h>

#include "ieliza.h"

static const GUID GUID_MfcEliza = {0x963a0c60, 0x1a2c, 0x11cf,
    {0x89, 0xe1, 0x0, 0xaa, 0x0, 0xa5, 0x80, 0x97}} ;

class CMfcEliza : public CCmdTarget
{
    <standard header contents omitted>

/*
Declaration of the member functions used in the IEliza interface. When
expanded by the preprocessor, it becomes:

    class XEliza : public IEliza
    {
      public:
        STDMETHOD_(ULONG, AddRef)();
        STDMETHOD_(ULONG, Release)();
        STDMETHOD(QueryInterface)(REFIID iid, LPVOID* ppvObj);
        HRESULT virtual __stdcall Complain (LPOLESTR, LPOLESTR) ;
    } m_xEliza ;
    friend class XEliza ;

*/
    BEGIN_INTERFACE_PART (Eliza, IEliza)
        HRESULT virtual __stdcall Complain (LPOLESTR, LPOLESTR) ;
    END_INTERFACE_PART (Eliza)

/*
Declaration of array of structures used by IUnknown::QueryInterface to
determine which interface(s) this object supports.
*/
    DECLARE_INTERFACE_MAP ( )
/*
Declaration of class factory object, one per class.
*/
    static COleObjectFactory ms_ElizaFactory ;
};
```

5. The base class CCmdTarget contains an implementation of IUnknown, so you don't have to write any of the code for it. What you do have to provide is an array of data structures that the inherited QueryInterface( ) can use to determine which interfaces your object supports and which nested classes contain the VTBLs used for accessing the methods of these interfaces. This is conceptually and operationally similar to the message and dispatch maps used in the MFC. You provide this array of structures via the macros **BEGIN_INTERFACE_MAP** and **END_INTERFACE_MAP**. Between these two macros, you place one **INTERFACE_PART** macro for each interface you support. If you look at the expansion of the macro in the comment block below, you will find that it contains simply the interface ID and the offset of the nested object within the CCmdTarget. Thus:

```
<file mfceliza.cpp>

///////////////////////////////////////////////////////////////////////
//////
// CMfcEliza message handlers

/*
On expansion, the INTERFACE_PART macro becomes:

    { &IID_IEliza, offsetof(CMfcEliza, m_xEliza) }

*/


BEGIN_INTERFACE_MAP (CMfcEliza, CCmdTarget)
    INTERFACE_PART (CMfcEliza, IID_IEliza, Eliza)
END_INTERFACE_MAP( )
```

314

6. When you used the BEGIN_INTERFACE_PART macro, it expanded as shown in the previous example to create a nested class with the letter X prepended onto the specified name. You must implement your interface's methods as member functions of the nested class. The linker will produce an error if you omit any of them. The IEliza::Complain( ) method is implemented as follows:

```
HRESULT CMfcEliza::XEliza::Complain (LPOLESTR pIn, LPOLESTR pOut)
{
    Eliza (pIn, pOut) ;
    return S_OK ;
}
```

7. The nested class's COM interface methods are called directly from the client application. Therefore, the implied C++ `this` pointer on the stack points to the nested class XEliza object itself, not the outer CMfcEliza object that contains it. The nested class's methods will almost certainly want to access the outer class's data or functions, but if you try to write code that does this directly, you will get a compiler error. The macro **METHOD_PROLOGUE** produces a pointer called **pThis** that points to the outer class and may be used to access its members.

8. You must provide function shells in the interface's VTBL for the nested class's QueryInterface( ), AddRef( ), and Release( ) methods; however, you don't have to write their actual code. The CCmdTarget base class contains an intelligent implementation of these methods, all you have to do is delegate to them as shown below. The MFC CCmdTarget is quite smart, even supporting a client request for aggregation (not discussed in this book; see Brockschmidt, pp. 101-105). The CCmdTarget methods **ExternalQueryInterface( )**, **ExternalAddRef( )**, and **ExternalRelease( )** will work properly whether your object is aggregated or not. The base class also contains internal versions of these functions, but the external versions shown are the ones you want. Thus:

```
/*
Implementation of nested class AddRef( )method.
*/

ULONG CMfcEliza::XEliza::AddRef( )
{
/*
Set up pThis pointer to access outer object.
*/
    METHOD_PROLOGUE (CMfcEliza, Eliza)

/*
Use pThis pointer to delegate to outer object's AddRef( ) method.
*/
    return pThis->ExternalAddRef( ) ;
}

ULONG CMfcEliza::XEliza::Release( )
{
    METHOD_PROLOGUE (CMfcEliza, Eliza) ;
    return pThis->ExternalRelease( ) ;
}

long CMfcEliza::XEliza::QueryInterface (REFIID riid, LPVOID *ppv)
{
    METHOD_PROLOGUE (CMfcEliza, Eliza) ;
    return pThis->ExternalQueryInterface (&riid, ppv) ;
}
```

316

9. You must also construct the class's **COleObjectFactory** static member variable, passing its constructor the parameters it needs to do its job. This creates the class factory object that produces CMfcEliza objects and sets the class factory's initial state. The first parameter is the class ID of the object manufactured by the class factory. Since App Wizard didn't generate it for you, you must use GUIDGEN.EXE to create a new one, which I have placed in the class header file which you saw on page 313. Thus:

```
AFX_DATADEF COleObjectFactory CMfcEliza::ms_ElizaFactory (
    GUID_MfcEliza,                          // class ID manufactured by this CF
    RUNTIME_CLASS(CMfcEliza),               // class to instantiate
    FALSE,                                  // multi-instance ?
    TEXT("EssenceOfOle.Eliza.MfcCustomInProc")) ;    // human-readable
                                            //name of object for registry
```

10. You must also call the static function **COleObjectFactory::RegisterAll( )**, which does the internal MFC bookkeeping that connects the class factory to the MFC object that it manufactures. This probably wants to be done in the CWinApp::InitInstance( ) method. Thus:

```
BOOL CMfcipelizaApp::InitInstance()
{

/*
Initialize OLE in the MFC.
*/
    AfxOleInit ( ) ;

/*
Do internal bookkeeping that binds class factory to the MFC object that
it manufactures.
*/

    return  COleObjectFactory::RegisterAll( ) ;

}
```

317

11. As shown in Chapter 2, in-proc servers must export the functions DllGetClassObject( ) to expose their class factories to the world and DllCanUnloadNow( ) to allow COM to monitor their internal states. You will probably also want to add the function DllRegisterServer( ) to perform self-registration of your in-proc server, as described in Appendix A. These are included automatically by App Wizard if you specify an OLE Automation in-proc server, but not if you specify a non-OLE DLL as we have done in the custom interface sample code. In this case, you must add them manually to your source code and export them from a .DEF file as shown below. All of these external entry points may simply delegate to internal MFC functions that perform the necessary operations. You will find the original code in the MFC source file DLLOLE.CPP. Thus:

```
<file mfceliza.cpp>

/*
Export class factory to COM.
*/

STDAPI DllGetClassObject(REFCLSID rclsid, REFIID riid, LPVOID* ppv)
{
    AFX_MANAGE_STATE(AfxGetStaticModuleState());

    return  AfxDllGetClassObject(rclsid, riid, ppv);
}

/*
Export internal state to COM.
*/

STDAPI DllCanUnloadNow(void)
{
    AFX_MANAGE_STATE(AfxGetStaticModuleState());
    return AfxDllCanUnloadNow();
}

/*
Export self-registration function to COM.
*/

STDAPI DllRegisterServer(void)
{
    AFX_MANAGE_STATE(AfxGetStaticModuleState());
    COleObjectFactory::UpdateRegistryAll();
    return S_OK;
}

<file mfcipeliza.def>

; mfcipeliza.def : Declares the module parameters for the DLL.

LIBRARY       "MFCIPELIZA"
DESCRIPTION  'MFCIPELIZA Windows Dynamic Link Library'
EXPORTS
    DllRegisterServer
    DllGetClassObject
    DllCanUnloadNow
```

12. Since you generated the custom interface local server without App Wizard OLE support, you must add the code shown below to initialize your app. The local server app first checks its command line to see if was launched as an OLE server. As you recall from Chapter 2, in this case a local server provides its class factory by calling the API function CoRegisterClassObject( ). In the MFC, this is wrapped up in the method **COleObjectFactory::RegisterAll( )**. If the app was not launched as an OLE server, it then calls the method COleObjectFactory::UpdateRegistryAll( ) to perform self-registration, as discussed in Appendix A.

This local server uses the IEliza interface. Since the marshaling code for the interface was set up in the standard marshaling local server example, you don't have to do anything else to get it to work.

```
BOOL CMfclosvApp::InitInstance()
{
/*
Initialize OLE.
*/
    AfxOleInit ( ) ;


/*
Check command line to see if launched as an OLE server.  If so, then
register class factories and return before showing the main window,
which is customary behavior in a server. The sample app has the return
line commented out, causing it to show itself for illustrative
purposes.
*/
    if (cmdInfo.m_bRunEmbedded || cmdInfo.m_bRunAutomated)
    {
      COleObjectFactory::RegisterAll();
      return TRUE ;
    }


/*
If not, then update the registry with the app's current settings.
*/
    COleObjectFactory::UpdateRegistryAll();

    if (!ProcessShellCommand(cmdInfo))
      return FALSE;

    return TRUE;
}
```

13. An MFC custom interface app does not know to shut itself down after the last object has been destroyed. If you want this to happen, you must write your own code to make it so. In the supplied example, when an object is created, we increment a global counter in the class constructor. When an object is destroyed, we decrement the counter, and when the object count reaches 0, we shut down the app. Thus:

```
/*
Global count of all objects in the app.
*/

UINT g_ObjectCount = 0 ;

/////////////////////////////////////////////////////////////////////
//////
// CMfcEliza

IMPLEMENT_DYNCREATE(CMfcEliza, CCmdTarget)

/*
Eliza object constructed, increment global object counter.
*/

CMfcEliza::CMfcEliza()
{
    g_ObjectCount ++ ;
}

/*
Eliza object destroyed, decrement global object counter.  Shut down app
if object count reaches 0.
*/

CMfcEliza::~CMfcEliza()
{
    g_ObjectCount -- ;

    if (g_ObjectCount == 0)
    {
      PostQuitMessage (0) ;
    }
}
```

This chapter contains more sample apps than the others. They are arranged as follows:

```
\EssenceOfOLE
    \chap09
        \Eliza
            \client          client app for all IEliza samples
            \dual            IEliza through a dual interface
            \inprocsv        in-proc server for IEliza interface
            \localsv         local server for IEliza interface, standard marshaling
            \marshprox       client-side proxy for IEliza interface, custom marshaling
            \marshsv         local server for IEliza interface, custom marshaling
            \mfcipau         MFC in-proc server for IEliza dispinterface, for comparison
            \mfcipsv         MFC in-proc server for IEliza interface
            \mfclocau        MFC local server for IEliza dispinterface, for comparison
            \mfclosv         MFC local server for IEliza interface, standard marshaling
            \typelibmarshaled  IEliza marshaled via a type library
```

Because of the volume and interrelatedness of these apps, this chapter does not contain a prefabricated lab exercise. Instead, this section contains detailed instructions for getting the sample code up and running, and provides suggestions for experiments you might like to make with it. The non-MFC apps all use Unicode; the MFC apps do not.

1. First you must register all the servers. The root directory \Eliza contains a registry file ELIZA.REG. Run this file from the Explorer; it will register the IEliza in-proc server and local server. It also registers the standard marshaling of the IEliza interface and the custom marshaling proxy and server apps.

2. The MFC apps contain MFC support for self-registration. Running the two local servers from the Explorer will cause them to make their own entries in the registry. The two MFC DLLs require the assistance of the system utility app REGSVR32.EXE. Running this app passing the name of the server DLL on the command line will load the DLL and cause it to make its own registry entries.

3. The directories \dual and \typelibmarshaled each contain a .REG file that registers that particular server and interface. Run these files from Explorer.

4. Run the client app.

5. The Time Test menu item makes a number of repeat calls. If "Perform Eliza Processing" box is checked, then Eliza will think about your response. If it is cleared, then Eliza will ignore it, allowing you to measure only the function call overheads.

This page intentionally contains no text other than this sentence.

Chapter 10
Distributed COM (DCOM)

This page intentionally contains no text other than this sentence.

This page intentionally contains no text other than this sentence.

A. Concepts and Definitions

1. Consider the model of COM shown in the diagram below (see Chap~
One of the major strengths of COM to date is that neither client nor server ne~
with whether the other party is in a .EXE file or a .DLL. *Distributed CO
transparency to apps running on different machines connected by a network. Thus.

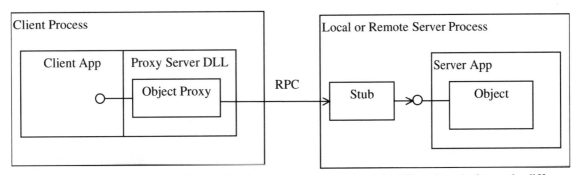

When a client creates an object which lives on a remote server, the client doesn't do much different than when it connects to an object on a local server. The functions to create the object might change a little (see page 330) or possibly not at all (see page 326). All objects appear to the client to reside in a DLL in the client's address space. Sometimes this contains the object's actual functionality (in-proc server), and sometimes it contains only proxy functions that communicate with the actual object functionality that lives in another process (local server) or another machine (remote server). The client neither knows nor cares which case it is.

The server of a remote object generally doesn't do anything different at all. Exposing its capability to clients on different machines is primarily an administrative task performed by the system administrator. Apps that want to can exercise microscopic control over their security, but reasonable behavior can usually be obtained simply through administrative settings. The server generally doesn't know or care if its clients are local or remote.

This transparency is enormously powerful for architecture, but like most things, comes at a price. The price in this case is slower performance. A network line isn't and cannot be made anywhere near as fast as a computer bus backbone, so remote object method calls will always be slower than if the server was running the same machine as the client. The architectural approaches that you can use to minimize this performance hit are described on page 358.

DCOM first appeared in Windows NT 4.0. It is also available as a separate service pack for Windows 95. Programming for DCOM is almost identical to programming for COM on the same machine. The two major additions are in the areas of security and optimization

B. Using Legacy Client Apps with DCOM

1. Legacy client apps that were developed without knowledge of DCOM may still use objects provided by remote servers. Remember that when a client app calls CoCreateInstance( ), COM reads the registry looking for the InProcServer32 or LocalServer32 entries to find the server for the specified class ID. With the addition of DCOM to the operating system, if this search fails, then COM will look for the registry key HKEY_CLASSES_ROOT\APPID\{object's app ID, usually the same as the class ID}, and find the named value "**RemoteServerName**". This contains a string value specifying the name of the remote system on which the requested object's server may be found. In the following example, the data3 sample from Chapter 2 will look for its server on the remote machine named REDTAILALE.

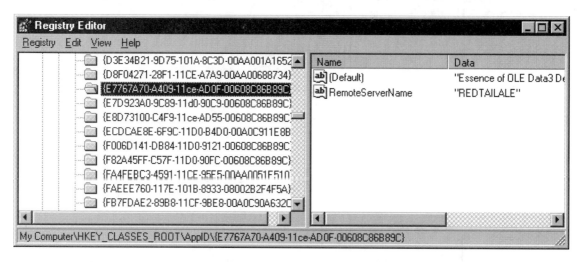

The AppID that corresponds to the specified CLSID is placed as a named value in the class's CLSID entry. For convenience, you usually choose the AppID to be the same as the class ID.

For this operation to succeed, a local server .EXE for the specified class ID must be registered on the named remote system, DCOM must be enabled on the remote machine and the client must have permission from the server machine's security system to launch that app There is not currently a lookup service whereby a server may advertise its availability for a client to examine at runtime. The client must explicitly specify a server machine.

2. It is easy to make these registry settings with the use of *dcomcnfg.exe*, the DCOM configuration utility app. Since it changes registry settings, this app may only be run from an administrator account. When you run it, you will see a list of all the objects with local servers registered on the system. If you select an object and click the "Properties" button, you will see the following view, which will allow you to make and change the registry settings described on the previous page.

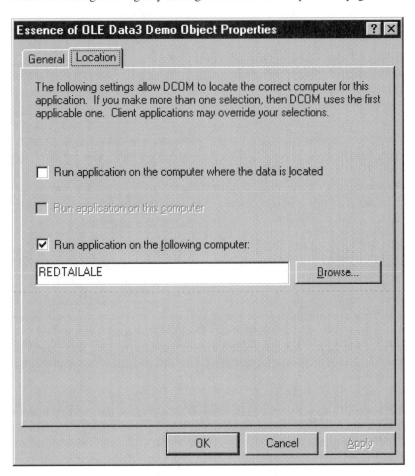

Note: Dcomcnfg only shows you objects that are registered with local servers. However, it is perfectly possible to have an EXE server on a remote machine take the place of an in-proc server on your local machine, although the call overhead will go up by about a factor of 1000. To do this, simply make the required registry settings via the registry editor.

3. How compatible is this backwards-compatible mode? It depends on what the legacy apps want to do. Some operations are simply not currently possible over a network because the operating system does not know how to share the objects that they require. For example, the operating system does not currently [NT 4.0, SP 2] know how to share a window handle from one machine to another. Any OLE/COM interfaces that depend on the sharing of window handles will not work correctly, which includes the interfaces used for in-place activation. This rules out remoting any full-featured ActiveX controls, such as those described in Chapters 5 and 6, as well as any of your own custom interfaces whose methods depend on window handles.

What other things do you have to worry about? Operating over a remote link is slower than on a local machine. If you set up the \chap02\data3 server to run on a remote system, as described in the lab exercises at the end of this chapter, you will find that accessing a remote server is slower than a local server by a ballpark factor of about 10. A local server is in turn slower than an in-proc server by a ballpark factor of about 100. Anything in your client-server operation that depends on timing is a candidate for trouble. Some individual calls can take much longer than they used to. In the first lab example, you may find that calling CoCreateInstance( ) can take 4 or 5 seconds to create an object on a remote machine the first time you call it, though it will be less on subsequent occasions as some of the operating system's infrastructure is loaded only on demand. When accessed from another domain, the call to IDataObject::DAdvise( ) inexplicably takes about 50 seconds [sic] to establish the advise sink, as opposed to almost nothing on a local server.

You will also have to negotiate several registry settings using dcomcnfg, as described later in this chapter. Many of them are non-intuitive, and you will probably need to experiment a bit before you get them right on your machine. For example, in the data3 experiment, IDataObject::GetData( ) works perfectly regardless of the settings of the authentication level (page 350) or the remote user identity (page 343). However, for the client app to receive callbacks from the circuit established via IDataObject::DAdvise( ), it is necessary either to set the default authentication level to "None" on both sides, or to set a specific identity for the server instead of impersonating the client by default. Otherwise the callback doesn't work.

When your user creates an object on a remote server machine and you look at the server's monitor expecting to see the object server app's window, don't be surprised not to find it there, although you can see the server app's process on Task Manager's process list. Unless you have specifically made registry entries to tell the *Service Control Manager* (SCM, pronounced "scum") to launch the server with the identity of the logged-in interactive user, the remote object will be created in an entirely separate area, described on page 343. Any windows created by the server app will be hidden so deeply that not even Spy++ will be able to show them to you. If the server app pops up a message box that you expect the user to click, the user won't see it and your app will hang. You may well want your production server to run invisibly, so that bone-headed users don't mess with it and screw up a remote client, although if the server is in a locked room where only administrators have access, you might want the window to display current status information for their benefit. But any legacy server that requires user input will need this registry setting in order to work.

4. Sometimes things just break. DCOM is a new piece of software, and no matter how much Microsoft touts its reliability, it's the first release and stuff is going to go wrong in strange ways and places that you aren't thinking about. Here's one example, and if there's one, there are others.

Consider the custom marshaling sample program in Chapter 9, particularly the method IMarshal::GetUnmarshalClass( ). It worked fine on NT 3.51 and Windows 95, but broke on NT 4.0, causing me to get all kinds of nasty e-mail. The reason why is that this app does not use the standard proxy/stub marshaler created by MIDL, which does work correctly. Instead, it chooses to marshal its custom interface by implementing the IMarshal interface. NT 4.0's implementation of DCOM contains a bug that causes it to pass an incorrect value of the parameter dwDestCtx to IMarshal::GetUnmarshalClass( ) when the object is first created. If you simply call CoCreateInstance( ) asking for the IEliza interface, as was done in the sample code of the first edition of this book, the NT 4.0 SCM calls this method with a value of MSHCTX_DIFFERENTMACHINE for dwDestCtx, even if the server resides on the local machine. The following code breaks:

```
extern CLSID CLSID_CustomEliza ;

case ID_ELIZA_CREATELOCAL:
{
    HRESULT hr ;

    hr = CoCreateInstance (
      CLSID_CustomEliza, NULL, CLSCTX_LOCAL_SERVER,
      IID_IEliza, (LPVOID *) &pEliza) ;

    <etc...>
    return 0 ;
}
```

The fix for it is to get the class factory first, then call IClassFactory::CreateInstance( ). It will be the class factory object that sees the incorrect dwDestCtx, and since this uses standard marshaling, it doesn't matter. Since the IEliza object is created after the server is launched, IMarshal::GetUnmarshalClass( ) is called from another place in DCOM which does not have the bug. Your custom marshaler will be called with a dwDestCtx of MSHCTX_LOCALMACHINE, which is correct. The following, seemingly identical, code works correctly:

```
case ID_ELIZA_CREATECUSTOMMARSHALING:
{
    HRESULT hr ;   IClassFactory *pcf ;

    hr = CoGetClassObject (
      CLSID_CustomEliza,
      CLSCTX_LOCAL_SERVER,
      NULL,
      IID_IClassFactory,
      (LPVOID*)&pcf) ;

    hr = pcf->CreateInstance (NULL, IID_IEliza, (LPVOID *)&pEliza) ;
    pcf->Release( ) ;

    <etc...>
    return 0 ;
}
```

C. REMOTE OBJECT CREATION

1. Apps that are built with knowledge of DCOM may explicitly create an object on a remote system via the API function **CoCreateInstanceEx( )**. An example of the use of this function is shown on the facing page. The flag **CLSCTX_REMOTE_SERVER** specifies that the object is to be created on a remote machine which may be anywhere on the network that is visible to the calling app. The server name is specified in a structure of type **COSERVERINFO**.

COM object method calls over a network are slow compared to calls made on the same machine. To improve performance, CoCreateInstanceEx( ) allows you to query for more than one interface when the object is created. In this way, you incur the network overhead of only a single function call when obtaining all the interface pointers you want to use. You pass a pointer to an array of structures of type **MULTI_QI** as the last parameter to CoCreateInstanceEx( ). Each structure contains a pointer to the ID of the requested interface, which you must set before making the call. Each structure contains an HRESULT and an interface pointer which are filled on output. When the function returns, these will be filled with the result of the request for the specified interface and a pointer to that interface. A return code of S_OK means that all of your requested interfaces were successfully retrieved. A return code of CO_S_NOTALLINTERFACES means that at least one but not all of the requested interface was successfully retrieved.

Because DCOM is not supported in the base release of Windows 95, the function declarations which require it have been conditionally compiled out of the header files. To have the compiler be able to see them, you must define the constant **_WIN32_DCOM** ahead of <windows.h> as shown, or define the value **_WIN32_WINNT** to 0x400 or higher. To make sure it appears everywhere, the sample code for this chapter defines the former constant in its project settings.

2. A sample app containing the code fragment on the facing page may be found in the directory \chap10\data4\client. It contains an upgraded version of the client app from the data3 example in Chapter 2. I have added menu choices to the app which allow you to specify a remote server for an object and create an object from the remote server. The performance test menu items and advise loop functionality have been left in, allowing you to compare local versus remote operation.

330

```c
#define _WIN32_DCOM
#include <windows.h>

extern WCHAR wServerName ; extern CLSID GUID_TimeData ;
extern LPDATAOBJECT lpd ;

case ID_DATAOBJECT_CREATEFROMREMOTESERVER:
{
/*
Set up COSERVERINFO structure specifying name of remote server.
*/
    COSERVERINFO si ;

    si.pwszName = wServerName ;
    si.dwReserved1 = 0 ;
    si.pAuthInfo = NULL ;
    si.dwReserved2 = 0;

/*
Set up array of MULTI_QI structures to specify requested interfaces and
hold returned pointers. Here we only have one.
*/

    MULTI_QI mqi [1] ;

    mqi [0].pIID = &IID_IDataObject ;
    mqi [0].pItf = NULL ;
    mqi [0].hr = 0 ;
/*
Create instance of object on remote machine.
*/
    HRESULT hr = CoCreateInstanceEx (
        GUID_TimeData,               // class ID of requested object
        NULL,                        // no aggregation
        CLSCTX_REMOTE_SERVER,        // remote server required
        &si,                         // name of remote server
        1,                           // # of interfaces to query for
        mqi) ;                       // array of MULTI_QI for each
                                     //   requested interface
/*
If call succeeded, use returned interface pointer.  Otherwise signal
error.
*/
    if (hr == S_OK)
    {
      lpd = (LPDATAOBJECT) mqi [0].pItf ;
    }
    else
    {
      MessageBox (hWnd, "Couldn't create object", "Error",MB_ICONSTOP);
    }
    return 0 ;
}
```

3. The function **CoGetClassObject( )**, which gets the class factory that manufactures a specified class of object, has also been upgraded to support DCOM. The third parameter to this function, which previously was reserved, now may contain a pointer to a **COSERVERINFO** structure which specifies the remote machine from which the class factory is to be obtained. Thus:

```
LPCLASSFACTORY lpcf ;
extern WCHAR wServerName ;
extern CLSID GUID_TimeData ;

case ID_DATAOBJECT_GETREMOTECLASSFACTORY:
{
    HRESULT hr ;

/*
Set up COSERVERINFO structure specifying name of remote server.
*/
    COSERVERINFO si ;
    si.pwszName = wServerName ;
    si.dwReserved1 = 0 ;
    si.pAuthInfo = NULL ;
    si.dwReserved2 = 0;
/*
Get class factory that manufactures objects of class GUID_TimeData. We
might use it later to create an instance of the object.
*/

    hr = CoGetClassObject (
      GUID_TimeData,            // class ID made by requested factory
      CLSCTX_REMOTE_SERVER,     // remote server required
      &si,                      // server on which to get class factory
      IID_IClassFactory,        // interface ID wanted on class factory
      (LPVOID *) &lpcf) ;       // output variable

    if (!SUCCEEDED(hr))
    {
      MessageBox (NULL, "Couldn't get remote cf", "", 0) ;
    }

    return 0 ;
}
```

Note: The preceding code fragment does not appear in the data4cl sample program. Implementing it is left as an exercise to the student.

4. DCOM adds the new helper functions **CoGetInstanceFromFile( )** and **CoGetInstanceFromIStorage( )**. The former creates a new object of the specified class, queries the object for IPersistFile, calls IPersistFile::Load( ) to initialize the object using the specified file, and finally queries for the requested interfaces. The latter does the same thing using the IPersistStorage interface.

You may specify the remote system, or pass NULL to accept the default as shown below. In this case, the function attempts to create the object first on the local system, next on the system specified by the "RemoteServerName" registry entry, and finally on the system on which the file resides. You may specify the class ID of the object, or pass NULL to accept the default as shown below. In this case, the class ID of the file's owner is determined by a call to GetClassFile( ), as described in Chapter 8, on the machine on which the object is instantiated. Thus:

```
case ID_DATAOBJCT_CREATEFROMFILE:
{
    OPENFILENAME of ;   char File [256] ;

    < fill OPENFILENAME structure >

    if (GetOpenFileName (&of))
    {
      HRESULT hr ;

      MULTI_QI mqi [1] ;
      mqi [0].pIID = &IID_IDataObject ;
      mqi [0].pItf = NULL ;
      mqi [0].hr = 0 ;

      WCHAR WideFileName [80] ;
      MultiByteToWideChar (CP_ACP, 0, File, -1, WideFileName, 80) ;

    hr = CoGetInstanceFromFile (
          NULL,              // server machine, NULL == default
          NULL,              // clsid, NULL means call GetClassFile( )
          NULL,              // IUnknown for aggregation
          CLSCTX_SERVER,     // context
          0,                 // mode, not documented
          WideFileName,      // file name
          1,                 // # of MQI
          mqi) ;             // array of MQI

          if (hr != S_OK)
          {
             MessageBox(NULL,"Can't get instance from file", "",0);
          }
          else
          {
             lpd = (LPDATAOBJECT) mqi [0].pItf ;
          }
    }
    return 0 ;
}
```

5. When a client creates an object on a remote machine, the remote machine's SCM looks in the registry for the server registered as handling the requested clsid, exactly as it does for a request originating on its own machine. The base release of NT 4.0 required a .EXE server to handle a remote creation request; a .DLL server wouldn't work. With the release of Service Pack 2, NT provided a *surrogate process* which the SCM will launch to allow .DLL servers to handle remote activation requests. The surrogate process acts as a shell, loading the DLL server, obtaining its class factory and registering it with COM.

To use a surrogate process for your .DLL server, you must add the named value "DllSurrogate" to the AppID registry settings for the server, as shown below. Dcomcnfg does not provide a UI for this; you must do it yourself. BTW, this works on the same machine as well as remotely. If there is a .DLL server on your machine that you like but don't trust inside your client app's address space, you can make this registry entry and create the object using the flag CLSCTX_LOCAL_SERVER.

If you add the named value DllSurrogate with an empty string, as shown above, COM will launch its standard surrogate process "dllhost.exe". This suffices for the great majority of cases. However, if you ever need to write your own custom surrogate, you can find instructions in the "ActiveX/COM Q + A" in the May 1997 Microsoft Systems Journal.

WARNING: One of the reasons for providing an object in a DLL server is that certain types of data, such as HDC's, cannot be marshaled across process boundaries. The IViewObject interface, for example, has this problem. If your remote DLL server requires or provides data that can't be marshaled to another process, you'll be able to launch it using a surrogate, but it won't work the way you want it to.

This page intentionally contains no text other than this sentence.

D. LAUNCH SECURITY

1. The security features described in this section deal with allowing or forbidding users to launch an app on a remote server. This is mostly a matter of administration, not programming.

DCOM settings are maintained in the system registry to tell the SCM which users are allowed to perform which operations. Most of the default server-wide items are listed as named values under the key HKEY_LOCAL_MACHINE\SOFTWARE\Microsoft\Ole. Thus:

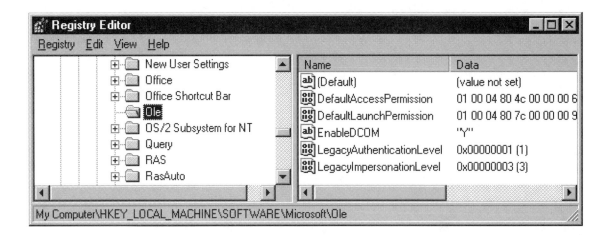

2. The first named value that we care about is "EnableDCOM". Setting it to "Y" as shown above allows remote requests to be received on the machine. Setting it to any other value, such as "N", disables incoming calls but still allows outgoing calls to proceed. Remember, however, that an object on the server machine more often than not makes callbacks to an interface provided by the client machine, such as asynchronous event notifications. With DCOM turned off on the client machine, these callbacks will fail with the error code 0x8001011C, "Remote calls are not allowed for this process."

336

3. These registry keys can be most conveniently set via the utility app *dcomcnfg.exe*, shown below. Since it modifies the registry, this app can only be run from an account with administrator privileges. Using it can be a little confusing, as some controls modify the server properties of the machine and some modify the client properties. The UI of the app does not always make the distinctions clear.

Checking the box shown below sets the "EnableDCOM" value to "Y", and clearing it sets the value to "N". The default on NT 4.0 is "Y". As discussed on the previous page, this value affects the server functionality of the machine. Thus:

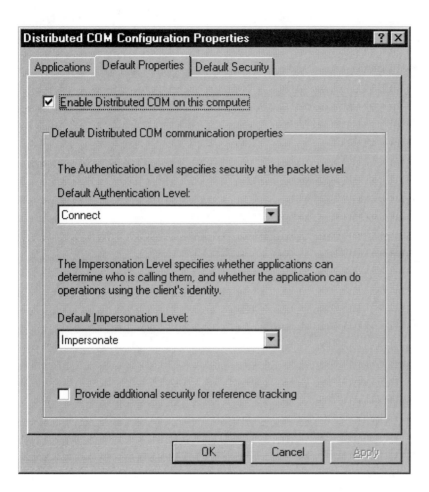

4. You may specify the users or groups that are allowed or forbidden to launch an individual app by setting the named value "LaunchPermission" in that app's AppID registry entry as shown below. This is most conveniently done via dcomcnfg as shown on the following pages.

The launch permission information is stored as an NT security descriptor in binary format. When a request for remote activation comes into a server machine from a remote client, the server's SCM looks in the registry to see if the requesting user has the authority to launch the app. If this named value is not present, then the SCM uses the value of the system's "DefaultLaunchPermission" shown on page 336. The default settings on NT 4.0 allow only administrators, the interactive user, and the system user to launch apps.

5. To configure an individual app's settings, first select the app on the "Applications" tab of dcomcnfg. Then click "Properties". Thus:

6. To configure an individual app's security settings, you use the "Security" tab of dcomcnfg. If you select the radio button for the default permission, dcomcnfg will remove "LaunchPermission" value from the app's AppID registry key. If you select the radio button for custom launch permission as shown, you will see a security administrator dialog box similar to that shown on the next page. Making selections in this dialog box will cause the editor to add the named values if necessary, and set their contents to the security descriptor containing the permissions that you have specified. Thus:

6. The dialog boxes that you use to edit security permissions are shown below. The first one shows the current settings. The default settings grant launch permission to administrators, the system user, and the interactive user. For development purposes, I have added lunch permission for the group "Everyone".

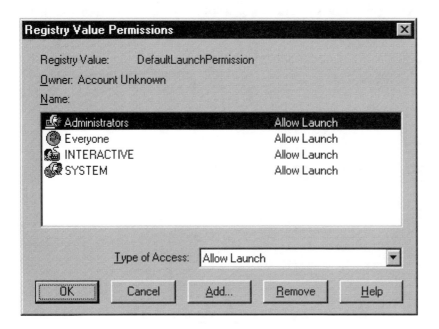

7. When you click "Add…", you will see the dialog box below. This shows you all the groups of users that your installation knows about. You select a group of users, then use the "Type of Access" control at the bottom to specify whether this group is allowed permission to launch as shown, or is denied that permission. Why would you want to explicitly deny access? The operating system checks denied accesses first, before looking for allowed access. You might set access allowed permission to Everyone, but put in an access denied permission for the group of "Disgruntled Ex-Employees". The operating system would check the latter group first, as an permission denial entry. When it did so, it would find that members of this group are denied launch permission, stop checking, and fail the call. Users who were not members of this group would be allowed access when the operating system checked far enough down the list to find that Everyone was allowed accessed.

You may also make entries for individual users, but this is rare. You generally grant permissions to groups and then set permissions on individual users by moving them into and out of the appropriate groups.

E. REMOTE CLIENT IDENTITY

1. When a client launches a server app on a remote server machine, which user ID does the server process run under? When the server process performs an action that requires the operating system to do security checking, such as opening a file, whose identity does the operating system use when checking if the operation is permitted or not?

By default, the server process runs by impersonating the launching user. Suppose an app running on George's machine calls CoCreateInstanceEx( ) to create an object on Mary's machine. Unless Mary has made registry entries directing otherwise, the server process will be launched on Mary's machine with George's identity. The server process is said to be "running as the activator." Any operations that George would have been unable to perform on Mary's machine via other channels, such as browsing her private files with Explorer, he will be unable to accomplish via DCOM either.

This makes sense from the point of not freaking out users and opening up gaping security holes when they upgrade to NT 4.0. However, it has two major drawbacks. First, it is very resource intensive. When you launch a process as the activator, the operating system creates an entirely new *window station*. A window station is a securable object that contains a desktop (where all the windows live), running object table, clipboard, and atom table. You can think of a window station as a clone machine that happens to inhabit the same physical box as all the other window stations. When a user logs on to NT, a window station called the *interactive window station* is created and given access to the keyboard, mouse, and display device. Other window stations on a machine cannot interact with the input or output devices, which is why you don't see the server's window when it runs as the activator. Window stations can only interact with each other if you specifically write code to make that happen, which hardly anyone ever does.

Window stations are expensive, costing at least 3 Megabytes of memory. Each different activator gets his own window station. The interactive window station is created when Mary logs on to her machine. If George creates an object on Mary's machine, COM will create a second window station and launch an instance of the server process on it. If Lee then creates the same class of object as activator on Mary's machine, COM will create a third window station and launch a third instance of the server process in it. This brings a server machine to its knees very quickly.

The second problem of running as the activator is that a process which is impersonating a user is allowed a lower level of privilege than one that is legally logged on as the same user. On NT 4.0, an impersonating process is allowed perform actions on its own machine, but not allowed to perform actions on other machines. If George launches a server process as activator on Mary's machine, the process will be able to do anything on Mary's machine that Mary has granted permission for George to do. However, since the server process is only impersonating George, the server process won't be able to do anything on any other machine, even George's. Any action on any other machine that requires any security checking at all will fail, even if George would normally be allowed to do it. In the data4 example, if you launch the remote server as activator and select "Data Object — DAdvise" from the main menu, you probably won't receive updates, although you will when you create the same object from a local server. The reason is that the server process is only impersonating the client, which won't allow the server to make calls to any other machine, even the original client's. The only way around this is to set the authentication level (see next section) on both machines to "none", which means that it won't even check to see if the caller is impersonating or not. Most real life administrators don't like to do this.

2. Is there a way around this? Fortunately, yes. A remote server app does not have to run as the activator. The administrator of the server machine may specify that the server process run as a specific user or as the interactive user, the one who is currently logged in via the user interface. Most real apps want one or the other. The "RunAs" named value in the AppID section of the registry, shown on the facing page, specifies the user whose identity the launched server will assume. You can set it with dcomcnfg, shown below, or via the registry editor.

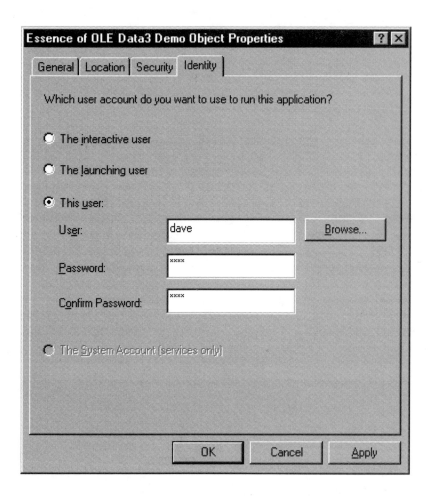

Note: Running as the interactive user or as a specific user does not require your app to supply a password at runtime. The identity of the remote user, as confirmed by the domain server, is all the ID required of a remote client. If there is no domain server, then the ID and password of the remote client need to match those of the specified user on the object's server.

2. If you choose "The interactive user", the RunAs registry setting will be "InteractiveUser". In this case, a server launched by a remote user shares the window station of the interactive user who is currently logged on. Any windows that the server shows will be visible on the desktop of the server machine. If George creates an object that launches a server and Lee comes along and creates another object of the same class, the same server app will handle both requests. The only drawback is that if no user is logged in, no app will run, and if the user logs out, any running servers will be terminated. Choose this option during development so you can see debugging information on the server app's window. You may also use it in production where you want the server's administrator to be able to see status information on the server app's window.

You may also elect to run a server app as a specific user. This will create one new window station, which isn't a terrible resource hit. A server here may still provide objects to multiple remote clients. The only real difference is that the interactive user won't be able to see the server's windows.

In either of these cases, the server process will not run under impersonation; it will be legally logged in as the specified user. If the server wants to make a call to another machine, it will be allowed to do so subject to the other machine's security.

345

3. It is frequently useful for a server to be able to temporarily impersonate the client that is making an object method call. You will need to do this when a remote server runs with any identity other than the activator. Server apps tend to have high levels of permissions, for example, frequently having the privilege of opening any file on their machines. The remote client generally has a much lower level of permission. When a DCOM client makes an object method call that requires opening a file, the operating should only succeed if the client making the call has permission to do so. Rather than write your own security checking and administration code, it would be great if the server could take on the client's identity and security attributes and attempt to open the file in the usual way. The operating system would treat the server as if it were the client, and refuse to open the file if the client was not permitted to do so, rather than using higher access privilege of the server.

A server impersonates a client via the API function **CoImpersonateClient( )**. The server takes back its own security identity by calling the API function **CoRevertToSelf( )**, which is called implicitly when the method returns if you haven't done it sooner. The sample app in \chap10\data4\server performs its impersonation on every call to IDataObject::GetData( ) and places the results on the main window for you to see. Thus:

```
extern HRESULT LastImpersonateResult ;
extern char LastImpersonatedName [] ;
extern HWND hMainWnd ;

STDMETHODIMP CTimeData::GetData (LPFORMATETC lpfe, LPSTGMEDIUM lpstg)
{

/*
Impersonate the calling client. Place the result code where it will be
shown on the server's main window for administrator to see.
*/

    LastImpersonateResult = CoImpersonateClient( ) ;



    < perform operations >

/*
Take back server's own identity.
*/

    CoRevertToSelf ( ) ;

    InvalidateRect (hMainWnd, NULL, TRUE) ;
    return retval ;
}
```

Note: This function might be slow because it may require a round trip to the domain controller to get the information of the client it needs to impersonate.

4. A client app sets an *impersonation level* that specifies which impersonation actions the client will allows the server to perform. DCOM-aware apps may provide this setting via the API function CoInitializeSecurity( ) shown in the next section. Apps which do not call this function are given the value specified in the LegacyImpersonationLevel registry setting shown on page 336. The settings available to the client are:

Name	Value	Operations allowed
Anonymous	1	Server cannot find out who client is.
Identify	2	Server can read identity of client, cannot perform operations as client.
Impersonate	3	Server can perform operations as client on server's own machine but not on other machine's, even the client's.
Delegate	4	Server can perform operations as client on other machines on network (not supported on NT 4.0, scheduled for 5.0)

A client may choose not to allow itself to be impersonated. However, a server may refuse to perform operations for a client that doesn't allow this. Good DCOM clients need to allow the server to impersonate them. If you don't trust the server, you shouldn't connect to it.

If the server calls CoImpersonateClient( ) and the client doesn't allow impersonation, the call will still return a value of S_OK. However, if the server then tries to perform any secured operations before reverting to itself, the call will fail, because the client has refused to provide the information necessary for the server machine's operating system to check if the operation should be allowed or not.

5. A server may need to find out the identity of a client that it is impersonating. The API function GetUserName( ) would seem to do the trick, but it only provides the user's name and not its domain. To get both user name and domain, it is necessary to open the thread's security token and read its actual data. A full discussion of the security mechanism is beyond the scope of this book, but the code shown on the facing page does the trick in the data4sv sample app. It can appear anywhere after the call to CoImpersonateClient( ) and before the call to CoRevertToSelf( ). It reads the domain and user information of the impersonated thread and displays it on the main window, as shown in the screen shot below.

```
Essence of OLE Data4 DCOM Local Server          _ □ ×
This window is displayed for demonstration purposes only.
Object Count == 1
Server Lock Count == 0
10:36:57

Main app running as user: Administrator
Last call to CoImpersonate client hr == 0x0
Last GetData call processed as domain: DOSEQUIS user: Administrator
Last GetData call auth level = 0x6
```

```
/*
Get user and domain name to display on screen.
*/

char LastImpersonatedName [80] = "", LastImpersonatedDomain[80] = "" ;

STDMETHODIMP CTimeData::GetData (LPFORMATETC lpfe, LPSTGMEDIUM lpstg)
{
    < code omitted >

    CoImpersonateClient ( ) ;

#define BUFSIZE 512
    HANDLE hToken ;
    char buf [BUFSIZE] ;
    DWORD bufsize = BUFSIZE ;
    SID_NAME_USE snu ;

/*
Open security token of this thread.
*/
    OpenThreadToken (GetCurrentThread(), TOKEN_QUERY,
      TRUE, &hToken) ;

/*
Get the information from the token that identifies the user thereof.
*/
    GetTokenInformation (
      hToken,
      TokenUser,    // const defined in system header file, see docs
      buf, bufsize,
      &bufsize) ;
/*
Query the operating system for the domain and user names that apply to
the user information from the token. Store in global variables that the
main window's WM_PAINT code draws on the screen.
*/

    DWORD NameSize = sizeof (LastImpersonatedName) ;
    DWORD DomainSize = sizeof (LastImpersonatedDomain) ;

    LookupAccountSid (
      NULL,
      ((PTOKEN_USER)buf)->User.Sid,
      LastImpersonatedName,
      &NameSize,
      LastImpersonatedDomain,
      &DomainSize,
      &snu) ;

    InvalidateRect (hMainWnd, NULL, FALSE) ;
    CoRevertToSelf( );
}
```

F. CALL SECURITY AND AUTHENTICATION

1. DCOM uses Microsoft's Secure RPC as its underlying communication mechanism. Secure RPC provides several *authentication levels* of security checking for a programmer to choose from.. The available authentication levels are:

Name	Value	Security checking done
None	1	No checking done at all.
Connect	2	Client identity checked only on first RPC to server. Automatically upgraded to Packet in NT 4.0.
Call	3	Client identity checked on first packet of every call. Automatically upgraded to Packet in NT 4.0.
Packet	4	Client's identity encrypted on each packet of every call (sometimes a call's data is split into multiple packets). Server checks identity to make sure the call came from the expected client.
Packet Integrity	5	Same as Packet, plus RPC calculates and encrypts a checksum of the packet's data. Server recalculates and checks this checksum to be sure that packet wasn't tampered with.
Packet Privacy	6	Same as Packet Integrity, plus RPC encrypts all the data in the entire packet so an eavesdropper can't read any of it.

The authentication level set by a client specifies the construction of the packets it sends to the server. The authentication level set by the server indicates the minimum level at which the server will accept an incoming call. If the client tries to make a call at a lower level than the server allows, the call will fail with an error. For example, Microsoft Transaction Server rejects any attempt to talk to it with an authentication level of less than Packet.

The levels Packet Integrity and Packet Privacy require the secure RPC mechanism to examine all the data in the packet, first to generate the checksum (and encrypt the data for Packet Privacy) on the client side; then to regenerate the checksum (and decrypt data for Packet Privacy) on the server side. This burns microseconds, so use them only for sensitive data.

RPC performs its authentication functions at a lower level than COM. On an outgoing COM call from a client, it takes place after the call is marshaled by the interface proxy. On an incoming COM call to a server, it takes place before the call is presented to the interface stub.

The secure RPC functionality is provided by a *security service provider* (SSP) , a package that lives on the operating system to provide security services. On NT 4.0, the only available security provider is the one that ships with the operating sytem. NT 5.0 is supposed to provide support for installable SSP's, notably Kerberos. When you see function calls refer to SSP's or authentication services, you may safely take the default values unless you have NT 5.0 and have gone to considerable trouble to buy and install a different one.

2. A DCOM app specifies the security settings for all interfaces in its process via the API function **CoInitializeSecurity( )**. If this granularity is too high, you can change it for individual interfaces as shown on the following pages. If an app has not called this function by the time it makes the first COM call that marshals an object pointer, such as CoCreateInstance( ), COM will automatically call it for you, specifying default settings from the registry.

The first parameter allows you specify a security descriptor instructing the secure RPC mechanism as to which users are or are not allowed access to interfaces of which this app is the server. This mechanism is somewhat complicated and is explained on page 356.

The authentication level that you set in this call is the outgoing level used in calls to interfaces of which this process is the client. The same value is used for the minimum authentication level that will be accepted for incoming calls to interfaces of which this process is the server. If COM calls this function automatically, it will use the "LegacyAuthenticationLevel" registry value shown on page 336.

The impersonation level set in this call is discussed in the previous section. If COM calls this function automatically, it will use the "LegacyImpersonationLevel" registry value shown on page 336.

The code shown below comes from the DCOM sample client app data4cl. It is called when you select "Data Object — Set Process Security..." from the menu. **For this feature to work in the sample app, you must make these settings before you create the remote object.** Thus:

```
DWORD g_AuthenticationLevel, g_ImpersonationLevel ;

case ID_DATAOBJECT_SETSECURITY:
{

/*
Pop up dialog box to get security settings from user.
*/
    if (DialogBox (hInst, MAKEINTRESOURCE (IDD_DIALOG3), hWnd,
      (DLGPROC) SecurityDlgProc) == IDOK)
    {
      HRESULT hr = CoInitializeSecurity (
              NULL,                       //security descriptor, use defaults
              -1,                         //count of authorization services
              NULL,                       //authorization srvc, NULL==default
              NULL,                       // reserved
              g_AuthenticationLevel,      // authentication level
              g_ImpersonationLevel,       // impersonation level
              NULL,                       // reserved
              EOAC_NONE,                  // additional capabilities
              NULL) ;                     // reserved

      if (hr != S_OK)
      {
            MessageBox (NULL, "Couldn't initialize security", "", 0) ;
      }
    }
    return 0 ;
}
```

3. The authentication level set in CoInitializeSecurity( ) specifies the authentication level used for all outgoing calls made by the client process. This granularity may be too coarse for your purposes. Suppose you had a distributed commerce client app that had two different interface pointers to the server. Interface IMarketingInfo has methods that the client app calls frequently but which transfer only non-sensitive information, like the latest unadvertised specials. You would not want to spend the microseconds on an authentication level higher than packet. On the other hand, you also have the interface IPurchase, whose methods transfer sensitive information such as the customer's credit card number. You want these calls to be made at the packet privacy level so that any eavesdropper can't see its information. What you really want is to be able to specify different authentication levels for different interface proxies.

You can do this via the API function **CoSetProxyBlanket( )**. This function sets the authentication level and impersonation level used on a single proxy without affecting any other proxies in the process. The API function **CoQueryProxyBlanket( )** will read the current security settings on an individual proxy. The sample app uses the latter to get and the former to set the authentication and impersonation level on the proxy to the remote data object, as shown on the facing page. The code shown is executed when you select "Data Object — Set Proxy Security ..." from the main menu. This code will work any time you have an object proxy for it to work on.

If you like fixups for kludges, you'll love the API function **CoCopyProxy( )** (not shown). This makes a new copy of an interface proxy so you can access the same remote interface at two different levels of authentication. When a single interface contains sensitive and non-sensitive methods, you make two copies of the proxy. You set one's authentication level low and use it to call the interface's non-sensitive methods. You set the other's authentication level high and use it call the interface's sensitive methods. It allows you to hack your way securely around a bad interface design.

```
typedef struct _MySecurityDlgParms {
    DWORD AuthenticationLevel ;
    DWORD ImpersonationLevel ;
} MYSECURITYDLGPARMS ;

case ID_DATAOBJECT_SETPROXYSECURITY:
{
    HRESULT hr ;   SECURITYDLGPARMS sdp ;
/*
Get current authentication and impersonation levels of this particular
IDataObject interface proxy. Store in a structure for passing to a
dialog box.
*/
    hr = CoQueryProxyBlanket (
        lpd,                        // proxy to obtain security settings for
        NULL, NULL, NULL,           // output we don't care about
        &sdp.AuthenticationLevel,// output of authentication level
        &sdp.ImpersonationLevel,  // output of impersonation level
        NULL, NULL) ;               // more stuff we don't care about
/*
Pop up dialog box passing current authentication and impersonation
level for end user to modify.
*/
    if (DialogBoxParam (hInst, MAKEINTRESOURCE (IDD_DIALOG3), hWnd,
        (DLGPROC) SecurityDlgProc, (LPARAM)&sdp) == IDOK)
    {
/*
If user clicks OK, then set authentication and impersonation levels on
this one proxy to those specified by the end user. This does not affect
other proxies in the same process, if any.
*/
        hr = CoSetProxyBlanket (
            lpd,                        // proxy to change settings on
            RPC_C_AUTHN_WINNT,
            RPC_C_AUTHZ_NONE,
            NULL,
            sdp.AuthenticationLevel, // new authentication level
            sdp.ImpersonationLevel,  // new impersonation level
            NULL,
            EOAC_NONE) ;
    }
    return 0 ;
}
```

4. The authentication level set in CoInitializeSecurity( ) specifies the minimum incoming authentication level that the server will accept on any of its objects. This, too, is very coarse granularity. Consider the hypothetical distributed commerce application discussed in the previous pages. If the server set packet privacy as its minimum level, both client and server would waste a lot of microseconds encrypting and decrypting non-sensitive marketing information. On the other hand, if the server sets its minimum security level lower, it might accept sensitive data at a low authentication level, thereby exposing it to eavesdropping. What you really want is for the server to be able to accept information at two different levels for two different interfaces.

Since the client initiates all conversations, the server can't prevent the client from sending sensitive information unencrypted. The server can, however, detect this situation and refuse to use the information. The API function **CoQueryClientBlanket( )** fetches the authentication level used by the client in the incoming call. If that level is lower than the one you think the client should have used, you can reject it. The sample app simply displays the level on the screen. The code isn't executed until the client actually makes a call to IDataObject::GetData( ). Thus:

```
DWORD g_AuthenticationLevel ;

STDMETHODIMP CTimeData::GetData (LPFORMATETC lpfe, LPSTGMEDIUM lpstg)
{

/*
Get authentication levels to display on screen.
*/
        CoQueryClientBlanket (
                NULL, NULL, NULL,           // don't care
                &g_AuthenticationLevel,  // output ptr
                NULL, NULL, NULL) ;         // don't  care either

    <other code omitted>
}
```

Note: If you run the client app and connect to the server on a local machine, you will find that the server always reports a level of 6 (packet privacy) no matter what the client sets. COM is saying that the data is as secure as it could possibly be because it hasn't been on the network at all. Furthermore, if the client app sets its authentication level to connect or call (2 or 3) and then creates an object on a remote server, you will see that NT has upgraded these levels to 4 (packet).

Note: This function has an output parameter that seems to want to return the impersonation level used by the client, but it doesn't currently work. You just have to try to impersonate the client, which will work or it won't.

This page intentionally contains no text other than this sentence.

5. The final piece of call security is specifying which users are or are not allowed to make calls to your app's interfaces. You can specify this in several ways, based on the first parameter you pass to called CoInitializeSecurity( ).

If you pass NULL as the first parameter, as in this example, access permission will be set based on registry entries. COM will first look at the security descriptor set in the "AccessPermission" value of your AppID section. This is set with dcomcnfg in a similar manner as the "LaunchPermission" value set on page 338. If your app doesn't have this registry setting, access permission will default to the global "DefaultAccessPermission" registry value shown on page 336. If this granularity and responsiveness is good enough for you, and it usually is, you can handle the entire access control issue administratively, without having to program anything.

Suppose that's not enough control. Maybe your system administrator is too lazy or maybe your permitted user set changes too quickly. For whatever reason, to sell your app and make money, your app needs to check when it starts up to see which clients are and are not allowed to access its objects. Your app can create an NT security descriptor at runtime based on its own private data and pass that descriptor as the first parameter of CoInitializeSecurity( ). COM will use the security descriptor to decide who is or is not allowed access. A demonstration of NT security descriptors and models is beyond the scope of this book, but they're not too terrible if you can find a prefabricated C++ class library that does it for you. This technique only works on Windows NT.

If you don't like NT security descriptors, you can pass as the first parameter to CoInitializeSecurity( ) a pointer to an interface of type *IAccessControl*, also adding the capability flag **EOAC_ACCESS_CONTROL** to the eighth parameter. This technique will work on Windows 95 as well as NT, although anyone who expects real security from Windows 95 would probably ask his barber for open heart surgery. The methods of this interface are:

GrantAccessRights	*// Add new access permissions to the existing list*
SetAccessRights	*// Replace existing access rights list with new list*
SetOwner	*// Set an item's owner or group*
RevokeAccessRights	*// Remove access permissions from existing list*
GetAllAccessRights	*// Get the entire list of access rights*
IsAccessAllowed	*// Decide if client is allowed access to the object/property*

DCOM provides a standard implementation of this interface, which you create by calling CoCreateInstance( ) with a clsid of **CLSID_DCOMAccessControl**. Although CoInitializeSecurity( ) is usually called implicitly with default parameters if you haven't done so before calling CoCreateInstance( ), this particular object is special cased by COM so that you can create it first and pass it as a parameter to CoInitializeSecurity( ). You use the first five methods of this interface to set up an access control list that specifies who is allowed to do what to the object. It requires using a number of complicated structures and isn't much less painful that the NT security descriptor. COM will then call the last method when it needs to know if a user is permitted access. The standard implementation of the object looks at the access control list that you have set up and says yea or nay.

7. Suppose checking at startup time isn't fine enough access control for your app. If you need to check for up-to-the-second access permission every time a client asks for access to an object, you can write your own implementation of the IAccessControl interface. You can stub out the first 5 methods. The only one that COM will ever call is the last one, **IAccessControl::IsAccessAllowed( )**. You place in this method whatever code you want to decide if the user is allowed access or not. Thus:

```
virtual HRESULT STDMETHODCALLTYPE IsAccessAllowed(PTRUSTEEW pTrustee,
    LPWSTR lpProperty, ACCESS_RIGHTS AccessRights,
    BOOL *pfAccessAllowed)
{

    if ( <whatever access checking I need to do succeeds> )
    {
      *pfAccessAllowed = TRUE ;
    }
    else
    {
      *pfAccessAllowed = FALSE ;
    }

    return S_OK ;
}
```

G. PERFORMANCE IN DCOM

1. When designing a DCOM server app, thinking about its performance in the initial design stages is vital to avoid writing and then trying to sell a pig-dog of an app. DCOM requires network traffic, and network calls are slower than local calls by at least one order of magnitude, frequently more. It's not just complex code that bogs down, either. It's anything that generates lots of network traffic. Look at the remote running object table sample in the next section for an example of very simple code that generates an awful lot of network traffic. You need to think about it at design time.

If you run the timing test on the sample app, you will find some interesting things. The table below sums up the performance data measured with the data3 legacy apps on two Pentium Pro 200 machines connected by a 10Mbit Ethernet with no other users:

bytes transferred	ms per call
100	1.2
200	1.4
10,000	11.0
20,000	21.8

As you can see, the call overhead is about 1 ms per call. Transferring data takes about 1 ms per 1000 bytes, which is just about the raw speed of a 10 MBit Ethernet. So for small amounts of data transferred, the call overhead dominates the timing. To optimize this, you need to minimize round trips. For example, if your server exposed an object representing a customer, you would make a performance profit by providing a method that returned a customer's first name, middle name, and last name in a single call, rather than exposing them as separate properties, each of which required a round trip to read.

As the amounts of data transferred get larger, then copying the data starts to dominate the overhead. The break-even point is somewhere around 1000 bytes transferred, which isn't a whole lot as data models go these days. To optimize this, you need to avoid transferring unnecessary data. For example, don't transfer the entire 1 Mbyte customer database to a client app that only cares about a single customer.

2. What else can you do? Here are a few ideas. First, make sure you are using the fastest hardware you can buy. I'm sure that 100 MBit Ethernet would make the numbers above go down considerably, probably more in the data transfer than the call overhead. But remember that your customers won't always have the latest hardware, and that future releases of software invariable get bigger and slower. It has long been a truism of the software industry that, "It doesn't matter how good the hardware boys are, the software boys will piss it away." Or, to put it somewhat less pungently, "Andy Grove giveth, but Bill Gates taketh away." Don't add your name to the end of the sentence.

Second, make sure that you can pass as many small properties as possible in the same call. Instead of exposing each property individually, or perhaps in addition so that designers using your server can choose what they want, have a method called GetCustomerData( ) which takes output pointers to all of a customer's properties and gets it all in one trip.

3. About the neatest way I can think of optimizing the performance is with a custom marshaling proxy. Your server app has a method like ISomeApp::GetCustomer( ), which returns a pointer to an ICustomer interface, for which you provide a custom marshaling proxy as shown in Chapter 9. When DCOM calls your server's method IMarshal::MarshalInterface( ), you write all the customer's data as a blob into the IStream used as a marshaling packet. On the client side, DCOM will create your custom marshaling proxy and call IMarshal::UnmarshalInterface( ). The proxy then unpacks the stream and uses its data, exposing methods that the client uses to access it locally. All the data is transmitted in a single call, and your client is none the wiser. If the client makes changes to the customer's properties, your proxy can cache them locally and only transmit them to the server when instructed to do so. This approach would work especially well for an object that had many small properties.

H. COOL BUT CAUTIONARY EXAMPLE: GLOBAL RUNNING OBJECT TABLE

1. One of the things that I get asked in every class on DCOM that I teach is if there is a global running object table. There really isn't, but I decided to sit down and write one as an exercise. Getting the running object table from a remote machine is trivial if you can place a server on that machine, which in turn is trivial using DCOM. The sample app server is found in the directory \EssenceOfOle\Chap10\drotdll. The subdirectory \test contains an app for testing the sample server. While very easy to write, this app demonstrates almost every possible pitfall in DCOM. Specifically:

A) Your remote server can only get the running object table of the window station on which it runs. If the remote server is configured to run as the interactive user, as is the sample, then it accesses the same running object table as the interactive user's apps on that system. If the server is running as a specific user, it will be on a separate window station and not be able to see the interactive apps, although it will see the running object table used by all other remote servers configured to run as the same user. This may be what you want in a distributed object application.

B) Even if you get a pointer to an object container in a remote running object table, unless the server that put the pointer there has granted you permission to use it, you can't call any of its methods.

C) This conceptually simple app generates a hellacious amount of network traffic. Looking at the source code on the following pages, the call to get the remote object table is one remote call, the call to IRunningObjectTable::EnumRunning is a second. Each call to IEnumMoniker::Next( ) is another, each call to IMoniker::GetDisplayName( ) is another. Furthermore, the bind context used in the latter call is on the client machine, so any call the moniker makes to the bind context in composing its display name is another remote call. You can really bog a system down by writing distributed code with a single-desktop mindset.

D) The moniker comes from a remote system. If you try to bind to it on the local machine, it might reference data on the remote machine and thus not work.

I wrote my own custom interface called IRemoteROT. It contains the single method GetRemoteRunningObjectTable( ). Thus:

```
interface DECLSPEC_UUID("23901471-FD2A-11D0-806E-006097418C73")
    IRemoteROT : public IUnknown
    {
        public:
          virtual HRESULT STDMETHODCALLTYPE
            GetRemoteRunningObjectTable(IRunningObjectTable **ppRot)=0;
    };
```

Implementing this interface is about as trivial as it gets. Thus:

```
STDMETHODIMP CRemoteROT::GetRemoteRunningObjectTable(
    IRunningObjectTable **ppRot)
{
    return GetRunningObjectTable (0, ppRot) ;
}
```

Note: I used the Active Template Library, described in Chapter 14, to write this server. I found it significantly quicker and easier than cutting and pasting my own code or using the MFC. I found its automatic generation of custom interface marshaling code to be particularly useful. I used the "Merge Proxy/Stub Code" option to bind the marshaling code into the same DLL as the server itself.

2. The test client app does about what you think it ought to do. It creates an object of the correct clsid on the specified remote system, then calls the method IRemoteROT::GetRemoteRunningObjectTable( ). Once it had the running object table, it enumerated the monikers in it and placed their display names in a list box for the user to look at. Its appearance is shown below. Its code is shown on the two following pages. Thus:

```
/*
This method called when user clicks "Connect"
*/

void CDrottestDlg::OnConnect()
{

/*
Create remote running object table server on specified machine. Query
for IRemoteROT interface.
*/

    CString RemoteSystemName ;
    GetDlgItemText (IDC_REMOTENAME, RemoteSystemName) ;

    USES_CONVERSION ;

    HRESULT hr ;
    COSERVERINFO si ;

    si.dwReserved1 = 0 ;
    si.pwszName = A2W(RemoteSystemName) ;
    si.pAuthInfo = NULL ;
    si.dwReserved2 = 0 ;

    MULTI_QI mqi [1] ;

    mqi [0].pIID = &IID_IRemoteROT ;
    mqi [0].pItf = NULL ;
    mqi [0].hr = 0 ;

    hr = CoCreateInstanceEx (
      CLSID_RemoteROT,
      NULL,
      CLSCTX_REMOTE_SERVER,
      &si,
      1,
      mqi) ;

    if (hr != S_OK)
    {
      char out [256] ;
      wsprintf (out, "Couldn't launch remote server, hr == 0x%x", hr) ;
      MessageBox (out, "RemoteROT") ;
    }

    IRemoteROT *pGet = (IRemoteROT *) mqi [0].pItf ;
```

```
/*
Now that we have the IRemoteROT interface, use it to get the running
object table from the remote machine.
*/

    hr = pGet->GetRemoteRunningObjectTable (&m_pRot) ;
    pGet->Release ( ) ;

/*
Iterate through running object table. Get each moniker's display name
and place in the list box for the user to see. First, get the
enumerator of all the objects in the running object table.
*/

    IEnumMoniker *pEnum ;
    hr = m_pRot->EnumRunning (&pEnum) ;

/*
Step through each moniker it
*/
    IMoniker *pMoniker ;

    while ((hr = pEnum->Next (1, &pMoniker, NULL)) == S_OK)
    {
      IBindCtx *pBindCtx ;
      CreateBindCtx (0, &pBindCtx) ;

      WCHAR wout [256], *pwout ;
      pwout = wout ;
/*
Get display name from moniker. Place in list box
*/

      pMoniker->GetDisplayName (pBindCtx, NULL, &pwout) ;
      m_List.AddString (W2A(pwout)) ;

/*
Clean up.
*/
      pBindCtx->Release ( ) ;
      pMoniker->Release ( ) ;
    }
    if (pEnum)
    {
      pEnum->Release() ;
    }
}
```

Directory: \EssenceOfOle\Chap10\data4
Directory: \EssenceOfOle\Chap10\drotdll

1. Make sure the data3 server from chapter 2 is registered according to its instructions on both client and server machine. For this quick demo, make sure that both machines are running with the same user ID and password. On both client and server machines, run dcomcnfg.exe and use it to enable DCOM. On the client machine, use dcomcnfg.exe to configure the client machine's registry as follows. From the "Applications" tab, choose "Essence of OLE Data3 Demo Object" and click the "Properties ..." button. Select the "Location" tab. Clear the "Run application on this computer" checkbox. Check the "Run application on the following computer" box, then click "Browse...". Use the browser to select the client machine, click OK. Click OK again to close DCOMCFNG. Run the data3 client app from the chap02 directory. Pick "Create from .EXE server". The object will run on the remote machine. Try the "Get Data" and "Get Data Time Test..." options.

2. On the client machine, run the registry editor, go to the CLSID for the server and comment out the InProvServer32 key, as you will see that dcomcnfg.exe has already done for the LocalServer32. Run the client app again, this time choosing "Create from .DLL server". The server app will appear on the server machine. There is at the time of this writing no way to make the server machine use an in-proc server for this request.

3. Register the data4 server app on local and remote machine. Run the data4 client app. Create objects both locally and remotely. The "Create from Remote Server" menu item will not be enabled until you have set a remote server name. Perform the time test.

4. Register the moniker server app from Chapter 8 on a remote machine. Run the moniker server app and save one of its files. Run the data4 client app, pick "Create from file..." from the menu. Note that the server app will appear on the remote machine.

5. Log in as different user on the client machine. Create a remote object using the data4 server. Note that server performs impersonation on remote machine.

6. Register the server \Chap10\drotdll\drotdll.dll on a remote system. Using dcomcnfg, set the security parameters so your client machine will have access. Run an app on the remote machine that registers a moniker, such as VC++ v5.0. Now go back to your client machine, run the app "drottest.exe" from the \test subdirectory. Type in the name of the remote machine, click the connect button. You should see the moniker from the remote system.

EXTRA CREDIT: Install netmon and see how many remote COM calls are generated by the seemingly simple remote running object table. Figure out how you would design a different interface to optimize this operation. Hint: What interface does IMoniker derive from?

Chapter 11
ActiveX Controls on the Internet

A. Component Download Service

1. To operate in an Internet environment, container apps need to be able to download ActiveX controls from the Internet and install them on the user's local system. In addition, container apps need some form of security checking to allow the user to download only controls from trusted sources and ensure that they have not been tampered with. This functionality is provided by the *component download service*.

The control download service is not restricted to downloading only ActiveX controls. It can download and use any OLE server, in-proc or local, provided that the server is self-registering as specified in Appendix A. It is also fully backwards compatible – the downloaded server need not contain any extra functionality in order to make it downloadable.

The examples shown in this section use the sample app found in the directory \CHAP11\CLIENT. For maximum flexibility and transparency, this app does not read its parameters from an HTML page. Instead, the user enters them through a dialog box. The app creates a single control of any class that you specify, downloading the control from the Internet if necessary. The app also allows you to specify the name and value of a single property. When the app finishes creating the control, it will set the named property to the specified value. Thus:

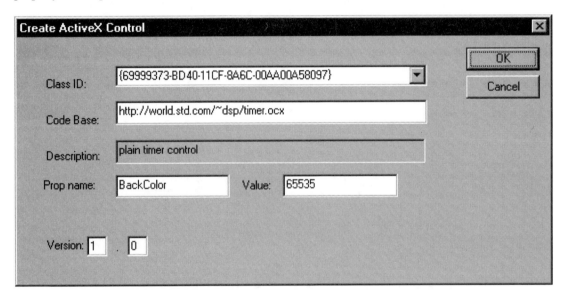

Note: This sample app was generated using App Wizard with "OCX Controls" box checked. However, to get CoGetClassObjectFromURL( ) to work, it was necessary to add a call to AfxOleInit( ) in the CWinApp::InitInstance( ) method. Otherwise, it came back with an error saying that OLE hadn't been initialized.

2. In HTML, an ActiveX control is signaled via the **<OBJECT>** tag, added to the HTML 3.2 specification by Microsoft. When you use the ActiveX Control Pad utility app (shown on next page) to add a timer control of the type built in Chapter 5 to an HTML page, you get the following HTML code, which may be found in the directory \CHAP11\DOWNLOAD\TIMER.HTM:

```
<OBJECT
    ID="Timer1" WIDTH=100 HEIGHT=51
    CLASSID="CLSID:69999373-BD40-11CF-8A6C-00AA00A58097"
    CODEBASE="http://www.rollthunder.com/timer.ocx">
    <PARAM NAME="_Version" VALUE="65536">
    <PARAM NAME="_ExtentX" VALUE="2646">
    <PARAM NAME="_ExtentY" VALUE="1341">
    <PARAM NAME="_StockProps" VALUE="1">
    <PARAM NAME="ShowSeconds" VALUE="-1">
</OBJECT>
```

The **CLASSID** attribute specifies the class ID of the OLE object to create. This is the same OLE/COM class ID that we've used throughout this book. The **CODEBASE** attribute specifies the URL from which the object's server (the .OCX DLL) can be downloaded if it isn't already on the user's system.

Each **<PARAM>** tag specifies the name and value of a property of the control. The properties that begin with an underscore, such as "_Version" in the above example, are not properties exposed by the control itself, but instead are for the use of the HTML browser. In the example shown above, the control's "ShowSeconds" property is set to -1 (TRUE).

3. You can place ActiveX controls on an HTML document using the ActiveX Control Pad, an HTML utility app available free from Microsoft's Web site. When you run the app and select "Edit – Insert ActiveX control", it reads the registry and shows you the following dialog box containing the names of all the controls registered on your system. As far as I can tell, it detects controls by looking for the "Control" registry key that OCX and now ActiveX controls place in their registry entries. Thus:

4. When you insert a control, the Control Pad loads the control's DLL, creates an instance of the control, and displays a window for editing the control's properties in a manner similar to Visual Basic. When you close the control's window, the Control Pad writes the appropriate HTML statements into its file. Thus:

5. Your container app will eventually need to create a new ActiveX control, either from reading an HTML file or, as in the sample app, because the user makes entries in a dialog box. The control might already be on your machine, or you might have to download it from the Internet. Even if a version of the control already exists on your system, the Web page may specify a newer version, so any time you see an <OBJECT> tag, you might need to download it or you might not.

The component download service of ActiveX is provided by the single function **CoGetClassObjectFromURL( )**. This function does its level best to return a pointer to the requested object's class factory.

The function first attempts to retrieve from the user's machine the class factory for the specified class ID and version of object. If this is successful, the function returns immediately with the success code S_OK and the output parameter contains a pointer to the class factory. In this case, the behavior is identical to the API function CoGetClassObject( ).

If this is not successful, the function attempts to download the control from the Internet using the specified URL. This process uses the asynchronous URL moniker with an IBindStatusCallback object, as discussed in the last section of Chapter 8. In this case, the function returns the code **MK_S_ASYNCHRONOUS**, meaning that the download has been successfully started. Further notifications of progress and final success or failure are signaled through the IBindStatusCallback interface's methods. The URL may indicate a single .EXE or .DLL, or it may point to compressed .CAB and .INF files.

After the download is successfully completed, the control's integrity is verified using the WinTrustVerify( ) mechanism discussed on page 378. The control is registered on the user's machine using the self-registration mechanism discussed in Appendix A. Finally, the control is loaded and the class factory returned in the method IBindStatusCallback::OnObjectAvailable( ) shown on page 373. Thus:

```
class CClientView : public CView
{
public:
    CBindStatusCallback *m_pCallback ;      IUnknown*   m_pUnknown ;
    IBindCtx*      m_pBindCtx ;              CProgressCtrl m_Progress ;

    <rest of class declaration>
}


void CClientView::OnControlCreate()
{
/*
Pop up dialog box asking user which control to create.
*/
    CCreateControlDlg dlg ;
    if (dlg.DoModal( ) == IDOK)
    {
      m_clsid = dlg.m_clsid ;
/*
Create a new bind status callback for asynchronous notifications during
the download. Create a bind context. Register the IBindStatusCallback
with it.
*/
      m_pCallback = new CBindStatusCallback (this) ;
      HRESULT hr = CreateBindCtx (0, &m_pBindCtx) ;

      IBindStatusCallback *pPrev = NULL ;
      hr = RegisterBindStatusCallback (m_pBindCtx, m_pCallback, &pPrev,
          NULL);
```

```
/*
Get class factory for specified control, downloading from the Internet
if necessary. Parameters entered by user via dialog box.
*/
        hr = CoGetClassObjectFromURL (
                dlg.m_clsid,                // class ID of control
                dlg.m_wUrlString,           // URL to download from
                dlg.m_VersionMajor,         // major version number
                dlg.m_VersionMinor,         // minor version number
                NULL,                       // mime type
                m_pBindCtx,                 //bind ctx with IBindStatusCallback
                CLSCTX_INPROC_SERVER,       // server context
                NULL,                       // reserved
                IID_IUnknown,               // interface ptr wanted on class fy
                (LPVOID *) &m_pUnknown) ;       // output variable

/*
Return code was S_OK, meaning control already existed on the user's
machine.  Create the control.
*/
        if (hr == S_OK)
        {
                ReallyCreateControl ( ) ;
                Cleanup ( ) ;
        }
/*
Return code was MK_S_ASYNCHRONOUS, meaning control must be downloaded.
Show progress control to user.
*/
        else if (hr == MK_S_ASYNCHRONOUS)
        {
                m_Progress.ShowWindow (SW_NORMAL) ;
                m_StatusText = "Control download Pending" ;
                Invalidate ( ) ;
        }
/*
Error condition.  Signal and abort.
*/
        else
        {
                AfxMessageBox ("Couldn't download control") ;
                Cleanup ( ) ;
        }
    }
}
```

6. The IBindStatusCallback object used in component download is a little different than that shown in Chapter 8. It must also support the interface *ICodeInstall*, which provides access to the UI for the component installation services. Supporting this interface is easily done via multiple inheritance. Its methods are pretty trivial. Thus:

```
class CBindStatusCallback : public IBindStatusCallback,
    public ICodeInstall
{
  public:

    < remainder of IBindStatusCallback declaration omitted>

    // ICodeInstall methods

    STDMETHODIMP GetWindow (REFGUID , HWND *) ;
    STDMETHODIMP OnCodeInstallProblem (ULONG, LPCWSTR, LPCWSTR, DWORD);
} ;


/*
Provide window handle used by OLE as parent for dialog boxes that OLE
will show relating to code installation.
*/

STDMETHODIMP CBindStatusCallback::GetWindow (REFGUID riid, HWND *phWnd)
{
    if (phWnd)
    {
      *phWnd = m_pView->m_hWnd ;
    }
    return S_OK;
}


/*
OLE has signaled a code installation problem.  Tell the user about it,
and return the code E_FAIL to abort the installation.
*/

STDMETHODIMP CBindStatusCallback::OnCodeInstallProblem (ULONG uiStatus,
    LPCWSTR pExistFile, LPCWSTR pSource, DWORD dwReserved)
{
    AfxMessageBox ("OnCodeInstallProblem") ;
    return E_FAIL ;
}
```

7. When CoGetClassObjectFromURL has downloaded, verified, and registered the specified control, it will call the method **IBindStatusCallback::OnObjectAvailable( )**. This is your signal that the object now exists and may be used. In the sample app, we create the control and clean up. Thus:

```
STDMETHODIMP CBindStatusCallback::OnObjectAvailable(REFIID riid,
    IUnknown* punk)
{

/*
Component download finished, control should now be installed. Use
helper function, shown on next page, to create it.
*/

    m_pView->ReallyCreateControl( ) ;

/*
Clean up after the control creation.
*/

    m_pView->Cleanup ( ) ;
    return S_OK;
}
```

8. Once you have the control's server installed on your system, you create the control exactly like any other OLE control, via the method CWnd::CreateControl( ). Why don't we use the IClassFactory interface pointer that we got from CoGetClassObjectFromURL( )? Because the CWnd proxy model used by control containers in the MFC requires so much other auxiliary setup, which is built into the CreateControl( ) method, that we can't skip it.

Once the control is created, you need to set its properties. In the MFC, it's dead easy to work with a control if you know at compile time which control you will be using. Class Wizard just generates a wrapper class based on the control's type info. It's much more difficult if you don't know until run time which control you will be using. The control in the sample app lives within a class called *CCtrlHolder*, which provides auxiliary functions for manipulating an arbitrary control.

If the <OBJECT> HTML tag contains an attribute with the name <DATA>, it represents a property stream saved by the control. You can query the control for the IPersistStream interface and pass the <DATA> stream to it. But you can't depend on this being present, so you need to be able to set the control's properties individually via its IDispatch interface, as represented by the **CCtrlHolder::SetPropByName( )** function called below and discussed on the following pages. Thus:

```
BOOL CClientView::ReallyCreateControl (void)
{

/*
Delete previous CWnd proxy that held our control, if there was one.
Then create CWnd proxy to hold new control.
*/
    if (m_pCtrlHolder)
    {
      delete m_pCtrlHolder ;
    }
    m_pCtrlHolder = new CCtrlHolder (m_clsid) ;

/*
Create the control as usual.
*/
    CRect r (10, 10, 200, 200) ;
    BOOL bOK = m_pCtrlHolder->CreateControl (
      m_clsid, "", WS_CHILD | WS_VISIBLE | WS_BORDER,
      r, this, 1, NULL, FALSE, NULL) ;

    if (!bOK)
    {
      AfxMessageBox ("Couldn't create") ;
    }
    else
    {
      m_pCtrlHolder->ShowWindow (SW_SHOWNORMAL) ;
      m_pCtrlHolder->BringWindowToTop( ) ;
    }
/*
Set property specified in dialog box.
*/
    m_pCtrlHolder->SetPropByName (m_PropName, m_PropVal) ;
    return bOK ;
}
```

374

9. The method **CCtrlHolder::SetPropByName( )** takes the name of a property and its value in the form of strings and sets it. First, we get the dispatch ID of the name and the type of the property via auxiliary functions shown on the following pages. To convert the string value of the property into whatever type is required, we instantiate an object of the MFC class *COleVariant* and use the method **COleVariant::ChangeType( )**.

The actual setting of the property is done via the method **COleControlSite::SetPropertyV( )**. The member variable m_pCtrlSite, introduced in Chapter 6, is a member of the CWnd class, which you have to include the header file "**occimpl.h**" in order to acces. Thus:

```
HRESULT CCtrlHolder::SetPropByName (CString PropName, CString PropVal)
{

/*
Get dispatch ID of named property via helper function shown on next
page.
*/
    DISPID id ;
    HRESULT hr = GetIDOfName (PropName, &id) ;

    if (hr != S_OK)
    {
      return hr ;
    }

/*
Get type of named property using helper function shown on subsequent
page.
*/
    VARTYPE vt ;
    hr = GetTypeOfProperty (id, &vt) ;

/*
Convert string value of property into requested type.
*/
    COleVariant var (PropVal) ;
    var.ChangeType (vt) ;

/*
Set the actual property. The method requires a pointer to the data
element of the VARIANT structure, which is 8 bytes from the start.
*/

    VARIANT *pv = (LPVARIANT)(&var) ;
    m_pCtrlSite->SetPropertyV (id, vt, ((char *)pv) + 8) ;

    return S_OK ;
}
```

10.   The   method   **CCtrlHolder::GetIDOfName( )**   is   a   simple   wrapper   for IDispatch::GetIDsOfNames( ). The IDispatch interface is present in the m_pControlSite's **m_dispDriver** element. Thus:

```
HRESULT CCtrlHolder::GetIDOfName (CString &Name, DISPID *pDispIdOut)
{
    DISPID id ;

/*
Convert property name into wide char.
*/
    WCHAR wName [256], *pNames ;

    MultiByteToWideChar (CP_ACP, 0, (LPCTSTR)Name, -1,
      wName, sizeof(wName)/sizeof(WCHAR)) ;

    pNames = wName ;

/*
Call IDispatch::GetIDsOfNames( )on the IDispatch that lives inside the
COleControlSite that lives inside the CWnd.
*/
    HRESULT hr = m_pCtrlSite->m_dispDriver.m_lpDispatch->GetIDsOfNames(
      IID_NULL, &pNames, 1, LOCALE_SYSTEM_DEFAULT, &id) ;

    *pDispIdOut = id ;
    return hr ;
}
```

11. The helper function **CCtrlHolder::GetTypeOfProperty( )** looks in the object's type info to read the type of the property associated with the specified dispatch ID. This is fairly simple using the principles shown in Chapter 4. The only tricky part is the types of stock properties. If you look them up in the type library, you will find that they have the value VT_USERDEFINED, so this method needs to special case them. Thus: :

```
HRESULT CCtrlHolder::GetTypeOfProperty (DISPID id, VARTYPE *pvt)
{
    ITypeInfo *pti ;

/*
Get type info describing this IDispatch.
*/
    HRESULT hr = m_pCtrlSite->m_dispDriver.m_lpDispatch->GetTypeInfo (
       0, LOCALE_SYSTEM_DEFAULT, &pti) ;

    if (hr != S_OK)
    {
      return hr ;
    }


/*
Check for stock property dispatch IDs. The type library does not tell
us what they are, but the Microsoft spec does.
*/
    switch (id)
    {
      case DISPID_BACKCOLOR:
      case DISPID_FORECOLOR:
      {
          *pvt = VT_I4 ;
          return S_OK ;
      }
    }


/*
Iterate through all the properties until we find the specified one.
*/
    int i = 0 ;   VARDESC *pVarDesc ;

    while (pti->GetVarDesc (i, &pVarDesc) == S_OK)
    {
      if (pVarDesc->memid == id)
      {
          *pvt = (pVarDesc->elemdescVar).tdesc.vt ;
          pti->ReleaseVarDesc (pVarDesc) ;
          return S_OK ;
      }
      i++ ;
      pti->ReleaseVarDesc (pVarDesc) ;
    }
    return E_FAIL ;
}
```

B. ActiveX Control Security

1. Downloading and running code from the Internet raises obvious concerns about security. How do you know that the full-motion belly dancer control that a page promises isn't a Trojan horse for code that formats your hard drive and cancels your subscription to the automatic backup service?

Microsoft had two options for designing control security. Internet controls could have been run in a heavily restricted space with a low level of privileges, for example, not allowing them to delete files. This "sandbox" design approach was rejected because it would have severely limited the usefulness of code from the net, and would have been impossible to implement on Windows 95.

The selected design approach uses a verification system, not a restriction system. It provides accountability, not safety. The operating system does not restrict the actions of a control once it has been installed. It doesn't keep a control from formatting your hard drive. It ensures that you know whom to kill if it does. The relatively few things you can do to protect against malicious controls that slip through are described at the end of this section.

A control from a responsible vendor will contain a digital signature, allowing the operating system to verify that it really does come from the vendor that it says it does. The control will also contain an encrypted hash value, allowing the operating system to detect if it has been altered since the vendor signed it. With this knowledge, you may decide intelligently whether or not to allow the control to be installed on your system. The process of generating a signature and placing it on a control is discussed in more detail on page 382.

2. CoGetClassObjectFromURL( ) uses the API function WinVerifyTrust( ) to inspect the newly downloaded control and check for the presence of the encrypted signature block. This signature block is decoded by a public key provided by a commercial security company such as VeriSign or GTE CyberTrust. The decoded signature block ensures that the file comes from a vendor that has registered with a security company, and contains a hash code that ensures it hasn't been tampered with since it was signed by its vendor.

When the function determines that the control contains a valid signature and hasn't been changed, it will pop up the following dialog box, thereby allowing the user to accept or reject the component. All the dialogs shown on this page and the next are shown directly by WinVerifyTrust( ). Thus:

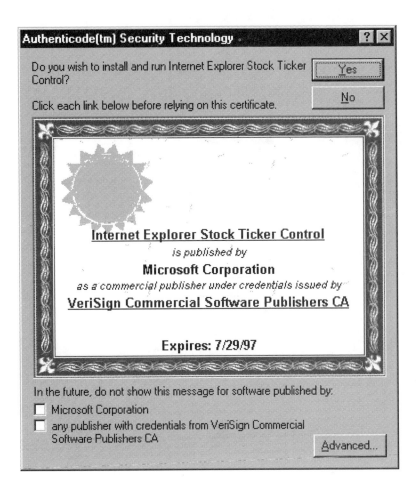

3. If the downloaded control does not contain a verifiable signature block, the user will see one of the following two dialog boxes. The first box is shown even if the control has in fact been signed but has later been tampered with, thereby invalidating the hash code. It is up to you to decide whether or not to allow the control to be installed. Good luck.

4. The user has the choice of designating certain vendors as trusted. In this case, any future downloaded component from any of the designated sources is automatically installed and the user not queried as on the previous page, provided that the control hasn't been tampered with. Thus:

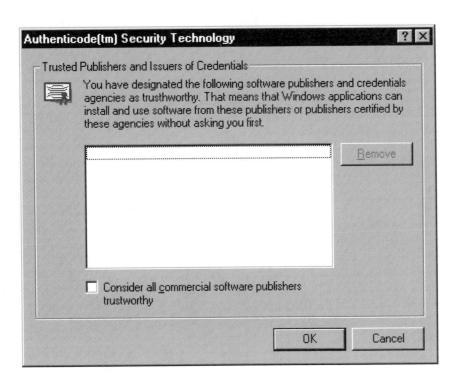

Note: Checking the bottom box to allow any commercial software vendor is not quite as stupid as it initially appears. Think what you do today in a software store. You don't worry about security problems because the boxes are shrink wrapped from commercial vendors. I still wouldn't check it myself.

5. The algorithm used by WinVerifyTrust( ) is based on the RSA public key encryption system. This system relies on two large prime number keys. A message encoded with one key can only be decoded with the other. The keys are large enough that one cannot reasonably be calculated from the other. You publish one, the public key, and keep the other, the private key, secret.

Suppose you are a vendor. You generate a private/public key pair and publish the latter half of it. Anyone wanting to send you a secure message encodes it using your public key before sending it to you. If someone intercepts the message, he will not be able to read it because decoding requires your private key. Conversely, if you encode a message with your private key and post the message on the Internet, anyone who downloads the message can be statistically sure that it came only from you if they can successfully decode it with your public key.

This works fine as long as the public keys are trustworthy. Suppose I were to post a malicious control on the Internet and claim that it came from Microsoft, and post a public key with which it could be decoded. You would take the control, decode it successfully with the key, and think everything was OK. The problem was that the public key didn't really come from Microsoft; instead it came from Trojan Horse Software and your hard disk is toast. You need a trustworthy repository of public keys for this scheme to work.

Enter the *certification authority* (CA), such as VeriSign GTE's or CyberTrust. These companies, for an annual fee, will verify your identity and provide a digital certificate that contains your public key. WinVerifyTrust( ) looks for such a certificate when it validates the control's signature.

You can sign up with a CA over the Internet, at www.verisign.com and www.cybertrust.gte.com. During the sign-up process, your browser will use the operating system's cryptography API to generate a private and public key pair. The private key will be saved on your machine in a file with the extension ".PVK". The public key will be sent to the CA. This outfit will do whatever verification of your identity it thinks it ought to, and if successful, send you a digital certificate, a file with the extension ".SPC". You need both of these files to sign a control.

Most certifying agencies provide several levels of authentication. In researching this book, I got an individual developer certificate from VeriSign, which costs $20 per year. To authenticate your existence, VeriSign looks you up in the Equifax credit bureau files. If your information matches theirs, you're in. Equifax had my age wrong and I wasn't able to sign up until I got a copy of my credit report from Equifax and signed up with VeriSign using the incorrect information. So much for trusting the individual certificate. A commercial developer's certificate costs $400 per year and requires a Dun & Bradstreet number or similar reference.

6. Once you get the key from a certifying agency, you sign your control using the utility app SignCode. This performs a hash of your control and encrypts it with your private key. It then places the encryted hash result and the CA certificate into your control.

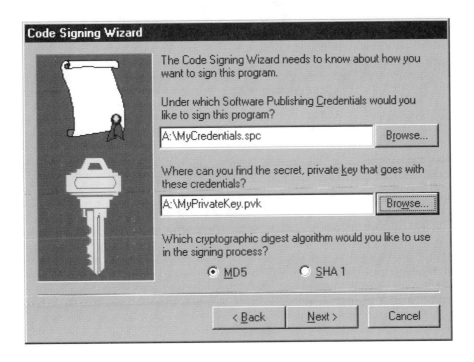

7. The final dialog box looks like this. The directory \CHAP11\SIGNEDTIMER contains a version of the timer control from Chapter 5 which has been signed. When you download it from the Internet, you will see the dialog box at the bottom of the page.

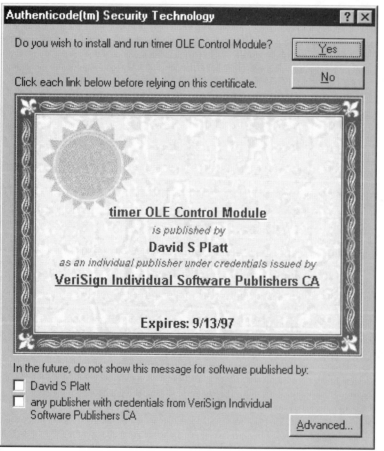

8. There is a limit to the amount of safety that the code signing approach can provide. If you're not comfortable with it, there are a couple of things that you can do. The first is to restrict the locations from which controls can be downloaded to places that you trust. This is accomplished via the code base search path. In the registry, there is a value called:

```
HKEY_CURRENT_USER\Software\Microsoft\Windows\CurrentVersion\
    InternetSettings\CodeBaseSearchPath
```

as shown in the screen shot below:

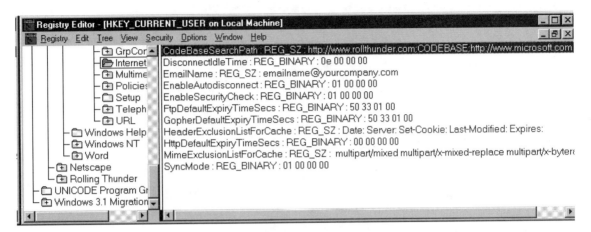

When an app running on this machine calls CoGetClassObjectFromURL( ), the function will attempt to download the code from the servers specified in this registry setting, in the order in which they appear. In the example above, the function will first attempt to download from www.rollthunder.com, then from the URL passed as a parameter to the function, then from www.microsoft.com. If you leave out the CODEBASE keyword, then downloads will only be possible from servers specified in the registry list regardless of what parameters are passed to the function. This is probably the first line of defense for a corporate intranet.

9. Anyone wanting more security and running Windows NT can use the NTFS file system. You make a separate account with no privileges that you use only for Internet surfing. If a malicious control tries to access or modify a disk file owned by another account, it will be blocked by the operating system. You still have the problem of it planting a malicious document and infecting global files such as a WinWord document template, but at least you've raised the intelligence and effort a vandal needs to damage your system.

385

C. ADVANCED FEATURES OF ACTIVEX CONTROLS

1. With the release of MFC 4.2, Microsoft added advanced properties to ActiveX controls. While these properties were originally inspired by the design needs of controls on HTML pages, they may be used any place you think they make sense. These are accessed via the "Advanced..." button in Control Wizard. Thus:

2. When you select the "Advanced..." button, Control Wizard shows you the following dialog box allowing you to select the advanced properties that you want. Loading properties asynchronously is a very useful property for an Internet control and the balance of this chapter discusses it in detail.

The other features are today mostly red herrings. You make little or no profit, and possibly incur a loss, from implementing them. They all depend on the active support of their container. At the time of this writing no container supports them, not even IE3 or the VC++ Test Container, so you can't tell if they work or not. I have to think that it will be a long time before Netscape supports them, if it ever does. This means that even if you want your control to use windowless activation if available, you will still have to support windowed activation as well in order to run properly in any environment. The small performance benefit that you might gain from windowless activation in one browser is probably not worth the additional development and testing time.

D. ASYNCHRONOUS DOWNLOAD OF PROPERTIES

1. Your ActiveX controls may require large pieces of data from the Internet. For example, a movie control might need to download the 5 Megabyte AVI file that it is to play. You want the control to become active as soon as possible and the page to be displayed without waiting for the download. The user may never actually play it, especially if he's on a 28.8 kbaud phone line. You would like the download to proceed asynchronously in background without gumming up the viewer. The source code examples in this section are from a very simple text control which downloads its text asynchronously. The source files may be found in the directory \CHAP11\ATEXT, and instructions for it are at the end of this chapter.

2. When you check the box on the previous page, Control Wizard adds to your control a property called "ReadyState", which tells the container the state of your control's asynchronous download, and also adds an event called "ReadyStateChange", which the control fires when its ReadyState property changes. For example, the control might set the property and fire the event when it finishes its download, and the container might respond by enabling the "Play" button. Thus:

```
[ uuid(8B159891-0429-11D0-B8A1-00608C876FB3),
  helpstring("Dispatch interface for Atext Control"), hidden ]
dispinterface _DAtext
{
    properties:
      //{{AFX_ODL_PROP(CAtextCtrl)
      [id(DISPID_READYSTATE), readonly] long ReadyState;
      //}}AFX_ODL_PROP
    methods:
      //{{AFX_ODL_METHOD(CAtextCtrl)
      //}}AFX_ODL_METHOD
      [id(DISPID_ABOUTBOX)] void AboutBox();
};


//   Event dispatch interface for CAtextCtrl

[ uuid(8B159892-0429-11D0-B8A1-00608C876FB3),
  helpstring("Event interface for Atext Control") ]
dispinterface _DAtextEvents
{
    properties:
     //   Event interface has no properties
    methods:
     //{{AFX_ODL_EVENT(CAtextCtrl)
     [id(DISPID_READYSTATECHANGE)] void ReadyStateChange(long NewState);
     //}}AFX_ODL_EVENT
};
```

WARNING: At the time of this writing, MFC version 4.2A contains a bug that causes the ReadyStateChange( ) event entry in the ODL file to contain no parameters, even though the code in COleControl actually passes the new ready state. The type library generated in this case will not match the actual code. I had to add the "long NewState" parameter shown in italics above by hand. You must do this for your apps as well until Microsoft fixes this.

Note: If you forget to check the box in Control Wizard, or want to add asynchronous downloading to an existing control, you can easily add this property and event by hand. Make sure you get the names and dispatch IDs right.

3. You don't want your movie control hard-wired to one specific movie; you want your customers to be able to place it on their pages and specify any AVI file anywhere on the Web that contains the flick they want to play. You do this by making the desired URL a standard synchronous property of your control, which the page designer can set. The name of this property can be anything you think the human Web page designer will recognize. The type of the property should be OLE_DATAPATH, which is typedefed as a BSTR. Thus:

Note: At the time of this writing, the property type OLE_DATAPATH only appears in the drop-down list when you check the Get/Set methods radio button as shown above. Also, this type is not defined in the standard header files, so I had to #define it myself.

389

4. As discussed in Chapter 8, asynchronous downloading of data from the Internet is accomplished via the URL moniker and the IBindStatusCallback interface. The MFC provides a class encapsulating this functionality called *CAsyncMonikerFile*. Derived from it is the class *CDataPathProperty*, which connects an asynchronous downloading file to an ActiveX control. The class *CCachedDataPathProperty*, derived from CDataPathProperty, adds the functionality of automatically storing the downloaded data in a memory file, so you don't have to worry about reading it in. The hierarchy is:

CFile	File base class
COleStreamFile	Adds IStream support
CMonikerFile	Adds binding via a moniker
CAsyncMonikerFile	Adds asynchronous downloading via URL moniker
CDataPathProperty	Adds connection to a control
CCachedDataPathProperty	Adds automatic reading and storage of data in a memory file

For each separate URL that you want to download, you need to derive a class from one of these. Thus:

```
/*
This class supports automatic asynchronous download of text from the
Internet.
*/

class CAsynchText : public CCachedDataPathProperty
{
    DECLARE_DYNAMIC(CAsynchText)

    < rest of class definition>
}
```

After deriving your asynchronous file class, add an object of that class to your control. Thus:

```
/*
This control contains an object of class CAsynchText to provide
asynchronous download of its property.
*/

class CAtextCtrl : public COleControl
{
    DECLARE_DYNCREATE(CAtextCtrl)

// Constructor
public:
    CAtextCtrl();
    CAsynchText          m_AsynchText ;

    < rest of class declaration >
}
```

5. In the control, you must make the download path property persistent via the method **PX_DataPath( )**. When the control is loading its property set, use the method **CDataPathProperty::Open( )** to begin the binding process. The data path needs to know which control it is attached to, so we pass the method our `this` pointer. Thus:

```
void CAtextCtrl::DoPropExchange(CPropExchange* pPX)
{
    ExchangeVersion(pPX, MAKELONG(_wVerMinor, _wVerMajor));
    COleControl::DoPropExchange(pPX);

/*
Load or save download path property.
*/

    PX_DataPath (pPX, "DownloadPath", m_AsynchText) ;

/*
If we are loading the property set, then start the binding process for
the asynchronous moniker.
*/
    if (pPX->IsLoading( ))
    {
      BOOL bOK = m_AsynchText.Open (this) ;

      if (!bOK)
      {
            AfxMessageBox ("Couldn't start download") ;
      }
    }
}
```

6. In the derived class, you have to override the method **CDataPathProperty::GetBindInfo( )**, in which you return the flags that control the asynchronous moniker binding operation. At the time of this writing, the data-push model specified as the default does not work. You need to override this method and add the flag **BINDF_PULLDATA**, thereby using the data-pull model which does work. Thus:

```
DWORD CAsynchText::GetBindInfo() const
{
    return BINDF_ASYNCHRONOUS | BINDF_ASYNCSTORAGE | BINDF_PULLDATA ;
}
```

7. As the downloaded data is received, the moniker will call the method **CDataPathProperty::OnDataAvailable( )**. The default implementation of the CCachedDataPathProperty base class automatically reads the data into a memory file. You should override this method if you want to invalidate the control so as to render its data as it arrives. If you do this, make sure you call the base class as shown below, otherwise the data will not be read from the incoming stream and the download operation will hang.

The method **CDataPathProperty::GetControl( )** returns a pointer to the control to which the asynchronous download object is attached. In the example below, we use this to invalidate the control to force a repaint. When the last OnDataAvailable( ) notification arrives, as indicated by the flags, the method **COleControl::InternalSetReadyState( )** both changes the ReadyState property and fires the ReadyStateChange event. Thus:

```
void CAsynchText::OnDataAvailable(DWORD dwSize, DWORD bscfFlag)
{

/*
Call the base class which actually reads the data into a memory file.
*/
    CCachedDataPathProperty::OnDataAvailable(dwSize, bscfFlag);

/*
Invalidate the control to which we belong to force a repaint. This
provides progressive rendering, with the data appearing on the screen
as it arrives.
*/
    GetControl( )->Invalidate( ) ;

/*
If this is the last OnDataAvailable( ) notification, set the ready
state flag and trigger the event.
*/
    if (bscfFlag & BSCF_LASTDATANOTIFICATION)
    {
       GetControl()->InternalSetReadyState(READYSTATE_COMPLETE);
    }
}
```

8. When the control's properties are reset in the method COleControl::OnResetState( ), you must stop any current download via the method **CDataPathProperty::ResetData( )**. Thus:

```
void CAtextCtrl::OnResetState()
{
    m_AsynchText.ResetData( ) ;

    COleControl::OnResetState();   // Resets defaults in DoPropExchange
}
```

9. The data path's Set( ) and Get( ) methods are shown below. When the download path property is set, calling the method **COleControl::Load( )** starts the download process. When a container wants to read the property, the method **CDataPathProperty::GetPath( )** returns the current value. Thus:

```
void CAtextCtrl::SetDownloadPath(LPCTSTR lpszNewValue)
{
    Load(lpszNewValue, m_AsynchText);

    SetModifiedFlag();
}

OLE_DATAPATH CAtextCtrl::GetDownloadPath()
{
    CString strResult;

    strResult = m_AsynchText.GetPath();

    return strResult.AllocSysString();
}
```

ActiveX Controls for the Internet

Directory: \EssenceofOLE\chap11\Download

This app uses the API function CoGetClassObjectFromURL( ) to download the control of your choice from the Internet. Run the app "client.exe" and select "Control – Create" from the main menu. When the dialog box appears, type in the class ID and URL of the control you want to download and install. The default points to a timer control on my Web site. If you have the timer control from Chapter 5 installed on your machine, it will give you a local copy of that. Unregister this control if you do not want this. You will see a progress bar as the control is downloaded from the Internet, and a security dialog box before the control is installed. If you like, type in the name and value of a property into the specified edit controls and the app will set the property to the specified value when the control is created. The default sets the background color, which most controls support, to yellow.

Directory: \EssenceofOLE\chap11\Atext

This is an extremely simple control that demonstrates asynchronous download of properties from the Internet. The control contains a property called "DownloadPath" which specifies the URL which it displays. Use the DLL Registering Tool app from Appendix A to invoke the self-registration code in "atext.ocx". After doing this, open the file "atextdemo.htm" using IE3. When IE3 runs the script, you should see the text of my home page appear. When the download is complete, the control will fire the "ReadyStateChanged" event and the "Ready" button will become enabled. It doesn't do anything if you click on it. Use the ActiveX control pad to set the "DownloadPath" property to point to different locations.

Directory: \EssenceofOLE\chap11\SignedTimer

This directory contains a timer control that has been signed with the Code Signing Wizard demonstrated in this chapter. Examine it with a binary editor and note the differences between it and the timer control from Chapter 5.

Chapter 12
ActiveX Scripting

A. CONCEPTS AND DEFINITIONS

1. Sitting on a page looking pretty is fine for a clock or a picture control. However, to use the full power of controls, you must be able to dynamically call their methods, set and get their properties, and respond to their events. A movie control, for example, is much more useful if it can be started, stopped, or positioned in response to commands from the user. Forms become much more convenient to use if you can validate their information on the client before submitting them to the server.

2. ActiveX makes this possible by means of *scripting*. A *script host* app, such as a web browser, reads a series of statements, the *script*, written in some interpreted language, such as Java or VB. The script host loads a *script engine*, a server provided by a vendor that knows how to read, interpret, and execute the script. While originally developed for and very useful on HTML pages, you can use ActiveX scripting any place and any time you want scripting capability.

3. The architecture of ActiveX scripting is independent of the script language. The script host and engine communicate via OLE interfaces, as described on page 400. Anyone who already has an interpreted language can make more money by packaging it into an ActiveX script engine, thereby allowing any host app that speaks ActiveX script to use it.

4. Microsoft provides the scripting engines VBScript and JavaScript, which provide the Visual Basic and Java languages, respectively. These are automatically installed when you install Internet Explorer, and are also available on Microsoft's Web site. The actual server files are VBSCRIPT.DLL and JSCRIPT.DLL. Their binary files are fully redistributable in accordance with Microsoft's license agreement.

B. Scripting in HTML

1. A script on an HTML page is indicated by the tag **<SCRIPT>**. Since scripts can use any interpreted language for which a script engine server is available, the value **"LANGUAGE"** tells the client app which script engine to load in order to interpret the script which follows. The tags **<!--** and **-->** keep the script's text from being displayed on browser apps that do not recognize the <SCRIPT> tag.

When the browser encounters the <SCRIPT> tag, it loads the specified script engine and sends it the script text that follows the tag. Code that is outside any procedure, such as the call to MsgBox( ) in the example below, is executed immediately upon page entry. Code in procedures is executed only when the procedure is called. In the example below, the subroutine Timer1_DblClick( ) is executed when the Timer1 object signals a double-click event.

The script shown below can be found in the directory \CHAP12\SCRIPTHOST\SIMPLE.HTM. You must have installed the timer control from Chapter 5 for it to work. If you open it with Internet Explorer 3.0 (IE3), you will see the message box. You will see the timer's About box when you double-click the mouse on it. Thus:

```
<HTML>
<HEAD>
<TITLE>New Page</TITLE>
</HEAD>
<BODY>
    <SCRIPT LANGUAGE="VBScript">
<!--

MsgBox ("Hello, World")

Sub Timer1_DblClick()
    call Timer1.AboutBox()
end sub

-->
    </SCRIPT>

    <OBJECT ID="Timer1" WIDTH=100 HEIGHT=51
     CLASSID="CLSID:69999373-BD40-11CF-8A6C-00AA00A58097">
        <PARAM NAME="_Version" VALUE="65536">
        <PARAM NAME="_ExtentX" VALUE="2646">
        <PARAM NAME="_ExtentY" VALUE="1323">
        <PARAM NAME="_StockProps" VALUE="1">
        <PARAM NAME="ShowSeconds" VALUE="1">
    </OBJECT>
</BODY>
</HTML>
```

397

2. The ActiveX Control Pad is a pretty good script editor. I used it to create the script on the previous page. Thus:

3. Selecting "Tools — Script Wizard..." from the menu brings up the Script Wizard dialog box, which allows you to easily choose events and specify the actions to be taken when they fire. In the example on the previous page, the event `Timer1_DblClick` was added using the Script Wizard, but the `MsgBox( )` line was added by hand. Thus:

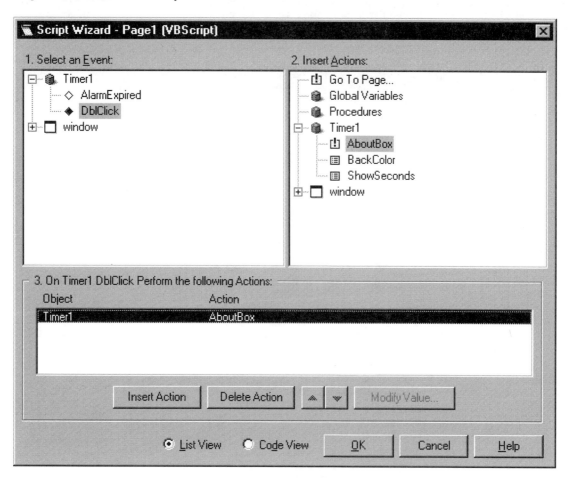

C. OLE ARCHITECTURE OF SCRIPTING

1. The connection between the script host and its engine is accomplished via standard OLE mechanisms. The "Language" value in the <SCRIPT> tag specifies the name of the script engine to use for interpreting the script that follows. That name must be registered with the "CLSID" key underneath it, exactly as is done with the name of any other OLE server. The key "OLEScript" designates that ID as belonging to an ActiveX script engine, and is required for proper operation of IE3. Thus:

2. Under the registry key HKEY_CLASSES_ROOT\CLSID, the script engine makes the standard InProcServer32 entry, pointing to the DLL in which the server's code resides. A script engine also must add the key "OLEScript" as shown below, thereby identifying the server as an ActiveX script engine, similar to the way the presence of the "Control" key marked that entry as belonging to a full-featured OLE control. Thus:

3. A script host and its engine communicate as shown in the following diagram:

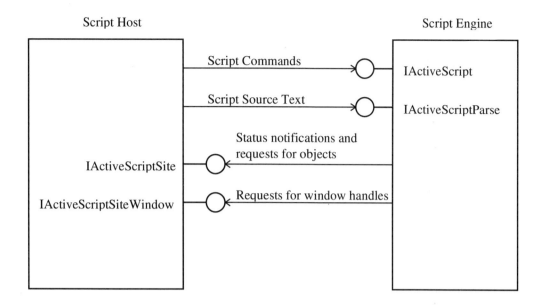

The script host must implement the *IActiveScriptSite* interface. The script engine uses this interface to communicate with the host while the script is executing, signaling such events as its entry, exit, and errors. This interface also provides the engine with pointers to automation objects required by the script. The methods of this interface are:

IActiveScriptSite::GetLCID	*// get locale of script, if other than default*
IActiveScriptSite::GetItemInfo	*// get IDispatch or ITypeInfo of an object in a script*
IActiveScriptSite::GetDocVersionString	*// get version string of document*
IActiveScriptSite::OnScriptTerminate	*// notify host that script has terminated*
IActiveScriptSite::OnStateChange	*// notify host that script has changed state*
IActiveScriptSite::OnScriptError	*// notify host of an error in the script*
IActiveScriptSite::OnEnterScript	*// notify script that execution has entered script*
IActiveScriptSite::OnLeaveScript	*// notify host that execution has left script*

If the host wants to allow the script any access to the Windows user interface, which is optional but customary, it must also implement the *IActiveScriptSiteWindow* interface. This provides the script engine with a window handle which it can use as a parent window for such things as message boxes. The methods of this interface are:

IActiveScriptSiteWindow::GetWindow	*// get hWnd to use as parent for script's dlg boxes*
IActiveScriptSiteWindow::EnableModeless	*// tell host to show or remove modeless dialog boxes*

4. A script engine is a DLL server that implements the *IActiveScript* interface. This interface allows the host to control execution of the script, for example, starting and stopping it. Its methods are:

IActiveScript::SetScriptSite	*// provide engine with IActiveScriptSite object*
IActiveScript::GetScriptSite	*// get current IActiveScriptSite used by engine*
IActiveScript::SetScriptState	*// set current execution state of script engine*
IActiveScript::GetScriptState	*// get current execution state of script engine*
IActiveScript::Close	*// politely shut down script engine*
IActiveScript::AddNamedItem	*// tell engine of existence of an object in the script*
IActiveScript::AddTypeLib	*// add new type library to script's name space*
IActiveScript::GetScriptDispatch	*// get IDispatch of object in currently running script*
IActiveScript::GetCurrentScriptThreadID	*// get ID of currently executing script thread*
IActiveScript::GetScriptThreadID	*// get ID of specified script thread*
IActiveScript::GetScriptThreadState	*// get state of specified script thread*
IActiveScript::InterruptScriptThread	*// stop an executing script thread*
IActiveScript::Clone	*// create clone of current script engine*

It is optional but customary for the script engine to also support the *IActiveScriptParse* interface. This allows the host to send the script to the engine in standard text format. The methods of this interface are:

IActiveScriptParse::InitNew	*// start new script*
IActiveScriptParse::AddScriptlet	*// add new piece to current script*
IActiveScriptParse::ParseScriptText	*// send script in text format to engine for execution*

If the host does not support this interface, then it must support the IPersistStream interface to allow the host to provide its script.

D. SCRIPT HOSTS

1. The examples shown in this section come from the sample script host app shown below. The code may be found in the directory \CHAP12\SCRIPTHOST, and full directions are at the end of this chapter. The app searches your registry for all registered script engines and makes an entry for each one on the "Engine" menu popup. The left-hand pane is a CEditView which allows you to open, edit, and save scripts. The right-hand pane contains a single ActiveX control which you can select using the "Control – Replace Existing" menu item. The scripts that you write may refer to the control by the name "Control1".

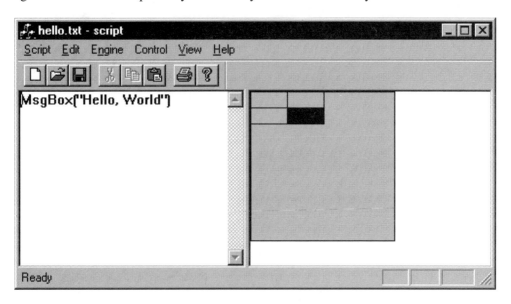

Note: Most Java apps require the host to provide a number of different objects, such as a window object and a document object. This host app does not support the object model, so don't be surprised if you can't do anything fancy with JavaScript.

2. When the user picks the menu command telling the sample app to run a script, we must first create the script engine object via our old friend CoCreateInstance( ). We ask the newly created object for the interface **IID_IActiveScript**, which we need to run the script. Note that the class ID that we pass to this function is the only difference between operating one script engine and another. The text in the script will probably vary, but the operation of the host need not.

Once we have this interface pointer to the script engine, we need to tell the engine about the site in which it runs. We do this by calling the method **IActiveScript::SetScriptSite( )**, passing a pointer to the IActiveScriptSite interface provided by the host. Our view contains a member variable of this class, whose implementation is shown beginning on page 408. Thus:

```
extern CLSID g_EngineClsid ;

void CScriptView::OnScriptRun()
{
    HRESULT hr;
/*
Create the active script engine to be used for the script in this
window.
*/

    hr = CoCreateInstance(
      g_EngineClsid,           // clsid of script engine server
      NULL,
      CLSCTX_INPROC_SERVER,
      IID_IActiveScript,       // need this interface to run a script
      (void **)&m_pActiveScriptEngine);

    if (hr != S_OK)
    {
      AfxMessageBox ("Couldn't create script engine object") ;
      return ;
    }

/*
Tell the IActiveScript about the site it lives in.
*/

    hr = m_pActiveScriptEngine->SetScriptSite(&m_ActiveSite);


    <continued on next page>
```

404

3. Now that we have connected the circuitry between the host and the script engine, we need to feed the script to the engine. Most script engines will support the interface IActiveScriptParse, which allows the host to feed the script in text format directly to the engine. If the engine does not support this interface, it must support IPersistStream and allow the script to be fed in that way. Once we have this interface pointer, we initialize the script engine's parser via the method **IActiveScriptParse::InitNew( )**, then send the script to the engine via the method **IActiveScriptParse::ParseScriptText( )**. Thus:

```
     <continued from previous page>
/*
We need the IActiveScriptParse interface to send the script to the
script engine.
*/
     hr = m_pActiveScriptEngine->QueryInterface (IID_IActiveScriptParse,
       (void **)&m_pActiveParse);

     if (hr != S_OK)
     {
       AfxMessageBox ("Couldn't get IActiveScriptParse") ;
       m_pActiveScriptEngine->Release( ) ;
       return ;
     }

/*
Initialize the script engine's parser.
*/


     hr = m_pActiveParse->InitNew( ) ;


/*
Fetch our text from our view's edit control.
*/


     char TextBuf [4096] ;
     GetEditCtrl( ).GetWindowText (TextBuf, sizeof(TextBuf)) ;


/*
Send it to the script engine in wide character format.
*/


     USES_CONVERSION

     hr = m_pActiveParse->ParseScriptText (
       A2W(TextBuf),        // text to parse, in wide chars
       NULL,                // item name
       NULL,                // debugging context
       NULL,                // end delimiter
       0,                   // cookie
       0,                   // start line number
       0,                   // flags
       NULL,                // buffer for processing results
       NULL) ;              // ptr to EXECEPINFO structure for results

     <continued on next page>
```

405

4. Scripts will frequently need to access automation objects such as controls. The whole point of a script is to tie one object to another. A script engine needs to know what objects the script contains. You tell it by calling the method **IActiveScript::AddNamedItem( )** once for each top-level object in the script, passing the object's name. This will cause the script engine to call the host's method IActiveScriptSite::GetItemInfo( ) to get the IDispatch and type info that it needs to use the object, as shown on page 409. The provided sample app contains a single control whose name is always "Control1".

Once all the objects have been named, you can run the script via the method **IActiveScript::SetScriptState( )**, passing it the somewhat obtusely named state SCRIPTSTATE_CONNECTED. Thus:

```
<continued from previous page>

/*
Tell the script that the control exists.
*/

    hr = m_pActiveScriptEngine->AddNamedItem (
      L"Control1",                               // obj name in script
      SCRIPTITEM_ISSOURCE | SCRIPTITEM_ISVISIBLE) ;   // flags

/*
Tell script engine to run the script.
*/
    hr = m_pActiveScriptEngine->SetScriptState (SCRIPTSTATE_CONNECTED);

    if (hr != S_OK)
    {
      AfxMessageBox ("Script wouldn't run") ;
    }
    else
    {
      m_bIsRunning = TRUE ;
    }
}
```

5. Stopping a script is fairly simple; you call the method **IActiveScript::SetScriptState( )**, telling the script engine to go into the disconnected state. The method **IActiveScript::Close( )** tells the script engine to empty its buffers and release all the interface pointers that it holds to the host, including the IActiveScriptSite and IActiveScriptSiteWindow. Finally, the host releases the engine. Thus:

```
void CScriptView::OnScriptStop()
{
    HRESULT hr ;

/*
Put script into disconnected state.
*/

    hr = m_pActiveScriptEngine->SetScriptState (
      SCRIPTSTATE_DISCONNECTED) ;

/*
Close the script engine. This causes the engine to release its pointers
to the host.
*/

    hr = m_pActiveScriptEngine->Close ( ) ;

/*
Release all pointers.
*/

    hr = m_pActiveParse->Release ( ) ;
    hr = m_pActiveScriptEngine->Release( ) ;
    m_pActiveScriptEngine = NULL ;

    m_bIsRunning = FALSE ;
}
```

6. The host must implement the IActiveScriptSiteWindow interface in conjunction with the IActiveScriptSite interface. This is probably most easily done via multiple inheritance. Thus:

```
class CActiveScriptSite: public IActiveScriptSite,
    public IActiveScriptSiteWindow
{

    <rest of class declaration>

}
```

7. The IActiveScriptSiteWindow interface is trivial, so I'll knock it out of the way now. If the script engine needs a window handle for any reason, such to use as the parent of a dialog box required by the script code, it will query the script site for this interface and call the method **IActiveScriptSiteWindow::GetWindow( )**. If you omit this interface from the host app, the VBScript engine will never be able to show a message box. The method **IActiveScriptSiteWindow::EnableModeless( )** tells the host app to show or remove its modeless dialog boxes in the event that the script is about to show a modal dialog box. Both of the implementations are trivial. Thus:

```
/*
Engine asking for window to use as a parent for a message box.  Respond
with main frame window.
*/

STDMETHODIMP CActiveScriptSite::GetWindow(HWND *phWnd)
{
    if (phWnd)
    {
      *phWnd = AfxGetApp( )->m_pMainWnd->m_hWnd ;
    }
    return S_OK ;
}


/*
Engine telling us to show/hide modeless dialog boxes.  We don't have
any, so ignore it.
*/

STDMETHODIMP CActiveScriptSite::EnableModeless (BOOL bModeless)
{
    return S_OK ;
}
```

8. When the host tells the engine that an object exists via IActiveScript::AddNamedItem( ), the engine will obtain the object's interface pointers via the method **IActiveScriptSite::GetItemInfo( )**. The engine might ask for the object's IUnknown method providing access to its IDispatch, or it might ask for the type info describing the methods and properties which the object supports and the events that it might signal. In the case of the type info, you must provide the type info describing the object's entire CoClass, not just the properties and methods IDispatch. In this example, the base class CCtrlHolder, which wraps the control, contains helper methods for providing these pointers. You can view them in the sample source code. Thus:

```
extern        CCtrlHolder*        g_pControl1 ;

STDMETHODIMP CActiveScriptSite::GetItemInfo(LPCOLESTR    pName,
    DWORD        dwReturnMask, IUnknown**  ppDispOut,
    ITypeInfo** ppTypeInfoOut)
{
    HRESULT hr;
    USES_CONVERSION

/*
See if the script engine is asking for our single control object.
*/

    if (wcsicmp (pName, L"Control1") == 0)
    {
/*
If they are asking for the object's IUnknown pointer, provide that.
GetDispatch( ) helper function provided in CCtrlHolder class.
*/

        if (dwReturnMask & SCRIPTINFO_IUNKNOWN)
        {
            hr = g_pControl1->GetDispatch ((IDispatch **)ppDispOut) ;
        }

/*
If they are also/otherwise asking for the type info, provide that. Make
sure it is the type info of the entire CoClass. GetTypeInfo( ) helper
function provided in CCtrlHolder class. See sample source code.
*/
        if (dwReturnMask & SCRIPTINFO_ITYPEINFO)
        {
            hr = g_pControl1->GetTypeInfo (ppTypeInfoOut) ;
        }
        return hr ;
    }

/*
Otherwise signal error.
*/
    MessageBox (NULL, W2A(pName), "Unknown object", 0) ;
    return TYPE_E_ELEMENTNOTFOUND;
}
```

9. If the script engine detects an error in the execution of the script, the engine will call the method **IActiveScriptSite::OnScriptError( )**, passing a pointer to an object which implements the *IActiveScriptError* interface. Its methods are: :

IActiveScriptError::GetExceptionInfo   *// get EXCEPINFO structure describing error*
IActiveScriptError::GetSourcePosition*// get line number and character position of error*
IActiveScriptError::GetSourceLineText   *// get text of script source code line causing error*

In the sample program, all we do is pop up a dialog box telling the user about the error.

The code returned from this method by the host tells the script engine what to do in response to the error. Thus:

```
STDMETHODIMP CActiveScriptSite::OnScriptError(IActiveScriptError *pse)
{
    HRESULT    hr;

/*
Get the EXCEPINFO structure describing the error.
*/
    EXCEPINFO ei;
    hr = pse->GetExceptionInfo(&ei) ;

/*
Get the position in the source code at which the error took place.
*/

    DWORD context,line ;
    LONG CharPos ;

    hr = pse->GetSourcePosition(&context, &line, &CharPos) ;

/*
Get the text of the source line that failed.
*/

    BSTR bstrLine ;
    hr = pse->GetSourceLineText(&bstrLine);

    <continued on next page>
```

410

```
/*
Format and display error for user.
*/
    CScriptErrorDlg dlg ;

    dlg.m_ErrorName = ei.bstrDescription ;
    dlg.m_AppName = ei.bstrSource ;
    dlg.m_ErrorStatement = bstrLine ;
    dlg.m_HelpFile = ei.bstrHelpFile ;
    dlg.m_HelpContext = ei.dwHelpContext ;

    int i = dlg.DoModal( ) ;

/*
Clean up BSTRS.
*/

    SysFreeString (ei.bstrDescription) ;
    SysFreeString (ei.bstrSource) ;
    SysFreeString (ei.bstrHelpFile) ;
    SysFreeString (bstrLine) ;


/*
Return codes to tell the script engine what to do based on user's
choice of the Ignore, Debug, or Quit buttons.
*/


/*
Abort button clicked, abort execution of script.
*/
    if (i == IDC_ABORT)
    {
      return E_FAIL ;
    }
/*
Tell engine to run script in a debugger if available, otherwise handle
as if aborted.
*/
    else if (i == IDC_DEBUG)
    {
      return S_FALSE ;
    }
/*
This tells the engine to ignore the error and keep trying to run.
*/
    else
    {
      return S_OK ;
    }
}
```

E. SCRIPT ENGINES

1. As previously stated, a script engine is an OLE server that exposes the IActiveScript and IActiveScriptParse interface. Writing the OLE wrapper of a script engine is several orders of magnitude less involved than writing the script interpreter itself. If you already have a scripting language, you can make it available to many more potential paying customers by packaging ActiveX script engine.

2. To make this happen, you simply write a standard in-proc OLE server that implements the IActiveScript interface. Microsoft says that IActiveScriptParse is optional, but support for it in other apps is so widespread that you ought to consider it mandatory as well. This section uses the sample app in the directory \CHAPTER12\SCRIPTENGINE. This is an extremely simple DLL that pops up a message box containing the script when you put it into the connected state. Instructions are given at the end of this chapter.

```
class  CScriptEngine : public IActiveScript, public IActiveScriptParse
{
    public:
      ULONG              m_RefCount;

      IActiveScriptSite *    m_pActiveSite ;
      SCRIPTSTATE            m_ss ;
      char *                 m_pScriptText ;
      DWORD                  m_ThreadId

      CScriptEngine  (void) ;
      ~CScriptEngine (void);

   < rest of class declaration >
}
```

3. As usual in OLE, many of the methods are trivial. For example, the **IActiveScript::GetSite( )** and **SetSite( )** methods work exactly like every other set and get in all of OLE. Thus:

```
STDMETHODIMP CScriptEngine::SetScriptSite(IActiveScriptSite *pass)
{

/*
Host is providing us with a pointer to the IActiveScriptSite interface.
Keep a copy of it, which means we have to AddRef( ) it.
*/

    if (pass)
    {
      m_pActiveSite = pass ;
      m_pActiveSite->AddRef ( ) ;
    }
    return S_OK ;
}


/*
Host is asking for the specified interface on the IActiveScriptSite
pointer that we are currently using. If it supports the specified
interface, AddRef( ) it and return a pointer to it.  Otherwise return
an error code.
*/

STDMETHODIMP CScriptEngine::GetScriptSite(REFIID riid, void **ppv)
{
    if (m_pActiveSite)
    {
      return m_pActiveSite->QueryInterface (riid, ppv) ;
    }
    else
    {
      *ppv = NULL ;
      return E_NOINTERFACE ;
    }
}
```

4. The host puts our engine into the connected state by calling the method **IActiveScript::SetScriptState( )**. When this happens, we need to spin off a new thread to execute the script, thereby allowing the call to return and the script to stay active. In this example, the thread function ScriptThreadFunc( ) simply pops up a dialog box containing the script's text so you can see it. Thus:

```
extern DWORD WINAPI ScriptThreadFunc (LPVOID) ;


STDMETHODIMP CScriptEngine::SetScriptState(SCRIPTSTATE ss)
{

/*
Save script state in a member variable.
*/
    m_ss = ss ;

/*
If host has told us to connect the script, spin off a thread to execute
it. The thread function in this simple example does nothing but pop up
a box containing the script text.
*/
    if (m_ss == SCRIPTSTATE_CONNECTED)
    {
     DWORD dwId ;

     HANDLE hThread = CreateThread (NULL, 0, ScriptThreadFunc,
           this, 0, &m_ThreadId) ;

     CloseHandle (hThread) ;
    }

    return S_OK ;
}
```

414

5. To get the sample script engine to work with IE3, it was necessary to implement the methods **IActiveScript::GetCurrentScriptThreadID( )**. This returns an integer that identifies the thread to the script engine. It might as well be the thread's ID from the operating system, stored when we created the thread.

```
STDMETHODIMP CScriptEngine::GetCurrentScriptThreadID(
    SCRIPTTHREADID *pstidThread)
{
    if (pstidThread)
    {
      *pstidThread = m_ThreadId ;
    }
    return S_OK  ;
}
```

6. When the host calls the method **IActiveScript::Close( )**, the engine must release the pointers that it holds to the host's interfaces. Thus:

```
STDMETHODIMP CScriptEngine::Close(void)
{

/*
Script  engine  closing  down.  Release  pointer  to  IActiveScriptSite
interface if we have been given one by the host.
*/
    if (m_pActiveSite)
    {
      m_pActiveSite->Release ( ) ;
      m_pActiveSite = NULL ;
    }
    return S_OK ;
}
```

7. The IActiveScriptParse interface is conceptually quite simple. All we do is remember the script code provided by the host. In the sample app, we use a simple character array. Thus:

```
/*
Host telling us to initialize a new script.   Release memory holding
previous script, if any.
*/

STDMETHODIMP CScriptEngine::InitNew( void)
{
    if (m_pScriptText)
    {
      free (m_pScriptText) ;
      m_pScriptText = NULL ;
    }

    return S_OK ;
}


/*
Host is providing us with a new script.   Allocate memory to hold it and
copy the script into that memory.
*/

STDMETHODIMP CScriptEngine::ParseScriptText(LPCOLESTR pstrCode,
    LPCOLESTR pstrItemName, IUnknown *punkContext,
    LPCOLESTR pstrDelimiter, DWORD dwSourceContextCookie,
    ULONG ulStartingLineNumber, DWORD dwFlags, VARIANT *pvarResult,
    EXCEPINFO *pexcepinfo)
{
/*
Get length of script string.
*/
    int length = wcslen (pstrCode) ;

/*
Allocate buffer of that size.
*/
    m_pScriptText = (char *)malloc (length + 1) ;

    if (m_pScriptText == NULL)
    {
      return E_OUTOFMEMORY ;
    }

/*
Copy script text into script engine's storage, converting it to ANSI.
*/
    WideCharToMultiByte (CP_ACP, 0, pstrCode, length+1, m_pScriptText,
      length+1, NULL, NULL) ;
    return S_OK ;
}
```

F. SCRIPT SECURITY

1. Using HTML pages containing scripts poses a far greater security risk than using a control from the Internet in your own apps. You can reliably know who wrote a control and that the control hasn't been tampered with, and decide to trust it or not. But there is currently no way of identifying and deciding to trust the author of a script.

Think about the WinWord macro viruses that exist today. WinWord is a relatively benign app, written by a relatively reputable vendor. Because of WinWord's power, a malicious macro can do essentially anything to your system. A control in a script has the same problem.

2. When IE3 is running in its medium security level and opens a page that contains a script, it shows the following dialog box, allowing the user to choose whether to run the script or not. This doesn't help much if the script is malicious, but at least the user won't be able to curse Microsoft when the script formats his hard drive.

IE3 also contains a higher level of security which will not run scripts at all, and a lower one that always runs scripts without asking first. You probably want to build in some similar security feature into your script-aware apps.

3. While today it is impossible to put trust certificates on Web pages, a control vendor can mark a control as being guaranteed safe in all situations. Consider the timer control that we developed in Chapter 5. It doesn't do anything except set a timer and draw on the screen. It can't possibly harm anyone or anything, no matter what methods a script calls or what properties are set to what values.

A control promises its complete harmlessness by making entries in the registry. A browser app that creates such a control may read the registry, check for the presence of these keys, and omit the security warning if they are present.

What if the control is lying about its harmlessness? There is no need for it to do so. If a control wanted to be malicious, it could trash your hard drive as soon as it passed WinTrustVerify( ). What if the control says it's harmless and honestly believes it, but some malicious Web page author finds a hole in it? You're scrod. See the previous chapter for ways to set up a sandbox for your apps.

4. In order to mark your control as safe, you must make entries under the new "Component Categories" registry key. This key was added to organize the entries that OLE servers make to identify the capabilities they promise to provide. It holds zero or more *category IDs*, 16-byte GUIDs, each of which identifies a particular capability that a registered class promises to support. It is conceptually similar to the "Control" or "OLEScript" registry keys, which promise specific, relatively large levels of functionality. Each category ID represents a similar promise, generally of a smaller level of functionality.

In the case of scripting, the category ID CATID_SafeForScripting indicates that a control is safe for using in scripts if no data is provided to it. The category ID CATID_SafeForInitializing indicates that the specified control is safe no matter what initialization data the script provides to it. If both of these category IDs are present in all controls used in a script, IE3 allows a script to run without a warning, even in the high-security mode that doesn't normally allow scripts at all. I don't know if I like to take a control's word for it, especially in the latter case, but that's how they wrote IE3. Thus:

418

5. You can make category ID entries in the registry by using the *component category manager* provided by the operating system. This is an OLE server that provides the *ICatRegister* interface, a set of methods used for manipulating categories. Its methods are:

ICatRegister::RegisterCategories   *// register human-readable category name*
ICatRegister::UnRegisterCategories   *// unregister human-readable category name*
ICatRegister::RegisterClassImplCategories   *// register a class as implementing a category*
ICatRegister::UnRegisterClassImplCategories   *// unregister a class as implementing a category*
ICatRegister::RegisterClassReqCategories   *// register a class as requiring a category*
ICatRegister::UnRegisterClassReqCategories   *// unregister a class as requiring a category*

You instantiate an object of this class via our old friend CoCreateInstance( ), creating an object whose GUID is **CLSID_StdComponentCategoriesMgr**, asking for the ICatRegister interface. You must include the header file **"comcat.h"**. The method **ICatRegister::RegisterClassImplCategories( )** actually places the category IDs in the registry. The IDs for the safety-related categories are in the file **"objsafe.h"**. Thus:

```
#include <objsafe.h>
#include <comcat.h>
extern GUID guid ;

STDAPI DllRegisterServer(void)
{
    <standard App Wizard registration code omitted>
/*
Register control component categories. First, open category manager
object.
*/
    ICatRegister* pcr ;
    HRESULT hr = CoCreateInstance(
      CLSID_StdComponentCategoriesMgr,
      NULL, CLSCTX_INPROC_SERVER,
      IID_ICatRegister, (void**)&pcr);
 /*
Use category manager to place entries in the registry.
*/
    if (SUCCEEDED(hr))
    {
      CATID catid[2] ;
      catid[0] = CATID_SafeForScripting ;
      catid[1] = CATID_SafeForInitializing ;

      hr = pcr->RegisterClassImplCategories(
            guid,       // GUID of control to make entries for
            2,          // number of CATIDs being added
            catid);     // array of CATIDs to add
    }
    if (pcr != NULL)
    {
        pcr->Release();
    }
    return NOERROR;
}
```

ActiveX Scripting

Directory: \EssenceofOLE\chap12\scripthost

This app is a simple script host. It searches your registry for all registered script engines and makes an entry for each one on the "Engine" menu popup. If it can't find any, it complains and exits. The left-hand pane is a CEditView which allows you to open, edit, and save scripts. The right-hand pane contains a single ActiveX control which you can select using the "Control – Replace Existing" menu item. The scripts that you write may refer to the control by the name "Control1". Several text files containing scripts are provided for you to use. Try the simplest one first, "Hello.txt". Commands for starting and stopping the script are found on the "File" menu.

Directory: \EssenceofOLE\chap12\scriptengine

This is an extremely simple script engine. Use the DLL Registering Tool app from Appendix A to invoke the self-registration code in "scriptengine.dll". After doing this, open the file "enginetest.htm" using IE3. When IE2 runs the script, you should see a dialog box appear containing the script text found on the HTML page. You may also see various message boxes informing you of the different methods of the script engine's interface being called by the host. After registering the engine, you will also see it appear on the menu of the host sample app discussed above.

Directory: \EssenceofOLE\chap12\safecntrl

This control makes entries in the registry that identify it as safe for use in scripts under all conditions. Use the DLL Registering Tool app from Appendix A to invoke the self-registration code in "safecntrl.ocx". After doing this, open the file "safecntrl.htm" using IE3. You will see a control appear on the page with the word "Safe" inside it. IE3 will not show you any warning messages regardless of the security setting, because it trusts the control's declaration that the control is safe at all times.

Chapter 13

Threads and COM

A. Concepts and Definitions

1. Using COM in multithreaded applications generates more *FUD* (Fear, Uncertainty, and Doubt) among programmers than any other area of COM. If you are writing a COM object server, might different objects in your server be called from different threads? Might one object's methods be called from different threads? Do you have to worry about serializing access to the object server's global functions and data? To each object's member functions and data? To anything?

And what about writing a client app that uses COM objects? Can your client app access the same object from two threads without screwing everything up? Can it access two different objects from the same server from two different threads? What if some classes of object work differently than others? What if an object's behavior changes from one version to the next?

Don't worry. As with most topics in COM, the reality isn't nearly as bad as the anticipation. COM supports threading in such a manner that neither side needs to know or care what the other is doing. The 'C' in COM stands for "Component". To require a client to have intimate knowledge of the internals of the objects that it wants to use, or to have an object need to care about the internals of its clients, would violate the most fundamental principle in all of COM — that it is a binary standard, so you don't need or want to know anything about the other guy except that he follows it, too. If you follow a few simple rules, COM will take care of the gory details of threading. It works according to the following principles:

A). A client app chooses a set of rules to follow for its handling of threads, from not knowing anything at all about threads to going completely crazy with them. The client app tells COM the rules that it intends to follow when it initializes COM via the function CoInitialize( ) or CoInitializeEx( ).

B). An object server chooses a set of rules to follow for its handling of threads, from not knowing anything at all about threads to going completely crazy with them. The server tells COM the rules that it intends to follow, either when it calls CoInitialize( ) or CoInitializeEx( ) for an .EXE server, or by making registry entries for a .DLL server.

C). Whenever a client creates or connects to an object, COM compares the rules that each party has said that it follows. If they have promised to play by the same rules, then COM sets up a direct connection between the two and gets out of the way. If they are different, then COM sets up inter-thread marshaling between the two parties so that each sees only the threading rules that it has told COM it knows how to handle. The latter case costs some performance, but allows parties following dissimilar threading rules to work together seamlessly without croaking or special casing. This is conceptually similar to the mechanism that COM uses for marshaling between processes and machines, so that neither client nor object needs to know or care where its counterparty is located.

422

2. I know more potential COM programmers that have run for the hills over the buzzwords "threading model", "apartment threading", and "free threading" than any other terms in all of Windows. They aren't that bad, although it doesn't help that the nomenclature keeps changing. A *threading model* is a set of rules describing the interaction of threading and COM that a client or an object server follows.

COM has not always supported threads. Sixteen-bit Windows didn't have threads, so the issue didn't arise. The first release of NT, version 3.1, had threads but didn't have OLE or COM, so the issue didn't arise there either. Windows NT 3.5 was the first release to support COM, but it did so on only one thread per process. All COM function and object calls had to be made from this thread. If a second thread tried to call CoInitialize( ) or any other COM API function, the call would fail with an error. At the time, this model didn't have a name because there wasn't any other from which to distinguish it. It was later called the *single threading model*, because only one thread per process could use it, or sometimes the "non threading model" because it is the default model used by COM objects that have no knowledge of threads whatsoever. It is still sometimes used today by lazy programmers and in legacy code. This model is described on page 426.

Windows NT 3.51 and Windows 95 added support for COM objects on multiple threads via the *apartment threading model*, described beginning on page 432. This approach was a logical outgrowth of the original single threaded model. Essentially, every thread in an app was now allowed to do what the single COM thread in a single threaded model application had previously done. Any number of threads could initialize COM and use objects, but each thread could only use objects that had been created on that thread. Turn your viewpoint around and you can think of the single threaded model as the degenerate case of the apartment threaded model — only one thread choosing to do what all are allowed to. This model is relatively easy to write and enjoys widespread support. Essentially all major market apps use it.

With the release of NT 4.0, COM added support for the *free threading model*, described beginning on page 446. This approach allows any thread to access any object at any time. It is good for cases in which many different threads need to access the same object. Windows 95 will support it if you install the DCOM service pack, which is automatically done when you install Internet Explorer 4.0. The DCOM service pack is also available separately from Microsoft's web site. Since support for it is not widespread, and since handling its synchronization and race condition requirements makes it harder to write code for than the apartment model, the free threading model is used much less widely than the apartment model at the time of this writing.

You will occasionally see the apartment threading model referred to as the "single-threaded apartment model" or STA, and the free threading model referred to as the "multi-threaded apartment model" or MTA. While this does accurately describe some of COM's source code internals seen only by a few system developers at Microsoft, a more confusing nomenclature for application programmers would be difficult to imagine — especially when you consider that your app will usually contain multiple single-threaded apartments, but only a single multi-threaded apartment. This book keeps to the nomenclature shown in italics above, which matches the registry entries that you have to make.

The beauty of how COM handles threads is that neither client nor server need to know or care about the model used by its counterparty. Each follows the rules of the model with which it was written, and COM intercedes and mediates between them to the extent necessary to make it work. It's not a matter of getting it to work at all, but getting it to work optimally.

WARNING: Even more than for other chapters in this book, follow this one through from beginning to end. Even if you only care about the free threading model, don't jump straight there. Read the entire chapter, or you'll get lost.

B. APARTMENT THREADED CONTAINERS

1. Threads are a very useful programming feature. COM is also a very useful programming feature. It makes sense that you would want to combine two such useful features when designing an app. The first mechanism available for doing this is the apartment threading model, which appeared in Windows NT version 3.51 and Windows 95. The other main alternative, the free threading model described on page 446, did not appear until NT 4.0, so essentially all major multithreaded container apps shipping today use the apartment threading model.

2. An apartment threaded container is simple to write. You just follow three simple rules and COM makes it all work. The first rule of apartment threading is that every container thread that wants to use COM objects must call the function CoInitialize( ) when it starts up and CoUninitialize( ) when it shuts down. The first thread to call CoInitialize( ) is COM's main thread in that process. It doesn't have to be the app's main thread, the one on which WinMain( ) was called, but for convenience it usually is. Unless otherwise stated, whenever I use the term "main thread" in the rest of this chapter, I am referring to COM's main thread. As the first thread to initialize COM, the main thread must also be the last thread to uninitialize COM.

Second, each thread that calls CoInitialize( ) must have a message loop and service it frequently. COM uses private messages to hidden windows for its own internal purposes, as described later in this chapter. If you fail to get and dispatch the messages that appear in a thread's message queue, you will break COM. You probably don't have to change your code a bit. The normal message loop you've been using in your main thread has been doing exactly this since day one, and you haven't heard a thing about COM and window messages. They've always been there; you just haven't had any reason to notice. If your new threads are going to create windows, you'll have to do it anyway. Just make sure you don't plan a design using a thread that wants to use the apartment model but doesn't check a message queue. An auxiliary thread that uses COM objects will contain code something like this:

```
DWORD WINAPI ThreadProc (LPVOID lpv)
{
/*
Initialize COM on this thread.
*/
    CoInitialize (NULL) ;

    <other initialization>
/*
Acquire and dispatch messages for this thread until a WM_QUIT message
is received.
*/
    MSG msg ;
    while (GetMessage(&msg, NULL, NULL, NULL))
    {
      TranslateMessage(&msg);
      DispatchMessage(&msg);
    }

/*
Shut down COM in this thread.
*/
    CoUninitialize( ) ;
    return 0 ;
}
```

3. The final rule that the container must follow is that when a thread obtains a pointer to a COM interface via any legal mechanism, that interface's methods may only be called from that thread. You may consider them as being locked inside the same apartment. For example, if a thread calls CoCreateInstance( ) and obtains a pointer to an interface, that interface's methods may only be called from within the thread that called CoCreateInstance( ). If this seems restrictive, fear not, there are legal workarounds described beginning on page 437. But keep this rule in mind and you'll have the right mental model.

You may use whatever mechanism you want to ensure that object's methods are only called from the thread on which the object was created. In the sample container program, when you create an object by selecting an item from the "Data Object" menu, I wanted that object to be created by the thread that owns the currently active child window, not the main thread which handles the menu messages. I did this by using the API function PostMessage( ) to forward the WM_COMMAND message sent from the menu to the active child window, which actually contains the code to process it. The posting and dispatching of the message cause the thread switch. The menu handling code in the main window looks like this:

```
/*
MainWndProc( ), case WM_COMMAND. Forward menu message from this main
window to the active child window to be handled on the child window's
thread.
*/
    case ID_DATAOBJECT_CREATEBOTHINPROC:
    case ID_DATAOBJECT_CREATEAPARTMENTTHREADEDLOCAL:
    case ID_DATAOBJECT_CREATEFREETHREADEDLOCAL:
    case ID_DATAOBJECT_RELEASE:
    case ID_DATAOBJECT_TIMETEST:
    case ID_DATAOBJECT_DADVISE:
    case ID_DATAOBJECT_DUNADVISE:
    {
      HWND hActive = (HWND) SendMessage (hMdiClient, WM_MDIGETACTIVE,
          0, 0) ;
      return PostMessage (hActive, message, wParam, lParam) ;
    }
```

In the child window I have a handler for these message. Thus:

```
/*
ChildWndProc( ), case WM_COMMAND. Handle menu message forwarded by main
window. Perform COM functions on the thread that owns the child window.
*/
    case ID_DATAOBJECT_CREATEAPARTMENTTHREADEDINPROC:
    {
      CLSID clsid ;
      CLSIDFromProgID(L"EssenceOfOLE.Data6.ApartmentThreaded", &clsid);

      MyOwnCreateAptObject (clsid, CLSCTX_INPROC_SERVER, hWnd) ;
      return 0 ;
    }
```

425

C. Simplest Example: Single-Threaded Control

1. Suppose you have a control that knows nothing at all about threads. How is this control handled when a multithreaded container app such as Internet Explorer tries to use it from different threads? To demonstrate, I created the simplest possible full-featured ActiveX control, using Control Wizard to generate a new ActiveX control project using MFC 4.0, accepting all the default settings. I then added two lines to the **COleControl::OnDraw( )**, using the API function **GetCurrentThreadId( )** to get the ID of the thread on which this function was called, and outputting that ID in the control's window. This code is shown below, and it's about as simple as it gets. Thus:

```
void CDemo40Ctrl::OnDraw(CDC* pdc, const CRect& rcBounds,
    const CRect& rcInvalid)
{
    pdc->FillRect(rcBounds,
        CBrush::FromHandle((HBRUSH)GetStockObject(WHITE_BRUSH)));
/*
Get the ID of the thread on which this function was called. Output it
in the control's window for the user to see.
*/
    char out [256] ;
    wsprintf(out, "MFC V4.0\nThread ID == 0x%x", GetCurrentThreadId());
    pdc->DrawText (out, -1, (LPRECT) &rcBounds, DT_CENTER) ;
}
```

You will find this control in the directory \chap13\demo40. Register the control according to the instructions at the end of this chapter, then open the page "demo40.htm" with Internet Explorer. The control will be created and shown in IE's window. Next, choose "File – New Window" from IE3's main menu, which will create another window showing the same page, containing another instance of the control. IE does this by launching a new thread, not a whole new process, which you can verify by using Spy++. Your screen will then look like the facing page. Both controls report the same the thread ID, even though IE3 created a new thread to handle the new page window and it was this new thread that called CoCreateInstance( ) to create the control. What is going on?

When the apartment threading model was first released, it became possible for multiple threads in an app to create objects from the same server. The rules require that each object be accessed only from a single thread; but different objects could be called from different threads and they could conflict over global data. The server could easily prevent this conflict if its designers had made its global data thread safe, but few spent the money on it at the time because it wasn't required. To keep from breaking every control in existence, COM had to provide a mechanism for detecting whether or not a server knew how to handle itself in a multithreaded environment and protecting the ones that couldn't while still allowing them to be used.

A control server which has taken the necessary precautions to allow itself to be accessed by multiple threads identifies itself as such by making an entry in the registry as described in the next section of this chapter. When a container app calls CoCreateInstance( ) to create a control, COM checks for the presence of this entry. In its absence, as in this case, COM assumes that the control's DLL server has no knowledge of threads whatsoever. If different threads were allowed to access objects in this server, they could trash the server's global data and chaos would result. COM makes sure that this doesn't happen by actually creating all objects from this server on the same thread, the container's main thread, regardless of the thread from which the container makes the creation request.

(If this doesn't make sense yet, read the next two pages.)

Two pages each containing an instance of a non-threaded control. COM creates both controls on the main thread. The first page has a direct connection to its control; the second page access its control via a marshaling proxy.

2. This thread safety problem for global data is universal. Every server must maintain a global object count so it knows when to shut itself down (for an .EXE server) or how to respond to DllCanUnloadNow( ) (for a .DLL server). The usual way of doing this is with a global variable that is incremented in an object's constructor and decremented in its destructor. Thus:

```
int g_ObjectCount = 0 ;

CSomeObj::CSomeObj ( )
{
    g_ObjectCount ++ ;
}

CSomeObj::~CSomeObj ( )
{
    g_ObjectCount -- ;
}
```

The problem is that the increment and decrement operations shown above are not thread safe in their accesses to the global variable g_ObjectCount. The assembler listing of the increment statement above usually looks something like this:

```
mov ax, [g_ObjectCount]        ; move global variable into register
add ax, 1                      ; increment contents of register
mov [g_ObjectCount], ax        ; move new value to global variable
```

Suppose that Thread A starts the above sequence near the end of its timeslice. It executes the first two statements, then gets swapped out before it can execute the third. Thread B now gets swapped in and executes all three statements. Eventually, Thread A will get swapped back in, execute the third statement, and overwrite the value stored in g_ObjectCount by Thread B. An operation that was safe in the non-threaded case is now fatal when objects can be called from multiple threads. Therefore, unless a control server identifies itself as knowing how to handle itself in a multithreaded environment, COM creates all of that server's objects on a single thread, thereby ensuring that this can't happen.

3. To solve this problem, COM sets up an *interthread marshaler*, conceptually similar to that used for marshaling calls to another process, which ensures that all controls provided by that DLL are created on the container's main thread, the one that first called CoInitialize( ). This marshaling code also ensures that all calls to all methods of these controls are made only from the container's main thread. In this manner, all calls to all objects in the server are serialized in the manner that the server expects.

Since the thread handling the second window in the previous example wasn't IE3's main thread, COM transparently marshaled the object creation into the main thread to avoid any possible conflicts over global data with other objects from the same DLL. The interface pointer returned to the second thread did not point directly to the code inside the object. Instead, it pointed to a marshaling proxy object on the second thread. When the second thread called a method on this object, the proxy marshaled the call to the main thread to be made and marshaled the results back to the second thread. This thread doesn't know or care whether it has a pointer to the actual object or to a marshaling proxy; it just calls the methods locally and the right thing happens. Each side follows the relatively simple COM rules, and COM intercedes to the extent necessary to make it work transparently. The flow is shown in the diagram below:

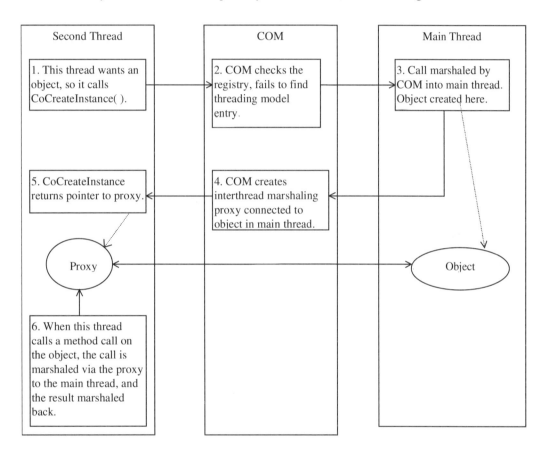

While this interthread marshaling may seem like an exotic and unusual thing for COM to do, it really isn't. Window message handling works the same way. Ever wonder why you don't have to serialize access to window message handlers? It's because the operating system marshals window messages to the thread that owns the window to which they are addressed. A window's response function will always be called from this thread; otherwise the switch to preemptive multitasking would have broken every Windows app ever written. In fact, COM accomplishes its marshaling by creating hidden windows and posting messages to them. You can see these windows in Spy++. They're the ones belonging to class "OleMainThreadWndClass" and having the text "OleMainThreadWndName".

4. OK, great, my control can run with any container app and vice versa, regardless of the threading used by either one. I get my app out the door quickly and don't break any existing code; what's the bad news ? The bad news is that this marshaling takes time and burns CPU cycles. A ballpark figure is that marshaling a call from one thread into another takes about as much time as marshaling to another process, a call overhead of a few milliseconds each. Obviously, this can vary widely. The more data you are passing, the longer it takes to copy, and if you are passing so much that the copy involves disk swapping, the delay can skyrocket. In performance measurements made for this book, a method call requiring interprocess marshaling was slower than a direct connection by a factor of about 200. A method call requiring interthread marshaling was slower than a direct connection by about a factor of 50.

The main problem, though, isn't just burning microseconds; it's the potential for deadly bottlenecks. The main thread to which a call is marshaled might be busy doing a calculation or reading a long file, in which case the thread that originates the call will have to wait until the main thread finishes. Imagine 5 or 6 threads each creating 10 controls, all needing all of their method calls marshaled back to the main thread. You've lost the prime benefit of multithreading, and even adding more CPU chips won't solve it. Life becomes a weary burden. There has to be a better way.

This page intentionally contains no text other than this sentence.

D. Somewhat More Complex Example: Apartment Threaded Control

1. Is there a way around the marshaling and attendant overhead in the previous section ? Fortunately, there is, and it's relatively easy. I generated and built the same control as the previous example, only this time using MFC 4.2, and put it on an HTML page called "demo42.htm". You will find this page and the control "demo42.ocx" in the sample code directory "\demo42". If you register the control, open the page with IE3 and then open another IE3 window showing the same page, you will find that the thread IDs are now different, as shown on the facing page. If you use Spy++, you will find that the thread ID being reported by the new control is the same as the new thread that IE3 created to manage the new window. Unlike the previous example, the control has somehow been created on the new thread. What has happened?

Every server that provides an object to COM needs to specify how its object's methods may be called from different threads, so that COM will know whether and how to intercede between the object and its client. There are three choices. The server can refrain from specifying anything, as in the first example. In this case, COM sets up marshaling code to force all calls to all objects from that server to be made from the app's main thread. Alternatively, the server may specify that any of the object's functions may be called from any thread at any time; that the object is reentrant or internally synchronized to whatever extent it requires, so it's perfectly safe for any thread to do anything to it at any time. This is the *free-threading model*, described beginning on page 446.

The middle ground that COM has provided in Windows 95 and Windows NT since version 3.51 is called the *apartment threading model*. A server that says it supports this model is promising COM that the server has serialized access to all of its global data, such as its object count. An apartment model server does not need to serialize access to its individual object's member variables and functions, because COM promises that each object will always be called from the same thread. The objects do need to serialize access to the server's global variables and functions, as different objects may try to access these from different threads. This also applies to class statics, which are just a politically correct form of global.

When a thread in IE3 calls CoCreateInstance( ) to create a control that supports apartment threading, COM will create the object on the calling thread instead of marshaling the creation into the main thread as was shown in the previous example. Since the creating thread is an apartment thread, COM knows that it promised to call the object's functions only from the thread that created the object. COM therefore does not set up the interthread marshaler as it did in the previous example, so the interface pointer returned is a direct pointer to the object's code, as you would otherwise expect from an in-proc object. The two kids promise to play together nicely, so Mom leaves them unsupervised. You avoid the marshaling operation, with its overhead and potential for bottlenecks.

Two pages each containing an instance of an apartment-threaded control. Each control lives in the apartment of the thread that created it. Each page accesses its control directly.

2. A control server that supports the apartment-threading model is saying to COM, "Hey, I've thought about threading a little bit, so I've serialized access to my own global data. You don't have to make all calls into all my objects on a single thread the way you did with the previous idiot. Just make sure you call each of my objects on the thread that created it, and I've made sure they'll never step on each other's toes as long as you follow that rule."

A control that supports the apartment threading model signals this to COM by making an entry in the registry as shown below. The control's InProcServer32 registry key contains a new named value called "ThreadingModel". If this value contains the string "Apartment", as shown here, the control is promising that it supports the apartment threading model.

ActiveX controls created with MFC 4.2 or later support the apartment threading model by default. So if you are creating controls with the MFC, then all you have to do is to serialize access to your globals and class statics as shown in the example on page 436. The MFC has already taken care of serializing access to the your control's global object count. If you are using the ATL, you have a choice of threading models, as shown in Chapter 14.

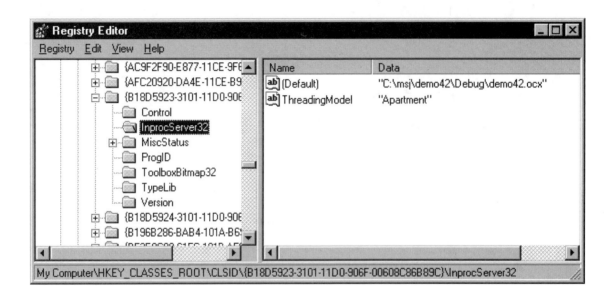

434

3. An MFC control registers itself as supporting the apartment model in the method COleControl::COleObjectFactory::UpdateRegistry( ), as shown below. Control Wizard automatically generates this method for you. Its primary feature is a call to the MFC function AfxOleRegisterControlClass( ), which makes the actual registry entries. The sixth parameter to this function is the constant **afxRegApartmentThreading**, which tells the function to register the control as supporting the apartment model. If you are writing a control with MFC version 4.2 or later and do not want to support apartment model threading, you must change this parameter to FALSE. Conversely, if you are upgrading a control which was originally generated with MFC version 4.1 or earlier and now want to support the apartment model, this parameter as generated in your original code will be FALSE and you must change it to afxRegApartmentThreading.

```
/*
This code generated by App Wizard, registers a control as supporting
the apartment threading model.
*/


BOOL CDemo42Ctrl::CDemo42CtrlFactory::UpdateRegistry(BOOL bRegister)
{
// TODO: Verify that your control follows apt-model threading rules.
// Refer to MFC TechNote 64 for more information.
// If your control does not conform to the apartment-model rules, then
// you must modify the code below, changing the 6th parameter from
// afxRegApartmentThreading to 0.

    if (bRegister)
        return AfxOleRegisterControlClass(
            AfxGetInstanceHandle(),
            m_clsid,
            m_lpszProgID,
            IDS_DEMO42,
            IDB_DEMO42,
            afxRegApartmentThreading,
            _dwDemo42OleMisc,
            _tlid,
            _wVerMajor,
            _wVerMinor);
    else
        return AfxOleUnregisterClass(m_clsid, m_lpszProgID);
}
```

4. Consider the code listing on page 428 that we used as an example of conflict potential. It isn't hard to write code that makes sure that different threads never conflict over the same global variable. Consider the example below. The API functions **InterlockedIncrement( )** and **InterlockedDecrement( )** as shown below, are thread safe functions for accessing a variable. The quickest, easiest, and cheapest way of serializing access to more complicated operations is with a critical section. If you are unfamiliar with these, you can find a quick introduction in my book *The Win32 API from Scratch* (Prentice-Hall, ISBN 0-13-121484-5). Thus:

```
int g_ObjectCount = 0 ;

/*
Object constructed. Perform a thread-safe increment of the server's
global object count.
*/

CSomeObj::CSomeObj ( )
{
    InterlockedIncrement (&g_ObjectCount) ;
}

/*
Object destroyed. Perform a thread-safe decrement of the server's
global object count.
*/

CSomeObj::~CSomeObj ( )
{
    InterlockedDecrement (&g_ObjectCount) ;
}
```

What if the thread creating your object isn't an apartment model thread? What if it's one of those nasty free threads that can hit you from anywhere at any time? Again, you don't have to care. Because of your control's registry entries, COM knows what it requires and will set up an interthread marshaler if necessary so that your apartment control sees what it expects. Short answer: don't worry about it; COM takes care of it.

E. MUCH MORE COMPLICATED EXAMPLE - INTERTHREAD OBJECT MARSHALING

1. The apartment threading model is easy to write and enjoys widespread support. Its primary disadvantage is the restriction against calling an object method from a thread other than the one on which the object was created. Suppose a good design for your application would require you to do that. It would be nice if there was a legal workaround so you could use the relatively simple apartment model. You could post window messages from one thread to another, but this is a pain. In this case, why does COM exist at all? There ought to be a better way, and in fact there is.

Suppose I have a control that performs an operation which could take a long time to complete, for example, searching a large or slow database. I would like my control to expose a method that starts the operation and returns immediately, rather than hanging the calling thread by not returning until the long operation completes, then performing an asynchronous notification when the search is completed. An easy way to do this would be for the control to create an auxiliary thread to perform the search operation and for the auxiliary thread to signal the completion of its search by firing an event back to the container. It seems simple enough, but there's a hidden problem.

The problem is that a control signals events by calling the IDispatch::Invoke( ) method of an object provided by its container. This object was created on the thread that contains the control itself. To comply with the apartment threading model, I can only safely call the event object's methods from the thread on which it was created. When the auxiliary thread tries to fire the event, it will be calling IDispatch::Invoke( ) from a different thread. That's a no-no in the apartment model.

Like most restrictions in Windows, such as the firewall between address spaces of different processes, this one too is negotiable. I can solve this problem by setting up an interthread marshaler for the event IDispatch interface from the auxiliary thread into the control's thread. This will create a proxy which the auxiliary thread can call to signal its event. Don't wince, it isn't hard; just two simple function calls with easy parameters. When the auxiliary thread calls IDispatch::Invoke( ) on the proxy, the call will be marshaled from the auxiliary thread into the control's thread, from which it will be made legally to the container, and the result marshaled back to the auxiliary thread. This exactly the same thing COM did behind the scenes in the first single threaded example shown in the diagram on page 429, just to and from different threads.

2. Consider the sample code in the directory \chap13\ThreadDB, which contains a control called "threaddb.ocx" and an HTML page called "threaddb.htm". If you register the former and open the latter with IE3, you will see the screen shown below. On it, I simulate a search program that takes a Social Security number and returns an automation object representing a customer, having such properties as first and last name. The VBScript listing is shown on the facing page. You enter a social security number and click "Start Search", thereby calling the method "**StartSearch**" on the ThreadDB control. For simplicity of this example, I didn't bother reading the Social Security number out of the edit control; I just pass an arbitrary value. When the operation completes, very quickly in this example, it fires back an event called "**SearchFinished**". This event passes as a parameter an automation object of class CustomerObj, from which VBScript fetches the properties which represent the customer's name and address and places them in the edit controls on the page. The VBScript listing actually lives in the file "threaddb.alx", a layout control that I used from ActiveX Control Pad to get the layout to look nice. Enter anything or nothing into the SSN box, click "Start Search", and hey, presto, that SSN has identified a client named John Smith. Thus:

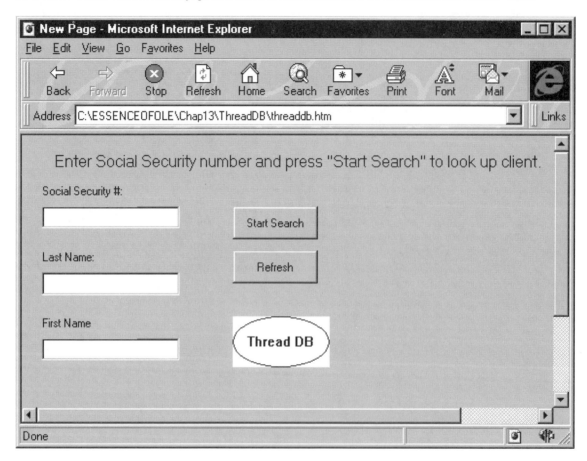

```
<SCRIPT LANGUAGE="VBScript">
<!--

rem ---- Variable to be store customer object

dim foo

rem ----- This function is called when "Start Search" button clicked.
rem ----- Call StartSearch method on ThreadDB control. SSN is
arbitrary.

Sub CommandButton1_Click()
  ThreadDB1.StartSearch (444)
end sub


rem ----- This function is called when ThreadDB control fires
rem ----- SearchFinished event. Set customer's first and last names
into
rem ----- edit controls. Save Customer object for future use in demo.

Sub ThreadDB1_SearchFinished(CustomerObj)
  set foo = CustomerObj
  TextBox2.Text - CustomerObj.LastName
  TextBox3.Text = CustomerObj.FirstName
end sub


rem ----- This function called "Refresh" button clicked.  Refresh
rem ----- customer's names from stored object

Sub CommandButton2_Click()
 TextBox2.Text = foo.LastName
 TextBox3.Text = foo.FirstName
end sub
```

3. Setting up the interthread marshaling is conceptually simple. It requires the following three steps:

A). The original thread, the one that created and legally owns the interface pointer, calls the API function **CoMarshalInterThreadInterfaceInStream( )**. This function creates a stream (see Chapter 7) containing all the information that COM needs to set up interthread marshaling into recipient thread. It returns the IStream interface pointer to this stream.

B). The original thread transfers the IStream interface pointer to the recipient thread by any convenient mechanism. Streams are designed in such a manner that transferring the IStream interface pointer directly to another thread as shown is allowed, even in the apartment model. In this example, I use a member variable.

C). The recipient thread calls the API function **CoGetInterfaceAndReleaseStream( )**, passing it the IStream pointer containing the marshaling information. COM uses the information in the stream to create the interthread marshaler. It returns a pointer to an interface proxy that the recipient thread may legally call.

The sample control exposes a single method called StartSearch( ), which VBScript calls when the user clicks the "Start Search" button. The code for this method is shown on the facing page. I first use the function AfxBeginThread( ) to create a new thread which pretends to perform a database search. The thread belongs to the class CSearchThread, which you will find in the sample code directory. I create the thread in a suspended state so I can initialize its member variables before it goes charging off into the database. In addition to normal member variables, such as the social security number of the customer I want to search for, I also need to give it the IDispatch interface pointer that I want it to use to signal its completion.

To find the IDispatch pointers used for signaling a control's events to its container, I traced down into the MFC source code to the function COleControl::FireEventV( ), the base function responsible for firing all events. When it fires an event, this function uses the IDispatch pointers that it has stored in a list member variable called **COleControl::m_xEventConnPt**. It would appear that more than one container IDispatch might want to be notified of an event. I lifted the relevant portions of the code, and bingo, I had the list of all IDispatch pointers that are listening for events from this control.

Remember, I can't just pass the IDispatch interface pointer directly. Doing so would violate the apartment threading model; that's the point of this whole exercise. In the example program, the method StartSearch( ) iterates over all the IDispatch pointers from the container and calls **CoMarshalInterThreadInterfaceInStream( )** for each of them, receiving an IStream interface pointer in return. I've never seen there be more than one, but better safe than sorry. The CSearchThread class contains a member variable called m_StreamArray, which represents an array of pointers to IStream interfaces. The control places each of the IStream interface pointers into this array. Finally, I resume the auxiliary thread, allowing it to proceed with its database search.

```
BOOL CThreadDBCtrl::StartSearch(long SocialSecurityNumber)
{
/*
Create thread object in suspended state. Set member variables.
*/
    m_pSearchThread = (CSearchThread *) AfxBeginThread (
        RUNTIME_CLASS (CSearchThread),
        THREAD_PRIORITY_NORMAL, 0,
        CREATE_SUSPENDED) ;

    m_pSearchThread->m_pCtrl = this ;
    m_pSearchThread->m_ssn = SocialSecurityNumber ;

/*
Find all the event IDispatch interface pointers and marshal them to the
thread.
*/

    IDispatch * pDispatch;    IStream *   pStream ;
    POSITION pos = m_xEventConnPt.GetStartPosition();

    while (pos != NULL)
    {
/*
Get next IDispatch in connection point's list.
*/
        pDispatch =
          (LPDISPATCH)m_xEventConnPt.GetNextConnection(pos);

/*
Create stream for marshaling IDispatch to search thread.
*/
        CoMarshalInterThreadInterfaceInStream(
            IID_IDispatch,    // interface ID to marshal
            pDispatch,        // ptr to interface to marshal
            &pStream) ;       // output variable

/*
Place stream in member variable where search thread will look for it.
*/
        m_pSearchThread->m_StreamArray.Add (pStream) ;
    }
/*
Allow thread to resume running now that we have initialized
all of its member variables.
*/
    m_pSearchThread->ResumeThread ( ) ;
    return TRUE;
}
```

4. The thread that performs the simulated search is an object of class CSearchThread. When the CSearchThread starts up, the MFC framework calls the thread's InitInstance( ) method, as shown on the facing page. Since the new thread wants to access COM, it must first call CoInitialize( ) as shown.

The thread now wants to get the interface pointers to the IDispatch interfaces that it will use to signal completion of its search. The CSearchThread contains the aforementioned member variable m_StreamArray, which holds the array of streams containing the information it needs to create these. It iterates over the array of IStream interface pointers provided by its creator on the previous page, calling **CoGetInterfaceAndReleaseStream( )** to convert each into an IDispatch pointer. As previously stated, these pointers are proxies, not direct connections.

On the following page, the thread then proceeds to simulate the results of a database search. It creates a CCustomer automation object with the name of John Smith to contain the result of the search. This is an automation object that I used Class Wizard to derive from CCmdTarget. It contains the properties of "FirstName", "LastName", and "SocialSecurityNumber", which I pass in the constructor. Finally, I use each IDispatch pointer to fire the SearchFinished event to each event sink that might be waiting, using the method COleDispatchDriver::InvokeHelper( ). I lifted the code straight from COleControl::FireEventV( ).

One thing looks strange here. The CCustomer automation object that the search thread provides as a parameter to the event is a COM object, but I don't seem to be marshaling it, even though its properties are being accessed by IE3 on another thread. Have I omitted something, or is this legal? It's legal. COM knows how to marshal method parameters. Because the parameter being passed to the event function is an IDispatch interface pointer and identified as such by the flags in the VARIANT structure that contains it, COM knows what type of marshaling is needed and sets it up automatically. The event function in VBScript actually receives not a direct connection to the CCustomer automation object, but rather a proxy that is valid in VBScript's thread. When VBScript calls the Invoke( ) method to get the FirstName and LastName properties, the call is marshaled to the search thread and the result marshaled back to VBScript. That's one of the beauties of COM, the dirty details are hidden away. You just follow a few simple and consistent rules for negotiating with COM and everything works more or less the way you think it ought to.

```
BOOL CSearchThread::InitInstance()
{
    HRESULT hr ;    int i ;
/*
Initialize COM in this thread.
*/

    hr = CoInitialize (NULL) ;

/*
Unmarshal interface pointers
*/
    IDispatch *pDispatch ;    IStream *pStream ;

    for (i = 0 ; i < m_StreamArray.GetSize( ) ; i ++)
    {

/*
Get stream pointer from array where control has placed it.
*/
        pStream = (IStream *) m_StreamArray [i] ;

/*
Use stream pointer to create IDispatch the I can call from
this thread.
*/
        CoGetInterfaceAndReleaseStream(
            pStream ,           // stream containing marshaling info
            IID_IDispatch,      // interface desired
            (void **) &pDispatch) ; // output variable

/*
Put resulting IDispatch in my array of those pointers.
*/
        m_DispatchArray.Add (pDispatch) ;
    }
```

<continued from previous page>

```
/*
Create new client object with arbitrary name
*/
    CCustomer *pCustomer = new CCustomer ("John", "Smith", 999) ;
    LPDISPATCH pDispOut = pCustomer->GetIDispatch (FALSE) ;

/*
Fire SearchFinished event to container
*/

    COleDispatchDriver driver;

    for (i = 0 ; i < m_DispatchArray.GetSize( ) ; i ++)
    {
/*
Place   the   proxy   IDispatch   interface   pointer   into   the
COleDispatchDriver.
*/
        driver.AttachDispatch((IDispatch *)m_DispatchArray[i],
            FALSE);
/*
Use the COleDispatchDriver utility method to fire the event.
*/
        driver.InvokeHelperV(
            m_pCtrl->eventidSearchFinished,
            DISPATCH_METHOD, VT_EMPTY, NULL,
            EVENT_PARAM(VTS_DISPATCH),
            (char *)&pDispOut);
        driver.DetachDispatch();
    }
/*
Release customer object. If event handler wanted a pointer to it,
it will have AddRefd it.
*/
    pCustomer->GetIDispatch (FALSE)->Release ( ) ;

    return TRUE;
}

/*
PostQuitMessage( ) is called from CCustomer::OnFinalRelease( ), thereby
ensuring that the thread stays around long enough to service any
customer objects that it created. When that happens, this function is
called. Uninitialize COM.
*/

int CSearchThread::ExitInstance()
{
    CoUninitialize( ) ;

    return CWinThread::ExitInstance();
}
```

444

5. If calls on the CCustomer proxy are marshaled back to the thread that created it, does this mean that the thread has to stay around as long as the object does? Yes, it does. To prove that to yourself, rebuild the control, adding a call to PostQuitMessage( ) at the end of the CSearchThread::InitInstance( ) method, thereby causing the thread to terminate as soon as it returns from signaling the event. When you click "Start Search", John Smith's name appears in the edit controls because the code that does that is executed during the event, while the thread is still alive. If you then click the "Refresh" button, attempting to access the CCustomer automation object again, you will see an error box from VBScript announcing an error of type 0x80010012L. If you look that up in the header files, you will find that this constant is defined as RPC_E_SERVER_DIED_DNE. You can't make a call into an object if the thread which created the object isn't around to service the call.

To solve this problem in the sample control, I overrode the OnFinalRelease( ) method of my CCustomer object. This is called when the last user of the object calls Release( ) and the object's reference count drops to zero. In it, I call PostQuitMessage( ), thereby sending the WM_QUIT message to the search thread. In the thread's ExitInstance( ) method, I uninitialize COM via the function CoUninitialize( ).

How do I know whether the interface really needed to be marshaled at all? It might have been a free-threaded interface that wouldn't care if it were called from another thread. I don't know, but fortunately I don't have to know or care. If I simply make the function calls to marshal the interface as shown above, and the interface actually belongs to an object that doesn't require marshaling, COM will simply not set up the marshaling code behind the scenes. Instead of a proxy, CoGetInterfaceAndReleaseStream( ) will return a direct pointer to the object's code. I follow a few simple rules and COM intercedes to the extent necessary. I don't have to know what that extent is in order to use it, and I'd usually just as soon not have to think about it.

F. FREE THREADING MODEL

1. This section describes the *free threading model*, sometimes known as the "multi-threaded apartment model", the other set of rules that an object or client may choose to follow. In the free threading model, an object method may be called from any thread at any time. It is up to the object to serialize access to its methods and instance data to whatever extent it requires to keep incoming calls from conflicting. It can provide more flexibility and better performance than the apartment model in a relatively small percentage of cases. The cost is that you have to write code to handle serialization and race conditions that COM handles for you in the apartment model. You don't choose the free threading model just for the heck of it, you choose it for the relatively small percentage of cases where its performance profits outweigh the increased development costs and time.

Where does using the free threaded model makes us a profit over the apartment model? Any place that a single object needs to be accessed fairly frequently by more than one thread. Suppose you have a DCOM server app accessed by remote clients. When the remote client calls a method on an object, the server machine receives that call on a random thread from a pool that exists for this purpose. This receiving thread makes the call locally to the actual object. If the object supports the free threading model, then the call into the object proceeds directly from the receiving thread. If the object supports the apartment threading model, then the call has to be marshaled into the thread on which the object was originally created and the results marshaled back into the receiving thread before being returned to the client, wasting microseconds. You also run the risk of the object's thread being busy servicing other objects, or, worse, blocked while waiting on some synchronization event. Finally, if all the objects live on the same apartment thread, you are unable to take advantage of multiple CPUs on the server, which is becoming more and more common.

The free threading model is especially good when the object doesn't need to remember its internal state from one call to the next. For another example, suppose that you have a single object that represents a connection to a database, or perhaps a piece of hardware such as a clock. The sample programs supplied with this article simulate the latter case. Suppose you now have four or five threads that need to access that object. In the apartment threading model, the object could reside on at most one of those threads. The others would have to set up interthread marshaling proxies to access the object from their own threads. You would incur the penalties of the code needed to set up the marshaling initially, and the marshaling overhead every time you made a call. If both object and client support the free threading model, then the multiple threads can all access the connection object directly, without any marshaling. The object itself will have to serialize its own calls to whatever extent they require, and you incur this overhead, but your intimate knowledge of its behavior allows you to optimize this case. Some calls can be made reentrant and won't need serialization at all. The ones we do have to serialize can frequently be done more cheaply than COM's generic marshaler.

2. When do we not want the free threading model? You don't want write an object that supports only the free threading model if most of your object's clients are going to use the apartment model. Remember, COM sets up marshaling proxies when client and server use different threading models. Accessing a free threaded object from an apartment thread incurs an interthread marshaling performance penalty of the same type shown previously on page 426, when an apartment thread created an non-threaded control. Why does COM do this when the control has stated that it can be called from any thread at any time, that it has already serialized its methods to whatever extent they require? The reason has to do with callbacks from the control to its container. It is a relatively rare case when a control is purely a server and its container purely a client. It is much more common for each side to call methods on interfaces provided by the other. For example, a container calls methods on a control by calling IDispatch::Invoke( ) on an interface provided by the control. A control fires an event to its container by calling IDispatch::Invoke( ) on an interface provided by its container. Each side is the server of one interface and the client of another. While a free threaded control has indicated its willingness to accept method calls from any thread, an apartment container is expecting its callback methods to be called only from within the thread which created them. By marking itself as "Free", the control is indicating that it doesn't have the discipline to do this. The control is saying, "You can call me from any thread at any time, but I reserve the right to call you back from any thread at any time." Since the apartment threaded container can't handle that, COM creates the free control in a separate thread and marshals all calls into it from or out of it to an apartment thread.

An apartment threaded control is much easier to write, so if your control is free threaded and your clients apartment, you'll have spend lots of extra time and money slowing your clients down. Not smart. However, if you expect a mix of clients for your objects, your in-proc server can support both threading models. In this case, both types of clients can have the speed of a direct connection and apartment threaded clients will have the thread safety they need. Making your app support the free threading model is expensive, so you don't do it without a reason. But if you do support the free threading model, then upgrading it to support both models doesn't cost much more. Supporting both threading models is discussed beginning on page 467.

You don't want to use free threading model for objects that provide or threads that deal with any sort of user interface. If a user interface thread depended on the state of a free-threaded object, the state of the object could change while the thread was in the middle of processing a message. Apartment threaded objects won't do this, as incoming calls arrive through a thread's message queue. The function OleInitialize( ) does not support a flag for the free threading model; it automatically and non-negotiably calls CoInitialize( ), thereby initializing the apartment model on that calling thread. Any functionality that requires OleInitialize( ), mostly user interface stuff such as object linking and embedding or drag and drop, is restricted to the apartment model. The container app used as a sample for this chapter uses the free threaded model in user interface threads, but this is done solely so you can see the results of the various options. A real world app wouldn't do this.

You don't want the free threading model if your object requires any kind of thread affinity for its method calls, for example, if your object uses thread local storage to remember its state from one call to the next. The MFC supports only the apartment model because it makes extensive use of thread local storage. OLE and COM support were added to the MFC relatively late in its life, when its internal architecture was already fixed. The ATL, described in the next chapter, does offer a choice of threading models for servers you create with it.

If you want your free threaded client or server to run on Windows 95, you will have to write an installation program to make sure that the DCOM service pack, which contains support for the free threading model, is installed on your customer's machine. Not all customers will allow this.

447

3. Free threaded client follow different rules from apartment threaded apps. A container app that wants to support the free threaded model must call the API function **CoInitializeEx( )**, passing a value of **COINIT_MULTITHREADED** as its second parameter. This initializes COM in the client app's address space and tells it that the calling thread follows the rules of the free threading model. Once it does this, the thread may call any COM function or object method from any thread at any time.

Previous writings, including some of mine, have stated that this only needs to happen one thread per process. This is now known to work in some situations but not in others, and will not be upwards compatible with NT 5.0. You need to make this function call from every thread that wants to call COM functions or object methods using the free threading model.

When the client app creates an object, COM detects via registry entries any object that cannot handle being called in this manner. For these objects, COM transparently sets up marshaling to serialize access to their methods in the way that the object is expecting. Your client app does not have to think about the threading model used by any of the objects that it creates. Your app tells COM which rules it is following and then follows them. COM checks the rules that the object says it follows, and transparently intercedes between client and object to the extent, if any, needed to make them work together properly.

There are two GOTCHAs here, both related to the fact that the free threading model is a recent arrival. First, you must either define the constant **_WIN32_DCOM** in your project, or define the constant **_WIN32_WINNT** to a value ox 0x400 or greater. In the samples supplied with this article, I defined the former constant in my project settings to make sure it applied everywhere. The system header files that come with Visual C++ version 5.0 omit the DCOM related functions, such as CoInitializeEx( ), unless this flag is defined.

The second problem is that the free threading model is present in Windows NT versions 4.0 and later. It is not supported in earlier versions of NT, nor is it supported in Windows 95 unless the DCOM extensions have been installed. If you build an app that calls CoInitializeEx( ) directly and run it on an operating system that doesn't contain it, the app will not run at all. It will halt with an undefined dynalink error before entering WinMain( ), so you won't even have a chance to detect the problem and try to explain it to the user. To work around this, I don't call CoInitializeEx( ) directly. As shown on the facing page, I first use the API functions LoadLibrary( ) and GetProcAddress( ) to check if the system DLL "ole32.dll" contains CoInitializeEx( ). If it does, I use the pointer returned from GetProcAddress( ) to call it indirectly. If not, I can try to explain the problem to the user.

```
// constant _WIN32_DCOM defined in project settings

int WINAPI WinMain(HINSTANCE hInstance, HINSTANCE hPrevInstance,
    LPSTR lpCmdLine, int nCmdShow)
{


/*
Check for presence of the function CoInitializeEx() in the operating
system DLL Ole32.dll. If not found, then the free threading model is
not supported. Inform user and exit.
*/

    HANDLE hMod = GetModuleHandle ("ole32.dll") ;


    typedef HRESULT (WINAPI *MYPTR)(void *, DWORD);
    MYPTR fpCoInitializeEx = (MYPTR) GetProcAddress (hMod,
        "CoInitializeEx") ;

    if (fpCoInitializeEx == NULL)
    {
      MessageBox (NULL, "This version of the operating system does not\
            Support the free threading model", "Error", MB_OK) ;

      return -1 ;
    }

/*
Initialize COM for free-threading model.
*/

    fpCoInitializeEx (NULL, COINIT_MULTITHREADED) ;

    <rest of WinMain>
}
```

4. The client app provided with this chapter is a multithreaded MDI app named 'data6cl.exe". The main frame window is handled by the app's main thread. It contains three MDI child windows, each of which is handled by its own separate thread. Two of the windows are controlled by free threads, the third by an apartment thread for a later demonstration. A screen shot may be found on page 455.

The data objects to which the client app connects support a private clipboard format called cfThreadId. When the client app child windows handle their WM_PAINT messages, they call IDataObject::GetData( ) and request this format, as shown below. When it receives the call, the server object calls GetCurrentThreadId( ) to find out the thread ID on which the call was received, as shown on the facing page. Thus:

```
extern IDataObject *pFreeObj ; extern UINT cfThreadId ;

case WM_PAINT:
{
    PAINTSTRUCT ps ;    HDC hDC ;
    char out [256] ;    int length ;
    hDC = BeginPaint (hWnd, &ps) ;
/*
If no object present, so inform user.
*/
    if (pFreeObj == NULL)
    {
      length = wsprintf (out, "<no object>") ;
      TextOut (hDC, 0, 0, out, length) ;
    }
    else
    {
/*
Call IDataObject::GetData() to make the object report the ID of the
thread on which it receives calls. Draw on screen.
*/
      FORMATETC fe ;    STGMEDIUM stm ;
      DWORD ThreadId = 0xFFFFFFFF, *pdw ;
      fe.cfFormat = cfThreadId ;
      fe.ptd = NULL ;
      fe.dwAspect = DVASPECT_CONTENT ;
      fe.lindex = -1 ;
      fe.tymed = TYMED_HGLOBAL ;

      if (pFreeObj->GetData (&fe, &stm) == S_OK)
      {
          pdw = (DWORD *)GlobalLock (stm.hGlobal) ;
          ThreadId = *pdw ;
          GlobalUnlock (stm.hGlobal) ;
          ReleaseStgMedium (&stm) ;
      }

      < output thread ID on screen >
    }
    EndPaint (hWnd, &ps) ;
    return 0 ;
}
```

```c
extern UINT cfThreadId ;

STDMETHODIMP CTimeData::GetData (LPFORMATETC lpfe, LPSTGMEDIUM lpstg)
{

/*
We support a private clipboard format, identified by the UINT
cfThreadId. The caller is asking for the ID of the thread on which we
receive the call. Allocate a new global, copy our thread ID into it,
and fill in the elements of the STGMEDIUM structure that we were passed
*/

    if (lpfe->cfFormat == cfThreadId
      && lpfe->tymed == TYMED_HGLOBAL
      && lpfe->dwAspect == DVASPECT_CONTENT)
    {
      DWORD *pdw ;
      pdw = (DWORD *)GlobalAlloc(GMEM_FIXED, sizeof (DWORD));

      if (!pdw)
      {
            return E_OUTOFMEMORY ;
      }

      *pdw = GetCurrentThreadId ( ) ;

      lpstg->tymed = TYMED_HGLOBAL ;
      lpstg->hGlobal = (HGLOBAL) pdw ;
      lpstg->pUnkForRelease = NULL ;

      return  S_OK ;
    }

/*
User asked for a format that we couldn't supply.  Return error code.
*/
    return DATA_E_FORMATETC ;
}
```

5. The client app has initialized itself to use the free threading model, but what happens if there is an apartment threaded object that the free threaded client app just can't live without? The client could certainly use the apartment threaded object, incurring the inter-thread marshaling penalty. Suppose that's too restrictive; you need the last microsecond of performance from the object, but you can't get its vendor to rewrite it for the free threading model. Is there a way around this ?

Yes, there is. COM deals with threading issues on a per-thread basis. You can create apartment threads within a free-threaded container. All a thread needs to do is to call CoInitializeEx( ) when it starts up, passing the flag COINIT_APARTMENTTHREADED. COM will then know that this thread uses the apartment model for all of its COM operations, even if the other threads in the app all use the free threading model. This thread must follow the rules of an apartment threaded container as discussed in my previous article, which include having a message loop and servicing it frequently, and calling its objects only from within the thread that created them.

The sample app shows how this is done. Go to the client app and restore the minimized window whose title bar contains the word "Apartment." This window is controlled by a thread within the client app the has initialized COM with the apartment threading model as described in the previous paragraph. As with the other windows, the thread ID of the thread controlling the apartment window is displayed in its title bar. The code for this thread is shown on the facing page.

Click on the "Apartment" window, then use the app's main menu to create an apartment threaded object. You will find that the thread ID reported by the object is the same as that of the thread controlling the window. This was previously the case when a free threaded window created a free threaded object. Now release the apartment control from the apartment window, and create a free threaded object in that window. The thread IDs are now different. COM sets up marshaling between client thread and object because it knew that they used different threading models.

```
DWORD WINAPI AptThreadProc (LPVOID lpv)
{
```

```
/*
Initialize COM on this thread as using the apartment model. The free
threads in the app omit this call, as the main thread has already made
it to use the free threading model.
*/

    CoInitializeEx (NULL, COINIT_APARTMENTTHREADED) ;

/*
Create MDI Child window, and perform other initializations.
*/

    <code omitted for clarity>

/*
Service the message loop, as required for the apartment threading
model.
*/

    MSG msg ;

    while (GetMessage(&msg, NULL, NULL, NULL))
    {
      TranslateMessage(&msg);
      DispatchMessage(&msg);
    }


/*
Shut down COM in this thread. The free threads omit this call as well.
*/

    CoUninitialize( ) ;

    return 0 ;
}
```

G. Free Threaded In-Proc Servers

1. To begin our investigation of the free threading model, run the sample client app "data6cl.exe" described in the previous section. It will look like the facing page, a main MDI frame window, two child windows tiled horizontally labeled "Free" and one minimized labeled "Apartment". Each window is created and controlled by a separate thread. The thread ID of the thread controlling the window is shown in that window's title bar. On the facing page, the main window is controlled by thread 0x67, which is the app's main thread, the top child window by thread 0x41, and the bottom child window by thread 0xb6.

Click on either of the tiled child windows, then choose "Data Object – Create Apartment-Threaded In-Proc" from the main menu. The WM_COMMAND message is received by the main window on the main thread, which contains code that posts it to the active child window. The message is thus processed by the window procedure of the child window on the thread which owns the child window. When you make this menu selection, the active child window calls CoCreateInstance( ) to create an object of the specified class, storing its pointer in a global variable called `pFreeObj` where all threads can access it. It then invalidates all the child windows, forcing them all to repaint themselves.

When it receives the WM_PAINT message, each free child window calls IDataObject::GetData( ) on pFreeObj. The child window makes this call from its own thread, whose ID is in its title bar. The child windows request the data in the format cfThreadId. As shown previously on page 451, this causes the object to report the ID of the thread on which it receives the call. The child windows display this ID for you to read. The transfer time shown on your screen will be 0 at this point; it will not change until you perform the time test two paragraphs from now.

In this example, both free-threaded windows report the same thread ID, which is different from the ID of the thread that owns the window and from which the call was originally made. COM has detected from the server's registry entries that the object supports only the apartment threading model, while COM knows from the container's initial call to CoCreateInstanceEx( ) that the container is using the free threading model. COM therefore creates a new thread, creates the object on that thread, and returns from the creation function not a direct pointer to the object, but rather a pointer to a marshaling proxy that marshals all calls into the object's thread. In this manner, the apartment threaded object sees only the threading behavior that it has told COM it knows how to handle. This is similar to the case on page 426 where an apartment container created a non-threaded control. COM is interceding between client and object to reconcile the differences between the threading models. Neither client nor object knows or especially cares about the threading model used by the other.

As in the previous example, it works seamlessly, but there's a price. Pick "Data Object – GetData Time Test" from the menu. This performs a timing test by repeatedly calling the method IDataObject::GetData( ), asking it to transfer a specified amount of data. The elapsed time is shown on the thread's child window. The numbers on the facing page were obtained on a Pentium Pro 200 CPU, transferring 10 k bytes on each of 10,000 repetitions. The total elapsed time was 1533 milliseconds, or about 0.15 ms per call. This overhead results as the call is marshaled from the window's thread on which it is made to the thread on which the apartment object lives and the results marshaled back.

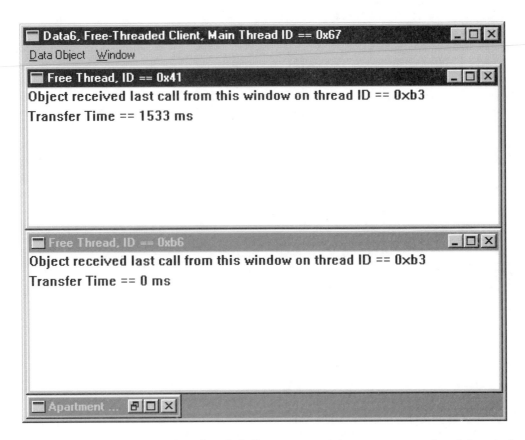

Results of time test on free-threaded client app containing an apartment-threaded control.

2. Suppose I don't want my customers to incur this overhead; I'm afraid they'll buy someone else's product instead. I want to write a object that provides a direct connection in the free threaded model without any of this marshaling overhead. Choose "Data Object — Release( )" from the menu, then "Data Object — Create Free-Threaded In-Proc". This calls CoCreateInstance( ), specifying the class ID of the object that has identified itself as supporting this model by placing the key "Free" under "Threading Model" in the InProcServer32 key in the registry, as shown below. The client app will then resemble the facing page. Note that the two free threaded windows are now reporting different values for the ID of the thread on which the object is receiving the call. Furthermore, the ID reported in each window is the same as the ID of the thread that owns the window and from which the call was made. Even though the call to CoCreateInstance( ) was made from one thread and not from the other, the pointer returned from CoCreateInstance( ) is to a direct connection to the free threaded object. Both threads can now call its methods directly. Perform the time test again, and you'll find that the transfer time has gone down to 70 ms, speeding up by a factor of about 22.

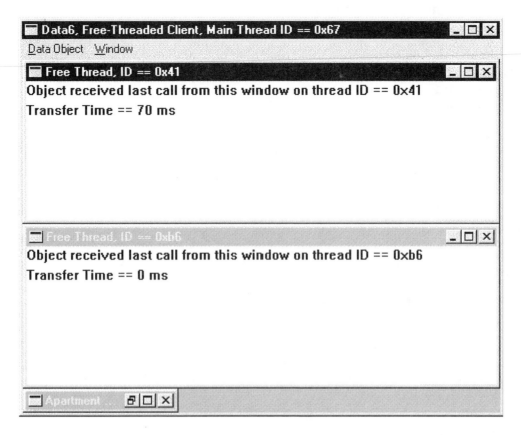

Results of time test on free-threaded client app holding a free-threaded control

457

3. All right, that's cool, but what about the case where the two threads might call the time test at the same time? In an apartment threaded object, COM would automatically serialize calls to each object's methods so I didn't have to worry. That isn't happening in this case. COM detected that both client and object are using the free threading model so it got out of the way. It means the object has to serialize its own methods to whatever extent they need. It is up to the programmer to determine what that extent is and to write the code that makes it happen.

Consider my object's implementation of IUnknown, shown on the facing page. My QueryInterface( ) method doesn't need to change at all. It is completely reentrant; everything is done on the stack. This illustrates one place where the free-threaded model can make you a performance profit — your objects only serialize only the calls that need it. Since it had no way of telling which calls needed serialization, the apartment model serialized all calls to all interfaces on its objects, whether they needed it or not.

In the apartment model, I used InterlockedIncrement( ) and InterlockedDecrement( ) in the object's constructor and destructor, because these functions changed my server's global object count and I had to serialize access to globals in the apartment threading model. Now I need to serialize access to my object's instance data as well, such as its internal reference count. AddRef( ) is pretty simple; I just use the function InterlockedIncrement( ). Release( ) is a little trickier; no harder to write the code for but you do have to think about threads. Suppose thread A and thread B each have a pointer to this object, whose reference count is 2. Suppose A, near the end of its timeslice, calls Release( ), which executes the InterlockedDecrement( ), returning a reference count of 1 and assigning it to the variable `retval`. Suppose thread A has now exhausted its timeslice and gets swapped out before it can execute the test for zero on the next line. Now suppose that thread B gets swapped in, calls Release( ), and because it has a new timeslice manages to execute the entire Release( ) method. The reference count is decremented to zero and the object destructed. Now suppose thread A gets swapped in, and goes to test for zero. The test will fail, because the reference count wasn't zero when thread A decremented it. Control passes to the last line, where the current reference count is returned. If we didn't use a stack variable, but instead returned `m_RefCount`, as in most of the examples in this book, we would be returning a garbage value because the object would have already been destructed and its member variables meaningless. Worse, if we put any real code after the test in Release( ), that did real things with member variables instead of just returning the reference count, it would probably croak on us. The things that you have to do aren't very hard, but the free threading model forces you to think in ways that the apartment model didn't. So even though I had to write this code, I've still made a performance profit because my serialization code has much lower overhead than the marshaling that COM would have provided for an inter-thread object access, with PostMessage( ).

It is important to remember that the performance profits I refer to on this page are profitable only where the same object needs to be accessed from multiple threads, which requires marshaling in the apartment threading model but not in the free threading model. Whether the marshaling would happen frequently enough to make the microseconds saved worth the trouble of writing (testing, debugging, maintaining, documenting) the additional code required for free threading is another issue.

```
/*
The QueryInterface() method does everything on the stack. It is thread
safe as is.
*/

HRESULT CTimeData::QueryInterface(REFIID riid, LPVOID FAR *ppv)
{
    if (riid == IID_IUnknown || riid == IID_IDataObject)
    {
        *ppv = (LPVOID)this;
        AddRef();
        return S_OK ;
    }
    else
    {
      *ppv = NULL;
      return  E_NOINTERFACE ;
    }
}


/*
AddRef() uses InterlockedIncrement()to serialize access to the member
variable m_RefCount, thereby making themselves thread safe.
*/

STDMETHODIMP_(ULONG) CTimeData::AddRef(void)
{
    return InterlockedIncrement (&m_RefCount) ;
}



/*
Release needs to not only call InterlockedDecrement( ), but also to
refrain from using its member variables afterwards, in order to make
itself thread safe.
*/

STDMETHODIMP_(ULONG) CTimeData::Release(void)
{
    UINT retval = InterlockedDecrement (&m_RefCount) ;

    if (retval == 0)
    {
        delete this;
    }
    return retval ;
}
```

4. What other types of serialization might we have to do? The answer for this example is in the methods IDataObject::DAdvise and DUnadvise( ), shown on the facing page. These methods are used to establish a callback circuit so the object can advise the client when its data changes. The client provides an object that supports the IAdviseSink interface, and the object calls the method IAdviseSink::OnDataChange( ) to notify the client when the data changes. This is discussed in more detail at the end of Chapter 2.

My data object as written only supports one connection at a time. A request for a second connection will fail until the first one is released. Since these methods access internal member variables, I need to write code to make sure that only one thread uses them at a time. I do this with a critical section that I set up as member variable of my object's class as shown below. Each method calls EnterCriticalSection( ) at its beginning and LeaveCriticalSection( ) at its end. If one thread gets swapped out in the middle of one of these methods, and another thread gets swapped in and calls one of them, the second thread will block until the first one finishes.

You may wonder why I am working directly with the IAdviseSink interface instead of following the standard practice of delegating these operations to a data advise holder, an object created by the API function CreateDataAdviseHolder( ). I don't do that in this example, because IDataAdviseHolder, even though it is a standard interface, does not seem to have a marshaler in my operating system (NT 4.0, service pack 2). I could write and install a marshaler for it, which would take under an hour, but I thought it was better to show how to run with the OS as shipped.

```
class CTimeData : public IDataObject
{

    public:
      long              m_RefCount ;
      LPADVISESINK      m_pAdvSink ;
      CRITICAL_SECTION  m_csDAdvise ;

    <rest of class declaration omitted>
}


CTimeData::CTimeData()
{
    InitializeCriticalSection (&m_csDAdvise) ;

    <rest of initialization omitted>
}
CTimeData::~CTimeData(void)
{
    DeleteCriticalSection (&m_csDAdvise) ;

    <rest of cleanup omitted>
}
```

```
STDMETHODIMP CTimeData::DAdvise (FORMATETC FAR* lpfe, DWORD dw,
    LPADVISESINK lpas, DWORD *lpdw)
{
    HRESULT hr, retval = S_OK ;

/*
Wait on the critical section so that no other threads making this
method call can interrupt this operation.
*/
    EnterCriticalSection (&m_csDAdvise) ;

    if (m_pAdvSink == NULL)
    {
        <set up callback circuit>
    }
/*
Leave the critical section.
*/
    LeaveCriticalSection (&m_csDAdvise) ;
    return  hr ;
}


STDMETHODIMP CTimeData::DUnadvise  (DWORD dw)
{
/*
Wait on the critical section so that no other threads making this
method call can interrupt this operation.
*/
    EnterCriticalSection (&m_csDAdvise) ;


    <perform cleanup>

/*
Leave the critical section.
*/
    LeaveCriticalSection (&m_csDAdvise) ;
    return S_OK ;
}
```

H. THREADING AND LOCAL SERVERS

1. COM reaches into a .DLL server via the function DllGetClassObject( ) and pulls out a class factory whenever it needs one. In an .EXE, it is up to your code to register class factories when it first starts up, maintain a global object count, and revoke the class factories and shut itself down when the object count reaches zero. This causes a multithreaded .EXE server to have timing and concurrency problems that a .DLL server doesn't. Fortunately, COM now contains auxiliary functions that make it easy to handle these situations, once you know where they are.

An .EXE server does not tell COM which threading model it supports by making registry entries, as did a .DLL server. Instead, it signals this to COM in the same way as a client app, by calling CoCreateInstanceEx( ), passing the flag **COINIT_MULTITHREADED** to support the free threading model or **COINIT_APARTMENTTHREADED** for the apartment model. When the server does the former, it is saying to COM that any objects that it provides to COM, including class factories, may be called from any thread; that the objects have already been internally serialized to whatever extent they require.

The first timing problem comes when the.EXE server registers its class factory. A single-threaded server could call CoRegisterClassObject( ) at whatever point in its initialization it felt like doing so. The server didn't have to worry about receiving incoming calls to IClassFactory::CreateInstance( ) until it checked its message loop, since that was necessary for receiving the call. A free threaded server doesn't have this luxury. It might receive calls to create objects at any instant after it registers its class factory. An apartment server may have a similar problem if the main thread creates auxiliary threads and the auxiliary threads register class factories. An object might get created and try to run before the server app had completed its own initialization. You could make registering the class factory your last piece of initialization, but that would needlessly tie your hands. And what about the fairly common case where .EXE server registers more than one class factory? At best, you would have to do a complicated timing dance to make sure everything happened in the right order. There has to be a better way.

This is an easy problem to solve. You create and register the class factories as before, but you add the flag **REGCLS_SUSPENDED** to the fourth parameter of CoRegisterClassObject( ). This registers the class factory with COM but leaves it in a suspended state, in which COM will not accepts incoming requests for that class factory. When your server has finished all its initialization, it tells COM that its class factories are open for business by calling the new API function **CoResumeClassObjects( )**. This allows all of your registered class factories to accept incoming calls. This code is shown on the facing page.

NOTE: In the sample code provided with this article, I use the same local server app to demonstrate both the free and apartment threading models. I have registered two different class IDs, one for each model. In the LocalServer32 entry of the apartment model server class ID, I have appended the string "-Apt" to the server's command line. When the server's WinMain( ) starts running, the first thing it does is to check its command line for this flag. If present, the server initializes itself to use the apartment threading model; otherwise it initializes itself to use the free threading model. Make sure that you understand that I did this for my own convenience in not having to write two server apps. It is not a standard part of COM, as is the "-Embedding" command line switch that tells a server app that it was launched by COM. While non-standard, you could certainly use this technique yourself if you wanted to have a switch-hitting local server.

462

```
int WINAPI WinMain(HINSTANCE hInstance, HINSTANCE hPrevInstance,
    LPSTR lpCmdLine, int nCmdShow)
{
    MSG msg;   WNDCLASS  wc;
    HRESULT hr ;

/*
Check which threading model the client wants us to support. This is my
own   addition   to   the   LocalServer32   key   for   convenience   in   the
demonstration app, not part of COM. Initialize COM accordingly.
*/

    BOOL bApartment ;

    if (strstr (lpCmdLine, "-Apt"))
    {
      bApartment = TRUE ;
      ClsidToRegister = GUID_ApartmentThreadedTimeDataLocal ;
      hr = CoInitializeEx (NULL, COINIT_APARTMENTTHREADED) ;
    }
    else
    {
      ClsidToRegister = GUID_FreeThreadedTimeDataLocal ;
      bApartment = FALSE ;
      hr = CoInitializeEx (NULL, COINIT_MULTITHREADED) ;
    }
/*
Check command line to see if launched as a COM server.  If so, register
the class factory for this app, but leave it in a suspended state.
*/

    DWORD dwRegister ;  BOOL bRegister = FALSE ;

    if (strstr (lpCmdLine, "-Embedding"))
    {
      LPCLASSFACTORY pCF = new CClassFactory ( ) ;

      hr = CoRegisterClassObject(
            ClsidToRegister, pCF,
            CLSCTX_LOCAL_SERVER,
            REGCLS_MULTIPLEUSE | REGCLS_SUSPENDED,
            &dwRegister) ;
    }
/*
Resume class objects, telling COM that all the class factories in this
process are now open for business.
*/
    CoResumeClassObjects ( ) ;

    < rest of WinMain >
}
```

463

2. The next problem comes in shutting down your local server. Your server app has probably controlled its lifetime with your own utility functions, which I call LockThisObjectsServer( ) and UnlockThisObjectsServer( ). You call these in the constructor and destructor of each object, as shown below, and also in your class factory's LockServer( ) method.

The problem is one of thread safe timing. When the last object on an .EXE server is destroyed, it usually starts the sequence of events that leads to the server shutdown, calling CoRevokeClassObject( ) and posting itself a WM_QUIT message, or perhaps WM_CLOSE if it has a main window. In a single threaded server, you never had to worry about a call to CreateInstance( ) coming in during this shutdown, because you just wouldn't service the message loop until you had revoked the class factory. This strategy doesn't work at all with a free threaded server and would require a complicated timing dance with an apartment model server having class factories on multiple threads. What happens if just after decrementing the server's global object count to zero and starting the server's shutdown code, but before the call to CoRevokeClassObject( ), a call comes into the class factory on another thread? It would try to create a new object on a server that was in the process of shutting itself down. At best, you'd have to write complicated code for aborting the shutdown; at worst, you'd croak.

COM has added two new API functions for solving this problem, **CoAddRefServerProcess( )** and **CoReleaseServerProcess( )**. These functions manipulate a global per-process reference count maintained by COM. They are serialized relative to each other, so you don't have to worry about them colliding. The important new feature is that when CoReleaseServerProcess( ) decrements this reference count to 0, COM immediately suspends all activity on all of your server app's registered class factories, by internally calling the API function **CoSuspendClassObjects( )**. When CoReleaseServerProcess( ) returns 0, you know that the object just destructed was the last one in your process and your server can safely initiate the shutdown – your class factories are already suspended; they won't be getting any incoming calls. If a client app now attempts to create an object of the class manufactured by your server, COM will launch another instance of it.

I've wrapped these functions into the utility locking and unlocking functions on the facing page. The critical section csShutdown is present only for serializing access to the server's global flag bShuttingDownNow. It has nothing to do with CoAddRefServerProcess( ) or CoReleaseServerProcess( ), which have their own internal serialization.

```
CTimeData::CTimeData()
{
    m_RefCount = 1 ;
    InterlockedIncrement (&g_ObjectCount) ;
/*
New object created, call utility function to lock server
*/
    LockThisObjectsServer ( ) ;
}


CTimeData::~CTimeData(void)
{
    InterlockedDecrement (&g_ObjectCount) ;
    InvalidateRect (hMainWnd, NULL, TRUE) ;
/*
Object destroyed. Call utility function to lock server.
*/
    UnlockThisObjectsServer ( ) ;
}
```

```
extern CRITICAL_SECTION csShutdown ;
extern BOOL bShuttingDownNow ;

/*
Caller wants to lock the server. Call the API function that increments
COM's per-process reference count.
*/

void LockThisObjectsServer ( )
{
    CoAddRefServerProcess( ) ;
}

/*
Caller wants to unlock the server.
*/

void UnlockThisObjectsServer ( )
{

/*
Enter the critical section that serializes access to the global flag
bShuttingDownNow.
*/
    EnterCriticalSection (&csShutdown) ;

/*
Call the API function that decrements COM's per process reference
count.
*/

    if (CoReleaseServerProcess( ) == 0)
    {
/*
Post a WM_CLOSE message to tell the main window to destroy itself, and
set the global state flag that says that shutdown is underway.
*/
        PostMessage (hMainWnd, WM_CLOSE, 0, 0) ;
        bShuttingDownNow = TRUE ;
    }

/*
Leave the critical section allowing other threads to access the global
flag bShuttingDownNow.
*/
    LeaveCriticalSection (&csShutdown) ;
}
```

3. This leaves us with one more hole to plug. Suppose client A creates an object from a local server. The server's process reference count is 1. Now suppose client B calls CoCreateInstance( ) to create another object, and the call reaches the first line of your class factory's CreateInstance( ) method before getting swapped out. Now suppose client A gets swapped in and calls Release( ) on its object, destroying it and decrementing the server's reference count to 0, thereby starting server shutdown. The creation of client B's object has started, but has not yet reached the point where it would keep the server alive. Eventually client A's thread will get swapped out, client B's will get swapped in, and try to create an object in a dying server. This is a problem.

It has always been possible to detect this situation and have the class factory fail the object's creation. The problem was that then the client wouldn't get the object that he wanted because of a simple timing problem. If the client tried it again a few seconds later, the original server would have been shut down, COM would launch a new instance, and the client would have his object.

Windows NT 4.0 added a new error code called **CO_E_SERVER_STOPPING**. When the method IClassFactory::CreateInstance( ) returns this error code, it tells COM that the object whose creation has been requested cannot be created because the server is in the process of shutting down. COM then launches a new instance of the server and creates the object from the new instance. Thus:

```
STDMETHODIMP CClassFactory::CreateInstance(LPUNKNOWN pUnkOuter,
    REFIID riid, LPVOID* ppvObj)
{
    HRESULT retval ;
/*
Wait on critical section that gates access to bShuttingDownNow.
*/

    EnterCriticalSection (&csShutdown) ;

/*
If shutdown flag set, then fail creation with the error code that tells
COM to launch another instance of the server to create the object.
*/
    if (bShuttingDownNow)
    {
      retval = CO_E_SERVER_STOPPING ;
    }

/*
Otherwise, create the object, which will increment the server process's
reference count.
*/
    else
    {
      <code omitted>
    }

    LeaveCriticalSection (&csShutdown) ;
    return retval ;
}
```

Note: If you want to try this, comment out all the other code in CreateInstance( ) and have it just return CO_E_SERVER_STOPPING. You will see COM launch instance after instance after instance of your server, trying to get one to work. Make sure you have saved your files in all your other apps first.

I. BOTH THREADING MODELS

1. As we saw in the previous section, it isn't always a good idea for a control to use the free threading model. A free threaded control actually loses performance when used by an apartment container because COM insists on marshaling all calls into and out of the control.

Is there a way in which a control can avoid any marshaling, providing direct connections to all clients? Yes, by marking itself as supporting both threading models, by setting the "ThreadingModel" registry value to "Both". A control that supports this model is saying that a) it will accept calls to any method on any object from any thread at any time, and b) that the control will ensure that any callbacks it might make into its container are made only on the thread on which the control received the callback object. The control is promising to be both robust and civilized. In this case, when the container creates a control, it will always be given a direct connection to the control, whether the container uses the apartment or the free threading model.

Supporting both threading models has a reputation for being difficult. Like most such reputations for difficulty in COM, it's far greater than it deserves. If you look through your registry, you will find that such servers as the VBScript engine, class ID {B54F3741-5B07-11CF-A4B0-00AA004A55E8}, support both threading models, although you'll also find that they are currently a small minority. As previously stated, supporting the free threading model is a little tricky and tedious, so you don't do it unless it will make you some money. The cost is mainly in going to the free threading model. Having done that, it doesn't cost much more to go ahead and support both models.

2. What do you have to do to write a control that supports both models? You have follow both of the disciplines that the two threading models require of their adherents. You must serialize access to your object's instance data as if it were a free threaded object, because a client might use it that way. And you must also make sure that your object makes callbacks into its client only from the thread on which it received the callback object, following the rules of the apartment threading model, because a client might use it that way.

Suppose we've done the first part, writing a free threaded control. What other things do we still have to do to upgrade to support for both models? Maybe not much. If all your callbacks are synchronous, you don't have to write any additional code. Your object can make callbacks into its client from within any of your object's methods called by the client. An apartment threaded client will always make that call on the right thread (or be responsible for the consequences if it doesn't), and a free threaded client won't care. However, if your object makes asynchronous callbacks to its client from other threads, you must set up marshaling so that every callback object is called on the thread from which it came, whether the callback object needs it or not.

Run the client app, select a free thread window, and create a free threaded object. Then pick "Data Object — DAdvise" from the main menu. This calls the method IDataObject::DAdvise( ), passing it a pointer to an IAdviseSink interface supplied by the client app. For the purposes of demonstrating when a call is marshaled and when it isn't, I wrote the object to create a new thread to make this callback. Whenever the data changes, hardwired to once per second in this simple example, the object will call the method IAdviseSink::OnDataChange( ), shown on the facing page, reporting the thread from which it made the call. The client then calls GetCurrentThreadId( ) on its own, getting the ID of the thread on which the callback was received, and displays them both to the user, as shown below. You will note that a free threaded client receives callbacks on the thread from which the object made the call (shown below), while an apartment thread always received callbacks on the thread on which the object was created.

468

```
STDMETHODIMP_(void) CAdviseSink::OnDataChange(LPFORMATETC pFEIn,
    LPSTGMEDIUM pSTM)
{

/*
Get ID of the thread from which this call originated. This is
in the data sent by the object.
*/
    DWORD *pdw ;
    UINT CallerThreadId ;

    if (pFEIn->cfFormat == cfThreadId)
    {
      pdw = (DWORD *)GlobalLock (pSTM->hGlobal) ;
      CallerThreadId = *pdw ;
      GlobalUnlock (pSTM->hGlobal) ;
    }

/*
Get the current thread ID, which is the ID of the thread on which
this call is received.
*/

    DWORD CurrentThreadID  = GetCurrentThreadId( ) ;

/*
Draw both on the screen for the user to see.
*/

    MessageBeep (0) ;

    HDC hDC = GetDC (m_hWnd) ;
    char out [128] ; int length ;

    length = wsprintf (out, "Callback originated on thread ID == 0x%x",
      CallerThreadId) ;
    TextOut (hDC, 0, 50, out, length) ;

    length = wsprintf (out, "Callback received on thread ID == 0x%x",
      CurrentThreadID) ;
    TextOut (hDC, 0, 70, out, length) ;

    ReleaseDC (m_hWnd, hDC) ;
    return;
}
```

3. When the client calls IDataObject::DAdvise, the object creates a new thread to keep track of time and make the actual call to IAdviseSink::OnDataChange( ). If my object implemented only the free threading model, the rules of the model allow me to pass this pointer to the new thread and have the new thread make the call directly. However, if an apartment thread was calling me, the pointer to IAdviseSink that I received would be a marshaling proxy, not a direct connection, precisely because my control could do this. Since my object wants avoid this penalty by supporting both threading models, I need to write code to do my own marshaling when making a callback from a different thread.

We set up our own marshaling in exactly the same manner as we did in the apartment threading example on page 437. The descriptively named API function CoMarshalInterThreadInterfaceInStream( ) takes the information necessary to set up marshaling for this interface and writes it into a stream, as shown on the facing page. I then pass that stream to the new thread. In the new thread's procedure, shown on the following page, I take the stream and call CoGetInterfaceAndReleaseStream( ). This reads the marshaling information from the stream and returns an interface pointer that is legal for the new thread to call. If original callback interface came from an apartment thread, which COM knows, this interface pointer is not a direct connection, but rather a proxy. When my new thread calls a method on this interface, the call will be marshaled back to the original thread, made from there where the apartment container is expecting it, and the result marshaled back to the caller.

What if the client uses the free threading model ? Do I incur all the marshaling overhead every time I make the callback, even though it isn't necessary? Fortunately not. My object doesn't know, care, or want to do either about the threading model used by the client. COM, however, knows the threading models used by both parties. If the client that supplied the callback object uses the free threading model, COM detects that. The final result of making the marshaling function calls is not a marshaling proxy, but rather a direct connection. You make the calls, COM figures out if you can have a direct connection or a marshaling proxy, and gives you back the right one. So you see, it isn't really hard to support both threading models, just a little tedious. You have to make two relatively simple function calls, one on each side of the thread. COM figures out the rest, and the right thing happens. Cool.

```
<file ctimedta.cpp>

STDMETHODIMP  CTimeData::DAdvise  (FORMATETC  FAR*  lpfe,  DWORD  dw,
LPADVISESINK lpas,
    DWORD *lpdw)
{
    HRESULT hr, retval = S_OK ;

    EnterCriticalSection (&m_csDAdvise) ;

    if (m_pAdvSink == NULL)
    {
/*
Make a copy of the advise sink pointer, which requires an AddRef.
*/
        m_pAdvSink = lpas ;
        m_pAdvSink->AddRef () ;

/*
Marshal the advise sink interface pointer into a stream.
*/
        IStream *pStream ;

        hr = CoMarshalInterThreadInterfaceInStream (
            IID_IAdviseSink,  // ID of interface to marshal
            m_pAdvSink,       // pointer to interface
            &pStream) ;       // output variable

        < error handling code omitted >
/*
Spin off a new thread to do timer notifications. Pass the
stream pointer to the new thread as its startup parameter.
*/
        g_ThreadShutdownFlag = FALSE ;

        m_hThread = CreateThread (NULL, 0, TimerProc, pStream, 0,
            &m_ThreadID) ;
    }
    else
    {
      retval = E_FAIL ;
    }

    LeaveCriticalSection (&m_csDAdvise) ;
    return retval ;
}
```

```
extern UINT cfThreadId ; extern CTimeData *g_pTimeDataObj ;
extern BOOL g_ThreadShutdownFlag ;

unsigned long __stdcall TimerProc (void *pStream)
{
    IAdviseSink *pAdvSink ;
/*
Unmarshal the interface pointer.
*/
    HRESULT hr = CoGetInterfaceAndReleaseStream (
      (IStream *)pStream,
      IID_IAdviseSink,
      (void **)&pAdvSink) ;

    for (;;)
    {
/*
Check shutdown conditions. Quit when signaled to do so.
*/
        if (g_ThreadShutdownFlag == TRUE || g_pTimeDataObj == NULL)
        {
            pAdvSink->Release() ;
            return 0 ;
        }
/*
Send data change to waiting client app.
*/
        FORMATETC fe ;     STGMEDIUM stg ;
        fe.cfFormat = cfThreadId ;
        fe.tymed = TYMED_HGLOBAL ;
        fe.dwAspect = DVASPECT_CONTENT ;
        fe.lindex = -1 ;
        fe.ptd = NULL ;

        DWORD *pdw ;
        pdw = (DWORD *)GlobalAlloc(GMEM_FIXED, sizeof (DWORD));
        *pdw = GetCurrentThreadId ( ) ;

        stg.tymed = TYMED_HGLOBAL ;
        stg.hGlobal = (HGLOBAL) pdw ;
        stg.pUnkForRelease = NULL ;

        pAdvSink->OnDataChange (&fe, &stg) ;
/*
Sleep for a second, then do it again.
*/
        Sleep (1000) ;
    }

    return 0 ;
}
```

This page intentionally contains no text other than this sentence.

4. The final issue for supporting both threading models is whether or not to support the free threaded marshaler. The free threaded marshaler is a piece of code that allows your apartment threaded clients to avoid creating marshaling proxies in certain situations where they don't need them. **WARNING: supporting the free threaded marshaler is a great way to get terrible, hard to reproduce, seemingly random crashes. Never add it to single, free, or apartment threaded controls. It will properly perform its functions of avoiding marshaling proxies, but that isn't what your object's clients need. Read this page thoroughly.**

Suppose apartment thread A creates an object from a server that supports both threading models. The object is created on thread A and the thread receives a direct, unmarshaled connection to the object. Now suppose that thread A gives a pointer to this object to apartment thread B so thread B can do some useful work with it. Knowing nothing about the object but simply following the rules of the apartment threading model, thread A calls CoMarshalInterThreadInterfaceInStream( ) and passes the resulting stream to thread B. Thread B calls CoGetInterfaceAndReleaseStream( ) and gets a proxy pointer to the object, which marshals all calls back to thread A to be made and then marshals the results back to thread B.

Since the object supports both threading models, setting up this proxy looks like it ought to be unnecessary. The vendor of the object has gone to great trouble to write it in such a manner that thread B could call it directly if only it knew that. So the vendor has gone one step further, by putting a free threaded marshaler in its object. The free threaded marshaler causes the pointer that thread B receives from CoGetInterfaceAndReleaseStream( ) be a direct connection instead of a proxy.

When threads go through the marshal/unmarshal process as described above, COM marshals the interface as described in Chapter 9. COM first queries the object for the IMarshal interface to see if the object wants to do custom marshaling. Our examples so far haven't done that, so COM set up standard marshaling proxies. The free threaded marshaler is an object supplied by COM that implements the IMarshal interface. All it does is pass a direct pointer to the interface in the marshaling packet and unpack that direct pointer on the other side. It thus overrides COM's standard marshaling mechanism. In this manner, when the threads call their marshaling functions as described above, thread B winds up with a direct connection to the object, not with a proxy.

Doing this, however, opens you up to tricky race conditions having to do with callbacks. The problem is that the object still resides on Thread A, even though Thread B has a direct connection to it. Suppose Thread A sets up a callback circuit with the object. Suppose Thread B now calls a method on the object which causes the object to make a callback into its client. Since Thread B has a direct connection, the method call is made on Thread B, so the callback will also be made on Thread B. However, the client was expecting this code to be called only from Thread A. Sometimes you'll get away with that, sometimes you won't, which isn't the gold standard for code reliability. At best, it will be a very frustrating bug to reproduce and track down. If your object didn't support the free threaded marshaler, Thread B would have gotten a proxy instead of a direct connection, and the potential bug would have been avoided. I'd suggest only using the free threaded marshaler if your object is purely an engine; if it doesn't support any callbacks to its client. Otherwise, the effort it takes to plug this hole isn't worth the performance improvement for the small percentage of cases that it helps.

Adding free threaded marshaler support is temptingly easy. The API function **CoCreateFreeThreadedMarshaler( )** creates the free threaded marshaler, which supports the IMarshal interface. You can create it in your object's constructor, as shown on the facing page, or you can wait and create it only when someone queries for it. Whichever you do, don't forget to release it in your object's destructor. You then connect the free threaded marshaler into your control via aggregation, as described in Appendix C. To do this, all you have to do is modify your QueryInterface( ) method to delegate requests for IMarshal to the free threaded marshaler, as shown on the facing page. But think twice before you put this in a product. Or three times.

```
/*
Object constructor. In the sample program, the same object is used for
the four different threading models, so I pass a parameter in the
constructor to tell the object if it is supposed to support both. In
this case, I create the free threaded marshaler.
*/

CTimeData::CTimeData (BOOL bBothThreadingModels)
{
    m_bBothThreadingModels = bBothThreadingModels ;

    if (m_bBothThreadingModels)
    {
      CoCreateFreeThreadedMarshaler (
            this,                      // outer IUnknown for aggregation
            &m_pFreeThreadedMarshaler) ;  // output variable
    }
    else
    {
      m_pFreeThreadedMarshaler = NULL ;
    }
}


/*
This QueryInterface( ) has been modified to support IMarshal through
aggregation.
*/

HRESULT CTimeData::QueryInterface(REFIID riid, LPVOID FAR *ppv)
{
    if (riid == IID_IUnknown || riid == IID_IDataObject)
    {
        *ppv = (LPVOID)this;
        AddRef();
        return S_OK ;
    }
/*
Caller is requesting IMarshal. Delegate this call to the free threaded
marshaler. The flag m_bBothThreadingModels only appears because this
example uses the same code for all threading models.
*/
    else if (riid == IID_IMarshal && m_bBothThreadingModels)
    {
      return m_pFreeThreadedMarshaler->QueryInterface (riid, ppv) ;
    }
    else
    {
      *ppv = NULL;
      return  E_NOINTERFACE ;
    }
}
```

Directory: \EssenceofOLE\chap13\demo40
Directory: \EssenceofOLE\chap13\demo42
Directory: \EssenceofOLE\chap13\ThreadDB
Directory: \EssenceofOLE\chap13\data6

1. Instructions for running the sample programs are given throughout the chapter. The instructions here deal only with registering the samples.

2. To register the controls needed for the apartment threading examples, use the command line utility RegSvr32.exe or the graphical registrar in Appendix A to register the following files:

\EssenceofOLE\chap13\demo40\demo40.ocx
\EssenceofOLE\chap13\demo42\demo42.ocx
\EssenceofOLE\chap13\ThreadDB\ThreadDB.ocx

3. To register the servers needed for the free threading examples, run the registry file

\EssenceofOLE\chap13\data6\data6.reg

Chapter 14
Active Template Library

A. CONCEPTS AND DEFINITIONS

1. The *Active Template Library* (ATL) is a collection of prefabricated code for writing COM objects that provides an alternative to the MFC. It first became popular when ATL version 2.1 shipped with Visual C++ version 5. If you know and like the MFC, which I do, you will find many of the ATL's features conceptually similar, with some cool new features.

The ATL is particularly good for writing low-level COM servers with custom or dual interfaces. Setting up custom VTBL interfaces in the MFC is a pain, as shown in Chapter 9, and then you still have to write the marshaling proxy/stub .IDL files, build them into a project, install and register the marshaling code, etc. The ATL easily sets up custom interfaces for you, and also takes care of the proxy and stubs required for marshaling. ATL servers may also use the apartment, free, or both threading models, whereas the MFC supports only apartment. The ATL's low-level toolbox has more tools in it than the MFC's.

The MFC, on the other hand, provides lots of user interface support, which the ATL does very little of. The MFC contains a cool application framework that supports embedding and linking in compound documents, as well as support for the Clipboard and drag-and-drop. It is also very good for OLE Automation using the IDispatch interface, particularly when these are tied into documents. MFC apps tend to be smaller than ATL apps with similar functionality, because the prefabricated code that you inherit lives in an external DLL. This external dependency occasionally causes logistical problems; but usually nothing too bad unless your downloading from the Internet, as discussed on the facing page.

The one frustrating hole in the ATL is its spotty Wizard support compared to what MFC users are used to, particularly when writing full featured ActiveX controls. You have to do an awful lot of cutting and pasting to have an ATL control fire events back to its container (see page 518), where the MFC Wizard does this with a few mouse clicks. A similar problem occurs with the property pages of controls (see page 524). When you are creating objects with custom interfaces, the ATL Wizard will generate one interface per object, but if you want to add a second one, you have to cut and paste. I hope that future versions of the ATL will spend some effort on making it easier to use.

Which architecture do you choose for writing your COM servers? Both ATL and MFC contain prefabricated COM functionality. The primary difference is that the latter ties this into a coherent application model with a user interface, whereas the former stands alone. You choose the MFC when you like this integrated functionality, where it fits your application model. You choose the ATL when you do not like this integrated functionality, when it costs you more than it buys you. Basically, I choose the MFC when there's a user interface involved, and the ATL when there isn't. I used the ATL to write the global running object table example in Chapter 10, and it was very convenient. The one user interface situation in which I sometimes use the ATL is explained on the facing page.

2. The ATL and MFC both provide the ability to write full-featured ActiveX controls. The MFC Wizard does this quickly and easily, as shown in Chapter 5. The controls are fairly small, about 25 Kbytes for the smallest one, because the prefabricated code that they inherit from the MFC lives in a separate DLL.

This dependency sometimes causes a problem. As long as you are shipping your MFC control on a disk, it's not a big problem. You make sure that your distribution disk contains the latest version of the MFC DLLs, and that your installation program updates any older versions that it finds. The big problem first appeared when Microsoft released the ActiveX Internet control spec, which allowed Web browsers to download and use controls from the Internet. Essentially all controls available at that time had been built with the MFC and achieved their small size at the cost of an external dependency on the MFC DLLs. The latest version of MFC42.DLL is almost a megabyte in size. Downloading this to a Web surfer's system is a non-starter. The problem wasn't terrible at first, because the only app the could download controls was Internet Explorer 3, which itself was an MFC app. The latest MFC DLLs were by definition already be on the user's system before the control could be downloaded. But soon, other non-MFC apps, such as WinWord, will acquire this capability, and versioning problems start cropping up. So this problem will only get worse in the future.

The ATL provided prefabricated classes to solve this problem. Instead of depending on a large external DLL, which contains code for lots of other features that your controls aren't using anyway, the ATL allows you to write controls that are completely self contained. Because the ATL omits anything not needed for its control framework, you can develop self contained controls at a size practical for downloading. They'll be larger than a similar MFC control, about 50 Kbytes for the smallest one, but they won't need a megabyte DLL.

So which framework do you choose for writing controls? If this dependency problem is a killer for you, then choose the ATL. If it isn't, you will find the MFC currently provides much better Wizard support so its controls are easier to write.

B. SIMPLE ATL DUAL INTERFACE SERVER

1. This section of the chapter demonstrates how to use the ATL to build the simplest automation server that I can think of, the same "Hello, world" server as we built in Chapter 3 using both the API and the MFC. The sample code can be found in the directory \EssenceOfOle\Chap14\atlhelloau.

We first need to create an ATL server project. Similar to an MFC project, this can contain more than one type of object. You create a project by selecting "File — New" from the main menu, selecting the "Projects" tab, and picking "ATL COM AppWizard". Thus

2. The ATL Wizard has only a single pane of questions, as shown below. About the only thing that it really needs to know is what type of project you want to build, a DLL, an .EXE, or a service (an .EXE automatically launched by the service control manager). The Wizard will generate code based on your choices as shown on the following pages. Thus:

This page intentionally contains no text other than this sentence.

3. The ATL COM Wizard creates a new project and the shell of a server without any COM objects inside it. The shell is represented by the ATL class *CComModule*, which is roughly analogous to the MFC class CWinApp. The server contains a single object of this class which is instantiated in the server's main file as shown on the next page. It contains methods to perform such .EXE-level or .DLL-level operations as incrementing or decrementing the global object count for locking or unlocking the server, registering or revoking class factories, and making or removing registry entries.

A .DLL server will instantiate an object of class CComModule directly, as shown in the timer control example on page 506. An .EXE server, as in this example, requires some additional support, which the Wizard provides by deriving a class called *CExeModule* from the CComModule. This overrides the base class's method CComModule::Unlock( ), adding code that shuts down the .EXE when the app's object count reaches zero. The declaration of this class is in the generated file "stdafx.h". Thus:

```
<file stdafx.h>

#define STRICT


#define _WIN32_WINNT 0x0400
#define _ATL_APARTMENT_THREADED


#include <atlbase.h>
//You may derive a class from CComModule and use to override
//something, but do not change the name of _Module

class CExeModule : public CComModule
{
public:
    LONG Unlock();
    DWORD dwThreadID;
};
extern CExeModule _Module;

#include <atlcom.h>

//{{AFX_INSERT_LOCATION}}
// Microsoft Developer Studio will insert additional declarations
// immediately before the previous line.
```

4. The ATL Wizard generates our server app's WinMain( ) function and places it in the project. The file name will be the same as that of the project, in this case "atlhelloau.cpp". Note that this files contains a global variable representing the one and only object of the CExeModule class, whose name is always "**_Module**", in the same manner as an MFC app contains one and only one global object of its CWinApp derived class, whose name is always "theApp".

When the server is launched, the code generated for the .EXE server checks its command line. If it finds the command "-RegServer" or "-UnregServer", it adds or removes its registry entries and exits. If it finds the string "–Embedding", it registers its class factories and continues to run. It does not register window classes or create windows as does an MFC local server. When you see that code in the sample, know that I had to write it myself. Indented and commented for clarity, the WinMain( ) generated by the ATL Wizard looks like this:

```
/*
Instantiate the one and only _Module for this .EXE.
*/


CExeModule _Module;

BEGIN_OBJECT_MAP(ObjectMap)
END_OBJECT_MAP()

extern "C" int WINAPI _tWinMain(HINSTANCE hInstance,
    HINSTANCE /*hPrevInstance*/, LPTSTR lpCmdLine, int /*nShowCmd*/)
{
    lpCmdLine    =    GetCommandLine();    //this    line    necessary    for
_ATL_MIN_CRT

/*
Initialize COM.
*/

    HRESULT hRes = CoInitialize(NULL);

/*
Initialize ATL internal bookkeeping.
*/
    _Module.Init(ObjectMap, hInstance);
    _Module.dwThreadID = GetCurrentThreadId();

/*
Parse command line. Look for COM commands.
*/
    TCHAR szTokens[] = _T("-/");

    int nRet = 0;
    BOOL bRun = TRUE;
    LPCTSTR lpszToken = FindOneOf(lpCmdLine, szTokens);
    while (lpszToken != NULL)
    {
```

```
/*
Command line contains string "-UnregServer". Remove this app's entries
from the registry and terminate.
*/
        if (lstrcmpi(lpszToken, _T("UnregServer"))==0)
        {
                _Module.UpdateRegistryFromResource(IDR_Atlhelloau, FALSE);
                nRet = _Module.UnregisterServer();
                bRun = FALSE;
                break;
        }
/*
Command line contains string "-RegServer". Add this app's entries to
the registry and terminate.
*/
        if (lstrcmpi(lpszToken, _T("RegServer"))==0)
        {
                _Module.UpdateRegistryFromResource(IDR_Atlhelloau, TRUE);
                nRet = _Module.RegisterServer(TRUE);
                bRun = FALSE;
                break;
        }
        lpszToken = FindOneOf(lpszToken, szTokens);
    }

    if (bRun)
    {
/*
We were launched to service an object. Register class factories.
*/
        hRes = _Module.RegisterClassObjects(CLSCTX_LOCAL_SERVER,
                REGCLS_MULTIPLEUSE);
        _ASSERTE(SUCCEEDED(hRes));

/*
Run standard message loop.
*/
        MSG msg;
        while (GetMessage(&msg, 0, 0, 0))
                DispatchMessage(&msg);

/*
Message loop terminated; revoke class factories.
*/
        _Module.RevokeClassObjects();
    }

/*
Uninitialize COM.
*/
    CoUninitialize();
    return nRet;
}
```

5. ATL servers perform their own registration, a very cool feature as we have seen with MFC apps. In the example on the previous page, the ATL server registered or unregistered itself via the method **CComModule::UpdateRegistryFromResource( )**, passing TRUE as the second parameter to add the registry entries and FALSE to remove them.

The ATL COM Wizard generates a *registrar script* for your app, which it adds to your project in a file with the extension .RGS. This contains the various keys and values that need to be added to the registry in an almost readable format called "Backus Nauer". When you build your app, the contents of this file are included in your .EXE or .DLL as a resource. The registrar script file for our sample automation server app is shown below. The registry entries that it creates are shown on the facing page. Note that no entries are made in the \CLSID section because no objects have yet been added to the project. If you want to add other registry entries, you can modify the registrar script file by hand. It's not very hard to figure out. Thus:

```
<file atlhelloau.rgs>

HKCR
{
    NoRemove AppID
    {
      {0B0E3311-C571-11D0-90FC-00608C86B89C} = s 'atlhelloau'
      'atlhelloau.EXE'
      {
            val AppID = s {0B0E3311-C571-11D0-90FC-00608C86B89C}
      }
    }
}
```

The code that actually reads the Backus Nauer resource and makes or removes registry entries based on it is called the *ATL component registrar*. The method CComModule::UpdateRegistryFromResource( ) creates the component registrar and feeds it the relevant scripts.

You may choose either to bind the component registrar statically into your app or to rely on the copy in the system .DLL "atl.dll", about 18 Kbytes in size. The former option makes your app about 5 Kbytes larger but removes this external dependency. Defining the compile-time constant _ATL_STATIC_REGISTRY, done automatically when you build the "Release MinDependency" project configuration, selects this option. The latter option will reduce the size of your app by about 5k, but leave you with an external dependency, albeit a small one.

This line in the script on the facing page:

```
{0B0E3311-C571-11D0-90FC-00608C86B89C} - s 'atlhelloau'
```

creates this registry entry:

These lines in the script on the facing page:

```
'atlhelloau.EXE'
{
        val AppID = s {0B0E3311-C571-11D0-90FC-00608C86B89C}
}
```

creates this registry entry:

487

6. Next, you have to add objects to your ATL project by selecting "Insert — New ATL Object..." from the main menu. This causes the ATL Object Wizard to appear, offering the selection of all the prefabricated object types that it knows about. For the Hello sample, we use the simplest case, a "Simple Object". This is an object that can provide prefabricated support for IUnknown and IDispatch. Thus:

The Wizard will then show you a property page asking you to specify the names of your classes and files. As you fill in one box, the Wizard will fill in the others. Thus:

488

7. The Wizard also needs to know several attributes of your new object, such as the desired threading model, before it can generate your new object's code. Your selections here will determine the ATL base classes and constant settings used for your new class. The ATL's internal code supports all threading models. The ATL won't step on its own toes no matter which one you choose. However, it is up to you to make sure that your own code follows the rules of whatever model you select, for example, serializing access to your own global variables if you select "Apartment", as in this example.

Selecting the "Dual" radio button will cause the Wizard to generate a dual interface, exposing your object's properties and methods through both a custom interface and an IDispatch as discussed in Chapter 9. Since you'll be getting it for free, you might as well take it. If don't want IDispatch, perhaps because you want to pass parameters of types not supported by automation, then selecting the "Custom" button will generate a custom VTBL interface without an IDispatch. The ATL does not support an IDispatch without a dual interface.

Selecting "Yes" for aggregation will select an ATL base class that allows itself to be created either as a standalone object or as part of an aggregate. Selecting "No", as in this example, allows creation as a standalone object only, the model used throughout this book. Selecting "Only" specifies an object that cannot be created as a standalone object, but only as part of an aggregate. The selections for the current example are shown below. Thus:

WARNING: This dialog box practically invites you to include the free threaded marshaler. You should only do this if you are supporting both threading models in an in-proc server, and frequently not even then, as discussed at the end of Chapter 13. Including it when you shouldn't will occasionally appear to give you extra speed, but I guarantee that it opens you up to the possibility of random crashes. Even if you don't see them in your development testing, your customers will.

8. Based on the selections that you made on the previous pages, the Wizard will generate a new class for your object. Naturally, it starts without any methods or properties; these will be added as shown on subsequent pages. The class declaration uses multiple inheritance to access the ATL's prefabricated functionality. It uses C++'s template mechanism to tell the ATL which custom classes to create. Commented for clarity, the class declaration of our simple example looks like this:

```
class ATL_NO_VTABLE CAtlHelloDisp :

/*
ATL's implementation of IUnknown, using the apartment-threaded model.
*/
    public CComObjectRootEx<CComSingleThreadModel>,

/*
ATL's implementation of a class factory, passing the name of the class
that the factory creates and the class ID to which it answers.
*/
    public CComCoClass<CAtlHelloDisp, &CLSID_AtlHelloDisp>,

/*
ATL's implementation of IDispatch, telling it the custom interface it
supports and the ID of the type library which contains the description
of that interface.
*/
    public IDispatchImpl<IAtlHelloDisp, &IID_IAtlHelloDisp,
      &LIBID_ATLHELLOAULib>
{
public:
    CAtlHelloDisp()
    {
    }
/*
Tell the component registrar which resource contains strings for this
class.
*/

DECLARE_REGISTRY_RESOURCEID(IDR_ATLHELLODISP)

/*
Tell class factory that this object is not aggregatable.
*/

DECLARE_NOT_AGGREGATABLE(CAtlHelloDisp)

/*
Data map telling IUnknown::QueryInterface( )   which interfaces this
object supports.
*/

BEGIN_COM_MAP(CAtlHelloDisp)
    COM_INTERFACE_ENTRY(IAtlHelloDisp)
    COM_INTERFACE_ENTRY(IDispatch)
END_COM_MAP()
};
```

490

9. When it first generated your project, the ATL App Wizard created an .IDL file. Since your project didn't then contain any COM objects, this file hasn't contained anything interesting until now. When you added the object to your project, the ATL Object Wizard made entries in your .IDL file describing the new object. Commented for description, the file now looks like this:

```
import "oaidl.idl";
import "ocidl.idl";

/*
Description of IAtlHelloDisp, the dual interface supported by this
object. It contains no methods or properties yet.
*/

    [
      object,
      uuid(0B0E331D-C571-11D0-90FC-00608C86B89C),
      dual,
      helpstring("IAtlHelloDisp Interface"),
      pointer_default(unique)
    ]
    interface IAtlHelloDisp : IDispatch
    {
    };

/*
Description of type library itself.
*/

[
    uuid(0B0E3310-C571-11D0-90FC-00608C86B89C),
    version(1.0),
    helpstring("atlhelloau 1.0 Type Library")
]
library ATLHELLOAULib
{
    importlib("stdole32.tlb");
    importlib("stdole2.tlb");

/*
Description of AtlHelloDisp object class
*/
    [
      uuid(0B0E331F-C571-11D0-90FC-00608C86B89C),
      helpstring("AtlHelloDisp Class")
    ]
    coclass AtlHelloDisp
    {
      [default] interface IAtlHelloDisp;
    };
};
```

491

10. When you added the object to your project, the Wizard also added a new registrar script containing all the Backus-Nauer code directives necessary to register the new object. When your app registers itself, these entries will be made as shown on the facing page. Thus:

```
<file atlhellodisp.rgs>

HKCR
{
    EssenceOfOleAtlHelloDisp.1 = s 'AtlHelloDisp Class'
    {
      CLSID = s '{0B0E331F-C571-11D0-90FC-00608C86B89C}'
    }
    EssenceOfOleAtlHelloDisp = s 'AtlHelloDisp Class'
    {
      CurVer = s 'EssenceOfOleAtlHelloDisp.1'
    }
    NoRemove CLSID
    {
      ForceRemove {0B0E331F-C571-11D0-90FC-00608C86B89C} =
            s 'AtlHelloDisp Class'
      {
            ProgID = s 'EssenceOfOleAtlHelloDisp.1'
            VersionIndependentProgID = s 'EssenceOfOleAtlHelloDisp'
            ForceRemove 'Programmable'
            LocalServer32 = s '%MODULE%'
            val AppID = s '{0B0E3311-C571-11D0-90FC-00608C86B89C}'
      }
    }
}
```

Registry entries made by file "atlhellodisp.rgs".

11. You will see that your object supports a custom dual interface named IAtlHelloDisp, as shown in the Workspace window below. Thus:

To add properties and methods to your interface, right-click on the interface. The resulting context menu will contain the items "Add Property" and "Add Method". When you pick "Add Property", you will get the dialog box shown below. It is conceptually similar to the automation property editors used in the MFC. There's nothing magic about them, nothing you couldn't do yourself by going to four or five different files and making entries yourself, but it's much more convenient this way. Thus:

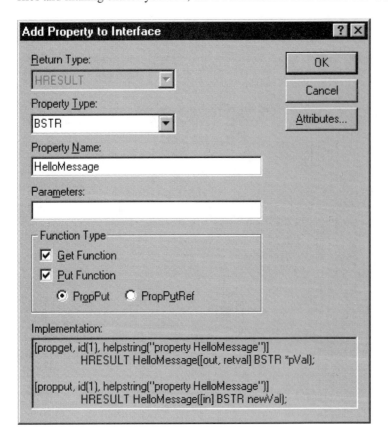

12. Adding a method is likewise simple. Thus:

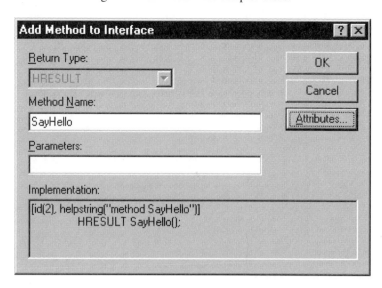

If you want to edit the attributes of a method or a property, such as hardwiring in a fixed dispatch ID, the "Attributes" button will bring up a dialog box allowing you to do this. Thus:

13. When you add a method or a property, the Wizard makes entries in your class's header file declaring handler functions for the method or property, in a manner similar to the MFC.

You will probably need to add member variables to your class, such as m_bstrHelloMsg below. This variable is of class **_bstr_t**, which is a Microsoft-specific class that encapsulates a BSTR, released as part of the smart pointer package that came with VC++ 5.0. Its function is discussed in more detail in Appendix D. While the ATL has its own BSTR class called CComBSTR, it doesn't contain automatic ANSI/Unicode conversion, which the _bstr_t does. To use this class, you must include the header file "**comdef.h**". Thus:

```
#include <comdef.h>

class ATL_NO_VTABLE CAtlHelloDisp :
    public CComObjectRootEx<CComMultiThreadModel>,        // IUnknown
    public CComCoClass<CAtlHelloDisp, &CLSID_AtlHelloDisp>, // class fy
    public    IDispatchImpl<IAtlHelloDisp,    &IID_IAtlHelloDisp,    //
IDispatch
        &LIBID_ATLHELLOAULib>
{
public:
    CAtlHelloDisp()
    {
    }

    _bstr_t m_bstrHelloMsg ;

DECLARE_REGISTRY_RESOURCEID(IDR_ATLHELLODISP)

BEGIN_COM_MAP(CAtlHelloDisp)
    COM_INTERFACE_ENTRY(IAtlHelloDisp)
    COM_INTERFACE_ENTRY(IDispatch)
END_COM_MAP()

// IAtlHelloDisp methods
public:
    STDMETHOD(SayHello)();
    STDMETHOD(get_HelloMessage)(/*[out, retval]*/ BSTR *pVal);
    STDMETHOD(put_HelloMessage)(/*[in]*/ BSTR newVal);
};
```

14. Likewise similar to the MFC, the Wizard adds shell functions to your object's implementation file, as shown in bold below. You fill in whatever code you need to make your object do what you want it to do. Thus:

```
<file atlhellodisp.cpp>

extern HWND hMainWnd ;

/*
Value of HelloMessage property being requested. Provide its current
value from our member variable.
*/

STDMETHODIMP CAtlHelloDisp::get_HelloMessage(BSTR * pVal)
{
    *pVal = m_bstrHelloMsg ;
    return S_OK;
}

/*
New value of HelloMessage property being set. Remember the BSTR in our
member variable.
*/

STDMETHODIMP CAtlHelloDisp::put_HelloMessage(BSTR newVal)
{
    m_bstrHelloMsg = newVal ;
    return S_OK;
}

/*
Controller wants us to show the value of our string in our window.
Output the current value of the HelloMessage property. The _bstr_t does
automatic conversion between its internal Unicode and the ANSI required
by the window.
*/

STDMETHODIMP CAtlHelloDisp::SayHello()
{
    MessageBeep (0) ;
    SetDlgItemText(hMainWnd, IDC_EDIT1, m_bstrHelloMsg);

    return S_OK;
}
```

15. The Wizard also makes the necessary entries in your .IDL file to describe the new interface's properties and methods. Thus:

```
import "oaidl.idl";
import "ocidl.idl";

    [
      object,
      uuid(0B0E331D-C571-11D0-90FC-00608C86B89C),
      dual,
      helpstring("IAtlHelloDisp Interface"),
      pointer_default(unique)
    ]
    interface IAtlHelloDisp : IDispatch
    {
      [propget, id(1), helpstring("property HelloMessage")]
            HRESULT HelloMessage([out, retval] BSTR *pVal);
      [propput, id(1), helpstring("property HelloMessage")]
            HRESULT HelloMessage([in] BSTR newVal);
      [id(2), helpstring("method SayHello")] HRESULT SayHello();
    };
[
    uuid(0B0E3310-C571-11D0-90FC-00608C86B89C),
    version(1.0),
    helpstring("atlhelloau 1.0 Type Library")
]
library ATLHELLOAULib
{
    importlib("stdole32.tlb");
    importlib("stdole2.tlb");

    [
      uuid(0B0E331F-C571-11D0-90FC-00608C86B89C),
      helpstring("AtlHelloDisp Class")
    ]
    coclass AtlHelloDisp
    {
      [default] interface IAtlHelloDisp;
    };
};
```

16. Finally, the object map in your project's main file is updated to tell the module which classes are manufactured by this app. The _Module uses this map when registering class factories. Thus:

```
CExeModule _Module;

/*
Map that tells which classes this app supports.
*/

BEGIN_OBJECT_MAP(ObjectMap)
    OBJECT_ENTRY(CLSID_AtlHelloDisp, CAtlHelloDisp)
END_OBJECT_MAP()


extern "C" int WINAPI _tWinMain(HINSTANCE hInstance,
    HINSTANCE hPrevInstance, LPTSTR lpCmdLine, int nShowCmd)
{

    <rest of WinMain>
}
```

C. INTERNALS OF ATL OBJECTS

1. If all you want to do was get your [expletive deleted] automation server out the door, you can stop reading now. This section goes under the hood to examine how ATL objects are connected to COM. Look at the declaration of your new dual interface class, excerpted below:

```
class ATL_NO_VTABLE CAtlHelloDisp :
    public CComObjectRootEx<CComMultiThreadModel>,          // IUnknown
    public CComCoClass<CAtlHelloDisp, &CLSID_AtlHelloDisp>, // class fy
    public IDispatchImpl<IAtlHelloDisp, &IID_IAtlHelloDisp, //IDispatch
      &LIBID_ATLHELLOAULib>
{
    <omitted>

public:
    STDMETHOD(SayHello)();
    STDMETHOD(get_HelloMessage)(/*[out, retval]*/ BSTR *pVal);
    STDMETHOD(put_HelloMessage)(/*[in]*/ BSTR newVal);
}
```

The first two classes in the derivation list, CComObjectRootEx and CComCoClass, contain no virtual functions; therefore they make no entries in the VTBL of the derived class CAtlHelloDisp. (Ignore the ATL_NO_VTABLE declaration for now, it is explained on page 504).

The ATL has also generated a C and C++ header file definition of your custom interface. In this example, you will find it in the file "atlhelloau.h". Excerpted for clarity, your new interface's definition looks like this:

```
<file atlhelloau.h>

interface DECLSPEC_UUID("0B0E331D-C571-11D0-90FC-00608C86B89C")

    IAtlHelloDisp : public IDispatch
    {
    public:
        virtual HRESULT STDMETHODCALLTYPE get_HelloMessage(
            BSTR __RPC_FAR *pVal) = 0;

        virtual HRESULT STDMETHODCALLTYPE put_HelloMessage(
            BSTR newVal) = 0;

        virtual HRESULT STDMETHODCALLTYPE SayHello( void) = 0;
    };
```

2. The third ATL base class in your object's derivation list is **IDispatchImpl**. Simplified for clarity, its definition reads:

```
template <class T, const IID* piid, const GUID* plibid >

class ATL_NO_VTABLE IDispatchImpl : public T
{
// IDispatch methods
public:
    STDMETHOD(GetTypeInfoCount)(UINT* pctinfo)
    STDMETHOD(GetTypeInfo)(UINT itinfo, LCID lcid, ITypeInfo** pptinfo)
    STDMETHOD(GetIDsOfNames)(REFIID riid, LPOLESTR* rgszNames,
      UINT cNames, LCID lcid, DISPID* rgdispid)
    STDMETHOD(Invoke)(DISPID dispidMember, REFIID riid,
      LCID lcid, WORD wFlags, DISPPARAMS* pdispparams,
      VARIANT* pvarResult, EXCEPINFO* pexcepinfo, UINT* puArgErr)
    <etc.>
}
```

The first parameter passed in the declaration template to this class is IAtlHelloDisp. So in your class, the IDispatchImpl expands to be:

```
class ATL_NO_VTABLE IDispatchImpl : public IAtlHelloDisp
{
    <etc.>
}
```

So you can see here that the ATL's implementation of IDispatch is actually implementing the four IDispatch methods required for the dual interface. Looking at the previous page, you can see that the additional methods of the interface, SayHello( ), get_HelloMessage( ) and put_HelloMessage( ), are implemented in the class CAtlHelloDisp.

So we can see where all the methods are implemented except for those of the IUnknown interface. Where are they ?

3. Surprise ! The ATL implements objects in a manner that at first glance appears to be completely ass backwards. As you study it and let it percolate, however, it will start to make a certain amount of twisted sense. Your class CAtlHelloDisp is not in fact the most derived class in the hierarchy. In reality, the ATL provides a class called *CComObject* that implements the outer IUnknown.

The class that you have taken such trouble to write is in fact an abstract base class. Since it does not provide vtbl entries for the IUnknown methods, you cannot create an object of your new class by saying "new CAtlHelloDisp ( )". Instead, you must use your class as a base for one of the ATL classes, such as CComObject. You would say:

IAtlHelloDisp *pHelloDisp = new CComObject <CAtlHelloDisp> ( ) ;

The derivation is actually done this way:

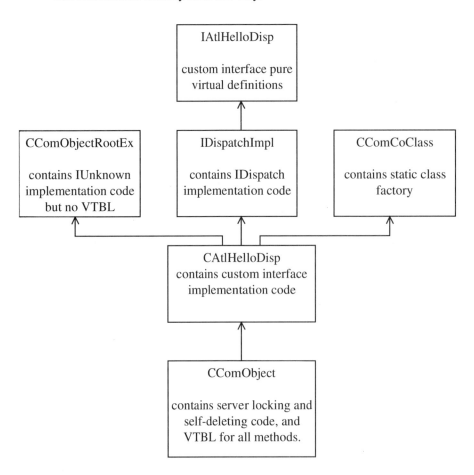

4. Why do they do such a seemingly crazy thing ? It actually makes sense for flexibility reasons. COM objects differ from each other in important ways. The ATL designers wanted to provide prefabricated functionality for all the eventualities they could think of. They did that by providing 10 different classes that can be used as the most-derived class, CComObject and its siblings listed in the table below. This means no cutting or pasting, or setting obscure member variables and flags. Just choose the ATL class that has the behavior you want.

For example, most COM objects, such as your CAtlHelloDisp in this example, lock the server when they are created and unlock it when they are destroyed. The ATL base class CComObject provides this behavior by looking for the global variable named "_Module", which belongs to class CComModule, and calling its Lock( ) and Unlock( ) methods. You could use CComObject as the most-derived class for an ATL object which you wanted to behave in this manner.

Other objects, such as the class factory in a local server, do not lock their servers. If you were writing an object that you didn't want to lock its server, such as a new kind of class factory, you might use an ATL class called CComObjectNoLock as the most-derived class for your object. This class provides the same functionality as CComObject except that it does not lock and unlock the server. By choosing the right ATL base class to as your most derived class, you can get the functionality you need without having to cut and paste.

These normal objects lock the server on creation, unlock server on destruction and destroy themselves on final release.

CComObject	Normal case, does not support aggregation
CComPolyObject	Same as CComObject but supports aggregation on request
CComAggObject	Same as CComObject but requires aggregation

These slightly strange objects do not lock the server. It is up to your server code to make sure that they are only used in cases where this behavior is appropriate:

CComObjectNoLock	No aggregation, deletes itself on final release. Used for local server class factories
CComObjectStack	No aggregation, does not delete itself on final release. Used for stack objects that are automatically destroyed. I'd be careful with this one.
CComContainedObject	Supports aggregation, does not delete itself on final release. Used where object is contained inside another and needs to stay alive as long as its owner, such as nested classes in the MFC

These objects have strange lifetime management for the case where an object is both used internally and exposed to outsiders. Neither supports aggregation.

CComObjectGlobal	Locks server on second and subsequent AddRef( ) calls. Does not delete itself on final release. Useful for objects which are global variables in an app, and need to stay alive as long as the app does.
CComObjectCached	Locks server on third and subsequent AddRef( ) calls. Deletes itself on final release. Useful for objects that are used internally by server and held by using pointers.

Tear-off object classes. Both support aggregation and delete themselves on final release, neither locks the server.

CComTearOffObject	tear-offs that are created at each request
CComCachedTearOffObject	tear-offs that are created at first request and then cached

5. Now you should be able to see what the ATL_NO_VTABLE macro is about. It means that your new class and its ATL base classes don't have their own VTBLs, that the most derived class, the CComObject class, will have a VTBL on their behalf. This saves a few bytes in object size and a few microseconds when constructing and destructing, as the intermediate classes won't need to have their VTBLs constructed and constantly patched up. The drawback is that you can't call any virtual functions in your class's constructor because the VTBL doesn't exist yet, or in the destructor because the VTBL has already been destroyed.

Suppose there is some functionality that you would normally place in your object's constructor, but can't because of this VTBL timing problem. The workaround is to use the method **FinalConstruct( )**, a member function of the base classes CComObjectRoot and CComObjectRootEx. The most-derived class, your CComObject relative, calls this method when its own construction process is complete and the VTBL set up. You override this method in your class and use it for your initialization that requires the VTBL. Thus:

```
class CAtlHelloDisp: public CComObjectRootEx< ... >
{

/*
Method called after most-derived class's construction is complete.
*/

    HRESULT FinalConstruct( )
    {
      < do initialization that requires the VTBL here >
    }


    <rest of class declaration omitted>
};
```

Note: If you can't live with or don't trust this feature, you can always remove the ATL_NO_VTABLE macro. Everything will continue to work correctly. It'll just run a little slower and take a little more memory

This page intentionally contains no text other than this sentence.

D. FULL-FEATURED ATL CONTROL

1. The full featured .OCX controls produced by the MFC are extremely popular, particularly for plugging into intelligent development environments such as Visual Basic. This section shows you how to build the timer control shown in Chapter 5 using the ATL instead of the MFC. The sample code may be found in the directory \EssenceOfOle\Chap14\atltimer. First, you use the ATL COM App Wizard to make a new project containing an empty shell of a server, this time specifying a .DLL. The shell code is shown below.

```
CComModule _Module;

// DLL Entry Point
extern "C" BOOL WINAPI DllMain(HINSTANCE hInstance, DWORD dwReason,
    LPVOID /*lpReserved*/)
{
    if (dwReason == DLL_PROCESS_ATTACH)
    {
      _Module.Init(ObjectMap, hInstance);
      DisableThreadLibraryCalls(hInstance);
    }
    else if (dwReason == DLL_PROCESS_DETACH)
      _Module.Term();
    return TRUE;    // ok
}


// Used to determine whether the DLL can be unloaded by OLE

STDAPI DllCanUnloadNow(void)
{
    return (_Module.GetLockCount()==0) ? S_OK : S_FALSE;
}


// Returns a class factory to create an object of the requested type

STDAPI DllGetClassObject(REFCLSID rclsid, REFIID riid, LPVOID* ppv)
{
    return _Module.GetClassObject(rclsid, riid, ppv);
}


// DllRegisterServer - Adds entries to the system registry

STDAPI DllRegisterServer(void)
{
    return _Module.RegisterServer(TRUE);
}


// DllUnregisterServer - Removes entries from the system registry

STDAPI DllUnregisterServer(void)
{
    _Module.UnregisterServer();
    return S_OK;
}
```

2. Next, you add your control's object to your project. Select the "Insert—new ATL Object" menu item, which will bring up the ATL Object Wizard. Selecting the "Controls", entry in the left-hand box, you pick the "Full Control" option in the right-hand box. This creates the ATL objects that provide the full control functionality. Thus:

3. When the Wizard is inserting your control into your project, you have the option of setting various properties on your control. Since a full control does in-place activation, a window-centric (and thus thread-centric) operation, the apartment threading model is the best choice. Since most containers look for an IDispatch interface, a dual interface is a better choice here than a custom. There is no reason for a control to support aggregation. If you want your control to fire events to its container, you should check the "Support Connection Points" box, which will add support for the IConnectionPointContainer interface. The container uses this interface to provide the control with the IDispatch that the control uses to signal events to the container. Thus:

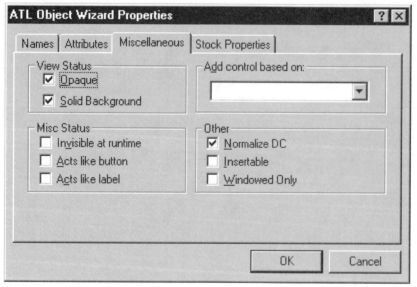

WARNING: The upper dialog box offers a choice of threading models for your control. When you are writing a visible control, you should choose only single or apartment model (and single isn't really recommended either.) If you choose free or both for a control that has a user interface, your control may look funny in certain situations which will be hard to diagnose. See the discussion in Chapter 13 of where not to use the free threading model.

4. The Wizard also allows you to specify your control's support for stock properties, such as the background color. When you select a property, a member variable is added to your control's class to represent it, in this m_clrBackColor (shown later). Entries are also made to various maps and to the .IDL file. The ATL base class knows how to handle the setting and getting of these properties; all you have to do is read or write the variable.

Unlike the MFC, this Wizard is invoked only when the project is first generated, not in the middle of development. If you want your project to support stock properties, it is much easier to add them now. Adding them later is much less convenient, although certainly possible. Thus:

5. The Wizard will generate a control class for you that supports all of the interfaces required for a full in-place activation control. As you can see, there are a lot of them. The ATL control base class, similar to the MFC's COleControl, is **CComControl**. The stock property "BackColor" is included in the variable **m_clrBackColor**. Commented for clarity, the header file looks like this:

```
class ATL_NO_VTABLE CAtlTimerCtrl :
/*
All the interfaces that this control supports by inheritance from the
ATL's base class implementation.
*/
    public CComObjectRootEx<CComSingleThreadModel>,
    public CComCoClass<CAtlTimerCtrl, &CLSID_AtlTimerCtrl>,
    public CComControl<CAtlTimerCtrl>,
    public CStockPropImpl<CAtlTimerCtrl, IAtlTimerCtrl,
      &IID_IAtlTimerCtrl, &LIBID_ATLTIMERLib>,
    public IProvideClassInfo2Impl<&CLSID_AtlTimerCtrl, NULL,
      &LIBID_ATLTIMERLib>,
    public IPersistStreamInitImpl<CAtlTimerCtrl>,
    public IPersistStorageImpl<CAtlTimerCtrl>,
    public IQuickActivateImpl<CAtlTimerCtrl>,
    public IOleControlImpl<CAtlTimerCtrl>,
    public IOleObjectImpl<CAtlTimerCtrl>,
    public IOleInPlaceActiveObjectImpl<CAtlTimerCtrl>,
    public IViewObjectExImpl<CAtlTimerCtrl>,
    public IOleInPlaceObjectWindowlessImpl<CAtlTimerCtrl>,
    public IDataObjectImpl<CAtlTimerCtrl>,
    public IConnectionPointContainerImpl<CAtlTimerCtrl>,
    public ISpecifyPropertyPagesImpl<CAtlTimerCtrl>
{
public:
    CAtlTimerCtrl()
    { }


DECLARE_REGISTRY_RESOURCEID(IDR_ATLTIMERCTRL)
DECLARE_NOT_AGGREGATABLE(CAtlTimerCtrl)


/*
This map tells the ATL's implementation of QueryInterface( ) where to
find the VTBL for each supported interface.
*/


BEGIN_COM_MAP(CAtlTimerCtrl)
    COM_INTERFACE_ENTRY(IAtlTimerCtrl)
    COM_INTERFACE_ENTRY(IDispatch)
    COM_INTERFACE_ENTRY_IMPL(IViewObjectEx)
    COM_INTERFACE_ENTRY_IMPL_IID(IID_IViewObject2, IViewObjectEx)
    COM_INTERFACE_ENTRY_IMPL_IID(IID_IViewObject, IViewObjectEx)
    COM_INTERFACE_ENTRY_IMPL(IOleInPlaceObjectWindowless)
    COM_INTERFACE_ENTRY_IMPL_IID(IID_IOleInPlaceObject,
      IOleInPlaceObjectWindowless)
    COM_INTERFACE_ENTRY_IMPL_IID(IID_IOleWindow,
      IOleInPlaceObjectWindowless)
    COM_INTERFACE_ENTRY_IMPL(IOleInPlaceActiveObject)
    COM_INTERFACE_ENTRY_IMPL(IOleControl)
```

```
        COM_INTERFACE_ENTRY_IMPL(IOleObject)
        COM_INTERFACE_ENTRY_IMPL(IQuickActivate)
        COM_INTERFACE_ENTRY_IMPL(IPersistStorage)
        COM_INTERFACE_ENTRY_IMPL(IPersistStreamInit)
        COM_INTERFACE_ENTRY_IMPL(ISpecifyPropertyPages)
        COM_INTERFACE_ENTRY_IMPL(IDataObject)
        COM_INTERFACE_ENTRY(IProvideClassInfo)
        COM_INTERFACE_ENTRY(IProvideClassInfo2)
        COM_INTERFACE_ENTRY_IMPL(IConnectionPointContainer)
    END_COM_MAP()

    /*
    This map keeps track of which properties are set via which property
    page. Its use is shown on page 529.
    */

    BEGIN_PROPERTY_MAP(CAtlTimerCtrl)
        PROP_PAGE(CLSID_StockColorPage)
    END_PROPERTY_MAP()

    /*
    This map keeps track of the IDispatch interfaces the control is
    expecting from its container for signaling events. Its use is shown on
    page 518.
    */

    BEGIN_CONNECTION_POINT_MAP(CAtlTimerCtrl)
    END_CONNECTION_POINT_MAP()

    /*
    This map connects window messages to their handler functions. Its use
    is shown on page 514.
    */

    BEGIN_MSG_MAP(CAtlTimerCtrl)
        MESSAGE_HANDLER(WM_PAINT, OnPaint)
        MESSAGE_HANDLER(WM_SETFOCUS, OnSetFocus)
        MESSAGE_HANDLER(WM_KILLFOCUS, OnKillFocus)
    END_MSG_MAP()


    // IViewObjectEx
        STDMETHOD(GetViewStatus)(DWORD* pdwStatus)
        {
          *pdwStatus = VIEWSTATUS_SOLIDBKGND | VIEWSTATUS_OPAQUE;
          return S_OK;
        }

    public:
        HRESULT OnDraw(ATL_DRAWINFO& di);
        OLE_COLOR m_clrBackColor;           // stock property
    };
```

6. The first thing we have to do is handle the drawing of our control. Like the MFC, the ATL base class CComControlBase contains the method OnDraw( ), the default implementation of which does nothing. The Wizard overrides this method for you, and you fill in the function shell with whatever drawing code you want. In this method, the ATL framework passes us a structure of type **ATL_DRAWINFO**, as shown below. This contains the information we need for drawing, particularly the HDC hdcDraw and bounding rectangle prcBounds. Thus:

```
struct ATL_DRAWINFO
{
    UINT cbSize;
    DWORD dwDrawAspect;
    LONG lindex;
    DVTARGETDEVICE* ptd;
    HDC hicTargetDev;
    HDC hdcDraw;                 // DC on which to draw
    LPCRECTL prcBounds;          //Rectangle in which to draw
    LPCRECTL prcWBounds;
    BOOL bOptimize;
    BOOL bZoomed;
    BOOL bRectInHimetric;
    SIZEL ZoomNum;
    SIZEL ZoomDen;
};
```

7. We use the standard SDK drawing functions to draw on the screen, using the HDC and bounding rectangle provided in the ATL_DRAWINFO structure. Thus:

```
HRESULT CAtlTimerCtrl::OnDraw(ATL_DRAWINFO& di)
{

/*
Get current time.
*/
    SYSTEMTIME st ;
    GetLocalTime (&st) ;

/*
Convert into colon-separated string.
*/
    char out [128] ;
    wsprintf (out, "%2.2d:%2.2d:%2.2d", st.wHour, st.wMinute,
            st.wSecond) ;

/*
Draw within bounding rectangle presented by framework.
*/
    DrawText(di.hdcDraw, out, -1, (RECT *)di.prcBounds,
      DT_CENTER | DT_VCENTER | DT_SINGLELINE);

    return S_OK;
}
```

8. The control already contains a window courtesy of the CComControl base class. To handle window messages, we first add the declarations of their handler functions to our control class as shown below. The ATL framework supports a message map, conceptually similar to that of the MFC. Entries in this map are used by the base class's internal window response function to call the correct handler function for each Windows message it receives. Unlike the MFC, we have to add entries to it by hand. Thus:

```
class ATL_NO_VTABLE CAtlTimerCtrl : <base classes omitted>
{
public:

    BOOL m_bShowSeconds ;
    UINT m_TimerId ;

    CAtlTimerCtrl()
    {
      m_bShowSeconds = TRUE ;
    }

/*
Declarations of message handler functions.
*/

    LRESULT OnCreate (UINT nMsg, WPARAM wParam,
                   LPARAM lParam, BOOL& bHandled);
    LRESULT OnDestroy (UINT nMsg, WPARAM wParam,
                   LPARAM lParam, BOOL& bHandled);
    LRESULT OnTimer (UINT nMsg, WPARAM wParam,
                   LPARAM lParam, BOOL& bHandled);

/*
Add handler functions to the map that tells which message is bound to
which handler.
*/

BEGIN_MSG_MAP(CAtlTimerCtrl)
    MESSAGE_HANDLER(WM_PAINT, OnPaint)
    MESSAGE_HANDLER(WM_SETFOCUS, OnSetFocus)
    MESSAGE_HANDLER(WM_KILLFOCUS, OnKillFocus)
    MESSAGE_HANDLER(WM_CREATE, OnCreate)
    MESSAGE_HANDLER(WM_DESTROY, OnDestroy)
    MESSAGE_HANDLER(WM_TIMER, OnTimer)
END_MSG_MAP()
```

9. We then manually add the message handler functions to the implementation file and write whatever code we think ought to go inside them. The method **CComControl::FireViewChange( )** is used for forcing a redraw in preference to InvalidateRect( ), because the control might be running in a windowless container. This method checks whether it is or not, calls InvalidateRect( ) if it isn't, and notifies the container if it is. Thus:

```
/*
Window created. Start the timer.
*/

LRESULT CAtlTimerCtrl::OnCreate (UINT nMsg, WPARAM wParam,
                 LPARAM lParam, BOOL& bHandled)
{
    m_TimerId = SetTimer (0, 1000, NULL) ;
    return 0;
}


/*
Window destroyed. Kill the timer.
*/

LRESULT CAtlTimerCtrl::OnDestroy (UINT nMsg, WPARAM wParam,
                 LPARAM lParam, BOOL& bHandled)
{
    KillTimer   (m_TimerId) ;
    return 0;
}


/*
Timer has signaled that a second has elapsed. Tell the ATL framework to
force a repaint.
*/

LRESULT CAtlTimerCtrl::OnTimer (UINT nMsg, WPARAM wParam,
                 LPARAM lParam, BOOL& bHandled)
{
    FireViewChange ( ) ;
    return 0;
}
```

515

10. When we made entries in the "Stock Properties" Wizard box, member variables were automatically added to the control's class header file. We can add our own properties, such as ShowSeconds, in the same manner as for the ATL automation server shown previously. The .IDL file will then look like this:

```
import "oaidl.idl";
import "ocidl.idl";

    [
      object,
      uuid(5595DC5E-D759-11D0-9119-00608C86B89C),
      dual,
      helpstring("IAtlTimerCtrl Interface"),
      pointer_default(unique)
    ]
    interface IAtlTimerCtrl : IDispatch
    {
      [propput, id(DISPID_BACKCOLOR)]
            HRESULT BackColor([in]OLE_COLOR clr);
      [propget, id(DISPID_BACKCOLOR)]
            HRESULT BackColor([out,retval]OLE_COLOR* pclr);
      [propget, id(1), helpstring("property ShowSeconds")]
            HRESULT ShowSeconds([out, retval] BOOL *pVal);
      [propput, id(1), helpstring("property ShowSeconds")]
            HRESULT ShowSeconds([in] BOOL newVal);
    };
```

Note: When exposed in this manner, the ActiveX Test Container app does not recognize these properties as properties. It thinks they are methods. You have to set and get them using the test container's "Methods" dialog box. Visual Basic is smart enough to recognize them as properties and work correctly.

As before, the Wizard adds shell functions for setting and getting the specified properties. We add the code that makes them work. The base class already contains handler functions for the stock properties. Thus:

```
STDMETHODIMP CAtlTimerCtrl::get_ShowSeconds(BOOL * pVal)
{
    *pVal = m_bShowSeconds ;
    return S_OK;
}


STDMETHODIMP CAtlTimerCtrl::put_ShowSeconds(BOOL newVal)
{
    m_bShowSeconds = newVal ;
    SetDirty ( ) ;
    FireViewChange ( ) ;
    return S_OK;
}
```

516

11. When using properties which are colors, it is necessary to differentiate between a hard-wired color and one which indicates a system color. In the MFC, this was provided by the method COleControl::TranslateColor( ), but the ATL does not provide this functionality. You must write code as shown below to do that yourself. If the high byte of an OLE_COLOR type variable is non-zero, it means that the low word does not contain a hard-wired RGB triplet, but rather the index of a system color whose RGB value you obtain via the API function **GetSysColor( )**. If the high byte is zero, then the low three bytes do indeed represent an RGB value which you should use. Thus:

```
HRESULT CAtlTimerCtrl::OnDraw(ATL_DRAWINFO& di)
{
/*
Get current time. Convert into colon-separated string.
*/
    SYSTEMTIME st ;      char out [128] ;

    GetLocalTime (&st) ;
    if (m_bShowSeconds)
    {
      wsprintf (out, "%2.2d:%2.2d:%2.2d", st.wHour, st.wMinute,
           st.wSecond) ;
    }
    else
    {
      wsprintf (out, "%2.2d:%2.2d", st.wHour, st.wMinute) ;
    }
/*
Get correct color.
*/
    COLORREF cr ;

    if (HIBYTE(HIWORD(m_clrBackColor)))
    {
      cr = GetSysColor(LOWORD(m_clrBackColor)) ;
    }
    else
    {
      cr = m_clrBackColor ;
    }

    HBRUSH hbr = CreateSolidBrush (cr) ;
    SetBkColor (di.hdcDraw, cr) ;

/*
Draw within bounding rectangle presented by framework.
*/
    FillRect (di.hdcDraw, (RECT *)di.prcBounds,hbr) ;
    DrawText(di.hdcDraw, out, -1, (RECT *)di.prcBounds,
      DT_CENTER | DT_VCENTER | DT_SINGLELINE);
    DeleteObject (hbr) ;
    return S_OK;
}
```

12. Adding an event to an ATL control is trickier than in the MFC, as the ATL does not have a slick Wizard for this feature. To add an event, you must first add a new dispinterface to your .IDL file, as shown below. Note that, unlike the dual interface used for the controls methods and properties, the event IDispatch must be place inside the "library" declaration in your .IDL file. To this dispinterface you add a method for each event that you want to fire. An event IDispatch may not contain properties, but you still need the "properties" keyword as the MIDL compiler will croak without it. Finally, you add a line to your control's coclass, using the IDL keyword "**source**" to mark your control as the source of the event IDispatch interface. This is exactly what the MFC's Class Wizard did for you, but with the ATL, you have to do it manually. Thus:

```
library ATLTIMERLib
{
    <omitted>

// 1. Add a new dispinterface for CAtlTimerCtrl events

    [
      uuid(5595DC5F-D759-11D0-9119-00608C86B89C),
      helpstring("IAtlTimerCtrl Event Interface")
    ]
    dispinterface _IAtlTimerCtrlEvents
    {
        properties:

// 2. Add a method for each event you want to fire.

        methods:
        [id(1)] void AlarmExpired (void);
    };


    [
      uuid(EE6E4F32-B113-11D0-8023-006097418C73),
      helpstring("AtlTimerCtrl Class")
    ]
    coclass AtlTimerCtrl
    {
      [default] interface IAtlTimerCtrl ;

// 3. Mark your control as the source of the event dispinterface

      [default, source] dispinterface _IAtlTimerCtrlEvents ;
    };
};
```

13. After you build the control project with these additions to the .IDL file, your control's type library describes the events that you want to fire. You now need to generate the code that calls IDispatch::Invoke to fire those events. The ATL provides a proxy generator to do generate this code. You pick "Project — Add to Project — Components and Controls", then select "Developer Studio Components". Thus:

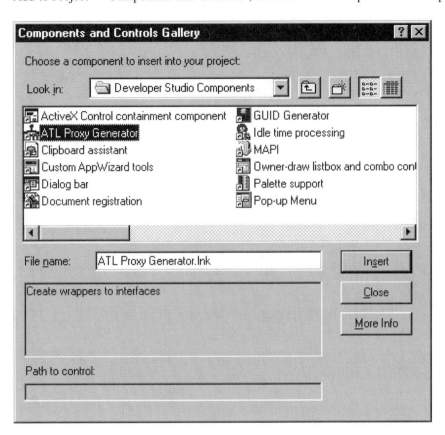

14. You will next see the ATL proxy generator dialog box as shown below. Use the "..." button to bring up a browser box and select your control's type library. You will see a list of the dispinterfaces in your type library; select the one that identifies your control's event IDispatch and click the ">" button to move it to the "Selected" list box. Thus:

The generator will create a class that implements the IConnectionPoint interface, which the control's container uses to pass to the control the IDispatch interface pointer that the control calls to signal events back to its container. The new class will also contain easily used wrapper methods for making the IDispatch::Invoke( ) calls, as shown on the facing page. This is conceptually similar to what Class Wizard does in the MFC when you generate a new IDispatch wrapper class from a type library. The new class will have all of its event firing function in-line in its header file, in the case of this example, "cpatlimer.h".

```cpp
template <class T>
class CProxy_IAtlTimerCtrlEvents : public IConnectionPointImpl<T,
    &DIID__IAtlTimerCtrlEvents, CComDynamicUnkArray>
{
public:
//methods:
//_IAtlTimerCtrlEvents : IDispatch

public:
    void Fire_AlarmExpired()
    {
      T* pT = (T*)this;
      pT->Lock();
      IUnknown** pp = m_vec.begin();
      while (pp < m_vec.end())
      {
            if (*pp != NULL)
            {
                  DISPPARAMS disp = { NULL, NULL, 0, 0 };
                  IDispatch* pDispatch =
                        reinterpret_cast<IDispatch*>(*pp);
                  pDispatch->Invoke(0x1, IID_NULL, LOCALE_USER_DEFAULT,
                        DISPATCH_METHOD, &disp, NULL, NULL, NULL);
            }
            pp++;
      }
      pT->Unlock();
    }
};
```

15. You connect your new event proxy into your control in the following manner. First, you include the proxy class's header file in your control class's header file. Next, you modify the IProvideClassInfo2Impl's template parameter list so that it knows the outgoing event dispinterface (note the double underscore caused by the event interface's name beginning with an underscore). Third, you add the new proxy class CProxy_IAtlTimerCtrlEvents to your control class's derivation, thereby making the method Fire_AlarmExpired( ) part of your control's class. Thus

Add to header file thus:

```
#ifndef __ATLTIMERCTRL_H_
#define __ATLTIMERCTRL_H_

#include "resource.h"        // main symbols

// 1. Include header file here

#include "cpatltimer.h"


class ATL_NO_VTABLE CAtlTimerCtrl :
    public CComObjectRootEx<CComMultiThreadModel>,
    public CComCoClass<CAtlTimerCtrl, &CLSID_AtlTimerCtrl>,
    public CComControl<CAtlTimerCtrl>,
    public CStockPropImpl<CAtlTimerCtrl, IAtlTimerCtrl,
      &IID_IAtlTimerCtrl, &LIBID_ATLTIMERLib>,

// 2. Add event dispinterface ID here

    public IProvideClassInfo2Impl<&CLSID_AtlTimerCtrl,
      &DIID__IAtlTimerCtrlEvents, &LIBID_ATLTIMERLib>,
    public IPersistStreamInitImpl<CAtlTimerCtrl>,
    public IPersistStorageImpl<CAtlTimerCtrl>,
    public IQuickActivateImpl<CAtlTimerCtrl>,
    public IOleControlImpl<CAtlTimerCtrl>,
    public IOleObjectImpl<CAtlTimerCtrl>,
    public IOleInPlaceActiveObjectImpl<CAtlTimerCtrl>,
    public IViewObjectExImpl<CAtlTimerCtrl>,
    public IOleInPlaceObjectWindowlessImpl<CAtlTimerCtrl>,
    public IDataObjectImpl<CAtlTimerCtrl>,
    public ISpecifyPropertyPagesImpl<CAtlTimerCtrl>,
    public IConnectionPointContainerImpl<CAtlTimerCtrl>

// 3. Add proxy class here

    public CProxy_IAtlTimerCtrlEvents<CAtlTimerCtrl>,

{
```

<continued on next page>

522

Finally, you add the event dispinterface ID to the connection point map with a macro entry as shown below. The ATL's prefabricated IConnectionPointContainer needs to know which outgoing interfaces this control uses. It looks to this connection point map for this information. Thus:

```
<continued from previous page>

BEGIN_COM_MAP(CAtlTimerCtrl)
    COM_INTERFACE_ENTRY(IAtlTimerCtrl)
    COM_INTERFACE_ENTRY(IDispatch)
    COM_INTERFACE_ENTRY_IMPL(IViewObjectEx)
    COM_INTERFACE_ENTRY_IMPL_IID(IID_IViewObject2, IViewObjectEx)
    COM_INTERFACE_ENTRY_IMPL_IID(IID_IViewObject, IViewObjectEx)
    COM_INTERFACE_ENTRY_IMPL(IOleInPlaceObjectWindowless)
    COM_INTERFACE_ENTRY_IMPL_IID(IID_IOleInPlaceObject,
      IOleInPlaceObjectWindowless)
    COM_INTERFACE_ENTRY_IMPL_IID(IID_IOleWindow,
      IOleInPlaceObjectWindowless)
    COM_INTERFACE_ENTRY_IMPL(IOleInPlaceActiveObject)
    COM_INTERFACE_ENTRY_IMPL(IOleControl)
    COM_INTERFACE_ENTRY_IMPL(IOleObject)
    COM_INTERFACE_ENTRY_IMPL(IQuickActivate)
    COM_INTERFACE_ENTRY_IMPL(IPersistStorage)
    COM_INTERFACE_ENTRY_IMPL(IPersistStreamInit)
    COM_INTERFACE_ENTRY_IMPL(ISpecifyPropertyPages)
    COM_INTERFACE_ENTRY_IMPL(IDataObject)
    COM_INTERFACE_ENTRY(IProvideClassInfo)
    COM_INTERFACE_ENTRY(IProvideClassInfo2)
    COM_INTERFACE_ENTRY_IMPL(IConnectionPointContainer)
END_COM_MAP()


// 4. Add macro for your connection point entry here.

BEGIN_CONNECTION_POINT_MAP(CAtlTimerCtrl)
    CONNECTION_POINT_ENTRY(DIID__IAtlTimerCtrlEvents)
END_CONNECTION_POINT_MAP()

    <rest of class declaration>
} ;
```

16. To make this control a useful commercial product, we need to provide a property page so that our customer, the application programmer, will have an easy job of setting our control's properties. Remember, a property page is an entirely new object, with a class factory and CLSID, so we have to go back to the ATL Object Wizard and add it. You will find the ATL's prefabricated property page on the Wizard's "controls" pane. Thus:

When setting the page's, attributes in the Wizard, the "Title" string is the name that will appear on the property page's tab when it appears in the property sheet's dialog box. Thus:

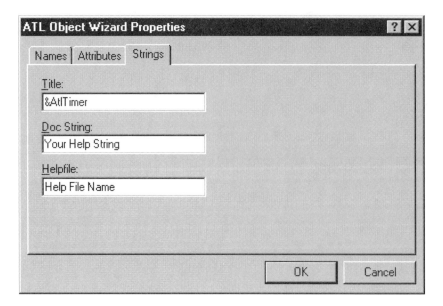

17. The Wizard will generate a new class for your property page. Note that the CComObjectRootEx and CComCoClass base classes are present, as they are for most objects. The **IPropertyPageImpl** class in the derivation list is the ATL's implementation of the IPropertyPage interface. The **CDialogImpl** base class is the ATL's implementation of a generic dialog box, conceptually similar to but much less versatile than the MFC's CDialog. The enum named **IDD** is the resource ID of the dialog box template to be used for this property page. Thus:

```cpp
#ifndef __CATLTIMERPROP_H_
#define __CATLTIMERPROP_H_

#include "resource.h"        // main symbols
EXTERN_C const CLSID CLSID_CAtlTimerProp;

// CCAtlTimerProp
class ATL_NO_VTABLE CCAtlTimerProp :
    public CComObjectRootEx<CComMultiThreadModel>,
    public CComCoClass<CCAtlTimerProp, &CLSID_CAtlTimerProp>,
    public IPropertyPageImpl<CCAtlTimerProp>,
    public CDialogImpl<CCAtlTimerProp>
{
public:
    CCAtlTimerProp()
    {
      m_dwTitleID = IDS_TITLECAtlTimerProp;
      m_dwHelpFileID = IDS_HELPFILECAtlTimerProp;
      m_dwDocStringID = IDS_DOCSTRINGCAtlTimerProp;
    }

    enum {IDD = IDD_CATLTIMERPROP};

DECLARE_REGISTRY_RESOURCEID(IDR_CATLTIMERPROP)
DECLARE_NOT_AGGREGATABLE(CCAtlTimerProp)

BEGIN_COM_MAP(CCAtlTimerProp)
    COM_INTERFACE_ENTRY_IMPL(IPropertyPage)
END_COM_MAP()

BEGIN_MSG_MAP(CCAtlTimerProp)
    CHAIN_MSG_MAP(IPropertyPageImpl<CCAtlTimerProp>)
END_MSG_MAP()

    STDMETHOD(Apply)(void)
    {
      ATLTRACE(_T("CCAtlTimerProp::Apply\n"));
      for (UINT i = 0; i < m_nObjects; i++)
      {

      }
      m_bDirty = FALSE;
      return S_OK;
    }
};
#endif //__CATLTIMERPROP_H_
```

18. The Wizard adds a dialog box resource to your project with the specified resource ID, here IDD_CATLTIMERPROP. This is the dialog box template will be shown when the property page appears on the screen. You modify it in the dialog box editor, adding whatever controls you think will provide your customer the programmer with the right degree of presentation and power. In this example, a simple check box turns on and off the "ShowSeconds" property. Thus:

19. Unlike the MFC, there is very little prefabrication of the dialog procedure that controls your property page. You need to add message handlers for important dialog messages. When your property page is first shown, you need to process the WM_INITDIALOG message to show the user the initial state of your control's properties. When the user clicks on the "Show Seconds" checkbox, you need to call the base class's SetDirty( ) method, which tells the outer property sheet to turn on the "Apply" button.

First, you need to include your project and control header files. Next, add a **MESSAGE_HANDLER** macro to the message map as before to handle the WM_INITDIALOG message. A **COMMAND_HANDLER** macro adds a handler for the WM_COMMAND message that the dialog box receives when the user clicks the check box.

The control to which the property sheet refers is found in the IPropertyPageImpl base class's member variable **m_ppUnk[]**. This is actually an array because it is reasonable for a user to place multiple controls of the same type on a form, select them all, and pop up the property page to set common properties all at once, as users can do with multiple files in Explorer. The number of controls is stored in the base class's member variable **m_nObjects**.

The sample shown below uses the ATL class CComQIPtr, which automatically queries for the specified interface. Its destructor automatically calls the Release( ) method on the interface pointer when the CComQIPtr goes out of scope. Thus:

```
#include "atltimer.h"
#include "atltimerctrl.h"

BEGIN_MSG_MAP(CCAtlTimerProp)
    MESSAGE_HANDLER(WM_INITDIALOG, OnInitDialog)
    COMMAND_HANDLER(IDC_CHECK1, BN_CLICKED, OnShowSecondsClicked)
    CHAIN_MSG_MAP(IPropertyPageImpl<CCAtlTimerProp>)
END_MSG_MAP()

LRESULT OnInitDialog(UINT uMsg, WPARAM wParam, LPARAM lParam,
    BOOL& bHandled)
{
/*
Get the custom interface of the first control to which the property
page refers. Get state of "ShowSeconds" property.
*/
    CComQIPtr<IAtlTimerCtrl, &IID_IAtlTimerCtrl> pTimer (m_ppUnk[0]);
    BOOL bCheck ;
    pTimer->get_ShowSeconds (&bCheck) ;
/*
Set property page checkbox to reflect control's state.
*/
    CheckDlgButton (IDC_CHECK1, bCheck) ;
    return 1;
}


/*
Show Seconds checkbox clicked, set property page's dirty flag to turn
on "Apply" button.
*/
LRESULT OnShowSecondsClicked(WORD wNotify, WORD wID, HWND hWnd,
        BOOL& bHandled)
{
    SetDirty(TRUE);
    return 0;
}
```

20. The Wizard generated your property page class with the Apply( ) method already overridden. This method is called by Windows when the user clicks either the "Apply" or the "OK" buttons. In it, you check the state of your dialog box controls, set the ATL control(s) properties to reflect that state, and clear the base class's dirty flag m_bDirty. Thus:

```
/*
User clicked "Apply" or "OK"
*/
    STDMETHOD(Apply)(void)
    {
/*
Get state of property page's checkbox.
*/

        BOOL bShowSeconds = IsDlgButtonChecked (IDC_CHECK1) ;

/*
Loop through all the controls that this property page might apply to.
*/
        for (UINT i = 0; i < m_nObjects; i++)
        {
/*
Get custom interface pointer to the control.
*/

            CComQIPtr<IAtlTimerCtrl, &IID_IAtlTimerCtrl>
                pTimer (m_ppUnk[i]);


/*
Set the control's "ShowSeconds" property to reflect the state of the
property page's checkbox.
*/

            pTimer->put_ShowSeconds (bShowSeconds) ;
        }
/*
Clear property page's dirty flag.
*/
        m_bDirty = FALSE;
        return S_OK;
    }
```

21. Finally, we need to tell the control which property pages it supports, which we do by making entries in its property map. Each PROP_ENTRY macro takes the name of the property, its dispatch ID, and the class ID of the property page that is used to edit the property.

This map is also used by the control base classes IPersistStream and IPersistBlob. Making entries here therefore also makes the properties persistent. Thus:

```
BEGIN_PROPERTY_MAP(CAtlTimerCtrl)
    PROP_ENTRY("ShowSeconds", 1, CLSID_CAtlTimerProp)
    PROP_ENTRY("BackColor", DISPID_BACKCOLOR, CLSID_StockColorPage)
END_PROPERTY_MAP()
```

Directory: \EssenceofOLE\chap14\atlhelloau
Directory: \EssenceofOLE\chap14\atltimer

1. First, let's test the hello, world automation server. You first need to register it. Open a command prompt window, change directory to \EssenceofOLE\chap14\atlhelloau, and enter the command "atlhelloau –RegServer".

2. Now to hook up a controller to it, run RegEdit. Go to the ProgID HKEY_CLASSES_ROOT\EssenceOfOleAtlHelloDisp.1, open its CLSID key, and copy the value of the CLSID to the Clipboard. Next, open the ProgID HKEY_CLASSES_ROOT\EssenceofOLE.HelloAutomation, which is the ProgID for the automation server in chapter 3. Replace its CLSID with the one on the Clipboard. Now run the controller program from Chapter 3. It will look under the latter ProgID, find the CLSID of the ATL server, and launch that.

3. The text provides step-by-step directions for creating the timer control using the ATL, so I won't duplicate them here. If you want to use the control that I've built for you, you must register the file \EssenceofOLE\chap14\atltimer\atltimer.dll, using either the command line utility RegSvr32, or the GUI utility that I provide in Appendix A.

Chapter 15

Java and COM

A. CONCEPTS AND DEFINITIONS

1. *Java* is a computer language developed by Sun Microsystems, originally for controlling intelligent household appliances such as toasters. It has lately evolved into the major language for apps delivered from the Internet, becoming Sun's main counterforce weapon against Microsoft's world domination. To learn more about Java, consult the book *Learn Java Now* by Stephen R. Davis, published by Microsoft Press. Java may have a great future as a better C++. The religious wars that swirl around it today center on two main features, platform independence and security.

2. When you build a Java app, the Java compiler converts your Java language source code not into native machine language instructions, as is the case in C++. Instead, it produces files with the extension *.class*, which contain *Java byte codes*. These are instructions written for the *Java Virtual Machine (JVM)*, a piece of software written for your specific operating system and processor. When your Java app runs on a machine, it is up to that machine's JVM to read the Java byte codes and interpret them into native instructions for the processor and operating system on which it runs. Thus:

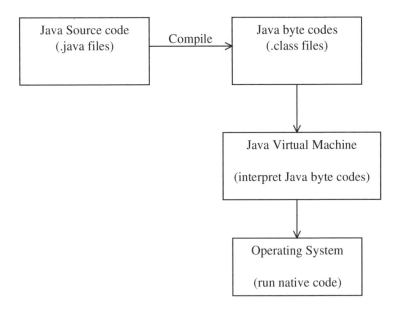

The idea is that Java byte codes are supposed to be universal. If you write an app once in Java, the JVM on any system should be able to interpret and run it. Sun's slogan is "Write once, run everywhere." In practice today, that's not even close to true. It's more like "Write once, debug everywhere." One vendor's JVM differs from another's by just enough to make you tear your hair out; you have to test your applet not just for every platform on which you want to run, but for every vendor's JVM that you care about supporting.

Furthermore, such platform independence as does exist is accomplished by reducing your Java applet to the lowest common denominator of all platforms. For example, since Windows supports object linking and embedding and other operating systems don't, your Java app will have to choose between skipping this feature (very bad if native apps provide it) or losing its platform independence. If you write anything larger than, say, Notepad, Java's architecture will be more of a hindrance than a help and a native app will clean your clock. Corel is currently trying to rewrite their entire business application suite in Java so as to cover the entire market with a single binary. Good luck.

3. Of more interest than platform independence is Java's ability to run applets in a sandbox where they can't hurt anything. If you download and run a native app from the Web, it can do nasty things like format your hard drive, which you don't usually want. Since Java applets execute via the JVM, the JVM can forbid the program from doing anything it shouldn't, such as altering files. This means that you can download Java applets from the Web run them without worrying that they will hurt your machine, which is not the case with native apps – provided, of course, that you trust your JVM.

If the JVM keeps applets in a sandbox, does this not severely restrict the usefulness of Java applets? Not necessarily. Java distinguishes between *trusted* and *untrusted* applets. An untrusted applet, the default, is restricted to the sandbox by the JVM. A trusted applet is allowed to go anywhere and do anything, such as modifying files. The administrator or user sets the rules about which applets are trusted and which are not. Applets installed from hard media or a local network are usually set up as trusted. Applets downloaded from the Internet are generally untrusted, unless they are signed with a digital certificate as shown in Chapter 11. In this case, since you know who wrote an applet and you know that it hasn't been tampered with, you might choose to trust it.

4. Since COM is a language-independent binary standard, it should come as no surprise to learn that you can write both COM clients and servers in Java. In order to accomplish this, you must have a JVM that supports COM. Some, notably Microsoft's, do, and some, notably Sun's and Netscape's, don't. So much for platform independence.

Why would you want to use or implement COM objects in Java ? For the same reasons as you use or implement COM objects in other any language. If you are writing a client app in Java, it's because you need to use the functionality that a component vendor has found it cost-effective to provide in a language-independent COM fashion, thereby maximizing potential customers, rather than in a language-dependent Java-only fashion that wouldn't sell nearly as many units. If you are a component vendor, it's because that, while Java might be the best language for solving your programming problem, you will sell a lot more units if your customers can use your products from any language.

You will find, as you write COM apps in Java, that it provides a higher level of abstraction and prefabrication than C++, a level similar to Visual Basic. As with VB, that's good news as long as you want to do things in exactly the way that Java thinks you ought to want to do them.

5. The Microsoft JVM looks for its Java class files in the directory \winnt\Java or \win95\Java. For development, you also need to make sure that VJ++'s utility directory \DevStudio\Vj\bin is in your command path.

This page intentionally contains no text other than this sentence.

B. COM CLIENTS WRITTEN IN JAVA

1. Suppose you want to write a Java applet that makes calls to a COM object. In this example, I show you how to write a Java client for the "Hello, World" automation server from Chapter 3. You will find the sample code in the directory "\EssenceOfOle\Chap15\javahellouauclient". Thus:

535

2. For your Java applet to use a COM object, you must first generate a Java wrapper class for the object via the *Java Type Library Wizard*, which is on the Tools menu of Developer Studio. To write the sample applet, I first generated a new Java applet using the Java Applet Wizard, accepting all the default options. This tool reads the registry and shows a list of all the type libraries registered on the system. You select the type library describing the COM objects that you want your Java applet to use. Thus:

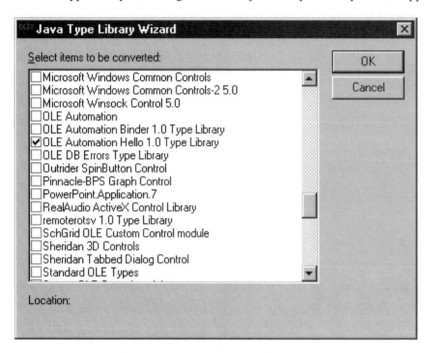

NOTE: At the time of this writing, the GUI of the Java Type Library Wizard does not contain a "Browse" button, thereby restricting you to type libraries that have been registered. If you need to generate Java classes for type libraries that are not registered, you can run the Wizard from the command line as shown on page 542.

3. When you do this, the Type Library Wizard will generate Java .class files for you based on the contents of the specified type library. There will be one .class file for each interface and each coclass specified in the type library. Since COM object do not run through the JVM, there is no way for the JVM to intercept any operations that the COM object performs, thereby sandboxing it. The new class is therefore placed in the TrustLib directory, where it can only be accessed by applets that are themselves trusted, as discussed on page 540. Thus:

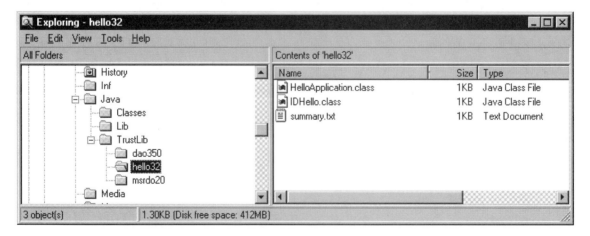

4. The .class file generated by the Wizard contains all the information that a COM-aware JVM needs to interpret Java byte codes into COM object calls. For example, if you look at the binary dump of the "HelloApplication" class shown below, you will see that the last 16 bytes (highlighted below) contain the CLSID of the automation sever, {6CED2900-A1DD-11cf-8A33-00AA00A58097} stored in Intel little-endian format. Thus:

5. You will also find a file named "summary.txt" which contains the human-readable description of the new class's contents. Note that IUnknown support is built into the Java class com.ms.com.IUnknown. Also note that access to the HelloMessage property is provided by a pair of functions with the prefixes "get" and "put". Thus:

```
<file summary.txt>
public class hello32/HelloApplication extends java.lang.Object
{
}
public interface hello32/IDHello extends com.ms.com.IUnknown
{
    public abstract void SayHello();
    public abstract java.lang.String getHelloMessage();
    public abstract void putHelloMessage(java.lang.String);
}
```

6. Once you have generated the wrapper classes, using them is fairly straightforward and sensible for a Java programmer. I used the **import** directive to include the names of the classes in the hello32 package. The app would still work if I omitted it; I would refer to objects by their full class names, such as "hello32.IDHello", instead of their short names as shown below.

As always, COM objects are accessed only via their interfaces. My Java applet contains a member variable of class **IDHello**, which represents the Java wrapper class for the dispinterface of that name.

To create the object, I use Java's **new** operator, specifying the name of the class. The JVM looks in the file "HelloApplication.class", sees that the requested class is a wrapper for a COM object, reads the CLSID from the file and calls CoCreateInstance( ), asking always for the interface IUnknown.

Using the new operator created the object and got me an IUnknown interface. I now need to get from that to the IDHello interface. In C++, you would call QueryInterface( ) directly. In Java, this is done automatically for you by the JVM when you cast the object returned from the new operator. The cast **(IDHello)** shown below tells the JVM to query the object for its support of the IDHello dispinterface. You would think that the call would happen immediately, but if you put MessageBox( ) calls into the server, you will find out that it doesn't. Instead, the JVM tries to be a little clever and do it just-in-time. The call to QueryInterface( ) actually takes place just before the first call to a method on the interface, shown on the facing page.

In Java, you don't call an object's AddRef( ) or Release( ) methods directly either. The JVM automatically calls AddRef( ) whenever you make a copy of an object pointer. The JVM's garbage collection automatically calls Release( ) when an object is set to null as shown below. You might think that just allowing the applet to terminate would release it, but it doesn't. Thus:

```
import hello32.*;

public class javahelloauclient extends Applet
{

/*
This member variable represents the IDHello interface.
*/
    IDHello m_hello ;

/*
When the applet starts, create the new class. The cast to (IDHello)
tells the JVM to query for this interface, but the call doesn't
actually take place until just before a method call is made to that
interface.
*/
    public void start()
    {
      m_hello = (IDHello) new HelloApplication ( );
    }

/*
When the applet shuts down, release object by setting its pointer to
null. If you omit this, the JVM will not call Release( ) and the
object's server will stay alive.
*/
    public void stop()
    {
      m_hello = null ;
    }

    < continued on next page >
```

538

7. The Java wrapper classes in the .class file expose all the methods of the COM object's interfaces as if they were Java object calls. To call a COM interface method, simply make the function call as if the COM object were a native Java object. The JVM automatically handles all of the conversion from Java's String class into the BSTR's that COM requires. Thus:

```
< continued from previous page >

/*
This method handles events from the components in the applet
*/

    public boolean handleEvent(Event evt)
    {
/*
User clicked "Say Hello" button. Call that method.
*/
        if(evt.target == m_SayHelloButton)
        {
            m_hello.SayHello ( ) ;
            return true;
        }


/*
User clicked "Set String" button. Fetch the text from the text field
and pass it to the object.
*/
        else if (evt.target == m_SetMessageButton)
        {
            m_hello.putHelloMessage(m_HelloMessageText.getText()) ;
            return true;
        }


/*
User clicked "Get Message" button. Call the method that fetches the
value of the property, place it into the text field.
*/
        else if (evt.target == m_GetMessageButton)
        {
            m_HelloMessageText.setText (m_hello.getHelloMessage()) ;
            return true;
        }
        return false;
    }
}
```

8. Security is a big deal in Java. You might say that the former is the main marketplace rationale for the latter's existence (certainly platform independence isn't). The distinction between trusted and untrusted applets is critical and counter-intuitive. "Trusted" means "this code does potentially dangerous things, such as modifying files, but I trust it not to hurt me when it does so, so I will allow it." "Untrusted" means "I don't trust this code not to hurt me, so the JVM will forcibly deny any attempt it makes to do potentially dangerous things." A trusted applet may create and use objects from either trusted or untrusted classes. The JVM will prevent the latter from hurting anything. An untrusted applet, on the other hand, may only create objects of untrusted classes, not of trusted classes. You trust your next door neighbor enough to let him borrow your potentially dangerous chainsaw (well, maybe). You don't trust his teenage son with it, but you might let him borrow your relatively safe garden hose.

Since COM objects do not execute via the JVM, they are considered trusted. This means that only trusted Java applets are allowed to use COM objects. An untrusted applet might use an otherwise benign COM object to do nasty things, for example, using WinWord to plant macro viruses.

In this example of a COM client written as a Java applet, the JVM will refuse to create the object unless the applet trying to create the object is itself trusted. How is an applet deemed to be trusted? The first way is that, for the convenience of developers, when Internet Explorer is launched from within Developer Studio, all applets within it are automatically considered trusted. If you install the sample code according to the instructions at the end of this chapter, then open and run the applet from within Developer Studio, it will work.

Your customers won't be using Developer Studio, so you have to find some way to make your applet trusted. At the time of this writing, IE3 will only allow a Java applet to access a COM object if the applet is in a digitally signed .CAB file. This uses the same code signing technology discussed for ActiveX controls in Chapter 11. You can find full details on doing this in the \CabAndSign sample code that comes with the Java SDK. For this book's sample code, you will find details on creating and signing your .CAB file in the directory \EssenceOfOle\chap15\javahelloauclient\cab.

C. Creating a COM Server in Java from a Type Library

1. If you like the Java language for itself, you will like using it for COM servers. In this example, I show you how to write a Java COM server that provides the same functionality as the "Hello, World" automation server from Chapter 3. You will find the sample code in the directory "\EssenceOfOle\Chap15\javahelloauserver".

Microsoft's JVM, "msjava.dll", prefabricates just about all of the infrastructure needed for a COM server. It contains the necessary COM server functions DllGetClassObject( ) and DllCanUnloadNow( ). It contains an implementation of IUnknown and IDispatch. It also contains a class factory that creates Java classes in response to requests from COM. You simply write the Java class that implements your custom methods and properties. Thus:

Note: since MSJAVA.DLL is, obviously, a DLL, the default location for a Java COM server is in-process. If you need the Java server to run out of process, you can use the DllSurrogate registry key as described in Chapter 10.

Note: MSJAVA.DLL does not provide the self-registration capabilities of DllRegisterServer( ) and DllUnregisterServer( ). Registration of Java COM servers must be done by a separate utility app, as described on page 545.

541

2. Suppose you already have a type library describing the objects and interfaces that represent some useful COM server functionality, and suppose that you want to implement this functionality in the Java language. You run the Java Type Library Wizard on the type library to create an abstract Java base class based on its description, which you will then write code to implement. This is the same type library wizard shown in this chapter's Java client example; however, since your type library will probably not have been registered at this point, you will probably have to run it from the command line. The app's name is "javatlb.exe". The command line switch "/U:T" (who thinks these things up?) causes it to output the class description in the file "summary.txt", as shown on the facing page.

In this example, the type library is in the file "JavahelloSv.tlb". The source may be found in the file "JavaHelloSv.odl." It contains the same methods and properties as the Chapter 3 automation server, but with different UUIDs, object names, and interface names. Thus:

3. The type library wizard creates Java classes in exactly the same manner as shown in the client example. It makes a new directory under the \Java\TrustLib, and creates a new .class file for each object and interface in the type library.

If I wanted to, I could have skipped this entire step and started straight from the classes generated in the client example, but that would have led to confusion between the Java automation server and the C++ automation server from Chapter 3.

When you use the "/U:T" switch on javatlb's command line, it produces the file "summary.txt", which lists the objects and interfaces in the generated classes. Note that all of the methods are designated as "abstract", meaning that you have to write the code to implement them. Thus:

```
<file summary.txt>

public class javahellosv/JavaHelloSv extends java.lang.Object
{
}
public interface javahellosv/IDJHello extends com.ms.com.IUnknown
{
    public abstract void SayHello();
    public abstract java.lang.String getHelloMessage();
    public abstract void putHelloMessage(java.lang.String);
}
```

543

4. Now you need to write a Java class that implements the interface class generated from the type library. To do this, use VJ++ to generate a new Java project, but don't use the applet Wizard, which will generate a lot of infrastructure that you don't want. Then add a new Java file to your project. In this file, write a Java class that implements the methods specified in the class definition, which you specify via the Java keyword **implements**. Note that in Java, the name of the class must be the same as that of the file in which it lives, and the name is case sensitive. Also, the import statement isn't absolutely necessary; it just allows you to refer to objects by their short names. Thus:

```
<file CJHello.java>

import javahellosv.* ;

public class CJHello implements IDJHello
{
    String m_String = "Java Text String" ;

/*
Client told us to say hello. Output our message string to Java's
standard output stream.
*/
    public void SayHello()
    {
      System.out.println(m_String);
    }


/*
Client is asking for the current value of our HelloMessage string
property. Return its current value.
*/
    public java.lang.String getHelloMessage()
    {
      return m_String ;
    }


/*
Client is passing us a new value for our HelloMessage property. Save it
in our member variable.
*/
    public void putHelloMessage(java.lang.String newString)
    {
      m_String = newString ;
    }
}
```

544

5. Finally, you register the Java server using the command line utility "javareg.exe". This makes the registry entries that you need for COM to find the JVM and for the JVM to create your class. It also registers the type library. The batch file that registers the sample code is:

<file RegisterJavaHello.bat>

```
javareg /register /class:CJHello
    /clsid:{A1779020-1248-11d1-916E-00608C86B89C}
    /progid:EssenceOfOLE.JavaHelloAutomation
```

As you can see from the registry, the COM server for any Java class is the JVM, msjava.dll. COM will load that DLL and get the class factory from it. When COM calls IClassFactory::CreateInstance( ), the JVM in turn will look at the "JavaClass" named value to know which Java class to create. The implemented category entry marks this COM object as being implemented by Java class. The .class files of the implementing class needs to be in the current directory or \TrustLib or \Classes or \Lib directory. Thus:

D. Creating a COM Server from an Existing Java Class

1. Now turn the preceding example around. Suppose you already have a Java class whose functionality you like, but you think you could sell a lot more units if you could expose its functionality via COM to any client in any language, rather than only being available to Java apps. VJ++ provides the ActiveX Wizard for Java, which reads an existing Java class and creates a COM wrapper for it.

Suppose I have a Java class named CJavaViaWizard, with functionality similar to the CJHello class in the previous example. The sample code may be found in the directory \EssenceOfOle\chap15\javatoactivexviawizard (I love long descriptive file names). Thus:

```
/*
Initial Java class looks like this.
*/

public class CJavaViaWizard
{
    String m_String = "Java Via Wizard Text String" ;

    public void SayHello()
    {
      System.out.println(m_String);
    }

    public java.lang.String getHelloMessage()
    {
      return m_String ;
    }

    public void putHelloMessage(java.lang.String newString)
    {
      m_String = newString ;
    }
}
```

2. When you run the Wizard from the Tools menu, it will ask you for the name of the Java class you want to wrap. The Wizard will then generate a new COM interface containing all the public methods in your original Java class, and a new .IDL file describing this interface and a COM object that implements it. The Wizard will also generate abstract Java base classes describing the interface and the COM object which implements it, as Javatlb did in the previous section. Since these base classes are rather sneakily generated after the fact, they will contain the methods that you have already implemented in your original Java class, so you won't have to write any additional code.

The basic design choices that the Wizard provides you are whether to generate a new .IDL file or write the information into an existing one, whether to generate a new random CLSID for your COM server or use one that you provide, and whether to expose your new COM server's functionality as a dual interface or as a dispinterface only. Pick the ones you want.

The Wizard generates a .IDL file immediately, but it offers you the choice of compiling it into a .TLB now or later. The Wizard also will generate a .REG file, as shown on a later page, but it offers you the choice of incorporating it into the registry now or later. Thus:

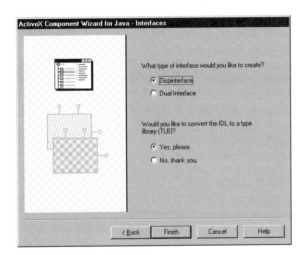

3. Now you've made your selections, the Wizard will generate the .IDL file. You will see that it contains the definition of a dispinterface that provides access to all the prublic methods in the original Java class. The .IDL file also contains the definition of a coclass that implements that interface. Thus:

```
[
    uuid(3cd76ff2-199f-11d1-917b-00608c86b89c),
    helpstring("CJavaViaWizardLib Type Library"),
    version(1.0)
]
library CJavaViaWizardLib
{
    importlib("stdole32.tlb");

/*
Dispinterface providing access to all public methods in the original
Java class.
*/

    [
        uuid(3cd76ff1-199f-11d1-917b-00608c86b89c),
        helpstring("ICJavaViaWizard Interface")
    ]
    dispinterface ICJavaViaWizard
    {
        properties:
        methods:
        [ helpstring("SayHello Method"), id(1) ]
        void SayHello();

        [ helpstring("getHelloMessage Method"), id(2) ]
        BSTR getHelloMessage();

        [ helpstring("putHelloMessage Method"), id(3) ]
        void putHelloMessage([in] BSTR p1);

    }

/*
Object that implements the dispinterface.
*/
    [
        uuid(3cd76ff0-199f-11d1-917b-00608c86b89c),
        helpstring("CCJavaViaWizard Object")
    ]
    coclass CCJavaViaWizard
    {
        [ default ]
        dispinterface ICJavaViaWizard;
    };

};
```

4. The abstract base classes are placed in your \TrustLib directory, just as they were in the previous two examples. Thus:

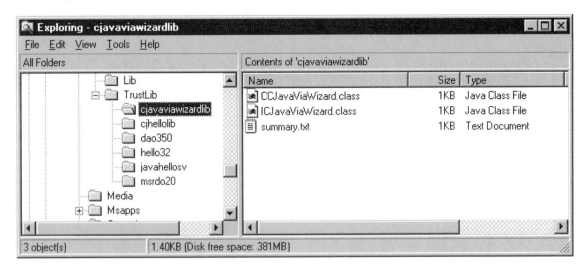

<file summary.txt>

```
public class cjavaviawizardlib/CCJavaViaWizard extends java.lang.Object
{
}
public     interface     cjavaviawizardlib/ICJavaViaWizard     extends
com.ms.com.IUnknown
{
    public abstract void SayHello();
    public abstract java.lang.String getHelloMessage();
    public abstract void putHelloMessage(java.lang.String);
}
```

5. The Wizard generates a .REG file containing the registry settings that you need to connect your Java class to COM. You will note that it does not provide a ProgID, nor does it provide entries to register the type library. You will have to add these yourself if you want them. Every time you run the Wizard on this class, this file will be overwritten, so be careful with it. Thus:

```
REGEDIT4

[HKEY_CLASSES_ROOT\CLSID\{3cd76ff0-199f-11d1-917b-00608c86b89c}]
@="Java Class: CJavaViaWizard"
"AppID"="{3cd76ff0-199f-11d1-917b-00608c86b89c}"

[HKEY_CLASSES_ROOT\CLSID\{3cd76ff0-199f-11d1-917b-00608c86b89c}\
    InprocServer32]
@="MSJAVA.DLL"
"ThreadingModel"="Both"
"JavaClass"="CJavaViaWizard"

[HKEY_CLASSES_ROOT\CLSID\{3cd76ff0-199f-11d1-917b-
00608c86b89c}\Implemented Categories]

[HKEY_CLASSES_ROOT\CLSID\{3cd76ff0-199f-11d1-917b-
00608c86b89c}\Implemented Categories\
    {BE0975F0-BBDD-11CF-97DF-00AA001F73C1}]

[HKEY_CLASSES_ROOT\AppID\{3cd76ff0-199f-11d1-917b-00608c86b89c}]
@="Java Class: CJavaViaWizard"
```

6. Finally, the Wizard tells you the modifications you need to make to your existing Java class to make it implement the abstract base class that connects it to COM. These changes are pretty trivial. You have to import the abstract base class as shown previously. You have to change your class declaration to say that the class now implements the abstract base class. And you have to include a string named "CLSID" which contains the value of this server's CLSID. Your class declaration now looks like this:

```
/*
1. Import new abstract base class package.
*/

import cjavaviawizardlib.*;

/*
2. Change derivation so your original class now implements the new
abstract base class.
*/

public class CJavaViaWizard implements
    cjavaviawizardlib.ICJavaViaWizard
{

/*
3. Add string named CLSID, containing your server's CLSID.
*/
    private static final String CLSID =
        "3cd76ff0-199f-11d1-917b-00608c86b89c";

    <code omitted>
}
```

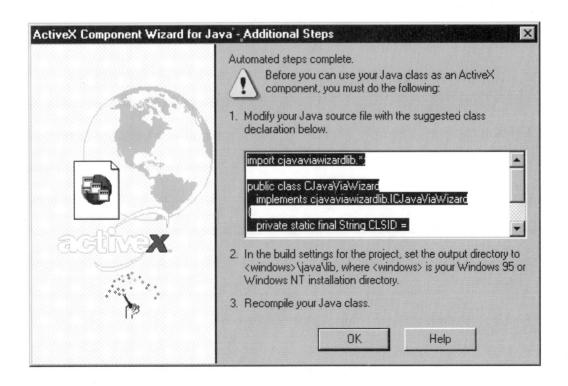

551

E. COM Error handling in Java

1. COM's binary standard calls for methods to signal their success or failure with simple result codes. Because exceptions are language dependent, and also very hard to implement across different processes and different machines, COM doesn't support them. However, Java programming depends heavily on exceptions to signal errors, and Java programming would be difficult and unwieldy if you couldn't use them. The JVM converts between these two divergent world views.

Microsoft provides the Java class **com.ms.com.ComFailException** to signal the failure of a COM function or method call. Whenever a Java applet makes a COM call, if the return code is anything other than S_OK, the JVM will create and throw an exception of this type. An applet that cares about error return codes will use Java's standard **try-catch** syntax to catch this exception as shown below.

The ComFailException object contains the methods **getHResult( )** and **getMessage( )**. The former provides you with the COM error code value used through this book, and should be valid at all times. The latter is inherited from the Java base class RuntimeException, from which ComFailException derives. Thus:

```
/*
Import Microsoft's COM package so you can refer to the ComFailException
by its short name.
*/

import com.ms.com.* ;

public boolean handleEvent(Event evt)
{
   if (evt.target == m_GetMessageButton)
   {

/*
Attempt COM method call within the try block
*/
         try
         {

m_HelloMessageText.setText(m_hello.getHelloMessage());
         }
/*
If it doesn't succeed, the JVM will create and throw a ComFailException
for you to catch.
*/
         catch (ComFailException cfe)
         {
                System.out.println( "COM Exception:" );
                System.out.println( cfe.getHResult() );
                System.out.println( cfe.getMessage() );
         }
         return true;
   }
   return false;
}
```

2. From the server side, all Java class methods that implement COM interface methods are implicitly defined as throwing a ComFailException. When your Java COM server method encounters an error that it wants to signal, you allocate an object of this class, fill in its elements, and throw it. The JVM will catch the exception, convert it back to a COM HRESULT, and pass it back as the return value of your method in the manner the COM client is expecting. Thus:

```java
public class CJHello implements IDJHello
{
    String m_String = "Java Text String" ;
    final int E_FAIL = 0x80004005 ;

/*
This method won't allow the text string to begin with the characters
'BAD'.
*/

    public void putHelloMessage(java.lang.String newString)
    {
      if (newString.startsWith ("BAD"))
      {

/*
Allocate a new ComFailException, passing it the result code and message
string in its constructor.
*/
            ComFailException MyException = new ComFailException(E_FAIL,
                "String can't start with the characters 'BAD'") ;

/*
Throw the exception. The JVM will catch it and package it into the
proper COM interfaces and structures.
*/
            throw  MyException ;
      }
      else
      {
            m_String = newString ;
      }
    }
}
```

Note: You will occasionally see a COM method, such as IPersistStream::IsDirty( ), return an HRESULT of S_FALSE, whose hex value is 0x00000001. This represents a funny intermediate state between success and failure. It essentially means that "Yes, I was able to successfully find out what you wanted to know, and the answer to your question is 'No'." Java provides a separate class to handle this case called ComSuccessException. Use it exactly as you would a ComFailException.

Directory: \EssenceofOLE\chap15\javahelloauclient
Directory: \EssenceofOLE\chap15\javahelloauserver
Directory: \EssenceofOLE\chap15\javatoactivexviawizard

1. To run the Java client applet, you must first set up a server for it to connect to. Make sure that the "Hello, World" automation server from Chapter 3 is registered and properly working.

2. Using Microsoft Developer Studio with Visual J++ installed, open the project file "javahelloclient.dsw". From the tools menu, select "Java Type Library Wizard". When the Wizard box appears, select "OLE Automation Hello 1.0 Type Library", the click OK. Use Explorer to verify that the class files have appeared in your \Winnt\Java\TrustLib directory as shown in the text. Pick "Build — Execute" from the main menu. You should see Internet Explorer launched with your applet in it. The automation server from Chapter 3 should appear.

3. Using Internet Explorer, open the file "javahelloauclient.html". You will not see the Java applet, nor will you see the automation server. You will probably see an error in IE's status bar saying something like "class not found". This is because IE3 requires the applet to be trusted in order to create a COM object, and this one isn't. Now go to the subdirectory \cab and use IE to open the file "javahelloauclientcab.html". You should see my security certificate appear on the screen, although it may have expired by the time you read this. If you allow the installation to proceed, you are telling IE to trust the applet. The automation server will appear.

4. Now for the Java COM server. In server directory, run "javatlb" as shown in the text to generate the wrapper classes. Then run Javareg via the batch file "RegisterJavaHello.bat" to register the Java server. Check the registry, as shown in the text, to make sure that the correct entries have been made. You will find a client app written in Visual Basic called "testjavahelloserver.exe". Run this app. The Set and Get buttons will work; the SayHello button will appear not to. This is because the Java server writes its message to the system output stream. Coming up with some way of tapping into this is left as an exercise to the student.

5. Now we need to use the ActiveX Wizard for Java. In the directory javatoactivexviawizard, open the project file javatoactivexviawizard.mdp. Run the Wizard from the Tools menu, making entries as shown in the text. The class file has already been edited for you. You will find a test app called "test.exe" in the directory.

Chapter 16
Shell Extensions and COM

This page intentionally contains no text other than this sentence.

A. CONCEPTS AND DEFINITIONS

1. The Windows 95 and NT 4.0 user interface shell is a great step forward from the old File Manager. Not only is it far better as shipped, but it also makes it easy for you to write your own shell extensions to customize the handling of your own files. This chapter discusses the various ways in which you can extend the shell's functionality. The code for all samples shown in this chapter may be found in the directory \EssenceOfOle\chap16\shellext.

These are the different features that you can customize:

When the user clicks the right mouse button on one of your app's files, he sees a context menu of the actions that the shell thinks make sense on that file at that time. The shell provides default operations, such as renaming or deleting a file, but you can also add your own menu items with operations that apply specifically to your own files. You can make these menu items the same for all of your files, or you can change them dynamically based on the contents of the individual file. This is done with a *context menu handler*, as described on page 564.

When the user drags files from Explorer and drops them on certain desktop icons, such as the Recycle Bin or a printer, the icon appears to take an action on those files, such as deleting or printing the files. You can easily set up a *drop target handler* which will receive notifications when files are dropped on an icon of yours, so you can take whatever action you want to. For example, if you are writing a utility app that wipes the contents of sensitive files, you might show a shredder icon on the desktop. When the user drops files on it, you might overwrite the contents of the file with garbage characters. An example of drop target handler is shown on page 574.

When the user right clicks on a file and selects "Properties" from the context menu, a dialog box appears containing a set of property pages pertaining to the file, displaying status information and allowing the user to change parts of it. For example, the shell provides a general property page, showing properties common to all files, such as a check box signaling the read-only attribute of the file. You can add your own property pages to this dialog box, allowing the user to see and change properties that are specific to your own files. An example of a *property sheet handler* is shown on 571.

An app generally provides a single icon for each type of file that it supports. This is fine for a word processor, but perhaps you would like each file to provide its own distinctive icon. For example, a paint program might want each of its painting document to display an icon showing what it looks like. You can dynamically provide your own custom icons via an *icon handler*, as shown on page 578.

B. SHELL EXTENSION ARCHITECTURE

1.   Shell extensions require you to write an in-proc COM server to provide the shell with the functionality necessary to handle your extensions. These COM servers tend to be relatively small, although quirkier than other areas of COM. The first quirk is that all servers mentioned in this chapter need to be registered as using the apartment threading model. If you do not do this, they will not load. The .REG file you use to do this must therefore use the REGEDIT4 syntax. Thus:

```
REGEDIT4
 [HKEY_CLASSES_ROOT\EssenceOfOle.ShellExtServer\CLSID]
    @ = "{1E392640-6E11-11d0-9097-00608C86B89C}"
 [HKEY_CLASSES_ROOT\CLSID\{1E392640-6E11-11d0-9097-00608C86B89C}]
    @ = "Essence of OLE Data3 Shell Extension Server"
 [HKEY_CLASSES_ROOT\CLSID\{1E392640-6E11-11d0-9097-00608C86B89C}\InProcServer32]
    @ = "c:\\EssenceofOLE\\chap13\\shellext\\debug\\shellext.dll"
    "ThreadingModel" = "Apartment"
```

WARNING: Shell extensions have nasty, non-intuitive quirks that other parts of COM don't, such as the threading model problem discussed above. I think that this was the first major OS-wide use of COM and that the programmers didn't fully understand it. This chapter will attempt to navigate you around them.

2. When developing and testing your shell extensions, you need to make sure that the shell unloads your extension DLL server whenever it finishes an operation with it. Otherwise you won't be able to rebuild the DLL as Explorer will keep it loaded in memory. This is easily accomplished by adding the following registry key:

HKEY_LOCAL_MACHINE\Software\Microsoft\Windows\CurrentVersion\Explorer
    \AlwaysUnloadDLL = 1

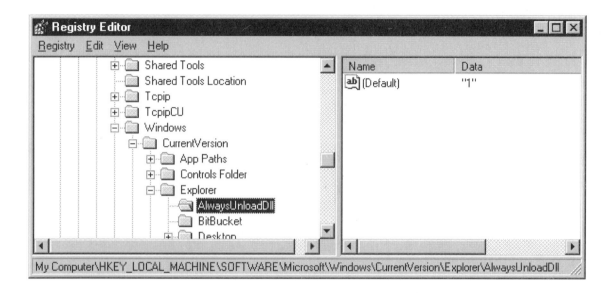

Warning: Debugging shell extensions is difficult in Windows 95. In addition to that platform's usual instability, it always launches a new Explorer window as a thread of the existing desktop process, not a new process. To use the debugger on this thread, you have to "Build — Start Debug — Attach to Process". You will find that debugging your shell extensions is much easier on Windows NT, although you will have to test your app on both operating systems because there are significant differences.

Note: Explorer will unload your DLL using the API function CoFreeUnusedLibraries( ), which in turn will call your server DLL's method DllCanUnloadNow( ). If you have a bug in this code, or more likely in the reference counting code of your server's objects, the unloading won't work. You can easily detect this situation by putting a message box in your DllCanUnloadNow( ) function.

3. Since the different types of shell extensions frequently share common code, such as that used to read the internal structure of a particular type of file, they are frequently put together in the same DLL, supporting all the required interfaces via multiple inheritance. That is the model used for the sample code of this book, as shown in the class CShellExt on the facing page. The interfaces required for the shell extension functionality are defined in the header file "**shlobj.h**", which you must include. These interfaces are:

IContextMenu   *// used for customizing context menus (page 567)*
IShellPropSheetExt   *// used for showing property sheets (page 572)*
IDropTarget   *// used for accepting files via drag-and-drop (page 575)*
IExtractIcon   *// used for providing different icons to Explorer (page 578)*

When it is initialized, a shell extension handler needs to be told the name of the file or files to which it pertains. Naturally, Microsoft decided to do this in two different ways for different types of shell extensions. You must provide the initialization interface required by the shell extension(s) that you want to support; in the case of the sample app provided with this chapter, both.

A context menu handler and a property page handler receive their initialization via the IShellExtInit interface. This interface has only one method, called Initialize( ), which passes the name of the single file or selection of files to which the menu or property sheet pertains. This method is shown on page 562.

A drop target handler and an icon handler are initialized with one and only one file name. For reasons known only to Microsoft, these shell extensions receive this file name via the IPersistFile interface, seen earlier in this book. Implementing this interface for a shell extension is shown in on page 563.

IShellExtInit   *// required for initializing context menu and property sheet handlers*
IPersistFile   *// required for initializing drop target and icon handlers*

```cpp
#include <shlobj.h>

class CShellExt : IContextMenu, IShellPropSheetExt, IDropTarget,
    IExtractIcon, IShellExtInit, IPersistFile
{
public:
    ULONG m_RefCount ;          char m_FileName [256] ;

    CShellExt(void);
    ~CShellExt(void);

    //IUnknown interface members
    STDMETHODIMP        QueryInterface(REFIID, LPVOID FAR *);
    STDMETHODIMP_(ULONG)    AddRef(void);
    STDMETHODIMP_(ULONG)    Release(void);

    // IContextMenu methods
    STDMETHODIMP QueryContextMenu (HMENU hmenu, UINT indexMenu,
        UINT idCmdFirst, UINT idCmdLast, UINT uFlags) ;
    STDMETHODIMP InvokeCommand (LPCMINVOKECOMMANDINFO lpici) ;
    STDMETHODIMP GetCommandString (UINT idCmd, UINT uType,
        UINT * pwReserved, LPSTR  pszName, UINT cchMax) ;

    // IShellPropSheetExt members
    STDMETHODIMP AddPages (LPFNADDPROPSHEETPAGE lpfnAddPage,
        LPARAM lParam) ;
    STDMETHODIMP ReplacePage (UINT uPageID,
        LPFNADDPROPSHEETPAGE lpfnReplaceWith, LPARAM lParam) ;

    // IDropTarget members
    STDMETHODIMP DragEnter(LPDATAOBJECT, DWORD, POINTL, LPDWORD);
    STDMETHODIMP DragOver(DWORD, POINTL, LPDWORD);
    STDMETHODIMP DragLeave(void);
    STDMETHODIMP Drop(LPDATAOBJECT, DWORD, POINTL, LPDWORD);

    // IExtractIcon methods
    STDMETHODIMP GetIconLocation (UINT   uFlags, LPSTR szIconFile,
        UINT   cchMax, int   * piIndex, UINT  * pwFlags) ;
    STDMETHODIMP Extract (LPCSTR pszFile, UINT   nIconIndex,
        HICON   *phiconLarge, HICON   *phiconSmall,
        UINT   nIconSize) ;

    // IShellExtInit interface members
    STDMETHODIMP Initialize (LPCITEMIDLIST pidlFolder,
        LPDATAOBJECT lpdobj, HKEY hkeyProgID) ;

    // IPersistFile methods
    STDMETHODIMP GetClassID(LPCLSID);
    STDMETHODIMP IsDirty(void) ;
    STDMETHODIMP Load(LPCOLESTR, DWORD) ;
    STDMETHODIMP Save(LPCOLESTR, BOOL) ;
    STDMETHODIMP SaveCompleted(LPCOLESTR) ;
    STDMETHODIMP GetCurFile(LPOLESTR FAR *) ;
};
```

4. When initializing a context menu handler or property sheet handler, Explorer will call your shell extension object's **IShellExtInit::Initialize( )** method to provide your context menu handler with the name of the file or files for which it is being invoked. In this example, we check that there is only one name as we don't know how to deal with more. We store the name in a member variable for later use.

The names are passed to us via an IDataObject interface. We must use the method IDataObject::GetData( ) to obtain the global memory block containing the actual file names. The block conforms to the CF_HDROP Clipboard format, allowing it to contain more than one name.

We access a CF_HDROP block's contents via the API function **DragQueryFile( )**. Passing -1 as this function's second parameter will give you the number of file names it contains. Passing a zero-based index as the second parameter will unpack the specified name into a string. Thus:::

```
STDMETHODIMP CShellExt::Initialize (LPCITEMIDLIST pidlFolder,
    LPDATAOBJECT lpd, HKEY hkeyProgID)
{
    FORMATETC fe = {CF_HDROP, NULL,DVASPECT_CONTENT,-1,TYMED_HGLOBAL};
    STGMEDIUM stg ;      HRESULT hr = E_FAIL ;

    if (lpd)
    {
/*
Get the file name(s) in a global memory block conforming to the
CF_HDROP Clipboard format.
*/

        hr = lpd->GetData (&fe, &stg);
/*
CF_HDROP might contain more than one file. This example only knows how
to handle one at a time.
*/

        if (hr == S_OK && DragQueryFile ((HDROP)stg.hGlobal, (UINT)(-1),
            NULL, 0) == 1)
        {
/*
Get the file name out of the global memory block. Store in a member
variable for later use.
*/
            DragQueryFile (
                (HDROP)stg.hGlobal,     // global memory block
                0,                      // # of file within block
                m_FileName,             // output buffer
                sizeof (m_FileName));   // output buffer size
            hr = S_OK ;
        }
        else
        {
            hr = E_FAIL;
        }
        ReleaseStgMedium (&stg);
    }
    return hr ;
}
```

5. When initializing a drop target handler or an icon handler, Explorer will query for the IPersistFile interface and call its **Load( )** method. It will not call any of the other methods; you can safely stub them out. In this example, we save the file name in a member variable for later use. Thus:

```
STDMETHODIMP CShellExt::Load (LPCOLESTR pFileName, DWORD grfMode)
{

/*
Convert file name from wide character to ANSI and store in a member
variable.
*/

    WideCharToMultiByte (CP_ACP, 0,(LPCWSTR)pFileName, -1,
      m_FileName, sizeof (m_FileName), NULL, NULL);

    return S_OK ;
}
```

C. CONTEXT MENU HANDLERS

1. When the user right-clicks on a file, Explorer shows a context menu of actions ("verbs") that might be taken with the file. This is a very useful feature because different types of files may have a variety of operations that could reasonably be performed on them, and double-clicking only provides access to one of them.

In the example below, the user has right-clicked on a file with the extension ".htm", an HTML file. The primary verb associated with a file of this type is to open it in the registered Web browser. But there are other things that the user might want to do with such a file, such as editing it, which use other apps. In the example below, the user has installed the ActiveX Control Pad for editing these files. It is a very cool feature to be able to add these auxiliary verbs to the context menu.

2. This turns out to be very simple to accomplish. It's all done with registry entries; you don't have to write any code. In the case of the ActiveX Control Pad, it was done by the installation program. First, you have to register the extension of the files whose context menu entries you want to modify. Add a key to the HKEY_CLASSES_ROOT with the file's extension, in this case ".htm". Set the value of this key to any unique name that you want to use as a program ID, in this case "htmlfile". Thus:

HKEY_CLASSES_ROOT\.htm = htmlfile

Second, you need to specify the entry to be made on the menu and the command to be executed. Under your file type's registered name, add the key "Shell". Under this key, add a subkey whose name is the text you want to appear on the context menu, in this case "Edit with ActiveX Control Pad". Under this key, add a subkey named "command", whose value is the command string that you want executed when the user selects the context menu item. This will usually be the name of a .EXE file with one or more command line arguments. Thus:

HKEY_CLASSES_ROOT\htmlfile\shell\Edit with ActiveX Control Pad\command
    = C:\Program Files\ActiveX Control Pad\ped.exe %1

3. Suppose this granularity is too coarse for your purposes. Suppose you want the context menu to vary depending on the name or content of the individual files. In this chapter's sample code, I provide a context menu with the capability of changing the file's first character from an 'A' to a space and back again, via utility functions IsFirstCharA( ) and SetFirstCharA( ). How do I hook this up to Explorer ?

Explorer provides a fairly easy way for you to add your own code which modifies the context menu before it is shown to the user and which responds to the user's selections. You do this by writing a *context menu handler*, a COM server that Explorer will load and call just before showing the context menu of your file. The interfaces exposed by the context menu handler contain the code you write to add items to the context menu and respond to their selection by the user.

Suppose I have a file type with the extension .EOO (as in Essence Of OLE). I want to specify a context menu handler to be invoked when the user clicks on a file of this type. This handler will look at the contents of the individual file and modify the menu accordingly.

First, I register the program ID for the specified file extension as shown on the previous page. Thus:

I then put in the key that tells Explorer where the context menu handler is found. Under the file's registered name, I add the subkey "shellex". Under this I add a subkey called "ContextMenuHandlers". Under this, I add one or more arbitrarily-named subkeys, each of which contains a value representing the class ID of the server that provides the code for handling the context menu. Thus:

HKEY_CLASSES_ROOT\EssenceOfOle.ShellExtensionFile\shellex\ContextMenuHandlers
    \DemoCtxMenu = {1E392640-6E11-11d0-9097-00608C86B89C}

4. When the user right-clicks on a file, Explorer looks in the registry for the class ID of the registered context menu handler or handlers, calling CoCreateInstance( ) for each class ID that it finds. Explorer will then query for the interfaces IShellExtInit and IContextMenu. The former was previously discussed on page 562. The methods of the latter are:

QueryContextMenu ( )   // *Allow your context menu handler to add items to context menu*
InvokeCommand ( )   // *Notify your context menu handler that one of its items was selected*
GetCommandString ( )   // *Get explanatory string to show in Explorer's status pane.*

5. Next, Explorer will call our object's **IContextMenu::QueryContextMenu( )** method. This is our chance to add our own menu items to the context menu that Explorer is about to show. The insertion is done via the API function InsertMenu( ). The index at which our items are allowed to be inserted is passed as the second parameter of this method. The command ID must be a zero-based offset from the third parameter of this method. Finally, the return value must be the number of menu items added (another quirk), so Explorer will know which menu items are ours and which are its. Thus:

```
#define    IDC_FIRSTCHARA    0

STDMETHODIMP CShellExt::QueryContextMenu(HMENU hMenu, UINT indexMenu,
    UINT idCmdFirst, UINT idCmdLast, UINT uFlags)
{

/*
Check the file's contents to see if its first char is a capital A. If
so, set flags for check mark, otherwise set flags for no check mark.
*/

    UINT flags ;
    if (IsFirstCharA (m_FileName) == TRUE)
    {
      flags = MF_BYPOSITION | MF_STRING | MF_CHECKED ;
    }
    else
    {
      flags = MF_BYPOSITION | MF_STRING | MF_UNCHECKED ;
    }
/*
Add item to context menu allowing user to toggle first character from
'A' to non - 'A' and back.
*/

    InsertMenu (hMenu, indexMenu, flags, idCmdFirst + IDC_FIRSTCHARA,
      "&First char 'A'");
/*
Return the one-based number of items we have added. This is the only
place I know of in all of COM where the return value of a method is
specific information and not a status code. The count should have been
returned via an output pointer in the parameter list.
*/
    return 1 ;
}
```

567

6. When the user selects from the context menu any of the items that we have added to it, Explorer will notify us by calling our **IContextMenu::InvokeCommand( )** method. The sole parameter is a pointer to a structure of type CMINVOKECOMMANDINFO, which contains information about the menu selection. The element *lpVerb* will contain zero in its high word and the command offset in its low word. We check this offset and take whatever action we think we should. Thus:

```
STDMETHODIMP CShellExt::InvokeCommand (LPCMINVOKECOMMANDINFO lpici)
{

/*
Check to see if it's the verb we added.
*/

    if (HIWORD (lpici->lpVerb) == 0 &&
      LOWORD (lpici->lpVerb) == IDC_FIRSTCHARA)
    {
/*
If so, toggle the first character from 'A' to non- 'A' or back again.
*/

      if (IsFirstCharA (m_FileName))
      {
            SetFirstCharA (m_FileName, FALSE) ;
      }
      else
      {
            SetFirstCharA (m_FileName, TRUE) ;
      }
    }
    else
    {
      MessageBox (NULL, "Illegal InvokeCommand", "", 0) ;
    }

    return S_OK ;
}
```

7. When the user is dragging the mouse along the context menu, Explorer will call our object's **IContextMenu::GetCommandString( )** method to obtain the menu explanation string to show in its status bar. You look at the command ID and return the string based on it.

WARNING: This function works differently in Windows NT than 95. The documentation specifies the 4ᵗʰ parameter as an ANSI string pointer, which is correct in 95 but wrong in NT. If you return an ANSI string in NT, as the parameters seem to be telling you to do, Explorer will show only garbage. In NT, this must be a Unicode string. You must use the API function **GetVersionEx( )** to find out what operating sytem you are running on, and return the correct type of string. Pain in the ass. Thus:

```
STDMETHODIMP CShellExt::GetCommandString( UINT idCmd, UINT uType,
    UINT * pwReserved, LPSTR  pszName, UINT cchMax)
{

/*
If the command ID is the same as the menu item we added, then return
the menu prompt string for Explorer to show in its status bar
*/

    if (idCmd == IDC_FIRSTCHARA)
    {
/*
Get version of OS.
*/
        OSVERSIONINFO osvi ;
        GetVersionEx (&osvi) ;

/*
If NT, the copy string as wide characters.
*/
        if (osvi.dwPlatformId == VER_PLATFORM_WIN32_NT)
        {
            wcsncpy ((WCHAR *) pszName,
                L"Toggle first character to 'A'", cchMax) ;
        }
/*
If Windows 95, copy string as ANSI characters.
*/
        else
        {
            lstrcpyn (pszName, "Toggle first character to 'A'", cchMax);
        }
    }
    return S_OK ;
}
```

8. When the user drags a file on the desktop using the right mouse button and drops it, he sees a context menu as well, as shown below. You can connect a context menu handler to modify this context menu as well. This is known as a *drag drop handler*, not be confused with a drop target handler discussed elsewhere in this chapter, which accepts dropped file names from Explorer. Hey, I didn't write the nomenclature.

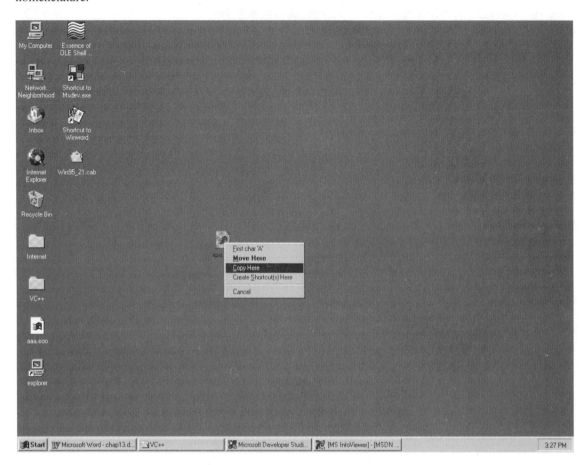

To add a context menu handler to the drag-and-drop menu, all you have to do is to make one registry entry, as shown below. This tells Explorer to use your regular context menu handler for this case. You could write a different one if you wanted to.

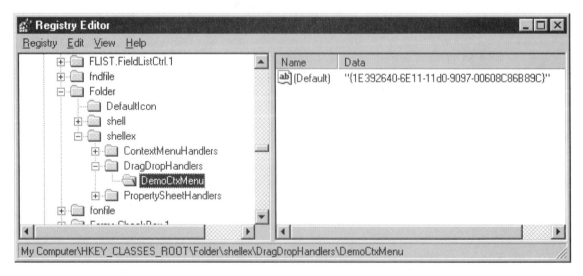

D. PROPERTY SHEET HANDLERS

1. When the user right-clicks on a file in Explorer or on the desktop and selects "Properties" from the context menu, Explorer pops up a property sheet dialog box containing property pages, presenting the user with information on the selected file and frequently allowing him to modify that information. For example, the read-only attribute of a file may be set in this manner. You can add your own property pages to the property sheet to present and allow the user to modify properties of your own files. In the source code example, a property page is used to tell the user whether or not the first character of the file is an 'A' and allowing him to change it. Thus:

2. Similar to a context menu, you add your own property pages to the property sheet by supplying a shell extension COM server that supports IShellExtInit and the new interface *IShellPropSheetExt*. The latter's methods are:

STDMETHODIMP AddPages ( ) // *add pages to a property sheet*
STDMETHODIMP ReplacePage ( ) // *replace an existing page in a property sheet. Used only by*
                       // *Control Panel applets, otherwise stubbed out*

To tell Explorer to use your shell extension, you must make entries in the registry. Under your registered file name's shellex key, you must add the subkey "PropertySheetHandlers". Under this key, you add one or more subkeys with any name, the value of each of which contains the class ID of the COM object to create when the property sheet for that type of file is being shown. Thus:

HKEY_CLASSES_ROOT\EssenceOfOle.ShellExtensionFile\shellex\PropertySheetHandlers
    \DemoPage = {1E392640-6E11-11d0-9097-00608C86B89C}

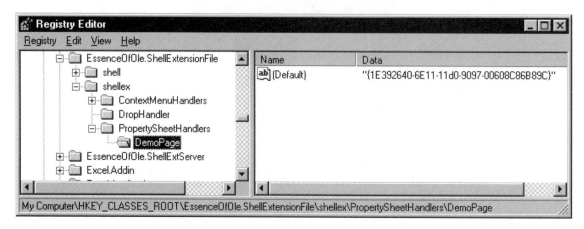

572

3. When the user tells Explorer to pop up the property sheet, Explorer will query the registry, create shell extension objects of the specified types, and initialize them via IShellExtInit::Initialize( ). Next, it will call the method **IShellPropSheetExt::AddPages( )**. In this method, you must create the property page or pages that you want to add by filling out a structure of type **PROPSHEETPAGE** and calling the API function **CreatePropertySheetPage( )**. These are standard parts of the Windows API, documented in Nancy Cluts's book, *Programming the Windows 95 User Interface* (Microsoft Press, ISBN 1-55615-884-X).

In this method you are passed a pointer to a function and an lParam. The pointer points to a callback function inside Explorer that will actually add your property page to the property sheet that Explorer is about to show. When you have created your property page, you must call that function via the pointer, passing the new property page handle and the lParam. Kind of kludgey, but it works. Thus:

```
STDMETHODIMP CShellExt::AddPages (LPFNADDPROPSHEETPAGE lpfnAddPage,
    LPARAM lParam)
{

/*
Create property page
*/
    PROPSHEETPAGE psp;

    psp.dwSize      = sizeof(psp) ;
    psp.dwFlags     = 0 ;
    psp.hInstance   = hDllInst ;

/*
This object will be released before the property page is actually
shown, so any data that we need to pass to the property sheet's handler
function must be explicitly allocated and copied. A reference to a
member variable won't work.
*/
    char *cp = (char *)malloc (sizeof(m_FileName)) ;
    lstrcpy (cp, m_FileName) ;
    psp.lParam = (LPARAM) cp ;
    psp.pszTemplate = MAKEINTRESOURCE(IDD_DIALOG1) ;
    psp.pfnDlgProc  = (DLGPROC)PropExtDlgProc ; // shown in sample code

    HPROPSHEETPAGE hPage = CreatePropertySheetPage(&psp);

/*
Call the specified function to add the page to Explorer's property
sheet. If it succeeds, it will destroy the page when the dialog box
goes away. Otherwise, we have to destroy it ourselves.
*/

    if (hPage)
    {
        if (!lpfnAddPage(hPage, lParam))
        {
            DestroyPropertySheetPage(hPage);
        }
    }
    return S_OK ;
}
```

E. Drop Target Handlers

1. You may have noticed that cool things can happen when you drop a file on a desktop icon, such as the printer or the recycle bin. It is easy to write and install your own handler for dropped files, containing a drop target whose methods will be invoked when a user drops files on a file of yours, either on the desktop or in an Explorer window. To do so requires a COM server, known as a *drop target handler*, which supports the interfaces IDropTarget and IPersistFile.

2. First you must register your drop target handler. Explorer supports only one drop target handler per file type. Under your file's "shellex" key, you add the subkey "DropHandler". The value of this key is the class ID of the COM server that handles drop requests on files of this type. Thus:

HKEY_CLASSES_ROOT\EssenceOfOle.ShellExtensionFile\shellex\DropHandler
   = {1E392640-6E11-11d0-9097-00608C86B89C}

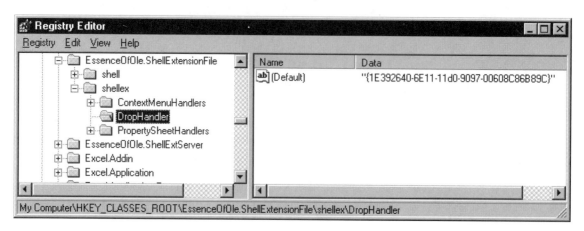

3. The IDropTarget interface for a shell extension works in exactly the same manner as the simple text example in Chapter 1. As was done in IShellExtInit::Initialize( ), the names of the files in the drag operation are passed in CF_HDROP format via an IDataObject. It's up to you to fetch the number and names of the files being dragged and do whatever you want to do with this information. In the sample below, the handler beeps once for each file when the drag operation enters the drop target icon. Thus:

```
STDMETHODIMP CShellExt::DragEnter(LPDATAOBJECT pIDataSource,
    DWORD grfKeyState, POINTL pt, LPDWORD pdwEffect)
{
    FORMATETC fe = {CF_HDROP, NULL, DVASPECT_CONTENT,-1,TYMED_HGLOBAL};
    STGMEDIUM stg;

/*
Get data from IDataObject in CF_HDROP format.
*/

    if (pIDataSource && (pIDataSource->GetData (&fe, &stg) == S_OK))
    {
/*
Query for number of files in drag operation. Beep once for each file.
*/

        UINT nFiles = DragQueryFile((HDROP)stg.hGlobal, (UINT)-1,NULL,0);
        for (UINT i = 0 ; i < nFiles ; i ++)
        {
            MessageBeep (0) ;
        }
    }

    DragOver(grfKeyState, pt, pdwEffect) ;
    ReleaseStgMedium (&stg) ;

    return S_OK ;
}
```

4. When the user drops the files on your icon, the IDropTarget::Drop( ) method will be called. The data is transferred and queried in the same manner as demonstrated in the DragEnter( ) case. In the example below, I fetch the name of each file, assemble a string with all the names, and pop up a message box to show it to the user. You will replace this with code that does what you want to do with the file names. Thus:

```
STDMETHODIMP CShellExt::Drop(LPDATAOBJECT pIDataSource,
    DWORD grfKeyState, POINTL pt, LPDWORD pdwEffect)
{
    FORMATETC fe = {CF_HDROP, NULL, DVASPECT_CONTENT,-1,TYMED_HGLOBAL};
    STGMEDIUM stg;

/*
Get memory block containing file names from data object.
*/
    if (pIDataSource && (pIDataSource->GetData (&fe, &stg) == S_OK))
    {

        char names [1024] ;
        int length = 0 ;
/*
Get number of files in memory block.
*/
        UINT nFiles = DragQueryFile ((HDROP)stg.hGlobal,(UINT)-1,NULL,0);


/*
Get the name of each file. Assemble into a string.
*/
        for (UINT i = 0 ; i < nFiles ; i ++)
        {
            length += DragQueryFile ((HDROP)stg.hGlobal, i, &names
                [length], sizeof (names)-length) ;
            names [length] = '\n' ;
            length ++ ;
            names [length] = 0x00 ;
        }
/*
Show names of files to user.
*/
        MessageBox (NULL, names, "Dropped Files", 0) ;
    }


    DragOver(grfKeyState, pt, pdwEffect) ;
    ReleaseStgMedium (&stg) ;

    return S_OK;
}
```

This page intentionally contains no text other than this sentence.

F. ICON HANDLERS:

1. Most file types, such as WinWord, instruct Explorer via registry entries to show a single icon for all files of that type. Sometimes you would prefer to show customized icons for files of different types. For example, a paint program might want each of its files to display as an icon showing the appearance of the painting. You may provide Explorer with a separate icon for each file by providing an icon handler, a COM server which supports the IExtractIcon and IPersistFile interfaces. The methods of the former are:

GetIconLocation( )   *// get file and resource ID of icon to display*
Extract( )   *// if GetIconLocation( ) fails, provide icon*

As always, you must register your icon handler. Explorer supports only one icon handler per file type. Under your file's "shellex" key, you add the subkey "IconHandler". The value of this key is the class ID of the COM server that handles icon requests on files of this type. Thus:

HKEY_CLASSES_ROOT\EssenceOfOle.ShellExtensionFile\shellex\IconHandler
    = {1E392640-6E11-11d0-9097-00608C86B89C}

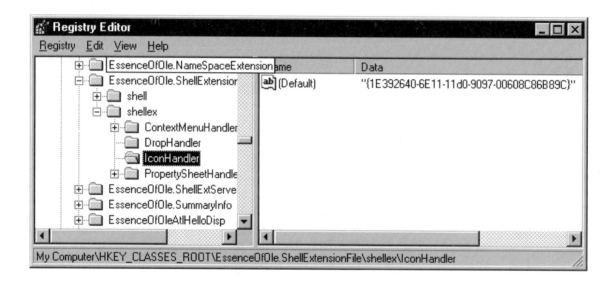

2. When it is time to display an icon for a file of your type, Explorer will load your icon handler and tell it the name of the file via the method IPersistFile::Load( ). Explorer will then query for the **IExtractIcon** interface and call the **GetIconLocation( )** method. Most icon handlers will provide icons that exist in a .EXE or .DLL file. To respond to this request, you copy the name of the file and the index of the icon within the file into the output parameters provided to this method and return S_OK. Explorer will use the API function ExtractIcon( ) to retrieve the specified icon from the specified file.

The sample program does not use this mechanism, so we return S_FALSE to indicate the yes, we got the request and were able to process it, but no, we aren't going to give back an icon location. Thus::

```
STDMETHODIMP CShellExt::GetIconLocation (UINT    uFlags,
    LPSTR szIconFile, UINT   cchMax, int   * piIndex, UINT  * pwFlags)
{
    return S_FALSE ;
}
```

Warning: The parameters of this method are different in Windows NT than in 95, in the same manner as shown previously in the method IContextMenu::GetCommandString( ) on page 569. The second parameter, szIconFile, is defined in the header file as an ANSI string pointer, and this is correct in Windows 95. However, in NT 4.0, the string is always passed in Unicode, regardless of what the header file says it is. If I was actually doing anything with it, I'd have to check which version I was running on and make sure I copied back the correct type of string. Pain in the ass.

3. If IExtractIcon ::GetIconLocation( ) returns S_FALSE, the icon handler is telling Explorer that it can't use a prefabricated icon; rather, it wants to roll its own icon on the fly. Explorer will then call **IExtractIcon ::Extract( )** to retrieve the actual handles to both large and small icons. It is up to your handler to create whatever icons it wants to use and provide them to Explorer via the output parameters.

In the sample icon handler, we create an icon that shows as much of the sample file's text as will fit. The internal structure of an icon is a little tricky, and a full discusssion is beyond the scope of this book, but the sample code below does work correctly. After editing the sample file, the icon will not change automatically, but you can cause Explorer to refresh it by pressing the F5 key. Sending that message to Explorer under program control is left as an exercise to the student. Thus: :

```
STDMETHODIMP CShellExt::Extract (LPCSTR pszFile, UINT    nIconIndex,
    HICON   *phiconLarge, HICON   *phiconSmall, UINT    nIconSize)
{

/*
Create a memory DC compatible with the user's screen. Create a bitmap
the size of an icon that is compatible with it.
*/

    HDC hScreenDC = CreateDC ("DISPLAY", NULL, NULL, NULL) ;
    HDC hdc = CreateCompatibleDC (hScreenDC) ;

    HBITMAP hbm = CreateCompatibleBitmap (hScreenDC, 32, 32) ;

/*
Open file and read enough of its contents to show in icon.
*/

    HANDLE hFile = CreateFile (m_FileName, GENERIC_READ,
     FILE_SHARE_READ, NULL, OPEN_EXISTING,FILE_ATTRIBUTE_NORMAL, NULL);

    if (hFile == INVALID_HANDLE_VALUE)
    {
      return S_FALSE ;
    }

    char buf [100] ; DWORD nActual ;
    ReadFile (hFile, buf, sizeof(buf), &nActual, NULL) ;
    CloseHandle (hFile) ;

/*
Select the bitmap into the memory DC, draw on it.
*/
    LOGFONT lf = {10, 0, 0, 0, 0, 0, 0, 0, 0, 0, 0, 0, 0,
      "Times New Roman" } ;
    HFONT hf = CreateFontIndirect (&lf) ;
    SelectObject (hdc, hf) ;
    SelectObject (hdc, hbm) ;

    RECT r = {0, 0, 32, 32} ;
    DrawText (hdc, buf, nActual, &r, DT_WORDBREAK)   ;
```

```
/*
Create a monochrome bitmap for the AND mask. Setting all bits to 0 says
to show the icon bit in that location. Any bit set to 1 says to show
the screen background bit in that location.
*/

    char bits [1024] ;
    FillMemory (&bits, 1024, 0x00) ;

/*
Actually create the icon based on the bitmap containing the text that
we drew.
*/

    BITMAP bm ;
    GetObject(hbm, sizeof(BITMAP), &bm) ;

    char MyBits [10240] ;
    GetBitmapBits (hbm, 10240, MyBits) ;

    HICON hIcon = CreateIcon (hDllInst, 32, 32,
        (BYTE)bm.bmPlanes, (BYTE)bm.bmBitsPixel,
        (const BYTE *) bits,
        (const BYTE *)MyBits) ;

/*
Give the icons to Explorer. In this case, we use the same icon for both
large and small representations. You can use different ones if you want
to.
*/
    *phiconLarge = hIcon ;
    *phiconSmall = hIcon ;

/*
Clean up.
*/
    DeleteDC (hdc) ;
    DeleteDC (hScreenDC) ;
    DeleteObject (hbm) ;
    DeleteObject (hf) ;

    return S_OK ;
}
```

Lab Exercises
Chapter 16
Shell Extension Sample

Directory: \EssenceofOLE\chap16\shellext

This lab provides a sample shell extension that demonstrates context menu handler, property sheet handler, drop target handler, and icon handler.

1. First, you must register your shell extension server. Open Explorer to the directory listed above and double-click on the file "shellext.reg" to place all of its entries in the registry.

2. Now in Explorer, right-click on the file "aaa.eoo". You should see a context menu whose first entry is "Open with Notepad". Try it, end edit the contents of the sample file. This connection is made by a simple "command" entry in the registry, as shown on page 565.

3. Now invoke the context menu again. Try the second menu item, which toggles the first character from 'A' to space and back again. Note the menu command string in Explorer's status bar. All of this is being done by the IContextMenu handler.

4. Now right-click on the file again and select "Properties" from the context menu. You will see a property sheet dialog box with the "General" page provided by Explorer, but also with a second property page provided by the sample property sheet handler as shown on page 571. Try toggling the check box to toggle the first character from 'A' to space and back again.

5. Now try the drop target handler of the sample shell extension. You can do this in an Explorer pane if you want, but you will find it easier if you copy the file "aaa.eoo" to your desktop. Go back to Explorer, select any number of files, and drag them over to the desktop icon. When the cursor first enters the icon, you will hear one beep for each file in the drag, as shown on page 575. If you drop the files on the icon, you will see a message box containing the names of each file in the drag, as shown on page 576.

6. It was probably hard to see in the Explorer pane unless you had large icons turned on, but when you placed the file on the desktop, you might have noticed that its icon contained recognizable characters showing the first few words of the file's contents. This customized icon was provided by the icon handler shown on page 578. Edit the file, change the first few characters (or toggle the first to 'A' or back), and press the F5 key. The icon will refresh itself to show the new contents.

Appendix A
Self-Registering Servers

This page intentionally contains no text other than this sentence.

1. As we have seen throughout this book, OLE servers need to place entries in the system registry so that OLE can locate the server when asked by a client app to create an object. For the sake of transparency the example code in this book has primarily provided this capability through a .REG file which the user must edit to contain the server's exact path and explicitly place into the registry. This need for user intervention is inconvenient and prone to error. How many times in the course of using this book have you mistakenly set the wrong path to a server? It would be very convenient if somehow the servers knew how to register themselves. For OCX and ActiveX controls, it isn't just convenient, it is required.

2. An in-proc (DLL) server provides self-registration capability by exporting the named function DllRegisterServer( ). An example of this is shown on the next page. When an external app wants to register the server, it loads the DLL, queries for this function, and calls it as shown on page 588. The code in this sample uses the registry API to make all the entries required by the server. The server should also provide a mechanism for unregistering itself by exporting the named function DllUnregisterServer( ) as shown on page 587. The sample code for a self-registering in-proc server can be found in the directory \chapAppendixA\SelfRegisteringDll.

3. A local server can perform self-registration in a slightly different manner. Since it cannot export functions by name, a local server should look on its command line for the switches /RegServer and /UnregServer, which should cause it to register or unregister itself accordingly. The local server should make API calls to register itself in a manner similar to the source code example for the DLL.

4. When used for OLE automation or controls, App Wizard automatically attaches the MFC's own self-registration functions. When you are writing custom interfaces, you can provide this functionality by tapping into the MFC object method COleObjectFactory::UpdateRegistryAll( ), as discussed at the end of Chapter 9. In an in-proc server, the MFC exports the named registration functions as described above. In a local server, as far as I can tell, the MFC ignores the command line flags described in the previous paragraph. An MFC local server simply registers itself every time it is launched as a standalone app (i.e., not by OLE), which is not a bad idea. That way, if a server gets moved, it will automatically patch up the registry the next time it is run, even if the user doesn't know about the /RegServer flag. An MFC local server does not seem to support the /UnregServer flag or any other form of unregistration, which is a bad idea.

```c
static char *pGuidString = "{351D1CE0-DCAA-11cf-B85F-00608C876FB3}" ;
HINSTANCE hDllInst ;

STDAPI DllRegisterServer( )
{
    HKEY hClsidKey, hMyKey, hNameKey ;
    char FileName [256] ; int length ; LONG retval ;
/*
Open key to HKEY_CLASSES_ROOT\Clsid.
*/

    RegOpenKey (HKEY_CLASSES_ROOT, "CLSID", &hClsidKey) ;

/*
Create subkey using object's GUID
*/

    RegCreateKey (hClsidKey, pGuidString, &hMyKey) ;

/*
Get file name of the DLL.  Create the InProcServer32 key based on it.
*/

    length = GetModuleFileName (hDllInst, FileName, sizeof(FileName)) ;
    retval = RegSetValue (hMyKey, "InProcServer32", REG_SZ, FileName,
      length) ;

/*
Create human-readable name keys.
*/

    RegCreateKey (HKEY_CLASSES_ROOT, "EssenceOfOLE.Data5", &hNameKey) ;
    RegSetValue (hNameKey, "Clsid", REG_SZ, pGuidString,
      lstrlen(pGuidString)) ;


/*
Close keys and return success or failure code.
*/
    RegCloseKey (hMyKey) ;
    RegCloseKey (hClsidKey) ;
    RegCloseKey (hNameKey) ;

    if (retval == ERROR_SUCCESS)
    {
      return S_OK ;
    }
    else
    {
      return E_UNEXPECTED ;
    }
}
```

5. To be a good citizen, your DLL also wants to provide a mechanism for unregistering itself, which it does by exporting the function **DllUnregisterServer ( )** in a similar manner. Thus:

```
STDAPI DllUnregisterServer( )
{
    HKEY hClsidKey, hMyKey, hNameKey ; LONG retval ;

/*
Open top-level key and our object's guid key.
*/
    RegOpenKey (HKEY_CLASSES_ROOT, "CLSID", &hClsidKey) ;
    RegOpenKey (hClsidKey, pGuidString, &hMyKey) ;

/*
Delete our InProcServer32 server key.
*/
    retval = RegDeleteKey (hMyKey, "InProcServer32") ;

/*
Delete our object's guid key.  Under NT, this will fail if there are
other subkeys, which is the behavior we want.  Under Windows 95, it
will succeed and delete any subkeys, which isn't.  See note below.
*/
    RegDeleteKey (hClsidKey, pGuidString) ;

/*
Remove human-readable name entries.
*/
    RegOpenKey (HKEY_CLASSES_ROOT, "EssenceOfOLE.Data5", &hNameKey) ;
    RegDeleteKey (hNameKey, "Clsid") ;
    RegDeleteKey (HKEY_CLASSES_ROOT, "EssenceOfOLE.Data5") ;
/*
Close registry keys, signal success or failure.
*/
    RegCloseKey (hMyKey) ;
    RegCloseKey (hClsidKey) ;
    RegCloseKey (hNameKey) ;
    if (retval == ERROR_SUCCESS)
    {
      return S_OK ;
    }
    else
    {
      return E_UNEXPECTED ;
    }
}
```

Note: Self-unregistration is only supposed to remove keys that the server itself placed in the registry. If another app added a key to this CLSID, such as a LocalServer32 key or a TreatAs key, the DLL should not remove it and therefore must not remove its guid key either. In Windows NT, the above sample complies with this requirement, as the function RegDeleteKey( ) will not remove a key which contains subkeys. If another key has been placed under the object's key, the call will fail. Windows 95 does not provide this extra security, however. If you run this code under Windows 95, the key will be removed even if there are subkeys, so you must do more extensive checking before you call it.

6. A DLL needs the assistance of an app to register itself. VC++ contains a command line utility called REGSVR32.EXE. I have written a GUI version and supplied it to you in the sample directory \chapAppendixA\DllRegisteringTool. The active portion of the code looks something like this:

```
void CRegdllDlg::OnDoitnow()
{
/*
Get file name selected by user in edit control.  Load specified
library. Signal error if unable to do so.
*/
    char FileName [256] ;
    GetDlgItemText (IDC_EDIT1, FileName, sizeof(FileName)) ;

    HINSTANCE hLib = LoadLibrary (FileName) ;

    if (!hLib)
    {
      AfxMessageBox ("Specified file could not be loaded.") ;
      return ;
    }


/*
Based on selection of Register/Unregister radio button, query for the
address of the named function DllRegisterServer. If unable to find it,
signal error.
*/

    FARPROC pRegisterProc ;
    if (IsDlgButtonChecked (IDC_RADIO1))
    {
      pRegisterProc = GetProcAddress (hLib, "DllRegisterServer") ;

      if (!pRegisterProc)
      {
            AfxMessageBox ("Specified DLL does not export the
                  function DllRegisterServer( )") ;
            return ;
      }

/*
Call registration function exported by the DLL. Signal success or
failure.
*/
      if ((*pRegisterProc) ( ) == S_OK)
      {
            AfxMessageBox ("DLL server successfully registered") ;
      }
      else
      {
            AfxMessageBox ("DLL register unsuccessful") ;
      }
    }
}
```

Appendix B
The ANSI-Unicode Problem

1. You will by now have noticed that every string parameter to every OLE API function or interface method is defined as the type LPOLESTR. In the 16-bit world, this was just a regular ANSI character string, so you could ignore the entire issue, but in the 32-bit world, an OLESTR is of type WCHAR. This is a wide character string, a string made up of 16-bit characters using the Unicode character set. For anyone who has to provide Far Eastern character sets that require Kanji and doesn't mind restricting himself to Windows NT, Unicode is an incredible advantage. For anyone who doesn't care about non-Western character sets or who needs to support Windows 95, it's nothing but a pain in the ass. For a complete discussion of exactly what Unicode is and how it works, see Chapter 11 of *Advanced Windows NT* by Jeffrey Richter (Microsoft Press).

2. Regardless of your philosophy, OLE demands to be fed Unicode, so if we want to make an OLE app run, that's what we have to feed it. The easiest solution is to build your app to be Unicode-only. It's quite simple to do, you just #define the constant **UNICODE** in your system header files. This was done on some of the more involved sample apps, such as the Eliza local server in Chapter 9. The entire app is compiled to use Unicode strings. Windows NT uses Unicode internally, and your app will actually get slightly faster if you do this. But Windows 95 does not speak Unicode, so your Unicode app will not run on it at all. Very few markets, and no large ones, are willing to restrict themselves to NT at the time of this writing. Too bad.

3. In the absence of a Unicode app, you have to handle all strings on a case-by-case basis. In places where strings are hardwired into code, prepending the capital letter 'L' (as in Long) onto a string causes the compiler to make it Unicode, even if the app around it isn't. Thus:

```
case ID_DATAOBJECT_CREATEDLL:
{
    HRESULT hr ;

/*
Read class ID from registry key. Must pass a Unicode string to this
function, so prepend 'L' to the string.
*/

    CLSID clsid ;
    hr = CLSIDFromProgID (L"EssenceofOLE.Data3", &clsid) ;

/*
Create object based on class ID read from registry.
*/

    hr = CoCreateInstance (clsid, ...) ;

    <rest of creation case>
}
```

4. To convert ANSI characters into Unicode, use the API function **MultiByteToWideChar( )**. In the example below from Chapter 8, we need a Unicode string to pass to the API function CreateItemMoniker( ). We assemble it in ANSI and convert it to Unicode. Thus:

```
extern WCHAR WideFileName ;

case ID_EDIT_COPYFILEITEMLINK:
{
    LPMONIKER pFileMoniker, pItemMoniker, pCompositeMoniker ;
    LPDATAOBJECT pData ;  char out [256] ; WCHAR wout [80] ;

/*
Create moniker for currently open file.
*/
    CreateFileMoniker (WideFileName, &pFileMoniker) ;

/*
Get selection of text, convert to wide chars, and create item moniker
naming it.
*/
    DWORD dwSel = SendMessage (hEdit, EM_GETSEL, 0, 0) ;
    wsprintf (out, "%d:%d", LOWORD(dwSel), HIWORD(dwSel)) ;

    MultiByteToWideChar (CP_ACP,        // code page
            0,                          // flags,
            out,                        // ANSI string to convert
            -1,                         // string is null-terminated
            wout,                       // output buffer for Unicode string
            sizeof(wout)) ;             // max # of characters to convert

    CreateItemMoniker (L"!",    // delimiter character
        wout,                   // object name
        &pItemMoniker) ;        // output variable

<rest of code omitted>
```

5. When OLE passes a string to one of your object's methods, the string is always in Unicode. In the following example, also from Chapter 8, OLE calls the method IOleItemContainer::GetObject( ), passing the name of the object which it has parsed from a moniker. We need to convert from the Unicode OLE gives us to the ANSI that we use internally. The API function **WideCharToMultiByte( )** performs this conversion for us. Thus:

```
STDMETHODIMP CFileTextData::GetObject(LPOLESTR pWideItemName,
    DWORD dwSpeed, LPBINDCTX pbc, REFIID riid, VOID **ppv)
{

    HRESULT hr ;
    char ItemName [256] ;

/*
Convert item name from wide to the ANSI that we use internally.
*/

    WideCharToMultiByte (CP_ACP,        // code page
            0,                          // flags
            pWideItemName,              // Unicode char string to convert
            -1,                         // string is null-terminated
            ItemName,                   // output buffer for ANSI string
            sizeof(ItemName),           // size of buffer
            NULL, NULL) ;               // not used

    <rest of function>
```

6. In an MFC app, the MFC handles most of the conversions for you. For example, when you specify the name of a method or property in OLE automation, the MFC implementation of IDispatch::GetIDsofNames( ) knows to convert the string from ANSI to Unicode. But you will occasionally have to convert manually. In the following example, also from Chapter 8, we need to pass a Unicode string to the API function CreateURLMoniker( ). The MFC macro **A2W( )** performs this conversion in place for us. The macro **W2A( )** performs the opposite conversion (not shown). Both macros requires that you include the MFC macro **USES_CONVERSION** within the scope of their functions. All of these macros are defined in the MFC header file "**afxpriv.h**", which must be included as well. Thus:

```
#include <afxpriv.h>

void CUrlmonikerDlg::OnBind()
{
    char name [256] ;
    HRESULT hr ;

/*
Get name from combo box control. It is in ANSI characters.
*/

    m_URLCombo.GetWindowText (name, sizeof(name)) ;


/*
Use name to create an URL moniker. Store moniker in a member variable.
This function, as do all OLE functions, requires a wide character
string.  The macro A2W( ) is an MFC macro that performs this
conversion.  The macro USES_CONVERSION must be inserted prior to it as
shown.
*/

    USES_CONVERSION ;
    hr = CreateURLMoniker (NULL, A2W(name), &m_pUrlMoniker) ;

    <remainder of code omitted>
```

Appendix C
Containment and Aggregation

A. CONCEPTS AND DEFINITIONS

1. "Code reuse" is the holy grail of the software industry, and much is made of COM as a mechanism for promoting this Good Thing. In one sense, an application programmer does this every time he uses a COM object, such as a calendar control, that he bought from some vendor instead of writing it himself. In another sense, developers would very much like to assemble COM components out of other components, instead of building the entire component from scratch. This section deals with two mechanisms for assembling COM objects into larger, hopefully more functional and profitable COM objects.

2. Throughout this book, when I wanted an object to support more than one interface, I've done it with multiple inheritance. This is the easiest way to do things if you have to write all the methods yourself. And usually I've had to do exactly that, because the interfaces shared common data. The interfaces were not independent black-box components, they were different views of the same thing. Consider the example at the end of Chapter 7, where one object supported both IDataObject and IPersistFile. The two interfaces did different things to the same data. That's usually the case in COM; when you are writing one component, it is relatively rare to find a prefabricated black box component that does useful things for you without needing to know your intimate details. There are a few, such as the free threaded marshaler described at the end of Chapter 13, but it's much less common than seekers of holy grails would like to admit. That's why I've put these two techniques in an appendix, instead of their own separate chapter.

Suppose I have the data object server data3sv from Chapter 2. Suppose I want to bring out a new version of it and I want to upgrade it by providing some type of user interface capability via OLE Automation. I have some choices. I could implement an IDispatch on it myself using multiple inheritance, thus:

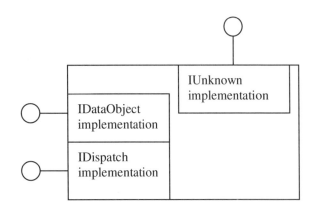

Or I could try to reuse an object that I already had. The code samples in this appendix deal with the case where I take the Hello,World Automation server from Chapter 3 and reuse it to provide a user interface for the data3sc in Chapter 2.

B. CONTAINMENT

1. One way I can reuse components is via containment, shown in the diagram below. My component consists of an outer object and an inner object. The outer object is the original CTimeData object, rewritten to add support for the IDispatch interface and therefore renamed CTimeDataDispatch. Its declaration is shown on the next page.

In the previous multiple inheritance examples, I've placed the code for implementing all the interfaces in the same object. The difference now is that the IDispatch VTBL on the outer object is an empty shell. My outer object provides a VTBL, but it accomplishes the work by creating a component, the inner or contained object, and delegating the IDispatch method calls to this object. Thus:

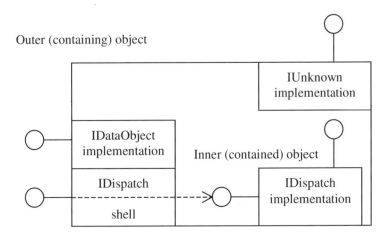

Containment is relatively easy to write. The contained object does not any special functionality to support it as is the case with aggregation; you can contain any object that can stand alone. Neither the outer object's client nor the inner object itself know or care that containment is taking place.

Better yet, the outer object can do all kinds of things to enhance the behavior of the inner object. For example, the outer object could inspect and modify method parameters before passing them to the inner object. Maybe the inner object speaks English and the outer object translates its input to and from French. Maybe the inner object provides useful functionality and the outer object meters it and sends bills to the client. If you think of subclassing a window in the Windows API, this is the COM version of it.

2. The outer object provides VTBLs for both interfaces via multiple inheritance as before. Thus:

```
class CTimeDataDispatch : public IDataObject, public IDispatch
{

    public:
      ULONG                       m_RefCount ;
/*
Pointer to inner object held by the outer object.
*/
      IDispatch *                 m_pInnerDispatch ;

      < rest of declaration omitted >
};
```

When the outer object is constructed, it creates the inner object via CoCreateInstance( ). Alternatively, the outer object could wait until the client actually queried for the inner object's interface and create it on demand. It releases the inner object in its destructor. Thus:

```
/*
Constructor/destructor
*/

CTimeDataDispatch::CTimeDataDispatch()
{
    m_RefCount = 1 ;
    g_ObjectCount ++ ;
/*
Create inner contained IDispatch
*/
    CLSID clsid ;
    CLSIDFromProgID (L"EssenceOfOle.HelloAutomation", &clsid) ;

    CoCreateInstance (
      clsid, NULL, CLSCTX_LOCAL_SERVER, IID_IDispatch,
      (LPVOID *) &m_pInnerDispatch) ;

    return;
}

CTimeDataDispatch::~CTimeDataDispatch(void)
{
    g_ObjectCount -- ;

/*
Release inner contained IDispatch
*/
    if (m_pInnerDispatch)
    {
      m_pInnerDispatch->Release( ) ;
    }
    return;
}
```

3. The outer object in this example implements the IDispatch interface by simply delegating the call to the inner object. If you wanted to mess with the parameters or do other work around this call, it would go here. Thus:

```
STDMETHODIMP CTimeDataDispatch::Invoke(DISPID dispidMember,
    REFIID riid,  LCID lcid, WORD wFlags, DISPPARAMS *pDispParams,
    VARIANT *pVarResult, EXCEPINFO *pExcepInfo, UINT *puArgErr)
{

/*
If inner dispatch interface pointer exists and is valid, delegate the
call to it.
*/

    if (m_pInnerDispatch)
    {
      return m_pInnerDispatch->Invoke (dispidMember, riid, lcid,wFlags,
          pDispParams, pVarResult, pExcepInfo, puArgErr) ;
    }
/*
If not, fail the call.
*/

    else
    {
      return E_FAIL ;
    }
}
```

C. AGGREGATION

1. Aggregation is the second technique for reusing existing objects. It gets airplay out of proportion to its importance. Kraig Brockschmidt himself said that he gave it far too much emphasis in the first edition of his book, and it is downplayed considerably in the second edition.

Aggregation differs from containment in that in the former, the inner object's interface is not wrapper by the outer object, but instead exposes its interface directly. The two object's IUnknown interfaces are wired together so that the inner object's IUnknown delegates its calls to the outer IUnknown. Thus:

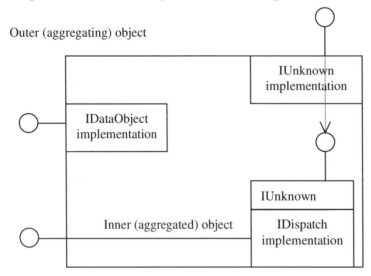

Another difference from containment is that to reuse an object via aggregation, the object must have been written to support it, and not all of them are. An object that is aggregatable is trickier to write than one that isn't, although both the MFC and ATL provide prefabricated support that makes it pretty easy. Furthermore, in aggregation, the outer object doesn't get the chance to examine or modify the calls to the inner.

So why would you use aggregation? You use it much less often than containment, because it's harder to write and doesn't do as much. You use it when containment won't work. Aggregation is required in cases where the component that you are reusing does useful work that requires a pointer to the outer IUnknown interface, as the rules of aggregation require that the inner component by given this pointer. An example is the free threaded marshaler described at the end of Chapter 13, a component that you can get from the operating system. It supports the IMarshal interface, handing out copies of the out IUnknown pointer to avoid interthread marshaling. Another place to use aggregation is where multiple inheritance is not available for technical or political reasons. The MFC uses aggregation extensively because it didn't support multiple inheritance when its COM support was first being designed. And some development shops still consider it politically incorrect today.

2. The code for aggregation looks like this. The outer object provides a VTBL only for its own interface, in this case IDataObject. Thus:

```
class CTimeDataOuter : public IDataObject
{

    public:
      ULONG       m_RefCount ;
      IUnknown*   m_pInnerUnknown ;

    <rest of class declaration omitted>
} ;
```

The outer object creates the inner object via CoCreateInstance( ) with two major new additions. First, when setting up aggregation, the outer object must pass a pointer to its IUnknown interface as the second parameter to CoCreateInstance( ). This will be passed to the class factory so that the inner object will know who it's inside of. Second, in aggregation, the outer object **MUST ask for the IUnknown interface** and only IUnknown when creating the inner object. Thus:

```
CTimeDataOuter::CTimeDataOuter()
{
    m_RefCount = 1 ;
    g_ObjectCount ++ ;

/*
Create inner object, passing pointer to outer object and requesting
IUnknown interface.
*/

    CLSID clsid ;
    CLSIDFromProgID (L"EssenceOfOle.HelloAutomation", &clsid) ;

    CoCreateInstance (
      clsid,
      this,                 // outer IUnknown for aggregation
      CLSCTX_LOCAL_SERVER,
      IID_IUnknown,         // in aggregation, must always ask for IUnknown
      (LPVOID *) &m_pInnerUnknown) ;

    return;
}
```

3. The outer object also modifies its QueryInterface( ). When the client queries for the interface that is supported by the inner object, the outer one delegates that call to the inner. Thus:

```
HRESULT CTimeDataOuter::QueryInterface(REFIID riid, LPVOID FAR *ppv)
{
    if (riid == IID_IUnknown || riid == IID_IDataObject)
    {
        *ppv = (LPVOID)this;
        AddRef();
        return S_OK ;
    }
    else if (riid == IID_IDispatch)
    {
      return m_pInnerUnknown->QueryInterface (riid, ppv) ;
    }
    else
    {
      *ppv = NULL;
      return  E_NOINTERFACE ;
    }
}
```

4. An object that supports being aggregated needs to be written for this purpose. It may choose either to require aggregation, or, as in this case, to run either aggregated or standalone. An aggregatable object needs TWO, repeat 2, IUnknown implementations. The first one, called the "delegating IUnknown", delegates all its calls to the outer IUnknown. This is the IUnknown that the inner component's exposed interface (here IDispatch) must derive from. The second one, called the "non-delegating IUnknown", implements what we consider to be normal IUnknown behavior. In this example, the class CAggrHelloDispatch derives directly from IUnknown, and its IUnknown methods will be the non-delegating IUnknown. I implemented the IDispatch and the delegating IUnknown from which it derives using nested classes. It would have been somewhat cleaner with multiple inheritance, but since aggregation is used where multiple inheritance can't, I wanted to show it this way.

Note that this class's constructor has been modified to require an IUnknown * as a parameter, which will be provided by this object's class factory. If it is NULL, it means that this object is not aggregated inside another, but instead is standing on its own. Thus:

```cpp
class CAggrHelloDispatch : public IUnknown
{
 public:
    IUnknown *m_pUnkOuter ;
    ULONG m_RefCount ;
/*
IDispatch and delegating IUnknown.
*/
    class CDelegatingDispatch : public IDispatch
    {
      public:
      IUnknown * m_pGuyToDelegateTo ;
      BSTR m_bstrHelloMsg;

      CDelegatingDispatch( ){m_bstrHelloMsg =SysAllocString(L"Hello");}

      STDMETHODIMP QueryInterface (REFIID riid, void ** ppv);
      STDMETHODIMP_(ULONG) AddRef (void);
      STDMETHODIMP_(ULONG) Release (void);
      STDMETHODIMP GetTypeInfoCount(UINT *pctinfo) ;
      STDMETHODIMP GetTypeInfo(UINT, LCID, ITypeInfo **pptinfo) ;
      STDMETHODIMP GetIDsOfNames(REFIID, LPOLESTR*,UINT,LCID,DISPID *);
      STDMETHODIMP Invoke(DISPID, REFIID, LCID lcid, WORD,
            DISPPARAMS *, VARIANT *, EXCEPINFO *, UINT *) ;

    }
    m_DelegatingDispatch ;
 /*
 Class constructor and destructor.
 */
    CAggrHelloDispatch(IUnknown *);
    ~CAggrHelloDispatch();

/*
Non-delegating IUnknown methods
*/
    STDMETHODIMP QueryInterface (REFIID riid, void FAR* FAR* ppv);
    STDMETHODIMP_(ULONG) AddRef (void);
    STDMETHODIMP_(ULONG) Release (void);
};
```

5. The object's class factory must also be modified. The outer IUnknown is passed as the first parameter of IClassFactory::CreateInstance( ). We pass this parameter to the CAggrHelloDispatch in its constructor. Thus:

```
STDMETHODIMP CHelloCF::CreateInstance(IUnknown FAR* pUnkOuter,
    REFIID riid,  void FAR* FAR* ppv)
{

/*
When asking for aggregation, the creator may only request the IUnknown
interface.
*/
    if (pUnkOuter != NULL && riid != IUnknown)
    {
      return CLASS_E_NOAGGREGATION ;
    }
/*
Create a new CAggrHelloDispatch object, passing the outer IUnknown we
are given as an aggregator. It might be NULL if this object is being
used standalone.
*/

    CAggrHelloDispatch * pHello = new CAggrHelloDispatch (pUnkOuter) ;

/*
Query interface to see if new object supports requested interface.
If found, go happily on our way.
*/

    if (pHello->QueryInterface (riid, ppv) == NOERROR)
    {
      pHello->Release ( ) ;
      return NOERROR ;
    }
/*
Object does not support requested interface. Delete it and return an
error code.
*/
    else
    {
      delete pHello ;
      return E_NOINTERFACE ;
    }
}
```

6. The inner object's constructor stores in a member variable the outer IUnknown pointer passed to it by the class factory. Unlike the usual case, it does NOT AddRef( ) the pointer. To do so would create a circular reference count situation, where the outer object held a reference on the inner and vice versa.

```
CAggrHelloDispatch::CAggrHelloDispatch(IUnknown * pUnkOuter)
{
    m_RefCount = 1;

/*
Remember the outer IUnknown. It will be NULL if we are being created
standalone and non-NULL if we are being aggregated. Do NOT AddRef( )
this pointer. That would give us an interlocking reference situation.
*/

    m_pUnkOuter = pUnkOuter ;

/*
Tell the delegating unknown who to delegate to. If we are aggregated,
it will be the outer IUnknown. Otherwise it will be out own
internal non-delegating IUnknown.
*/
    if (m_pUnkOuter)
    {
      m_DelegatingDispatch.m_pGuyToDelegateTo = m_pUnkOuter ;
    }
    else
    {
      m_DelegatingDispatch.m_pGuyToDelegateTo = this ;
    }
}
```

7. When the class factory first creates the object, it calls QueryInterface( ) on it to get the interface pointer requested by the creator. I wrote the object so that this call comes in to the non-delegating QueryInterface( ). Thus:

```
STDMETHODIMP CAggrHelloDispatch::QueryInterface(REFIID riid,void **ppv)
{

/*
Caller asking for IUnknown. Give back a pointer to the non-delegating
IUnknown.
*/

    if (riid == IID_IUnknown)
    {
      *ppv = this ;
      AddRef( ) ;
      return S_OK ;
    }


/*
Caller asking for IDispatch. Give back a pointer to the IDispatch that
derives from the delegating IUnknown. AddRef the delegating IUnknown.
If we are aggregated, the AddRef( ) will be delegated to the outer
object. Otherwise, the AddRef( ) will be delegated right back here to
our own non-delegating IUnknown::AddRef( ).
*/

    else if (riid == IID_IDispatch)
    {
      *ppv = &m_DelegatingDispatch ;
      m_DelegatingDispatch.AddRef( ) ;
      return S_OK ;
    }

    return S_OK ;
}
```

606

8. The delegating IUnknown simply delegates its calls to the right party, either the outer IUnknown when aggregated, or to its own internal non-delegating IUnknown if running standalone. Thus:

```
STDMETHODIMP CAggrHelloDispatch::CDelegatingDispatch::QueryInterface(
    REFIID riid, void **ppv)
{
    return m_pGuyToDelegateTo->QueryInterface (riid, ppv) ;
}

STDMETHODIMP_(ULONG) CAggrHelloDispatch::CDelegatingDispatch::AddRef()
{
    return m_pGuyToDelegateTo->AddRef ( ) ;
}

STDMETHODIMP_(ULONG) CAggrHelloDispatch::CDelegatingDispatch::Release()
{
    return m_pGuyToDelegateTo->Release ( ) ;
}
```

This page intentionally contains no text other than this sentence.

Appendix D
Smart Pointers

1. One of the biggest problems in COM is getting the reference count right. You spend an awful lot of your debugging time tracking down nasty and hard-to-reproduce bugs that invariably turn out to be caused by an extra or missing call to AddRef( ) or Release( ). With the release of VC++ 5, Microsoft added a new C++ wrapper class to automate reference counting or at least make consistent. The class is called **_com_ptr_t**. It contains a member variable called m_pInterface, which represents a raw interface pointer (the type used throughout this book). The idea is that you will no longer call AddRef( ) or Release( ) directly. Instead, the class contains overloaded methods and operators which call AddRef( ) and Release( ) on the internal pointer in a consistent and (relatively) logical manner, thereby preventing you from forgetting. For example, the destructor of this class automatically calls Release( ) on the internal interface pointer if it is non-NULL when the outer wrapper is destructed.

The facing page shows the Clipboard sample program from Chapter 1 rewritten to use smart pointers. The sample code may be found in the directory \EssenceOfOle\ChapAppendixD. First, you must include the system header file **<comdef.h>,** which defines smart pointer classes for all standard interfaces. The name of the smart pointer class is the name of the interface with the characters "Ptr" added to the end. You generally use these classes instead of using _com_ptr_t directly. Remember, IDataObject is a binary, language-independent interface specification. IDataObjectPtr is a convenient, Microsoft C++ specific utility wrapper class. In this case, instead of a dumb pointer LPDATAOBJECT or IDataObject*, we instantiate on the stack a smart pointer of the class **IDataObjectPtr**, which wraps an internal pointer to an IDataObject interface.

WARNING: Nothing will screw your project up faster or worse than using dumb pointers in some places and smart ones in others. Pick <u>ONE</u> model and follow it throughout your entire app, better yet, your entire company, no matter what.

When we call OleGetClipboard( ), we use the & operator to pass the address of the IDataObjectPtr. The _com_ptr_t base class overloads this operator to return the address of the internal interface pointer m_pInterface. In this way, OLE returns the clipboard data object pointer straight into the wrapper. The wrapper does not AddRef( ) the pointer in this case because it knows that, since this operator is used for obtaining interface pointers returned from functions, the AddRef( ) should have already been done before the function returns.

When we compare the IDataObjectPtr to NULL, we use the == operator. This, too, has been overloaded to operate on the inner interface pointer. We then call QueryGetData( ) using the arrow operator, which has also been overloaded to operate on the inner interface pointer.

Finally, the IDataObjectPtr goes out of scope and its destructor is called. When using dumb pointers, we had to remember to release it ourselves, first checking for NULL. The smart pointer contains this functionality prefabricated inside its destructor, so we don't call Release( ). If you forget and in fact do call Release( ) on the smart pointer, you will have one too many calls to Release( ) and the destructor will crash.

```
#include <comdef.h>

case WM_INITMENU:
{

/*
Get a data object pointer to the current Clipboard contents. Assign it
into a smart pointer. The & operator is overloaded so as to assign the
raw pointer returned by the function directly into the smart pointer's
m_pInterface variable. Smart pointer does not AddRef( ) it because it
knows that as the return value from a function, it already has been.
*/
    IDataObjectPtr lpd ;
    HRESULT hr ;

    hr = OleGetClipboard (&lpd) ;

/*
Fill out a FORMATETC structure
*/

    FORMATETC fe ;

    fe.cfFormat = CF_TEXT ;
    fe.ptd = NULL ;
    fe.tymed = TYMED_HGLOBAL ;
    fe.dwAspect = DVASPECT_CONTENT ;
    fe.lindex = -1 ;

/*
Smart pointer overloads the == operator to compare directly to its
internal interface pointer m_pInterface, so the test for NULL works
correctly. It also overloads the -> operator so the call to
QueryGetData is made correctly from the internal interface pointer.
*/
    if (lpd == NULL || lpd->QueryGetData (&fe) != S_OK)
    {
      EnableMenuItem ((HMENU)wParam, ID_DEMO_PASTETEXT, MF_GRAYED) ;
    }
    else
    {
      EnableMenuItem ((HMENU)wParam, ID_DEMO_PASTETEXT, MF_ENABLED) ;
    }

/*
Smart pointer releases Clipboard data object in its destructor when it
goes out of scope. Don't you do it, or you'll have one too many and
crash.
*/

    return 0 ;
}
```

2. What happens with smart pointers that don't live on the stack ? Suppose In the same example we rewrote our drop target class to use a smart pointer. Thus:

```
class CDropTarget : public IDropTarget
{

    protected:
      ULONG               m_RefCount ;
      IDataObjectPtr      m_pIDataSource ;


    <rest of class definition>
};
```

3. Our DragEnter( ) method would be similar, except that we would not call AddRef( ) on the source IDataObject pointer when we saved a copy of it. The smart pointer class overloads the = operator to do that for us automatically if the pointer is not NULL. It will also automatically release any previous pointer it might have held. Thus:

```
STDMETHODIMP CDropTarget::DragEnter(LPDATAOBJECT pIDataSource,
    DWORD grfKeyState, POINTL pt, LPDWORD pdwEffect)
{
/*
Check to see if the data is in a format we can handle (in this case,
only text).  If so, keep a copy of the data object pointer and add to
its reference count.
*/
    FORMATETC fe ;
    < fill out FORMATETC>

    if (pIDataSource->QueryGetData (&fe) == S_OK)
    {
/*
Smart pointer automatically does an AddRef( ) in its assignment. It
also releases any previous object that might have been held (in this
case, there shouldn't be one).
*/
        m_pIDataSource = pIDataSource ;
    }
    else
    {
/*
This sets the internal interface pointer to NULL, which is the result
that we want.
*/
        m_pIDataSource = NULL ;
    }
/*
Call our own DragOver( ) method to set the effect code.
*/
    DragOver(grfKeyState, pt, pdwEffect) ;
    return S_OK ;
}
```

4. When we are finished with the data object pointer, we cause the smart pointer to release it by assigning the smart pointer the value of NULL. Thus:

```
STDMETHODIMP CDropTarget::Drop(LPDATAOBJECT pIDataSource,
    DWORD grfKeyState, POINTL pt, LPDWORD pdwEffect)
{
    if (m_pIDataSource != NULL) // != operator overloaded by smart ptr
    {
/*
Get point on screen where data was dropped.  Convert to client
coordinates, store in global variables xText and yText, which will
cause main window to display the text where it was dropped.
*/

        <code omitted>
/*
Fetch text from data object and display it
*/

        STGMEDIUM stg ; FORMATETC fe ;
        <code omitted>

        m_pIDataSource->GetData (&fe, &stg) ;


/*
Copy data into string for display in main window and Invalidate to
cause a repaint.
*/
        <code omitted>

/*
Release storage medium. This isn't a smart pointer, in fact it isn't
any type of COM object, so we have to do it ourselves.
*/

        ReleaseStgMedium (&stg) ;

/*
Smart pointer releases internal pointer when its value is set to NULL.
*/
        m_pIDataSource = NULL ;

    }

/*
Call our own DragOver( ) method to set the effect code
*/

    DragOver(grfKeyState, pt, pdwEffect) ;
    return S_OK;
}
```

613

5. Smart pointers are especially useful when your app uses exception handling. When a function throws an exception which is caught higher up the stack, any pointers on the stack are discarded when the stack is unwound, possibly leaking away objects. With smart pointers, the objects are released when their pointers are discarded. Thus:

```
/*
This top-level function calls a middle function from within a try-catch
block.
*/

TopFunc ( )
{
    try
    {
      MiddleFunc ( ) ;
    }
    catch (CSomeException)
    {
      HandleException ( ) ;
    }
}


/*
The middle function gets a data object from the Clipboard and stores it
in a dumb pointer. It then calls the deepest function.
*/

void MiddleFunc ( )
{
    IDataObject lpd ;
    OleGetClipboard (&lpd) ;
    DeepestFunc ( ) ;
    if (lpd) lpd->Release ( ) ;
}


/*
The deepest function does some work and throws an exception to be
caught by the top function, causing the stack to be unwound. If
MiddleFunc( ) above uses a dumb pointer as shown, the object to which
it points will be leaked away as the stack is unwound, because the dumb
pointer doesn't know to call Release( ). If MiddleFunc( ) had uses a
smart pointer instead, the smart pointer's destructor would have
released the Clipboard data object when the smart pointer got discarded
during the stack unwinding.
*/

DeepestFunc ( )
{
    if (DoSomeWork())
    {
      throw new CSomeException ;
    }
}
```

6. As always, there's one place where the magic bullet doesn't work. When you write a function or method that returns a pointer to an object, such as OleGetClipboard( ) or QueryInterface( ), the rules require you to AddRef( ) the pointer before the function returns. The smart pointer class is not smart enough to detect this situation and automatically AddRef( ) the pointer being returned. You must call it manually.

You'd like smart pointers to free you ever having to think about reference counts, but they don't, so now you have to think about when you need to think about them and when you don't. Thus:

```
IDataObjectPtr pMyDataObject ;

HRESULT CSomeObject::QueryInterface(REFIID riid, LPVOID *ppv)
{

/*
Caller is asking for the IDataObject interface, which I keep in a
separate pointer for this example.
*/

    if (riid == IID_IDataObject)
    {

/*
Give caller a pointer to the IDataObject interface. The smart pointer
knows that the = operator means to give back the raw internal pointer.
*/
        *ppv = pMyDataObject ;

/*
Since this pointer is being returned from an interface method, the
rules require that its AddRef( ) be called. The smart pointer is not
smart enough to differentiate the situation where its value is being
returned, as here, which requires an AddRef( ), from that where it is
simply being examined, which wouldn't. Therefore we must manually call
AddRef( ) on the smart pointer.
*/

        pMyDataObject->AddRef( ) ;

        return S_OK ;
    }

    <rest of QueryInterface( )>
}
```

This page intentionally contains no text other than this sentence.

D

E

F

G

620

LICENSE AGREEMENT AND LIMITED WARRANTY

READ THE FOLLOWING TERMS AND CONDITIONS CAREFULLY BEFORE OPENING THIS CD PACKAGE, *THE ESSENCE OF COM AND ACTIVE X: A PROGRAMMER'S WORKBOOK.* THIS LEGAL DOCUMENT IS AN AGREEMENT BETWEEN YOU AND PRENTICE-HALL, INC. (THE "COMPANY"). BY OPENING THIS SEALED CD PACKAGE, YOU ARE AGREEING TO BE BOUND BY THESE TERMS AND CONDITIONS. IF YOU DO NOT AGREE WITH THESE TERMS AND CONDITIONS, DO NOT OPEN THE CD PACKAGE. PROMPTLY RETURN THE UNOPENED CD PACKAGE AND ALL ACCOMPANYING ITEMS TO THE PLACE YOU OBTAINED THEM FOR A FULL REFUND OF ANY SUMS YOU HAVE PAID.

1.   **GRANT OF LICENSE:** In consideration of your purchase of this book, and your agreement to abide by the terms and conditions of this Agreement, the Company grants to you a nonexclusive right to use and display the copy of the enclosed software program (hereinafter the "SOFTWARE") on a single computer (i.e., with a single CPU) at a single location so long as you comply with the terms of this Agreement. The Company reserves all rights not expressly granted to you under this Agreement.

2.   **OWNERSHIP OF SOFTWARE:** You own only the magnetic or physical media (the enclosed CD) on which the SOFTWARE is recorded or fixed, but the Company and the software developers retain all the rights, title, and ownership to the SOFTWARE recorded on the original CD copy(ies) and all subsequent copies of the SOFTWARE, regardless of the form or media on which the original or other copies may exist. This license is not a sale of the original SOFTWARE or any copy to you.

3.   **COPY RESTRICTIONS:** This SOFTWARE and the accompanying printed materials and user manual (the "Documentation") are the subject of copyright. The individual programs on the CD are copyrighted by the authors of each program. Some of the programs on the CD include separate licensing agreements. If you intend to use one of these programs, you must read and follow its accompanying license agreement. You may <u>not</u> copy the Documentation or the SOFTWARE, except that you may make a single copy of the SOFTWARE for backup or archival purposes only. You may be held legally responsible for any copying or copyright infringement which is caused or encouraged by your failure to abide by the terms of this restriction.

4.   **USE RESTRICTIONS:** You may <u>not</u> network the SOFTWARE or otherwise use it on more than one computer or computer terminal at the same time. You may physically transfer the SOFTWARE from one computer to another provided that the SOFTWARE is used on only one computer at a time. You may <u>not</u> distribute copies of the SOFTWARE or Documentation to others. You may <u>not</u> reverse engineer, disassemble, decompile, modify, adapt, translate, or create derivative works based on the SOFTWARE or the Documentation without the prior written consent of the Company.

5.   **TRANSFER RESTRICTIONS:** The enclosed SOFTWARE is licensed only to you and may <u>not</u> be transferred to any one else without the prior written consent of the Company. Any unauthorized transfer of the SOFTWARE shall result in the immediate termination of this Agreement.

6.   **TERMINATION:** This license is effective until terminated. This license will terminate automatically without notice from the Company and become null and void if you fail to comply with any provisions or limitations of this license. Upon termination, you shall destroy the Documentation and all copies of the SOFTWARE. All provisions of this Agreement as to warranties, limitation of liability, remedies or damages, and our ownership rights shall survive termination.

7.   **MISCELLANEOUS:** This Agreement shall be construed in accordance with the laws of the United States of America and the State of New York and shall benefit the Company, its affiliates, and assignees.

8.   **LIMITED WARRANTY AND DISCLAIMER OF WARRANTY:** The Company warrants that the SOFTWARE, when properly used in accordance with the Documentation, will operate in substantial conformity with the description of the SOFTWARE set forth in the Documentation. The

Company does not warrant that the SOFTWARE will meet your requirements or that the operation of the SOFTWARE will be uninterrupted or error-free. The Company warrants that the media on which the SOFTWARE is delivered shall be free from defects in materials and workmanship under normal use for a period of thirty (30) days from the date of your purchase. Your only remedy and the Company's only obligation under these limited warranties is, at the Company's option, return of the warranted item for a refund of any amounts paid by you or replacement of the item. Any replacement of SOFTWARE or media under the warranties shall not extend the original warranty period. The limited warranty set forth above shall not apply to any SOFTWARE which the Company determines in good faith has been subject to misuse, neglect, improper installation, repair, alteration, or damage by you. EXCEPT FOR THE EXPRESSED WARRANTIES SET FORTH ABOVE, THE COMPANY DISCLAIMS ALL WARRANTIES, EXPRESS OR IMPLIED, INCLUDING WITHOUT LIMITATION, THE IMPLIED WARRANTIES OF MERCHANTABILITY AND FITNESS FOR A PARTICULAR PURPOSE. EXCEPT FOR THE EXPRESS WARRANTY SET FORTH ABOVE, THE COMPANY DOES NOT WARRANT, GUARANTEE, OR MAKE ANY REPRESENTATION REGARDING THE USE OR THE RESULTS OF THE USE OF THE SOFTWARE IN TERMS OF ITS CORRECTNESS, ACCURACY, RELIABILITY, CURRENTNESS, OR OTHERWISE.

IN NO EVENT, SHALL THE COMPANY OR ITS EMPLOYEES, AGENTS, SUPPLIERS, OR CONTRACTORS BE LIABLE FOR ANY INCIDENTAL, INDIRECT, SPECIAL, OR CONSEQUENTIAL DAMAGES ARISING OUT OF OR IN CONNECTION WITH THE LICENSE GRANTED UNDER THIS AGREEMENT, OR FOR LOSS OF USE, LOSS OF DATA, LOSS OF INCOME OR PROFIT, OR OTHER LOSSES, SUSTAINED AS A RESULT OF INJURY TO ANY PERSON, OR LOSS OF OR DAMAGE TO PROPERTY, OR CLAIMS OF THIRD PARTIES, EVEN IF THE COMPANY OR AN AUTHORIZED REPRESENTATIVE OF THE COMPANY HAS BEEN ADVISED OF THE POSSIBILITY OF SUCH DAMAGES. IN NO EVENT SHALL LIABILITY OF THE COMPANY FOR DAMAGES WITH RESPECT TO THE SOFTWARE EXCEED THE AMOUNTS ACTUALLY PAID BY YOU, IF ANY, FOR THE SOFTWARE.

SOME JURISDICTIONS DO NOT ALLOW THE LIMITATION OF IMPLIED WARRANTIES OR LIABILITY FOR INCIDENTAL, INDIRECT, SPECIAL, OR CONSEQUENTIAL DAMAGES, SO THE ABOVE LIMITATIONS MAY NOT ALWAYS APPLY. THE WARRANTIES IN THIS AGREEMENT GIVE YOU SPECIFIC LEGAL RIGHTS AND YOU MAY ALSO HAVE OTHER RIGHTS WHICH VARY IN ACCORDANCE WITH LOCAL LAW.

ACKNOWLEDGMENT

YOU ACKNOWLEDGE THAT YOU HAVE READ THIS AGREEMENT, UNDERSTAND IT, AND AGREE TO BE BOUND BY ITS TERMS AND CONDITIONS. YOU ALSO AGREE THAT THIS AGREEMENT IS THE COMPLETE AND EXCLUSIVE STATEMENT OF THE AGREEMENT BETWEEN YOU AND THE COMPANY AND SUPERSEDES ALL PROPOSALS OR PRIOR AGREEMENTS, ORAL, OR WRITTEN, AND ANY OTHER COMMUNICATIONS BETWEEN YOU AND THE COMPANY OR ANY REPRESENTATIVE OF THE COMPANY RELATING TO THE SUBJECT MATTER OF THIS AGREEMENT.

Should you have any questions concerning this Agreement or if you wish to contact the Company for any reason, please contact in writing at the address below.

Robin Short

Prentice Hall PTR

One Lake Street

Upper Saddle River, New Jersey 07458